THE CIRCASSIAN

BENJAMIN C. FORTNA

The Circassian

A Life of Eşref Bey, Late Ottoman
Insurgent and Special Agent

HURST & COMPANY, LONDON

This English edition published in the United Kingdom in 2016 by
C. Hurst & Co. (Publishers) Ltd.,
41 Great Russell Street, London, WC1B 3PL
© Benjamin C. Fortna, 2016
All rights reserved.
Printed in India

A Cataloguing-in-Publication data record for this book
is available from the British Library.

ISBN: 9781849045780 *cloth*

This book is printed using paper from registered sustainable
and managed sources.

www.hurstpublishers.com

For Will, Nick and Benjy

.

CONTENTS

ACKNOWLEDGMENTS

Many people contributed to the writing of this book and I gratefully acknowledge the help and kindness they showed me at various stages along the way.

The peripatetic nature of Eşref's life means that its documentary trail is more diffuse than most historical figures. I tried to trace its record wherever possible and received much needed help in the process. I thank Dr Philipp Stoddard, who interviewed Eşref in the course of writing his PhD dissertation in the early 1960s. Dr Stoddard generously took the time to speak with me on several occasions and sent me a number of documents and photographs he had received from Eşref and recounted anecdotes that enlivened the narrative. More conventional archives offered up their sources and I am grateful for the archivists and librarians who helped me find my way among their collections. In particular I thank Mesut Güvenbaş at General Staff Military History and Strategic Studies Archive (ATASE) in Ankara who was extremely helpful in aiding me negotiate that remarkable resource. His colleagues at the archives of the Institute for the History of the Turkish Revolution (TİTE) in Ankara, the Prime Ministry's Ottoman archives (BOA) and the Orient Institut in Istanbul, where Drs. Richard Wittmann and Aléxandre Toumarkine were extremely generous with their time and conviviality, and numerous other collections in Turkey were extremely helpful. While in Ankara I benefitted from the help of Mühittin Ünal, Ahmet Özcan, my former student Nazan Çiçek and old friends and neighbors Martin Reiser and Gertrud Müller and their family who hosted me in their characteristically warm and welcoming way.

ACKNOWLEDGMENTS

Back in England I benefitted from the staff and collections of the National Archives, the British Library, the Bodleian Library, the Imperial War Museum, the House of Commons Parliamentary Papers, the Middle East Centre Archive at St Antony's College, Oxford, and SOAS Special Collections. Meanwhile, I was lucky to receive the help of colleagues such as Talha Çiçek who informed me about the Taha Toros collection and İbrahim Şirin, the Cihangiroğlu letters.

To make sense of these sources I was fortunate to be able to rely on the help of a great many colleagues, among them Şükrü Hanioğlu, Erik-Jan Zürcher, Rashid Khalidi, Nader Sohrabi, Fred Anscombe, Christine Philliou, Ryan Gingeras, Mesut Uyar, Polat Safi, David Roxburgh, Lucienne Thys-Şenocak, Fatmagül Demirel, Yiğit Akın, Dimitris Stamatapoulos, Vemund Aarbakke, İsmet Erarpat, Emre Erol, Ümit Eser, and Stefano Taglia. Nuray Özdemir and İrem Gündüz deserve special thanks for helping me decipher important parts of Eşref's papers. Conversations with my last group of SOAS doctoral students Caner Yelbaşı, Cihan Çelik, Erman Şahin and Yusuf Osman helped me think through the challenging historical period covered in this book.

I gratefully acknowledge research support from the Faculty of Arts & Humanities and the History Department of the School of Oriental & African Studies for granting me research leave during the 2010–2011 academic year, which allowed me to begin the research for this book. Special thanks go to Carol Miles for all her help and friendship during my eighteen years at SOAS. I also thank the Research Center for Anatolian Civilizations of Koç University in Istanbul for a residential fellowship in Spring 2014. Thanks to Büket Coşkuner and Özge Ertem for their generous collegiality in Istanbul.

When I started writing my friend and SOAS History colleague John Parker read two early draft chapters. I'm grateful to him for his sage editing which helped immensely as I groped for a narrative style to match Eşref's story. At Hurst Michael Dwyer kindly agreed to take on this project and was an encouraging editor, while Jon de Peyer, Kathleen May, Daisy Leitch and Brenda Stones patiently helped in countless ways.

I reserve special thanks for my family. My inimitable wife Sarah was a constant inspiration throughout the lengthy period of research and

ACKNOWLEDGMENTS

writing, while our wonderful boys Will, Nick and Benjy tolerated my obsession with Eşref and his world and dutifully read and commented on my draft chapters when they clearly had better things to do. I dedicate this book to them with love.

London and Tucson
May 2016

LIST OF ILLUSTRATIONS

LIST OF ILLUSTRATIONS

1

INTRODUCTION

TALES FROM THE TRUNK

A few years ago I found myself on the western coast of Turkey following the trail of a promising collection of private papers. This trip had been set in motion by a set of unexpected circumstances involving a death in the family of a college friend from Turkey; this led to reestablishing contact with a mutual friend, also Turkish, whom I had known for about thirty years. All this was well before the history of the late Ottoman Empire or the Turkish Republic was remotely a part of my life, as it has now become. Although I did not know it then, this mutual friend, whom I came to meet in the US in the 1980s, was the direct descendant of one of the most fascinating, if controversial, historical characters from the last years of the Ottoman Empire. This is the individual whose story became the center of this book.

I returned to a once familiar hill overlooking the Aegean, where I had been a guest in the mid-1980s, to discover that the neighborhood was now almost completely unrecognizable. Concrete blocks of flats had claimed many of the old olive groves on the lower slopes of the hill. Beyond this radically altered landscape lay the object of my trip: a trunk containing papers that had remained undisturbed since the 1960s and promised to shed new light on the Middle East in the turbulent period before, during, and after World War I; in other words, the period that witnessed the end of the Ottoman Empire and the birth of the Turkish Republic. Specifically, the chest contained the papers of a man known variously as Kuşçubaşızâde Eşref, Kuşçubaşı Eşref, Eşref Kuşçubaşı, İzmirli Eşref, Çerkes Eşref (Eşref the Circassian), and Eşref Sencer. Later the trunk would reveal another name, the alias or *nom de guerre* that he used during his career as an Ottoman special operations field officer.

I had heard of Eşref, as I'll be calling him here for brevity's sake, for his name appears from time to time in accounts of this tumultuous period. It was a decade of almost constant warfare that brought an unedifying end to over 600 years of Ottoman rule, dramatically altering the map of the region and affecting the lives of millions, often in devastating ways. I couldn't say that I knew terribly much about him, but the more I looked into his story in preparation for my visit, the more intrigued I became; intrigued and, to be honest, somewhat apprehensive. My curiosity was piqued because Eşref had been involved in many of the key events of the tumultuous final years of the Ottoman Empire. He was the child of recent immigrants, so his very existence in the empire was symptomatic of the many migrations that shaped the empire's final decades.

Like hundreds of thousands of inhabitants of the North Caucasus, Eşref's family had taken refuge in Ottoman territory as part of the great Circassian exodus, the tragic product of Russia's southward push during the second half of the nineteenth century. Eşref's upbringing in a Circassian family in the milieu of the Ottoman Palace reflected both the mix of continuity and rupture and the blend of traditional patrimonial rule and modernizing tendencies that characterized the Ottoman Empire in the late nineteenth and early twentieth centuries.[1] His career embodied a great many of the major events of his time, including the opposition movement to Sultan Abdülhamid II in the first decade of the twentieth century, the coming to power of the activist Committee of Union and Progress (the "Unionists") in the "Young Turk" revolution of 1908, the Italian–Ottoman war over Libya of 1911–12, the Balkan Wars of 1912–13, the various campaigns of the Great War, and the conflict known in Turkey as the "National Struggle" or "War of Independence" that ended with the establishment of the Turkish Republic in 1923. Although not a household name outside Turkey, Eşref is well known and still highly controversial there to this day.

INTRODUCTION

The prospect of opening his trunk and reading some as yet unseen papers left behind by such an active and contested figure was tantalizing. It is perhaps every historian's dream to explore an unknown cache of sources with the potential to change the way we look at the past.[2] Or maybe I had simply spent too much time pursuing what one colleague called the "dry delights" of social and institutional history. My previous work on the history of education and the history of learning to read in the late Ottoman and early Turkish Republican periods had been intellectually rewarding, at least to me. But as my nearest and dearest were very quick to point out, its almost total absence of action or even basic narrative plot might just have failed to capture the interest of the educated general reader, much less my own kin. Thus the chance to investigate the lively career of Eşref presented a welcome change of pace, if only to appease my domestic critics.

Yet as I got closer to this trunk, my apprehensions grew. First, I had to receive permission from Eşref's descendants to examine the papers, almost all of which were unreadable to them, being written in the old script. As part of the early Turkish Republic's *Kulturkampf* against the old regime, the Turkish "Language Revolution" of the late 1920s had Latinized the Ottoman Turkish alphabet. The result of this "reform" is that most Turks today cannot read the writings of their ancestors. Eşref's family quickly and very kindly granted me permission, and I am very grateful to them for their generosity and their ongoing trust and cooperation. Despite the sensitivities involved, they have never asked to exercise editorial control over my research.

The second and main reason for my apprehension was Eşref's highly controversial reputation. Indeed, one could say that he has become a legendary figure, blurring the boundaries between historical reality and popular imagination. It is partly because of this legend and partly because Eşref fought directly opposite another legendary figure that Eşref has been referred to as the "Turkish Lawrence of Arabia." This tag is problematic—Eşref was an Ottoman of Circassian background and, somewhat ironically in the circumstances, he considered T. E. Lawrence to have developed into a legendary figure who far surpassed his historical role—but the tag has stuck. The legend that has grown up around Eşref is due in part to the writings of Cemal Kutay, a prolific journalist and amateur historian who tended to lionize Eşref by presenting him in heroic terms and exaggerating his status; but subsequently it produced a negative counter-reaction. Efforts to debunk the mythical Eşref were led by Kemalist historians bent on puncturing the legend and guarding the nearly sacred Kemalist version of Turkish history. The most prominent of these efforts is the book by a secondary school teacher and amateur historian named Ahmed Efe.[3] Its subtitle, "From Legend to Reality," pithily summarizes its intention to cut the romanticized Eşref down to size. Often highly prosecutorial in tone, it amounts to a series of corrections, deflations, and accusations, rather than being a well-rounded and critical approach to history. There are those in Turkey who are hostile to the mythical Eşref and do not want his story to be told.

A third worry would emerge as I began to comprehend the sheer size of the project I was taking on. Eşref's peripatetic life was so full of movement and incident, much of it by definition occurring far from the spotlight of history, that simply assembling the basics of his whereabouts, let alone subjecting them to meaningful interpretation, would soon prove daunting. Also, during the many years he devoted to writing and compiling his notes, documents, and memories, he assembled a formidably large collection of materials. The size of his trunk quickly proved deceptive. Out of it came a remarkably varied and large trove of documents. Some are quite pithy and to-the-point, while others are long-winded and occasionally rambling. I often felt as though I could only scratch the surface of his papers, each of which seemed to touch on another episode behind which lay an almost impenetrable thicket of events, personalities, relationships, and, perhaps inevitably, controversies. Eşref's trunk offered many piecemeal clues, but assembling them to form a complete and rounded picture of his life story seemed increasingly remote.

Trying to tell his life according to his papers soon turned up other, more mundane, but no less persistent challenges. As I quickly discovered, simply establishing some of even the most basic facts of his life would prove highly difficult, if not impossible. For example, as we shall see, the most commonly cited year of Eşref's birth is probably off target by a decade. Similarly, he was for many years incorrectly considered to have been the head of the late Ottoman intelligence organization, and even recently written accounts routinely identify him this way. The Turkish intelligence agency (MİT) for many years listed him as one of its progenitors on its website before removing the relevant page. Today there is an anonymous but heavily followed Twitter site that has taken the name Eşref Kuşçubaşı and purports to speak in Eşref's voice from beyond the grave; there is also a novel based on his story.[4] It is no coincidence that the most exaggerated claims and counter-claims blossom on the internet where, for example, one finds him both accused of being a traitor but also lauded as "The World's Greatest Spy."[5]

Such hyperbole is mainly due to two interrelated aspects of Eşref's career. The first is his intimate involvement with a secret group of especially committed military officers known as the Special Organization (*Teşkilat-ı Mahsusa* in Turkish), which was established by Enver Paşa, the most important Ottoman military figure of the last decade of the empire's history, as his own *force spéciale*.[6] The Special Organization was a paramilitary force dedicated to intelligence-gathering, warfare, propaganda, and what we would today call "special operations." It is infamous for having carried out a number of dirty deeds for the Committee of Union and Progress, including political assassinations, clandestine operations, and, most controversially, the suppression of the empire's non-Muslim groups, including but not limited to the campaign to eliminate large sections of the empire's Armenian population during the Great War, an event that has aptly been termed a "shameful act."[7] The organization brought together a diverse group of agents, often referred to as "self-sacrificing officers" (*fedaî zabitan* in Turkish), from across the Ottoman lands and beyond whose common objective was to keep the empire intact at all costs. Eşref's intimate involvement with this organization is enough for some to have decided that he was responsible for many of its heinous activities. At the time I went to look into his trunk, I had most recently seen his name mentioned in the midst of a bitter academic dispute that appeared in the back pages of the leading journal in the field. At contention was whether something Cemal Kutay quoted Eşref as saying about his time on Malta could or could not be taken as evidence for his involvement in the Armenian Genocide.[8] In other words, the stakes involved in studying Eşref were about as high as they can get.

But there is a further reason for Eşref's negative reputation, and it lies in the very last years of the empire. When their "world collapsed around them," as Eşref put it, at the end of the First World War, the self-sacrificing Ottoman officers reacted in different ways. Many took what became known as the "nationalist" side in the fighting that led to the establishment of the Republic and went on to prominent careers in Turkey. But a significant number broke with the nationalists and were either purged, killed, or forced to leave the country. Eşref initially fought with the national forces but parted ways with the leadership coalescing around Mustafa Kemal, later known as Atatürk, and switched sides along with a number of Ottoman officers of Circassian descent. The anti-nationalists, or royalists, were from that point on effectively fighting under the aegis of the occupying Greek army, earning the bitter enmity of those who established the Turkish Republic. Given the almost monopolistic Kemalist control over the foundational writing of Turkish history, however much its grip has begun to loosen in recent years, Eşref has routinely been referred to as a "traitor to the nation" (*"vatan haini"*). Attempts to write Eşref back into a history from which he was excluded by the long-dominant Kemalist approach were taken to be affronts to the established version. Eşref's historical role is thus doubly loaded.

His name therefore appears on the remarkable list that emerged out of the drawn-out negotiations at Lausanne, ending in the establishment of the Turkish Republic. The men on this roster, called simply "The 150ers" (*Yüzellilikler*), were declared *personae non gratae* and banned from the new Turkish state. They were a disparate group, including Ottoman palace functionaries, members of the cabinet who served under Allied occupation after the war, those who signed the Treaty of Sèvres with its plans for dismemberment of what was left of the empire, various officials and journalists, and, relevant here, two large groups of Ottomans of Circassian background, one of which included Çerkes Edhem and his brothers along with Eşref and his younger brother Selim "Hacı" Sami.[9] Eşref and Selim Sami appear as numbers 60 and 61 on this infamous list. As a result, Edhem and Eşref have been treated as national traitors, mainly because they sided against Ankara in the dispute that emerged at the end of 1920. That both men moved to the Greek zone of control was the chief reason that they were accused of treason in Turkish national history.[10] The fact that Eşref's brothers Sami and Ahmed died in an attempt to infiltrate

1. Eşref's trunk. (Photograph author's own)

the Turkish Republic in 1927 did nothing to soften the official verdict of Kemalist historiography.

Eşref's papers were thus potentially quite exciting, but not without their dificulties and the prospect of controversy. I must admit that there were times when I reckoned I was mad to show interest in such a case. But as I began to look through the trunk, two things became readily apparent: 1) the material was both plentiful and captivating but 2), less hopefully, its haphazard arrangement perhaps accurately reflected the peripatetic and multi-episodic nature of Eşref's career. In other words, I was in for a potentially fascinating but seemingly long and bumpy trip.

Eşref's trunk of papers might be considered akin to what Ann Stoler has called a "charged site."[11] Its very presence and the fact that it had lain unopened for so long reflects some of the ruptures and erasures inherent in the troubled transition from the Ottoman Empire to the Turkish Republic. Given the tensions that surround such a collection of sources, there will surely be those who question the intentions behind bringing them to light. It should go without saying that my approach has been to take as neutral an approach as possible, trying always to discern the relationship between the man and his times. Given the contested historiography of this period and of Eşref in particular, there will no doubt be those who will criticize whatever I have to say and perhaps even my decision to write on this topic. To them I say only that the historian must try to weigh all of the evidence and come up with the most plausible account. I am thus not trying either to defend Eşref or to prosecute him, but simply to understand his world.

The missing memoir

For all their problems, Eşref's papers are important because the memoirs to which he devoted many years of his life no longer exist. Since his time as a prisoner of war during World War I, Eşref had been working on a massive account. It was intended to run to as many as twelve volumes. It is clear from various surviving notes and pieces of its table of contents that it was to include not only his eyewitness accounts of the many events in which he was involved, but also original documents and his own illustrations, many of them executed in watercolor. This large work, entitled "Tarihe Benden Haberler" ("My Reports to History"), seems to have perished in the fire that destroyed the library of Cemal Kutay in Kadıköy, Istanbul in 1987.[12] Eşref chose Kutay as his literary executor because Kutay had taken an interest in Eşref when others shunned him. Kutay had collected not only Eşref's memoirs but also those of Eşref's brother Selim Sami and other figures from the period. Kutay used these writings for his own voluminous but not terribly careful publications; but, for unknown reasons, he did not publish the memoir as Eşref had intended. Unless these writings somehow avoided destruction in the fire, they are now lost. There is one exception: the volume of his work covering his mission to Yemen during 1917 was transliterated, edited, and published in both English and Turkish versions.[13] This lone surviving book provides a sense of the degree of detail and colorful narrative that Eşref's larger work would have contained.

Because Eşref's memoir is missing, his papers take on additional significance. They contain a variety of materials, ranging from a few brief sections and partial tables of contents from "Tarihe Benden Haberler" to telegrams, battlefield notes, photographs, letters, legal documents, press clippings, personal memorabilia, etc. One of the most remarkable of the contents was an incomplete but still substantial memoir written by Eşref's second wife, Pervin. Covering the years between 1914, when they married, and 1920, when Eşref broke with the Ankara movement led by Mustafa Kemal, it provides a fascinating account of the war years. Once she enters Eşref's life, it takes on a more rounded shape, emphasizing the importance of the domestic arena to understanding any individual and serving as a reminder of how little we know about the family lives of many key figures of the late Ottoman and early Turkish Republican era. Other interesting contents include Eşref's own battlefield sketches, the recovered memoir of his comrade and Special Organization colleague Süleyman Askerî, and a number of photographs and vignettes from Eşref's time as a prisoner of war on the island of Malta during the final years of World War I. Intriguing and important though these papers are, they do not compensate for his missing memoir. The material is at times very rich, affording insights into some key encounters, but it is essentially scattered and fragmentary. More significant and often frustrating is the fact that Eşref often remained silent about the more controversial aspects of his life. These silences can at times seem deafening. They have often been filled by either the orthodoxies of official Kemalist history or by romanticized versions of the events in question. Because Eşref's mammoth work does not exist, it has been necessary to try to piece together information relating to a number of silences and gaps in Eşref's eventful life by using a variety of other source materials. Drawing on a range of archives both in Turkey and Britain, I have tried as well as I can to fill in those missing pieces.

Approach and organization

Because Eşref's life story played out on such a vast scale and was so full of incident, I have tried, perhaps rashly, to write this book in a more accessible style than most academic historians, myself included, usually manage. I am sure that the result, which by design includes far more narrative than theory, will not please all readers; but I hope it will be received as an attempt to make more accessible a period crucial for understanding the modern history of the region.

Despite the curiously low regard among professional historians for biography, it is an essential means to understanding any historical period. This is especially pertinent to late Ottoman and Turkish history, which has so heavily privileged the state over the individual. As Christine Philliou has so ably shown,[14] centering a study on one individual helps to question and to destabilize the rigid boundaries between state and society and opens up the possibility of a much more nuanced and complicated historical reality. Apart from the several studies on Atatürk,[15] the remarkable paucity of serious English-language biographies for this period makes it tempting to see a causal relationship between that absence and the persistent predominance of fixed ideas about this crucial period.

Focusing on a man such as Eşref, whose career frequently transgressed expected patterns of behavior, calls into question some of these assumed certainties in late Ottoman and Turkish history. Eşref's life story complicates the way we perceive such crucial questions as state service, loyalty, ethnicity, nationality, and as a result the relationship between the individual and the state and society as a whole. What is more, the glimpses into Eşref's domestic life provided by Pervin's memoir allow us to observe the complicated relationship between state service and private life, and between the military world and the domestic front, that is so crucial to capturing the lived experience of this troubled time.

Eşref's life story also affords us the opportunity to ponder the powerful emotional pull associated with victimization and victimhood that continues to flow from the conflicts in which he was involved. On the one hand, as a prominent member of the Special Organization, Eşref is inevitably associated with the acts committed by that diverse group. There are thus many who assume Eşref to have been a victimizer, particularly of the non-Muslim subjects of the empire in its last years. It will become clear that Eşref was probably responsible for the ethnic cleansing of some of the Greek (Rum) population from Western Anatolia in the period between the Balkan Wars and World War I. I have, however, found no direct evidence that he was involved in the uprooting and devastation of the empire's Armenian inhabitants. Nevertheless, the statement that he is recorded to have made about the presence of "tumors" in the Ottoman lands and his hypothetical comments about what he would have done if he had been counterfactually instructed to expel the Armenians make it likely that, like other members of the inner core of Committee of Union and Progress activists, he was not opposed to such devastating deportations *per se*.

On the other hand, Eşref considered himself to have been a victim of injustice occasioned by his banishment from the Turkish Republic at its creation. He published a pamphlet in 1953 decrying the ill-treatment he received at the hands of a government whose independence he helped to secure, but which confiscated his beloved Salihli estate and deprived him of the right to live in his own country with his family.[16] Pervin expressed similarly bitter sentiments in her memoirs, blaming the "sycophants" and "upstarts" around Mustafa Kemal for poisoning relations between the two erstwhile friends and comrades.[17] Without wanting even to approximate equivalence between such claims of victimization, it is perhaps a useful reminder that this period, especially the World War I era, generated deep and long-lasting feelings of suffering and bereavement amongst almost all of its population. Eşref's story shows the fragile line separating insider and outsider, perpetrator and victim.

Stepping back from the personal claims and specific grievances that find their root in this period, we can observe a few larger themes or trends that the study of Eşref's life helps us understand. Mobility, ethnicity, and the sense of belonging to a tight-knit group are common denominators in Eşref's story. Beginning with the experience of his fellow Circassians as refugees to the Ottoman lands, Eşref's life reflects the combination of the pre-modern and the modern that was peculiar to the last decades of the nineteenth century and the early decades of the twentieth. The juxtaposition of seemingly timeless aspects of transhumance and migration with the only recently diffused instruments of mobility such as the railway, the steamship, the telegraph and even the airplane—all of which he used at one point or other—created arresting counterpoints in Eşref's life. The Ottoman state, as reflected in both the traditional institution of the palace and the rapidly modernizing military, took advantage of the influx of the Circassian refugees.[18] Eşref's father was given a position in the palace and Eşref was offered places in some of the best schools of the expanding Ottoman military. Eşref's peripatetic career would combine aspects of that modernizing military, keen to embrace new technologies for warfare and communication, while adhering to long-standing patterns involving the recruitment of volunteers and based on networks of kinship, households, personal loyalty, and a sense of a shared duty or higher calling. Rapid change has meant that all modern lives are lived between two eras, and Eşref's was no exception.

The Circassian connection

The background to Eşref's story lies in the Caucasus. During the nineteenth century, Imperial Russia's drive to subdue and eventually colonize the mountainous terrain of its Caucasian hinterland resulted in a catastrophe for its many peoples, languages, and folkways. Largely ignored in the West, the Russian policy of forced migration in the Caucasus, involving expulsions, the destruction of property and livelihood, and resettlement with Slavs and other Christians, had profound effects first and foremost on the people driven out and secondly on the Ottoman Empire, the place of refuge for most of those who survived. Links between Istanbul and the Caucasus were long-standing. For centuries Circassians had entered Ottoman service, whether as female slaves in the imperial harem or as males in the imperial army; many rose to positions of considerable prominence, either as mothers of sultans or as decorated military officers.[19] Russia's southward drive changed these dynamics drastically. The Russo-Circassian War began in 1830 and lasted for over thirty years, reflecting the Circassians' tenacious defense of their territory. When it became increasingly clear that the brutal Russian campaign would eventually defeat the Circassians, they naturally sought refuge in the Muslim Ottoman Empire. By 1864 the Russian conquest of the North Caucasus was complete. Hundreds of thousands of Muslim refugees were effectively herded to the Black Sea ports where they were to be transported from their homelands to Ottoman territory. Those who lived through the horrific Russian attacks often succumbed to infectious disease. Large numbers did not survive the passage: of the estimated 1.2 million Caucasians forced to emigrate, approximately 800,000 survived and settled in the Ottoman lands.[20]

To the Ottomans these unfortunate people appeared to be an undifferentiated mass and were referred to collectively if inaccurately as "Circassians" (Çerkes in Turkish), despite the important differences that defined them in terms of language, ethnicity, clan, and social status, especially whether they were considered free or slave.[21] This influx came at a time when the empire could perhaps least afford it. The Ottoman state was increasingly in debt, having borrowed on the international capital markets since the Crimean War,[22] and was gradually witnessing its borders shrink at the expense of restive ethnic cum national groups and the Great Powers, with the remaining territory increasingly beset by internal divisions, ethnic strife, and the arrival of hundreds of thousands of refugees from the Balkans and the Caucasus.

The Circassians who arrived in the Ottoman domains were therefore greeted by an ill-equipped and often inept if well-intended Ottoman effort to care for and resettle them in the midst of an increasingly apprehensive population. While there was considerable sympathy among the Ottoman subjects for the plight of the refugees, the circumstances of their immigration also provoked dismay and not inconsiderable fear.

One of the many Circassians who bucked the trend and prospered in the Ottoman lands was Eşref's father. Although little is known about Mustafa Nuri's emigration from the Caucasus or his arrival in the Ottoman Empire, it is clear that at some point during the reign of Sultan Abdülaziz he entered the service of the Ottoman palace in the falconer's corps. Eventually he rose to the position of Chief Falconer. It is because of this position that Eşref and his brothers were referred to as "Kuşçubaşızâde," or son of the Chief Falconer. The patronymic was frequently dropped, leaving the more commonly used name of Kuşçubaşı. But Mustafa Nuri's experience was exceptional. The vast majority of Circassian immigrants to the Ottoman lands were far less fortunate.

Many of the Circassian immigrants had been radicalized and militarized in the process of resisting the Russian onslaught, and were understandably reluctant to trust others with their defense in future. To make matters worse, mortality stalked the new arrivals. The diseases with which they were afflicted, such as typhus and smallpox, spread quickly to the local inhabitants of the empire. The Muslim population, with whom they naturally had the most interaction, was particularly affected. Exacerbating the situation was the fact that the Ottoman state was able to offer only limited financial support, leaving local authorities to cope as best they could. Still, scarce central funds were diverted to help feed and house the immigrants, often provoking local resentments. Many of the Circassians were settled on marginal land, often with a view to altering the local demographic patterns so as to shore up regions where loyalty to the imperial center was perceived to be weak. This policy often did little to ensure the sympathy of the local population. Nor did the reputation for lawlessness and plundering that many Circassians were building do much to help their reception. Suspicion and apprehension frequently accompanied their settlement.

The paramilitary factor

One sector of Ottoman officialdom viewed the new arrivals more positively. The expanding military and security services saw in the Circassians a welcome source of manpower. Many had arrived battle-hardened from their experience fighting the Russians. Indeed, their reputation as a martial force was particularly fearsome. It has been observed that by the period of the empire's demise, the army, police, and gendarmerie forces were disproportionately comprised of Circassians.[23] They were not the only group represented. Albanians took their place alongside Arabs, Kurds, Laz, and of course Turks. But the Circassian presence was particularly prominent. Circassian fighters were recruited because, as we have seen, having been only recently and indifferently settled in the Ottoman lands after the trauma of their expulsion from the Caucasus, they were available to be recruited. The demand for their services was created by the decade of almost constant warfare in the Ottoman Empire in the period from 1911 onwards. Even when the empire was not at war it was heavily engaged in lower-level but still significant counterinsurgency operations, particularly in the Balkans but also in more remote areas such as Yemen, heavily taxing its military capacity.[24] Another factor contributing to the strong reliance upon Circassian officers and recruits by the various branches of the Ottoman military was its increasing appetite for volunteers. The range of tasks facing the Ottoman War Ministry militated in favor of a diversified approach. In particular, the Ottoman military began to replicate the gang or "cheta" (çete in Turkish) mode of organization exhibited in the Balkans, where all the key late Ottoman officers cut their teeth militarily-speaking. This guerrilla-style approach seemed to cry out for volunteers whose loyalty could be relied upon. As recent refugees who had in many cases been radicalized by the experience of expulsion from their homeland, the Circassians were ideally suited to such recruitment. Living in concentrated settlements and with their own languages and kinship structures, they appeared almost tailor-made for the expanding ranks of the Ottoman volunteer forces, especially those of the clandestine or semi-clandestine variety that were newly being established. Although ultimately a unique character with some extraordinary dimensions, Eşref's trajectory nevertheless shares elements with many other lesser-known figures among the empire's Circassian population.

Mobility

A final theme running through this book is that of movement and mobility. In this respect Eşref's life story represents a fascinating coming together of two trends, one long-standing and one only recently made possible by technological change. The scope of Eşref's movements during the active phases of his career would have been impossible even a generation earlier. Railroads took him first into internal exile while he was a student and later into battle. Steamships transported him on missions to the Persian Gulf and later carried him into captivity on Malta and then back to Istanbul and freedom. Another fairly recent contraption, the motor car, also features in his narrative, although it is usually associated with ill-fated voyages of one kind or another. He even had a few turns as a spotter pilot, testing primitive military aircraft in the years before World War I. Machine guns, automatic rifles, and hand grenades became his stock-in-trade. But his most constant companion was undoubtedly the telegraph, a mode of communication on which he depended heavily for both his profession and domestic arrangements. Like his contemporary Diaghilev in almost no other respect, Eşref shared his devotion to the rapid communication afforded by the telegraph. While the Russian impresario used it to orchestrate his dance productions across Europe,[25] Eşref relied on it to conduct operations on three continents at various times in his career. Eventually he had a telegraph apparatus installed in his farm at Salihli. But it was in the field, even in far-flung locales such as the Sinai desert, where it proved invaluable. Eşref used it not only to send and receive orders but also to cajole, threaten, and demand. And he used it for both military and domestic purposes. He sent telegrams both to his comrades-in-arms and to his wife and family, although his domestic messages usually contained only the barest of clues to his otherwise often clandestine whereabouts.

Eşref's activities were thus inscribed across the map by the latest technological contraptions. And yet his career also simultaneously reflects one of the oldest trends in Ottoman history, namely the importance of ethnic affinity, personal networks, and household structures. As Reşat Kasaba has so vividly shown, one constant across the centuries of Ottoman rule was the empire's reliance on mobile, especially tribal, human resources.[26] As the empire modernized, instead of disappearing, dependence on mobile manpower ironically increased. This was particularly evident in the military sphere. The rapid sequence of wars which the empire fought after 1911 quickly revealed the lack of preparedness of the Ottoman armed forces. The old solution was adopted by necessity; volunteers were quickly pressed into service. In many cases these were tribal fighters or "bandits," men who had lived on the margins of the modernizing empire but now were recruited to help save it by joining in the growing number of irregular units. But there was now an increased emphasis on loyalty. In the years before World War I, Enver Paşa oversaw a clear-out of officers who could not be trusted, replacing them with those whom he considered personally loyal.[27] Modern military professionalism combined with old-fashioned patronage was seen as the way forward. Such a combination would open possibilities for men like Eşref. As will become clear, Eşref internalized and took pride in his role as the most committed of the self-sacrificing officers and his loyalty to Enver, even to the point of risking his future in the Turkish Republic.

The Ottoman Ministry of War increasingly adopted paramilitary tactics. This was partly out of necessity, because of the opponents they were becoming accustomed to confront in battle, and partly due to an almost unshakable confidence in both the rightness of their cause and their innate leadership abilities. The experience in Macedonia against a variety of small groups of fighters organized into "*cheta*" units proved decisive. Counter-guerrilla warfare against Bulgarian, Greek, and Serb bands defined their experience in the Balkans. The Macedonian experience was also crucial to the organization of these officers into an oppo-sitional movement dedicated to overthrowing Sultan Abdülhamid II.[28] A number of Eşref's close colleagues such as Enver, Niyazi, Süleyman Askerî, and Aziz Ali Al-Masri joined the predecessor organization of the Committee of Union and Progress during this period, swearing an oath of loyalty on a Qur'an and a revolver. In the field, Ottoman forces began to replicate the organization of their Balkan opponents. Enver and Niyazi Beys, the heroes of the 1908 revolution that brought the Committee of Union and Progress to power, although trained in con-ventional tactics, quickly saw the advantages of guerrilla warfare. Enver fought over fifty such engagements and became known as an expert in counterinsurgency tactics.[29] Rapid movement and communication paired with decisiveness and the recruitment of volunteers were the hallmarks of the emerging military doctrine of the "Young Turk" period. The first test of these methods outside the Balkans came in what is today Libya. Limited to sending a small core of Ottoman offi-cers, almost all of whom had fought in Macedonia, the Ottomans under Enver trained the Sanusi tribal fighters to take on the larger, better equipped but traditionally trained Italian army. Using hit-and-run tactics and avoiding pitched battles, the Ottoman–Sanusi forces achieved impressive results.

The shock of the Balkan Wars forced the Ottoman brass to pull out of the North African campaign prematurely, but it left a lingering conviction that a handful of Ottoman officers coupled with a supply of determined fighting men would lead to victories. The Balkan Wars were fought along more traditional lines and were a disaster for the empire. But after they were over, Eşref played a leading role in another unconventional military operation. Deployed in a highly mobile raiding force, Eşref and his close associates led the unofficial reconquest of Western Thrace. There they established a provisional government and raised a militia force from among the local population. Istanbul's support eventually evaporated in the face of international pressure and the mini-state proved short-lived. Traditionally-minded senior officers voiced their disapproval of the use of irregular, voluntary formations, but to the committed the experience in Western Thrace provided further ammunition for the belief that the "self-sacrificing officers" with their paramilitary tactics were on to a suc-cessful formula.

But the Balkan Wars instilled other, more dangerous lessons. The horrors of that series of increasingly brutal conflicts turned into something very close to total war. Demographic engineering, ethnic cleansing, propaganda, and the battle for popular opinion were becoming almost as important as pitched battles. For the inner circle of the Unionist leadership, the impact of the Balkan Wars was almost immediately directed toward Anatolia. Even before the Great War began, the Unionists orchestrated campaigns to remove the Greek (Rum) population from areas considered to be strategically important. They started with boycotts, but these soon led to physical intimidation and harassment and eventually expulsions. A pattern had been established that would be carried out with even more venom—and with far more disastrous effects—on the empire's Armenian population, especially in Eastern Anatolia.

On other fronts as well, such as in the Caucasus, Iraq, and the Sinai desert, the Ottomans deployed mobile units of volunteers led by committed officers. Many of them, like Eşref, were skilled in irregular combat. Mobile units largely comprised volunteer recruits who were in the thick of the action throughout the Great War. This pattern then continued and was even reinforced during the "National Struggle" period after World War I. These units and their officers were often drawn from outside the normal chain of command. Regular rank had less meaning for these men, who could rely on their personal connections to trump seniority and circumvent the normal military hierarchy. As a result they were often mistrusted by the rank-and-file officers and either marginalized or excluded from the official histories written after the fact. Given that many of these men, Eşref included, were sidelined during the "National Struggle" period and the early years of the Turkish Republic, their contributions were minimized even further.

Although difficult to reconstruct with anything close to the completeness they deserve, the personal connections that linked Eşref with his colleagues and comrades-in-arms form a vital component of this story. His personal papers make it abundantly clear that Eşref considered himself very much part of a group of men who shared a common cause, the sacred mission of what Zürcher has aptly termed "Muslim nationalism." They were all members of a group of about forty or fifty men who considered themselves "self-sacrificing officers" (*fedaî zâbitân* in Turkish).[30] This is a term with clear religious overtones. All of these men were Muslim officers who were willing to die for the cause of defending their religion and their state, the famous Ottoman pairing of *din ü devlet*. Like many in this group, Eşref felt a sense of allegiance to his fellow officers, but it was even more powerfully displayed through his personal loyalty to Enver, the charismatic hero of the revolution of 1908. To Eşref and many of his peers, Enver was the only one who had the qualities to lead the empire from a military point of view. There was a degree of competition among Enver's acolytes, but it rarely seems to have become fractious. In contrast was the long-standing quarrel between Mustafa Kemal and Enver, which seems to have begun in Libya but grew much more serious after a botched attempt to coordinate a marine landing during the Balkan Wars and then continued during World War I. Zürcher has noted that it is unlikely that such quarrelsomeness, "breaches of army discipline and … political meddling" would have been tolerated in any other military.[31] Mustafa Kemal was junior in rank to Enver and, despite subsequent attempts by Kemalist historians to insist that he was always in the right, this amounted to a serious breach of military protocol. This rift would have lasting implications for a number of those who had fought with both, including Eşref.

What is even more striking than Eşref's sense of belonging to the "self-sacrificing officers" was his self-designation in another, more select sub-group of these committed men. Among Eşref's papers there is an extraordinary list on which he had written the top ten names of the self-sacrificing officers. Eşref called them the "Ten Promised Paradise" (*aşere-i mübeşşere* in Turkish) which is a calque on a term that appears in early Islamic history to denote ten men present at the battle of Badr in 624 CE. This was the first military test for the young Muslim community and the Prophet Muhammad promised the glad tidings of paradise to those who had fought with him in that seminal victory. In the list Eşref produced more than thirteen centuries later he placed himself at the top. Second place belonged to his brother Selim "Hacı" Sami, third was Süleyman Askerî, the future head of the Special Organization. In fourth place was Yakup Cemil, perhaps the wildest of them all. And so on. More than half of them were Circassians. All of them were highly motivated, mobile, and had direct experience of countersinsurgency fighting. All were close to Enver. We shall encounter most of them in the following chapters. As Eşref later said, "None of us had anything to lose. We were convinced that our cause was just."[32]

Chapter plan

This book is arranged as an episodic biography. It attempts to follow the main periods of Eşref's life against the backdrop of the major conflicts of his times and to try to see the unfolding of events through the lens of his activities. In other words, it does not try to provide Eşref's complete life story, but rather to focus on the main historically relevant episodes of his life from 1908 to 1920. About his early childhood and later years there is simply less reliable documentation available.

After having set out the main lines of Eşref's life in this introductory chapter, subsequent sections of the book take up its major passages of activity. Chapter 2 traces his early years from the environment around the Ottoman palace to his military education, his first brush with internal exile, and then a much longer period of estrangement when he was sent with his father and brother Sami to Arabia. There he was moved between prisons before escaping and taking up the life of an outlaw. Fashioning himself and his small group of followers as the Arabian Revolutionary Committee, Eşref kidnapped the son of the Medina garrison commander in broad daylight, among other deeds intended to demonstrate to the Ottoman authorities the wisdom of bringing him back onto the side of the law. This eventually came to pass. Together with his father and brother, Eşref returned to the Ottoman fold and was established on one of the imperial estates near Izmir. After the revolution of 1908, Eşref was given a position in the gendarmes and seems to have played the role of a Unionist activist in the Izmir region. Then again he reverted to a period of brigandage before being reconciled to state service once more.

Chapter 3 follows Eşref and his fellow "self-sacrificing officers" as they traveled to Libya to organize the resistance against the Italian invasion of 1911. He was tasked with leading a detachment of Ottoman officers and Muslim VIPs through British-controlled Egypt. Disguised as theology students, Eşref and his men snuck across the border and into the Libyan desert where they raised a local Bedouin force that scored some notable successes against the Italians. Photographs show Eşref and fellow officers such as Enver Paşa, the future Minister of War, and Mustafa Kemal, later Atatürk, in their thick wool uniforms alongside the flowing robes of the Sanusi tribesmen.

The outbreak of the Balkan Wars in 1912, the subject of Chapter 4, represented a much more serious threat to Istanbul. The key officers were stood down from Libya and ordered to Macedonia. Eşref participated in the defense of Istanbul in the later stages of the First Balkan War when he was wounded alongside his brothers Sami and Ahmed. During the second conflict Eşref took part in the recapture of Edirne and then directed guerrilla operations behind enemy lines in preparation for an offensive against Bulgaria. He was instrumental in establishing what has been referred to, somewhat incorrectly, as the "first Turkish republic," the short-lived Independent Government of Western Thrace, with its own flag and currency. Although it quickly collapsed, this mini-state embodied the revanchist spirit and the belief in irregular forces championed by the Unionist leadership.

Eşref's adventures intensified with the outbreak of World War I, as followed in Chapter 5. Thinking his military service over, Eşref had returned to his farm and married a young woman, also of Circassian heritage, named Pervin. But a telegram from Enver at the Ministry of War interrupted the newlyweds' honeymoon, calling Eşref away on another series of missions. First he went to Europe to meet with representatives of the Indian Revolutionary Committee, now potential anti-British allies. His report encouraged Enver to envision a pan-Islamic resistance network to destabilize the Russians in Central Asia and the British in India. When war was declared, Eşref was on a ship bound for Bombay. Recalled from his voyage, he was tasked first with shoring up the allegiance of the Arabian tribes to Istanbul and then with leading a detachment of volunteers in the Ottoman attempt to seize the Suez Canal from the British.

Next, and fatefully for him, Eşref accepted a mission, as described in Chapter 6, to deliver a shipment of gold to the Ottoman forces in Yemen who had been cut off by the "Arab revolt." Ambushed in the desert and wounded during a fierce firefight, Eşref was captured by rebel forces loyal to Emir Faysal. After being paraded among his captives and nearly dying from his wounds, he was given a remarkable local medical treatment that probably saved his life. He was then handed over to the British and taken to Cairo.

Chapter 7 covers his life as a prisoner of the British. From Egypt he was sent to the POW camp on Malta where he led the Turkish contingent. Normal daily life on Malta could be tedious for an active, restless character like Eşref. He spent his time writing to Pervin, solving—and at least once instigating—problems that arose among the colorful conglomeration of German, Italian, Greek, Armenian, Arab, and Turkish prisoners, teaching boxing lessons, and learning to paint. The British released him by mistake and he returned to Istanbul in early 1920.

Far from ending there, Eşref's problems were only beginning. Chapter 8 tells the story of Eşref's involvement in the emerging resistance movement which rose up to challenge the Allied occupation that came with the armistice. Eventually unified by Mustafa Kemal, this group incorporated a variety of actors with differing aims. At first Eşref's role was a promising one. He was appointed regional commander in the movement, but was soon faced with a rebellion raised by his fellow Circassians in the town of Adapazarı. Ankara increasingly viewed Eşref with suspicion, but he remained involved in the movement albeit with smaller roles to play. Finally, he fell out with the emerging leadership in Ankara who grew wary of his independent actions and probably his lingering connections with Enver. Like Çerkes Edhem, Eşref went over to the Loyalist/Greek side and played a role in the increasingly desultory attempts to supplant Mustafa Kemal.

The book concludes with Chapter 9, a brief summary of Eşref's life after 1920. He was eventually placed on the list of "the 150" who were banned from the Turkish Republic at its creation. Living first in Greece and then in Egypt, Eşref tried to rehabilitate his reputation but met with little success. That his brothers Selim "Hacı" Sami and Ahmed died while apparently trying to assassinate Mustafa Kemal, the future Atatürk, only added to the awkwardness of his relationship with the Turkish Republic. In the meantime he had to resort to clandestine night visits by sea in order to see his wife and glimpse his sleeping children. As an old man he was eventually allowed to return to Turkey, where he kept in touch with his wartime friends but stayed clear of political activity until his death in 1964. The book ends with a discussion of Eşref's place in the history of the late Ottoman Empire and the Turkish Republic.

2

FROM PALACE TO REBEL AND BACK AGAIN

The early years

Eşref's early years were shaped by his father's position in the sultan's palace, their family's Circassian origins and the increasingly tumultuous nature of life in the Ottoman Empire. His emerging but clearly head-strong personality played no small part in his ability to insinuate him-self into the turbulent events of the day. As we shall see, Eşref's life narrative seems determined to explore the borderline between insider and outlaw. Given his childhood of relative privilege, thereafter his phases of exile, banditry, and return to the center of power made for an unusually checkered career. This restless, occasionally transgressive dimension of Eşref's life helps explain both its inherent interest and its enduring controversy.

Kuşçubaşızâde Eşref's story begins in Istanbul. Although many aspects of his early years remain obscure, it is clear that he was born and grew up in the quarter of Beşiktaş on the European shores of the Bosphorus. Eşref's family seem to have first settled in a village with a large concentration of Circassians of Ubıh lineage called Hacıosmanköy in the region of Manyas on the southern shores of the Marmara Sea.[1] Unlike the majority of the Circassian refugees who were spread across the breadth of the Ottoman provinces, however, Eşref's father had a useful connection in the Ottoman palace and moved to Istanbul as a result. Through the intercession of his sister who was married to a palace official, Eşref's father Mustafa Nuri obtained a position in the imperial falconry corps, eventually rising to its head, or Kuşçubaşı as it was known in Turkish.[2] At some point Mustafa Nuri married a woman named Tevhide Hanım and together they had several children, the oldest male being Eşref. Remarkably little is known about Mustafa Nuri Bey, apart from his position, his apparent closeness to Sultan Abdülhamid II, and the fact that he was sent into internal exile in 1900, perhaps as a result of a palace or a political intrigue.[3] The fact that Eşref and his brother Sami grew up and attended schools in Istanbul and not among the Circassian population of the Southern Marmara would later create problems for Eşref during the "National Forces" period.

Sultan Abdülhamid II had come to power in 1876, the "year of the three sultans" in which both of his predecessors had been removed from office under extraordinary circumstances, one by *coup d'état* and the other on the grounds of insanity. As a result, young Abdülhamid followed a policy of extreme caution and adopted the secluded grounds of Yıldız Palace as his residence. Like many palace officials, Mustafa Nuri chose the adjacent quarter of Beşiktaş as a convenient place to live. Their house was located in the neighborhood known as "behind the Has Fırın (bakery)," a location preserved in a street with the same name that leads off from the main Barbaros Boulevard in Beşiktaş today. In the late nineteenth century the region was far less crowded than today's incarnation. The quarter featured large houses with ample gardens that would seem impossible in today's urban conglomeration. Apart from being convenient for the palace, the Kuşçubaşıs' house was also not far from a family with which, unbeknownst to them at the time, they would later become related through marriage, the Osman Ferid Paşa family on Serencebey Hill.[4] Fellow Circassians Osman Ferid and his siblings were direct descendants of Imam Shamil, the legendary leader of the resistance to the Russian invasion of the Caucasus. Like Mustafa Nuri, they had been forced to leave their beloved ancestral homeland for the safety of the Ottoman lands. From the time of the great exodus of the various peoples of the North Caucasus in the 1860s, the Ottoman sultans took special interest in the Circassian refugees, welcoming them into the empire despite its lack of resources and infrastructure. Given their resistance to the Russian invasion of their homeland, many of the refugees became enthusiastic servants of the Ottoman state, particularly in the palace and the military.

Many aspects of Eşref's life are difficult to establish with any degree of certainty, beginning with the year of his birth. Most accounts give his birthdate as 1873. Like much of what has been written about Eşref, they follow Philip Stoddard's pioneering 1963 doctoral dissertation on the Special Organization (Teşkilat-ı Mahsusa) in the Arab lands. Dr Stoddard's study remains one of the very few serious academic studies featuring Eşref Bey, and Stoddard interviewed Eşref several times in the early 1960s.[5] But Eşref's family—and his gravestone—suggest 1883 as the more likely birthdate. That is in fact the date shown on his census record.[6] Furthermore, in the pamphlet that Eşref published in 1953 to state his case for vindication and the restoration of confiscated property, he gives his age as 70, which would confirm the date of 1883. According to his family, Eşref himself used a simpler and in Turkey a more common temporal yardstick: he always insisted that he was a bit younger than Mustafa Kemal who was born in 1881. Part of the chronological problem undoubtedly stems from the fact that children were born at home and their dates of birth were recorded only much later. Another problem stems from the different calendars in operation at the time. That even such basic facts are difficult to ascertain provides a cautionary note about how difficult it can be to recover the historical record of the not so distant past.

Eşref was one of a large number of brothers and sisters but not many of them lived to maturity, a result of the mortality typical of that era as well as the particular profile of two of his brothers who were killed in an apparent attempt to infiltrate the Turkish Republic in 1927. In his papers, Eşref lists six maternal siblings and six half-siblings. Of these, several died in childhood of illness—scarlet fever was particularly deadly[7]—and at least one in childbirth. One sister named Aliye drowned when a steamship sank in Izmir harbor; her body was found clutching her children in a grim embrace. Compared with his siblings, Eşref's longevity was exceptional, particularly given the lengthy list of armed conflicts in which he fought. Years later he would tell his son-in-law that the reason he lived as long as he did despite his dangerous line of work was his predilection for proactive tactics. Whenever possible he avoided placing himself in a position vulnerable to attack, always

25

taking the offensive instead. It was a strategy that naturally earned him a few enemies along the way. It would not be long before the young Eşref began to demonstrate the pre-emptive and pugnacious sides of his personality.

Eşref's first interactions with the late Ottoman world took place in Istanbul. Although he would at times later be known as "İzmirli Eşref," or Eşref from Izmir, because of the land and power base he acquired in the Aegean region, it was clear that he identified with the neighborhood of his birth. Writing of his brother Selim Sami, four years his junior, Eşref identified him as he would presumably have described himself: "Selim Sami was Istanbullu and Beşiktaşlı."[8]

The two brothers experienced a similar educational trajectory. This began in the neighborhood *mektep* or Qur'an school, but was augmented by private tuition given by a local cleric. From this religious type of instruction they passed on to the educational institutions of the Ottoman state, first of the civil and then the military variety.[9] After attending the local state school, named the Hamidiye after the reigning sultan, at both primary and middle school level, they were enrolled in the imposing Kuleli military academy. Located on the Asian side of the Bosphorus, Kuleli was a prestigious institution. As sons of palace officials, the boys attended the "special" or "sons of officials" class. Eşref entered in 1893,[10] with Sami joining four years later.[11] They would both later enroll in the Imperial Military Academy (Mekteb-i Harbiye). Because he was sent into exile with his father, Eşref would not graduate but Sami later would.[12] The military schools played a decisive role in inculcating both an ethos of elitist solidarity and an oppositional spirit,[13] characteristics that would mark Eşref's subsequent career. As Gingeras aptly puts it when analyzing the small but important group of men (including Eşref and Sami) who formed the core of the late Ottoman clandestine service, these were "individuals born and groomed for power."[14]

For Eşref, however, the path to power was far from smooth. At Kuleli, Eşref was at the center of a major incident among the students which came to be known as the "big Kuleli fight." The altercation was one that pitted different factions of the school against each other. The groups were largely determined by the cadets' ethnicity and place of origin, with the fault lines separating those from Istanbul and the

Balkans against those from the Arab provinces. Eşref's group included a student from Podgorice in Montenegro named Ömer and three students from the capital: the future early Republican cabinet member İhsan Eryavuz, a certain Hasan Hoca from Beylerbey, and Eşref.[15] It was a violent encounter; Eşref was among the wounded but it seems that he gave at least as good as he got. An inquest ensued in which students from Yemen identified Eşref as the one who had beaten them up. The ringleaders were dispersed to military preparatory schools in different parts of the empire, all except Eşref. For a period of six months he remained at Kuleli as a boarding student in a kind of limbo until his case was decided. He heard others saying that he had been spared exile due to his father's influence. In fact, Mustafa Nuri Bey did eventually intervene with the sultan but not in the way that the gossips had assumed. Eşref's father objected to the fact that appearances suggested that his son was receiving special treatment. Sultan Abdülhamid II indicated to his Chief Falconer that the incident among the students was hardly a major cause for concern. But Mustafa Nuri insisted that the event was weighing heavily on him and that he was losing sleep over it. He pleaded for an imperial decree that would address Eşref's role in the fight. The sultan advised Mustafa Nuri to address his request to the director of the military schools.

Soon an officer from the War Ministry appeared at Kuleli. He took Eşref, severed his relations with the academy, and escorted him to his family's house. The officer gave Eşref one day's home leave to prepare and said he would return the following morning before sunrise to take Eşref to the train station, all without telling Eşref where he would be headed. With his father accompanying him to see him off, Eşref arrived at Sirkeci station the following morning. Mustafa Nuri was given Eşref's first-class ticket and told that the train was bound for Europe and that Eşref would be getting off in Edirne, a former capital of the Ottoman Empire. On arriving in Edirne that evening Eşref was taken to a hotel room, still not fully aware of what was happening to him. The next morning a military policeman arrived and escorted Eşref to the military preparatory school, handing him over to the duty officer. Amid great confusion the school's director, a certain Ragıb Bey, appeared in the late morning, asking a flurry of questions and casting suspicious, hostile glances in Eşref's direction.

Finally, Ragıb Bey began to interrogate his new arrival. It was not a respectful beginning to Eşref's time in Edirne. "Why were you sent here?" the director demanded. "Because of the Kuleli dispute," Eşref responded. "This isn't Kuleli," the director replied, "you should know that I punish people ruthlessly, gouge out their eyes and put them in the palms of their hands." These threats brought out the combative side of Eşref's personality. "Sir," he retorted, "you can send me to an enlisted unit, throw me in prison and block my future. But you won't be able to gouge out my eye and put it into the palm of my hand." Eşref was indicating that his father would provide a powerful deterrent. The director then asked whose son Eşref was. When he got his answer, the director's manner changed. "Ah, he's someone I respect. You can treat me like an uncle," before making an about-face.[16] Not for the last time Eşref showed a confidence bordering on cockiness in the face of authority.

It is difficult to gauge the full effect of the years in Edirne on Eşref, but it is clear that he formed lasting connections there with two of his schoolmates, both of whom shared his Circassian origins. One was Yenibahçeli Şükrü (Oğuz). Their career paths would cross several times in the years ahead, first as militant members of the Committee of Union and Progress, then in the Special Organization, and finally during the "national" resistance period. The other was with Süleyman Askerî.[17] Eşref's bond with Askerî seems to have been particularly strong. They eventually became related by marriage, marrying sisters, and their professional relationship was forged in Libya, the Balkan Wars, and particularly during the period in which they together founded the independent government of Western Thrace at the very end of that conflict. Askerî would subsequently be made head of the Special Organization, in which position he would have many opportunities to work together with Eşref before Askerî would take his own life in Iraq during World War I. Eşref placed Sülyeman Askerî just after himself and his brother Sami on his list of the inner core of the self-sacrificing officers, the "Ten Promised Paradise" (aşere-i mübeşşere).[18] Eşref couldn't have known it at the time but his banishment to Edirne would leave lasting marks on his career.

Eventually Eşref managed to return to Istanbul and to Kuleli where he finished secondary school and entered the Military Academy, known as Mekteb-i Harbiye, or Harbiye for short. Harbiye was the key institution in the formation of the Ottoman officer corps. With only a few exceptions, the central figures in the dramas that would unfold during the empire's final years had all been trained at Harbiye.[19] Although some sources claim that Eşref graduated from Harbiye, it seems clear that because of his being sent into internal exile in Arabia with his father and his brother Sami, he did not. Nevertheless Eşref's links with his Harbiye classmates remained an important factor, along with shared combat experience and networks of ethnicity and political affinity, in constructing his social milieu and his professional career.

A guest comes to stay

During the time when Eşref was a military student, his family hosted an unusual guest. A young, passionate theological student from eastern Anatolia came to stay with the family for an extended period. His name was Said Nursî and he would go on to play an extraordinary role in shaping the religious landscape of modern Turkey. Said Nursî's career reflects the close but sensitive relationship between religious and political life in both the empire and the Turkish Republic. Born into a Kurdish family in a village in the eastern province of Bitlis in 1877, Said Nursî quickly became known for his prodigious knowledge of the Islamic sciences. Unlike most theological students of the time, however, Said Nursî demonstrated a strong impetus for political and indeed military engagement. He was one of the founding members of the Muhammadan Union (İttihad-i Muhammedi Fırkası) and a writer for its organ *Volkan* ("The Volcano"). Nevertheless, during the anti-Unionist counter-revolution of 1909 he preached to the rebels and encouraged them to abandon their rebellion and submit to their officers in the name of Islamic unity. During World War I he joined the army and served as a member of the Special Organization in fighting against the Russians, who took him prisoner in 1916 and held him as a POW. He later supported Mustafa Kemal and the nationalist cause in the early 1920s. Said Nursî would go on to write several theological treatises, in particular the massive Epistle of Light (Risale-i Nur), stressing the need for positive action—his interventions in Turkish politics in the 1950s seem to have been influential in the success of the Democrat Party— that would inspire the creation of the "Nurcu" or "Nur" movement with its millions of followers around the world today.

But in the 1890s all that lay in the future. The circumstances leading to Said Nursî's stay with Eşref's family are obscure, but it seems that the young firebrand had been attempting to attract the interest of the sultan with his outspoken defense of Islam and his plan for reform in the eastern provinces, particularly those with a high concentration of Kurds. While in the eastern city of Erzincan, Said Nursî created some kind of disturbance. Having climbed a minaret, he was observed shouting about the sultan from one of its balconies in order to attract attention. The commotion caught the attention of an Ottoman official of Circassian origin named Yahya Nüzhet Paşa who was in Erzincan at the time, carrying out his duties as inspector of the eastern provinces. Nüzhet Paşa apparently took an interest in Said Nursî and decided that he should go to Istanbul, either to keep a better watch over him or to keep him from getting into further trouble in the provinces. As Şerif Mardin notes, "It was through such trusted aides rather than through the formal governmental structure that the sultan carried out his more secret policies."[20] Through Nüzhet Paşa's intercession with his fellow Circassian, Said Nursî went to stay at Mustafa Nuri's house in Istanbul. He remained there for a year and a half, taking his meals with the family.[21] He and Eşref became good friends and, as noted, the connection between Eşref and Said Nursî would continue during the war years when the theologian saw active service in a Special Organization unit fighting against the Russians. What influence Said Nursî had on Eşref is unclear, but it has been noted that Eşref's later attempts to implement the pan-Islamic propaganda during the Great War was a point of shared interest and activity. Ultimately failing to attract the attention of the sultan that he craved, Said Nursî eventually returned to Van in 1899. He would reappear in Istanbul in 1907, where he would meet the poet and fellow Special Organization propagandist Mehmet Akif, among other Islamist intellectuals. He would move to Salonica the following year where he met and was on "good terms" with several of the key Young Turk activists, including Dr Nazım, Talat, and Ali Fethi.[22]

One of Eşref's daughters remembers that in later years when Said Nursî's name came up in conversation and someone referred to him as a religious fanatic, her father said that no one had any right to assume anything about Said Nursî. Recalling the young man's time as a guest in his father's house and his military service as a volunteer in a detachment that included a number of graduates from the Galatasaray Lycée, Eşref referred to him as a patriot and a good man, a correction that she remembered vividly long afterwards.[23]

Arabian exile

Meanwhile, Eşref continued his studies. He got as far as the second year of the cavalry section of Harbiye when in 1900 his education was again cut short.[24] He was sent into internal exile in Arabia with his father Mustafa Nuri and his brother Selim Sami. The reason for this second and much more substantial period of exile remains obscure— Eşref says that despite their long friendship, the sultan apparently took exception to a coarse answer with which Mustafa Nuri responded to a question[25]—but it is likely that Mustafa Nuri and his sons were increasingly attracting the suspicion of the palace for their suspected opposition to the sultan. By this point Sultan Abdülhamid II had been the target of several assassination attempts and failed coups. The palace took on an increasingly suspicious air. The military, whose officers had been involved in past attempts to overthrow the sultan, came under particular scrutiny. Whatever its ultimate cause, Eşref's next period of banishment was to have important long-term consequences.

The ensuing Arabian phase of his life seems to have been formative for Eşref, both in terms of his experience among the Bedouin Arabs and with respect to his relationship with the Ottoman authorities, but it is also a period that remains frustratingly mysterious. One of the most colorful periods of a colorful career, it is almost completely without corroborating evidence beyond Eşref's own recollections. Some accounts of Eşref's life say that after Harbiye he was assigned to duty in Macedonia. There he apparently got involved in political activity and was banished to the Hicaz, the region along the Red Sea coast of Arabia where Islam began, together with his father and Selim Sami.

Although the cause of this banishment remains obscure, it is clear that this period of exile, first in Mecca and then Medina, was when Eşref and Sami got their first taste of life on the wrong side of the law. According to the terms of their father's exile, the boys were to be confined to the fortresses of the region, first at Mecca, then at Taif in September 1900. Eşref managed to escape from the Taif prison but was later recaptured and sent to the larger Ottoman military base in Medina. There, in the city where the Prophet Muhammad created the first Muslim community, Eşref was "thrown into a cellar that didn't see the light of day."[26]

Eşref stayed there for a year and a half, confined alongside political exiles associated with a number of plots against Sultans Abdülaziz and Abdülhamid, some as long ago as sixteen years. Waiting in his cell opposite those that had housed the likes of Midhat Paşa, the constitutional champion and fall guy for the coup that had deposed Abdülaziz,[27] who had died in captivity under mysterious circumstances, Eşref must have felt that he was languishing in a remote Arabian jail cell, similarly discarded and forgotten. Eşref was at first simply confined to the fortress of Medina; but at some point in 1901 after having wounded a man named Şihab, Eşref was shackled in a kind of serial leg stocks called a *tomruk*, designed to hold several prisoners in a row by their ankles. The restless Eşref considered this device a particular affront. He describes the device as a vestige from another time and as evidence that only in a backwater like the Hijaz could such an instrument, "unknown in our own day," have been deployed. It was, he said, as if the Tanzimat reforms and even *shari'a* law did not exist there in the city that gave birth to Islam and its holy law. Eşref seems to have been so insulted by the existence of the *tomruk*, which he describes as an instrument of "oppression and torture," that he sketched it several times from memory in his later writings, both on its own and showing it fastened around the ankles of its human captives as they lay on simple reed mats.[28] At one point in his confinement he was shackled for a month across from a man named Musa who was being punished for insulting Osman Ferid Paşa, the Custodian of Medina (and, ironically, someone to whom Eşref would later be related by marriage).[29]

Eventually, he escaped. With the help of his brother Sami and a fellow Circassian named "Çerkes" Tahir who was the assistant commandant at the Medina prison, Eşref managed to break out of the jail along with a number of political prisoners and took to the desert. The others managed to get transferred to Beirut and Damascus, even with a salary increase to boot. But Eşref was either unwilling or unable to reconcile himself with Ottoman authority. He chose the path of banditry instead. For several years, it seems, Eşref lived among the Arab tribes of the

FROM PALACE TO REBEL AND BACK AGAIN

2. Gone native in Arabia, c. 1905. (Source: EK papers)

Nejd desert, adopting the ways and dress of the Bedouin, as a lone photograph from this period shows. For the swiftness of the raids he made out of the desert upon the sedentary population, he supposedly earned the nickname "Shaykh of the Birds" or the "Flying Shaykh." Eşref pithily describes this as a rough-and-tumble period in which he provided an armed response to the despotic administration: "I hit and I was hit. I remained free from the despotism of that period and I worked in the name of liberty."[30] Together with an Arab named Faraj ibn-al-Masri, he apparently organized a guerrilla band they named the Arabian Revolutionary Committee.[31] Beginning operations in 1903, this unit, or perhaps gang, engaged in raiding and banditry.

Eşref's precise activities during this period are difficult to discern. In later years he claimed that the purpose behind the Arabian Revolutionary Committee was the toppling of Sultan Abdülhamid II. Like many episodes in Eşref's career, this claim has both a plausible and an unlikely side. It is believable to the extent that Abdülhamid's reign generated a wide range of oppositional activity. Groups dedicated to resisting and in some cases overthrowing the sultan sprouted across the Ottoman lands, especially among the students of the military academies. Influenced by the writings of a variety of European thinkers, many of which were only partially read or understood, some of the students of these schools developed a loose network of opposition. This in turn reinforced the sultan's innate apprehension about the possibility of another coup and resulted in an elaborate regime of censorship and a counter-opposition apparatus. Rumor and intrigue added to the mix.

Abdülhamid's reign is usually equated with the term "despotism," particularly in the official historiography of the Turkish Republic which sought to denigrate the rule of the last important Ottoman sultan. Indeed, many aspects of the Hamidian era, as this long period is known, were autocratic, as the sultan attempted to modernize the empire while maintaining strong central authority. His brand of rule has been described as "neo-patrimonial," by which is meant a form of rule that was grounded in rationalized structures but was ultimately reliant on personal connections and individual loyalty. In its most simplistic interpretation this was a period in which the cause of liberty and freedom were struggling to emerge from a time of stultifying authoritarianism. Such a simplification misses much of the nuance of the period but it makes for clearly delineated rivalry between good and bad forces. The situation was frequently far more complicated. It was tempting for all of those who opposed the regime in one way or other to present themselves as engaged in such a clear-cut battle. As we have seen, Eşref would later make such claims while acknowledging that his family's links with the palace complicated matters.

Eşref would later emphasize the comforts that came with his father's palace position as a means to underscore the sacrifice involved in his break with the sultan. Portraying his rebellion in the imperial military academy as one of the first instances of a revolt against the oppressive regime of Abdülhamid II, Eşref emphasizes the privileges on which he was turning his back by going against his family's benefactor. He describes the high-level connections that his family enjoyed with the palace, connections that ensured a life of affluence and ease. For example, trays of food would be delivered to their house from the palace. Despite this, Eşref says, he became worried about the "future of this holy nation and innocent community" and chose to forgo the benefaction of the sultan, thus becoming one of the first of his contemporaries to rebel.[32]

Patriotism, Samuel Johnson said, is the last refuge of a scoundrel and there are some who would define Eşref that way. But for our purposes it is important to note the complicated relationship between Eşref and central authority that begins in the Hamidian era. In subsequent years he would both fight against such authority, whether sultanic or Kemalist, and rely on its forgiveness. He benefited from the sultan's pardons on more than one occasion. Not surprisingly Eşref presents himself in different ways depending on the changing, tumultuous conditions of late Ottoman rule. When the Committee of Union and Progress came to power, Eşref would by contrast represent the full force of central authority, sometimes in the most violent fashion, and be trusted with important assignments. However, when Mustafa Kemal put his stamp on the "National Forces" in the early 1920s, Eşref would find that the forgiveness to which he had grown accustomed was far less forthcoming. Afterwards, whether defending his role in opposition to or in support of power, Eşref used his considerable rhetorical skills to his best advantage.

The years in Arabian exile taught Eşref and Sami some hard truths about power, but also showed them how to uncover its vulnerable spots. Getting involved in both brigandage and skirmishing between the tribes, the brothers Eşref and Sami seem to have developed both a taste and a talent for the marginal side of life. In Arabia such a way of life was not altogether unusual, given the propensity of the tribes for raiding and revenge-taking among themselves and on occasion against the Ottoman forces. After a period in which, Eşref says, Sami distinguished himself in this kind of skirmishing, Sami returned secretly to Istanbul where the government tried unsuccessful to find him.[33] But for Eşref in Arabia, the faraway government in Istanbul remained the most important intended audience. His strategy seems to have been calculated to demonstrate his capacity for disrupting Ottoman rule in the Hijaz, where both the economy and the prestige of sultanic rule rested on pilgrimage.[34] By attacking the Hijaz railroad, a prized project of Sultan Abdülhamid, kidnapping the son of the Ottoman commander of Medina, and raiding the official pilgrimage caravan to Mecca, Eşref's efforts were all aimed at the sensitive points of Ottoman rule and therefore designed to impress the authorities with his resourcefulness and fearlessness. They were also undertaken in the knowledge that despite the increasingly tense stand-off between the palace and the opposition, Sultan Abdülhamid II tended to show a remarkable degree of forgiveness towards his wayward subjects. As Eşref put it, "there was always 'one last pardon'. The sultan was not fundamentally a cruel man and much preferred banishment to execution, even though the exiles always worked against him. Besides, he was fond of my father."[35]

Eventually, Eşref's Arabian strategy seems to have worked. The audacity of Eşref's activities combined with Abdülhamid's tendency towards leniency led to reconciliation. By 1905 Eşref and his brother were pardoned, allowed to return to Western Anatolia, where they joined their previously pardoned father, and given imperial sinecures. Paid a daily stipend if they were to stay out of trouble, they were allowed to settle with their father on a large imperial estate near Izmir. Besides money and freedom, this move would afford Eşref and Sami a way back towards the center of power. But it would not mean the end of their complicated relationship with imperial authority.

Eşref's activities in Arabia were also noted beyond the Ottoman domains. The British in particular took notice. For example in *Seven Pillars of Wisdom*, that other, far better known Arabian adventurer T. E. Lawrence mentions Eşref's exploits in Arabia from this period. Lawrence gets some of his facts wrong, for example that Eşref's boyhood took place "near his Smyrna home," but he was clearly impressed with Eşref's derring-do. Lawrence recounts a number of episodes, including the kidnapping of the son of the Ottoman commander of Medina from the parade ground in broad daylight.[36] Lawrence and Eşref would later square off during the "Arab Revolt," but Eşref was characteristically disdainful of Lawrence and his legend. Eşref always insisted, with some justification, that Lawrence's role was exaggerated and that the Ottomans were far more interested in Lawrence's colleagues. Ironically, similar claims have often been raised about Eşref himself and the "legend" that has grown up around his name. Despite the antipathy between them, both men have been bracketed together under the term "Arabian adventurer," for better or worse.

During his stay in Arabia, Eşref seems to have engaged in all sorts of activities. With his education truncated in order to accompany his father into exile and the normal path of progression cut off, the energetic Eşref soon ran foul of the local officials in the Hijaz. His penchant for getting into trouble was not confined to the schools of Istanbul and Edirne. His account leaves some gaps but includes the fact that he bought a Luger pistol, presumably his first such weapon, "in order to protect himself from the Bedouin."[37] This is just about possible as the gun was invented in 1898. He seems to have used it to threaten someone in the Ottoman administration of the Hijaz and thus had to leave Medina for the Necd desert. There, by his own account, he was a guest of Abdülaziz Al-Rashid, the sixth Al Rashid emir who ruled from 1897 to 1906. The Al Rashids were traditional allies of the Ottomans in Arabia, but would soon be defeated and usurped by the rising Saudi dynasty. There, he says, the Rashidi emir wanted to employ Eşref right away; but, Eşref explained, his aim was to serve his ultimate benefactor, the Ottoman sultan.

In an unusually aimless period, Eşref left for Iraq, uncharacteristically to try his hand at commerce. In Basra he bought a sufficient quantity of dates and attar of rose to sell. Setting out from Basra he traveled along the Tigris, making his way around Iraq, including stops in Baghdad (where he apparently made a pilgrimage to the tomb of the medieval Sufi saint Abulqadir Gilani), Suleymaniya, and the holy sites of Kerbela and Najaf. Eventually he returned to the Necd where, learning that his father had been recalled from internal exile, he contacted Ahmed Ratib Paşa, the Governor of the Hijaz, but did not apparently risk—or perhaps trust—seeing him in person lest he be recaptured. Eşref then made his way up the route of the Hijaz railroad, passing through Madain Salih and Maan in Transjordan. From there he passed among the Howaytat, Sahur, and Banu Atiyya tribes before turning to the west and reaching Gaza on the coast of Palestine. From there he took a coastal lighter to Port Said, then possibly stopped in Cyprus, after which he boarded a French ship bound for Piraeus. Here Eşref explains that he didn't have permission to return to Istanbul so didn't dare to return to the Ottoman capital. Disembarking by chance in the Greek port, Eşref made his way to the Ottoman embassy in Athens and petitioned the authorities to be allowed to return to the Ottoman fold, informing them of his full loyalty and his long-standing desire to sacri-fice himself for the sultan. He was told that he would have to wait fif-teen days for a response, but he had insufficient money to stay in Athens, and got accosted and threatened by a group of local bandits; he therefore made his way to Thessaly and then on to Montenegro. Learning that the reforming Inspector General of Rumelia Hüseyin Hilmi Paşa happened to be in Üsküp (Skopje), Eşref entered Ottoman territory from Berane in Montenegro on his way to Kosovo. He was subsequently arrested by the Ottoman authorities, who described him as wearing "traveling clothes," in other words out of uniform.[38]

Eşref's account makes no mention of his arrest, only that he was questioned. A substantial correspondence ensued as the authorities tried to decide what to do with this former military cadet who had made his way from one end of the empire to the other. "Throwing himself before the Gate of Justice," Eşref appealed to be allowed to return to Ottoman lands and take up a post for the sake of his poor mother who had shed tears of longing for many years during his exile. Finally, he writes, he was able to catch the sympathetic attention of Ottoman officialdom and his plea was heard. He was authorized to return to Izmir, where his father had been recently settled on imperial lands. By 20 December 1905 Eşref had landed in Izmir. Both he and his father wrote letters to the sultan to express their gratitude for his benevolence. They had been returned to the loyal fold, at least for the time being.

The Izmir years

With imperial forgiveness came generosity. As part of the settlement that his father made with the palace, Mustafa Nuri, Eşref, and Sami were given positions on the imperial Tepeköy estates at Torbalı to the south-west of Izmir.[39] Eşref and Sami were paid a salary of 25 gold liras per month to stay out of trouble. The money was paid up front and it seems that they were happy to collect it for a while before some time in 1906 when they turned again to banditry. Although this sinecure was a fairly comfortable one, it seems likely that being paid to do nothing on the sultan's estate was excruciatingly boring for the energetic Eşref, a more pleasant situation but still a kind of exile. His drive to be recognized and to insert himself into the center of things was a likely factor in his return to banditry. If so, this was a strategy that eventually worked, for within a few years he came to the attention of Enver, the rising star of the late Ottoman Empire.

Eşref and his companions took to the mountains, becoming outlaws once again. In a move that would have critical later repurcussions, they joined forces with a man named Çerkes Reşid, one of several brothers of a Circassian family from the Bandırma region. The brothers, the most famous of whom would prove to be the younger Edhem, would play important roles in Eşref's story. From 1906 until at least 1923 their lives would be intertwined, sometimes in rather murky circum-

3. "Çerkes" Edhem. (Source: EK papers)

stances. Further blurring the lines between the two sides of the law, Eşref is believed to have recruited them into the Special Organization.[40]

Reşid was at that time serving as an officer in the Ottoman gendarmes (*jandarma*), the organization tasked with wiping out the brigands operating in the Izmir region. Reflecting the conflicted relationship between central authority and the refugees to the Ottoman lands who were prone to lawlessness, the gendarmes recruited heavily from the immigrant population of north-western Anatolia, espcially the Circassians. At the same time, the Ottoman state was committed to combatting brigandage. In 1909 it adopted a "Law for the Prevention of Brigandage," (Men-i şekavet kanunu).[41] Çerkes Reşid epitomized the contradictions inherent in such a recruitment policy. Demonstrating a propensity for playing both sides of the game, Reşid had joined the outlaws instead of hunting them. This anti-authoritarian turn seems to have been fueled by a desire to avenge the deaths of his older brother İlyas, who had been shot and killed in a roadside ambush, and his younger brother Nuri, who had been killed during a nighttime raid on their family home.[42] Helping himself to some officially issued Mauser rifles and cases of ammunition, Reşid had taken to the hills, joining Eşref and Sami and living the life of brigands, roving the territory in the hinterlands of Izmir and Afyon. When the pressure of the authorities grew too great, they moved northwards into the Bursa region. Here they wandered through Soma, Balıkesir, Kazdağı, Gönen, and Manyas, regions with a heavy Circassian population.

Life on the wrong side of the law was not easy. Eşref claims that the palace put a bounty on his head of 1,000 gold liras and a promise of promotion in rank for whoever could manage to suppress him and his colleagues. An important development during this period of brigandage was the arrival of Reşid's younger brother Edhem, who joined the group fresh out of his military service. Tall and lean and with an intense gaze, Edhem seems despite his youth to have possessed a masterful command of the territory in which they maneuvered and, perhaps even more important, an unsurpassed rapport with its population. Eşref clearly favored Edhem, whom he regarded with an avuncular affection and considered a very close friend. Eşref says that unlike his older brother Reşid who was, as we shall see, prone to outrageous and "overly familiar" or "crazy" behavior, Edhem was respectful, polite, and discreet.[43] A report written by a captain who had been sent to oppose the outlaws noted that Edhem was acting as a guide for Eşref and Sami and that he was far more knowledgeabe about the region. Edhem was arrested on the basis of that report, but despite being threatened and beaten while in handcuffs and transported here and there, he refused to divulge any incriminating information about his colleauges. When finally he had to make a confession, he gave the authorities only a very non-defamatory account of Eşref, saying that Eşref never asked anyone for money and treated kindly the villagers who willingly hid him. Eşref, he said, only stayed in the villages for half an hour at a time before returning to the mountains. Edhem reported that Eşref addressed the people this way:

> O people. If the government ask about me, don't conceal it but rather say that I have come. You won't be beaten. If anyone does get beaten or experiences oppression, whisper it secretly in my ear. God is merciful and will certainly show him ease. The oppressors will get their punishment.[44]

Despite such signs of allegiance between Eşref and Edhem and the apparent support of the population, not everything in the band of outlaws was so positive. There were signs of major problems with Çerkes Reşid, who began to demonstrate a sustained pattern of behavior that was outrageous even by the standards of those beyond the law. We shall see how Reşid was involved in a number of crimes, including wartime atrocities in Western Thrace and then the kidnapping of the son of Mustafa Rahmi Bey, the Unionist governor of Aydın, in 1919. Such behavior reflected badly on Eşref, who of course had himself once kidnapped the son of the Ottoman commander of the Medina garrison, and he went to some lengths to disassociate himself from Reşid's activities. These were, Eşref later recalled, "our weak, quite broken and down-and-out days."[45] They were on the outside, far from the circles of power and influence for which they believed themselves to be destined.

But as would often prove to be the case in Eşref's career, the tumultuous events that defined the last decades of Ottoman rule provided an opening. At some point, the details of which are unclear, Eşref and Sami were given positions in the gendarmerie and police forces in Izmir respectively. The city of Izmir and its hinterlands in the province of Aydın consituted one of the few places in Anatolia where the Committee of Union and Progress had enjoyed success in organizing, largely due to the efforts of Dr Nazım, an influential Unionist from Salonica.[46] Although Eşref's precise connections with the Unionist movement are unclear, it seems likely that the key to his return to the Ottoman fold was Eşref's involvement in the Committee of Union and Progress and the seemingly unending demand of the armed forces for officers who were both capable and politically trustworthy. Almost all of the key officers of the late Ottoman period served in Macedonia and the Balkans, regions synonymous with the ethnic tension and guerrilla warfare that characterized the period and that informed the strong sense of "Islamic nationalism" among them. Eşref was no exception. Already by January 1908 he was carrying out assignments in the region for Enver, the rising force of the Committee of Union and Progress and the man with whom Eşref's career would increasingly be linked. For example, he is described as a gendarme lieutenant carrying out a house search and turning up a cache of important papers for Enver in a village in Kosovo.[47] Other accounts, including that of his second wife, hold that Eşref served in Rumelia during this period. By one account, Eşref was an organizer for the Committee of Union and Progress in Rumelia before the revolution of 1908 and then served as one of its "militants" afterwards.[48] Eşref had what today might be called "transferable skills" that could as easily be deployed for the government as against it. His strategy had paid off; he had managed to get himself noticed amidst the tutmultuous events of the late Ottoman era. The ethnic antagonisms prevalent in the empire's European provinces would increasingly be transported to other parts of the empire, with disastrous consequences. This meant that a man like Eşref would henceforth be increasingly in demand. As we shall see, Eşref would be directly involved and the consequences for him would include both intimate involvement with the center of power but also a harsh estrangement.

In the meantime Eşref's life was about to become even busier. When the Committtee of Union and Progress came to power after the "Young Turk" revolution of 1908, more such assignments would come his way. The exact relationship between Eşref and the Committee of Union and Progress in this period is obscure, but it seems clear that he was an important figure in the region. Some have claimed that Eşref and Çerkes Reşid had established a key Committee of Union and Progress cell in Izmir before the revolution.[49] Further clues to Eşref's world are to be found in his private life, which seems increasingly to converge with his career during this period. For it was during this time that Eşref married a woman named Feride Hanım. Very little is known about Feride, but two points stand out. First, it seems likely that she was the daughter of an Ottoman officer from Izmir who is likely to have had links with the political oppostion to Abdülhamid. After a period of internal exile as an army commander in Yemen, her father Cemil Paşa returned to Izmir around 1888.[50] Secondly, Feride was a first cousin of Süleyman Askerî, a key player in the Special Organization, who would become a close friend of Eşref's. Süleyman Askerî and Feride's father were apparently brothers, adding another level to the bond that linked the two "self-sacrificing" officers, a connection that would be strengthened by their shared military service and their common bond with Enver. The date of Eşref and Feride's marriage is unknown, but probably took placed in 1908 or 1909. Their son Feridun was born sometime in 1909 and Feride apparently died shortly after his birth. Although it is difficult to say more, it seems that both Eşref's personal and professional lives were increasingly intermixed and increasingly complicated.

As well as becoming a father, Eşref also seems to have become a landowner during his Izmir years. Again, details are in short supply but there are enough clues to suggest that he acquired at least two farms and a house in Izmir sometime during the period between his return to the Izmir region and the outbreak of World War I. The farms were in Aydın and in Salihli. The transaction that landed him the former property involved more than a straightforward purchase. He seems to have bought a share in a farm collectively owned by an influential Greek family named Fotiadis. Eşref purchased a one-seventh share in this farm, and with it something he refers to as a "right of pre-emption" (hakk-ı şufa); subsequently he managed to take over the property as a result of quarrels among the Fotiadi siblings. "I did what I did," he says in an account that denigrates the Fotiadis for taking advantage of the Capitulations, arrangements that allowed foreign citizens legal and commercial advantages in the Ottoman Empire.[51] Many in the Muslim population resented these privileges, and the Committee of Union and Progress was quick to seize on and indeed to stir up anti-foreign and anti-minority sentiment in the region, as we shall see.

The second estate was in Salihli and, unlike the farm in Aydın, it remained in his possession for longer and was the one with which he is more closely associated. In fact, Eşref seems to have adored the Salihli property. According to his descendants, this property was a gift from Sultan Abdülamid II to Eşref's father. Exaclty when he took it over is not entirely clear, but from a few property deeds that still exist it is clear that he was adding to it by buying neighboring parcels at various times. The estate was an extensive one that included holdings in several villages around Salihli. When it was later confiscated by the Turkish Republic, it exceeded 15,000 dunums,[52] the equivalent of over 3,700 acres. Some of the deeds indicate that Eşref was purchasing relatively small parcels as late as 1918, while he was imprisoned on Malta, and that he registered the land under three names: his own as well as those of Çerkes Reşid and his brother Hacı Sami.[53] During the war the Salihli estate would serve first as the main residence for Eşref's family. Afterwards it became a headquarters in the national movement that arose to counter the Greek invasion of Western Anatolia.

In the period before and after 1908, Eşref and Sami were soon tasked with a number of jobs of the "enforcement" variety in the region of Izmir. One of the first of these reportedly saw Eşref involved in suppressing a strike being carried out by Italian railway workers in Izmir in October. The Committee of Union and Progress were notoriously opposed to labor activism, despite their having adopted the rhetoric of the French Revolution. During this incident in Izmir, Eşref apparently encouraged his armed force to fire on the crowd, killing an Italian bystander. Eşref was subsequently held for questioning but freed on Enver's personal intervention.[54] The temperature in this volatile and ethnically delicate region was rising.

The next major event to highlight Eşref and Sami's activity for the Committee of Union and Progress was the counter-revolution of 1909. In April a combination of Islamic divinity students, mutinying soldiers and liberal opponents of the Committee of Union and Progress carried out a coup with the aim of restoring Islamic law and reversing a number of Unionist changes. At the center of this counter-revolution was a shaykh of the Nakşibendi Sufi order named Derviş Vahdeti, whose journal *Volkan* ("The Volcano") was instrumental in encouraging the anti-Unionist rising. Less than two weeks later the Unionists suppressed the counter-revolution by sending the "Action Army" under the command of Mahmud Şevket Paşa from its stronghold in Macedonia to Istanbul.

The countercoup had repercussions in Izmir, mirroring the factional-ism of the capital. Eşref's telegraphic account of the period reads: "We were in Izmir. We gave no quarter. Even though the revolt reached as far as the police force in Izmir, Sami, Çerkes Reşid and I took matters into our own hands."[55] Eşref and his colleagues had a trick in store for the rebels. They got some of their men to change into officers' uniforms and put down the revolt in Izmir. When the Action Army threatened Istanbul, Derviş Vahdeti fled by sea. The ship carrying him and a number of his associates called at Izmir on 21 April. The Istabul police had learned of his departure and sent word to their colleagues in Izmir.[56] When Eşref received a bulletin informing him that Vahdeti and his men, whom he labels "reactionaries," were in the vicinity, he captured them and sent them to Istanbul where they were subsequently hanged.[57]

Wyndham Deedes and brigandage

A curious coincidence allows an insight into some of Eşref's activities during this otherwise relatively sketchy period. At two important points, first in Izmir and then in Cairo during World War I, Eşref found himself squaring off against a uniquely British antagonist named Wyndham Deedes. The youngest son of a family of East Kentish gentry and Eton-educated, Deedes was a veteran of the Boer Wars and one of a number of British officers on secondment to the Foreign Office who were assigned to help reform the Ottoman gendarmes in the period after 1907. Deedes learned Turkish and later translated several books, including those of Reşat Nuri (Güntekin), into English. His first assign-ment in the Ottoman lands was in Libya. He happened to be on leave when the Italo-Ottoman war broke out and thus returned to Izmir, the headquarters after the 1908 revolution of the British officers in the Ottoman gendarmerie.

It was there, in a country "haunted by robbers and outlaws as was Europe in the Dark Ages,"[58] that Deedes came up against Eşref and his brother Sami. In many respects they were complete opposites. Deedes was a fastidious ascetic who hated being dirty and thus always traveled with a sponge bag when he had to tour the countryside for his gendar-merie duties. He complained of the squalor of the villages where he stayed on his inspection tours, enumerating his many discomforts in his diary and letters to his mother. A characteristic entry in one of them reads: "Saturday. Had a very good night. Only killed three bugs."[59]

In the years before World War I, Deedes and the Kuşçubaşı brothers were on parallel career trajectories that converged in the Izmir region. After 1908 Eşref and Sami were, as we have seen, given posts in the police and gendarmerie forces before crossing over into brigandage. During Deedes' Foreign Office secondment he learned Turkish to a very high standard and was sent to Turkey to serve with the Ottoman gendarmerie in 1911. In Izmir under the command of Colonel Harker, with whom he would later be posted to the Arab Bureau in Cairo during World War I,[60] he worked on reforming the Ottoman gendarmes. This meant that his primary preoccupation was combatting the very brigands that included Eşref, Sami, and Reşid.

Deedes identified brigandage as one of "the greatest evils of this country" but found combatting it an uphill battle. Over the course of his time in Izmir, Deedes launched a series of initiatives to suppress this particular form of lawlessness that had a long history in the area but which had particularly flourished in recent years, in part due to the influx of refugees from lost Ottoman lands. One of his schemes was to create what he later referred to as a "'Bureau D'information' [sic]—a body of Trained Spies to go about amongst the Village people to ascertain the whereabouts and movements of the Brigands."[61]

That was easier said than done. In fact, Deedes more than met his match in facing off against the outlaws of the region. In time he even developed a grudging respect for the outlaws that he was meant to be pursuing. One of these was almost certainly Eşref's brother Sami.[62] In the summer of 1911 Sami had resigned from his post as a police inspector and moved from Istanbul to Izmir.[63] Still wearing his uniform, he encountered a gendarme unit in the town of Ödemiş to the east of Torbalı where he had earlier been stationed on the sultan's estate. Sami apprently informed the gendarmes that he was investigating a deadly incident between the gang of the infamous Çakırcalı Mehmet Efe, a legendary brigand of the Robin Hood variety, and some Circassians from the village of Çerkez İhsaniye, possibly related to the Kuşçubaşıs, who had been killed. After taking some information about the Circassians, Sami seized the unit commander's horse and weapon and fled.[64] Sami then proceeded to the Circassians' village. Recruiting five or six of them, he formed his own gang and proceeded to Çakırcalı's village in the vicinity of Ödemiş. Saying that they were wanted for questioning, Sami's band took away six of Çakırcalı's relatives. On 5 September their bodies were found: four had been killed and two were heavily wounded.[65] Sami had taken revenge for the killing of the Circassians. He would go on to expand his practice of brigandage, for example kidnapping a number of landowners for ransom. "Hacı" Sami was demonstrating the fluid boundary between outlaw and law enforcer. His links with the gendarmerie, his Circassian background, and his apparent ability to carry out violence with impunity further complicated the relations between the Circassians, the government, and the local population.

Into this volatile scene came the fastidious Wyndham Deedes. A few months later, in late February of 1912, Deedes made one of his many inspections upcountry to visit the van Lenneps, a Levantine family of Dutch origin who owned a large farm outside Izmir. At a time when "brigandage had acquired the status of a profession" and one of its mainstays was the ransoming of individuals from wealthy families, van Lennep himself had been abducted a few years earlier. He had been held until a ransom of the large sum of £6,000 was produced by his brother-in-law, a member of the wealthier Whittall family. At the time of his 1912 visit, Deedes describes the head of the band operating in the region as "an ex-police and gendarme officer who is out 'on band' as the Govt. want him on account of a family feud murder and other cases," a description which fits Sami well.

Even though they were on opposite sides of the game, Deedes was quite impressed with Sami. After a local kidnapping stunt, Deedes wrote:

> He is giving us a lot of trouble tho' he has only bagged one man for whom he got £1,000. £400 of which he returned to the father of the boy he bagged whom he met when he brought up the ransom money, saying he was sorry he had put him to so much trouble in getting £1,000, but his men had mis-informed him telling him that he was wealthier than he was. So gentlemanly.[66]

Later that year a major outbreak of violence took place between Sami's "gang" and Deedes' gendarmes. The contest seems to have come to a head during a skirmish in June 1912 near Aydın that left both a long casualty list and an even longer paper trail reaching all the way to the Council of Ministers and the Grand Vizier. By that point Sami's band had grown to include at least forty men. The battle with the gendarmes ended with three of Sami's men dead and two wounded and taken prisoner, while the gendarmes suffered two dead and one lightly wounded.[67] After the fighting was over, each side attempted to mobilize the bureaucracy in its favor. The state's agents, including the governor of Aydın, sent a number of telegrams to the neighboring provinces to ask for help in catching Sami and his men "dead or alive" and requesting money from the central authorities to compensate the families of the dead gendarmes.[68] Meanwhile, some of the captives petitioned the highest levels of the Ottoman state. Şirin Tahir, a Circassian from İzmit, pleaded that he had been pardoned under a general amnesty but not permitted to go free, a crime, he argued, not only against the law but also the Holy Qur'an.[69] Later, Eşref and Sami used their Unionist connections with Talat Bey, who had become Interior Minister in January 1913, in an attempt to get their colleagues released from prison in Izmir. Once the Balkan Wars began, Ottoman officialdom looked much more kindly on granting amnesties to those who had already demonstrated the ability to fight, even if on the wrong side of the law.

Remarkably, Sami's violent conduct seems not to have reduced his stock in Deedes' eyes but rather to have raised it. Deedes was transferred to Istanbul in the autumn of 1913,[70] and then moved on to Cairo where his high view of Sami was reflected in a description that appeared in *The Arab Bulletin*, the secret publication of the Arab Bureau, where he was working. There he describes Eşref as "an unredeemed ruffian" before continuing (referring to himself in the third person):

> but Haji Sami his brother has distinct sporting instincts, and used obviously to enjoy avoiding the great drives of the Smyrna provincial gendarmerie organized against them by Colonel Hawker and Major Deedes.[71]

Deedes had developed a sense of admiration for Sami, despite or perhaps because of their rivalry.

Deedes' account, with its combination of foreign adventure and "sporting instincts," almost appears to have jumped out of a John Buchan novel. In *Greenmantle* Buchan himself portrayed Enver and his men with a spirit of grudging admiration and played up the Great Game spirit of the times. But the reality for many in the Ottoman lands was far more serious and more dangerous than that created for literary amusement. As the Unionists tightened their grip on power, the trend towards autocracy grew. The very men who had launched the Constitutional Revolution of 1908 were growing increasingly minded to overlook constitutional niceties. Drawing lessons from their fellow revolutionaries in Russia, the Committee of Union and Progress preferred an elitist to a populist approach, particularly as the latter would necessiate the involvement of the non-Muslim minorities. The Russians had demonstrated that a skilled martyr–assassin (*fedaî*) was more effective than 10,000 revolutionaries.[72] Intimidation and violence went hand-in-hand with the Unionists' turn towards autocracy,[73] and *fedaî*s like Eşref, Sami, and Çerkes Reşid had the requisite skills. As we've seen, the emergence in the empire of a serious oppositional movement began around 1905, the year when Eşref returned from internal exile, and ultimately produced the 1908 revolution. These developments gave Eşref and his colleagues a second chance. As the new guard of Unionists first organized their opposition and then seized the levers of power, men like Eşref were increasingly in demand.

Even though he and his family had benefited from Abdülhamid's rule, the rise to power of the Unionists in the "Young Turk" revolution of 1908 presented Eşref with a variety of new opportunities, most but not all in the region around Izmir. But the Italian invasion of Libya in 1911 offered an even more direct route towards imperial prominence. During the tumultuous years since Eşref's return from Arabian exile he had married, become a father, obtained property, and managed to make himself indispensable among the activist wing of the party running the Ottoman Empire. But with his restlessness and remarkable energy undiminished, Eşref seemed determined to make his mark on the imperial stage. Libya provided that opportunity.

3

VOLUNTEERS IN THE DESERT

THE OTTOMAN–ITALIAN WAR FOR LIBYA

When Eşref heard the news, he was for unknown reasons deep in Eastern Anatolia. Moving from village to village in the remote and rugged country between Bitlis, Van, and Muş on horseback, by motor car when the primitive roads would permit, or simply on foot, Eşref was touring the area and meeting with local officials. They offered him the customary hospitality of the region. He stayed here in an officers' guest room or the house of a local official, there with an officer of the Hamidiye cavalry regiments. These units had been established under Sultan Abdülhamid II to maintain order in the east, but their Kurdish troops had terrified the local Armenian and Turkish population. Eşref's brief diary entries show that he was staying in Armenian villages from time to time and being treated well. But he had a serious problem: he was by his own account "terribly ill" and had broken limbs.[1] He could only travel at a fraction of his normal, demanding pace. But now time was in short supply. On 30 September 1911 he wrote in his diary: "News came that the Italians had declared war against us."[2] Eşref's life—like those of all the empire's subjects—was about to change dramatically. The Ottoman–Italian war, though of relatively brief duration, would be the first engagement of what would prove to be over a decade of warfare. Disease, displacement, deprivation, and death would affect

hundreds of thousands. When it was over the Ottoman Empire would
have vanished and the new nation state of Turkey would be established
in its central lands. Although Eşref couldn't have known it at the time,
this would mean banishment and personal tragedy.

Eşref's friend and former schoolmate Süleyman Askerî was in
Baghdad when word of the Italian invasion of Libya traveled down the
telegraph wires. Despite the distance between them, there was much
that linked Askerî and Eşref. As we have seen, they were related by
marriage, Eşref having married Askerî's first cousin Feride. Feride died
young but not before giving birth to a son, Feridun, in 1909.[3] The
relationship between Askerî and Eşref seems to have been close but not
without a certain frisson of rivalry. On the one hand, the men appeared
to have been close friends since their time as classmates in the military
preparatory school in Edirne.[4] Beyond the marital link, Eşref and
Süleyman shared the intense experiences of belonging to the group of
"self-sacrificing officers" that coalesced under Enver Bey to form the
clandestine Special Organization. Indeed, Süleyman and Eşref are
thought by some to have been two of its first leaders.[5] They would
serve together in Libya, the Balkan Wars (where they were both major
figures in the Temporary Government of Western Thrace) and in World
War I. Beyond the intersection of career paths there are signs of a
closer friendship. Eşref had given Askerî one of his prized horses, an
Arabian thoroughbred named Enis (Companion).[6] Years later, long after
Askerî had taken his own life in wartime Iraq, Eşref tracked down his
surviving kin and spent hours copying the pages of Askerî's Libyan
diaries by hand. On the other hand, there was a certain competitive
friction between the two, both rising stars in the constellation of officers under the same patron, Enver, the man of the hour. Later, when
copying out Askerî's diary of his journey to Libya, Eşref could not
refrain from making a snide comment that it was the writing of a "hero"
who had returned without seeing any action.[7] But for now all of that
lay before them.

Meanwhile in Baghdad, the mercurial Askerî and his fellow gendarmerie officers began agitating for permission to cross the width of the
empire to join the fight in Libya. They would have to overcome not
only the large distances and infrastructural obstacles that stood
between them and the front, but also the sometimes equally formidable

resistance of the military hierarchy. For Askerî, the series of wars that began with the Libyan conflict, or Tripolitanian as it was also known, would translate into both career opportunities and fatal decisions. After his service in Libya and the Balkan Wars, where he would again serve alongside Eşref, Askerî was to be selected by Enver to run the clandestine Special Organization. But for this zealously committed and highly spirited officer, it would all end tragically. Askerî was sent back to Iraq in December 1914 to take charge of the overall defense of that theater and to halt the British advance there. After an ambitious reorganization of the Ottoman forces in Iraq, which included integrating Teşkilat-ı Mahsusa units, regular forces, and tribal levies and sending raiding parties into southern Iran to attack the oil pipeline near Abadan, Askerî's Iraq strategy ended disastrously. Heavy rains and superior British firepower frustrated Ottoman actions. The Ottoman forces were finally routed on 14 April 1915 at Şuayyibe, losing half their men. The survivors were then set upon by their erstwhile tribal allies.[8] Askerî was severely wounded and, realizing the extent of his failure, turned his service revolver on himself. He was only thirty.

To the shores of Tripoli

In 1911, when this grisly turn of events was impossible to foresee, the imminent danger to the Ottoman Empire lay in Libya. The Ottoman province of Tripolitania (Trablusgarp), or "Tripoli in Libya" as it was sometimes known, was in many respects an unlikely proving ground for the Young Turk officers, most of whom were born and raised in the much more advanced parts of the empire, places like Istanbul, Salonica, and Manastır (modern-day Bitola in Macedonia). By contrast Trablusgarp was isolated, sparsely populated and poor. It held little intrinsic worth to a regime busy with a plethora of pressing issues. This was not a battle that the late Ottoman Empire chose to fight. As was so often the case during the empire's last decades, it was the European powers who set the agenda. During the course of the nineteenth century—what one historian labelled the empire's longest[9]—Istanbul watched impotently as the colonial powers helped themselves to its North African territories. The first to go was Algeria, taken by the French in 1830 and incorporated as three *départements* of the Republic in 1848. France seized

Tunisia in 1881; and Britain, eyeing the strategic route to India, took Cyprus in 1878 and Egypt in 1882. So much for the promises that Britain and France had made to protect Ottoman territorial integrity as recently as the Treaty of Paris in 1856 after their common cause in the Crimean War.

The carve-up of the southern Mediterranean littoral left the Italians only one option if they were to make good on their plans for restoring long-lost imperial pride. Fearful of being left empty-handed and bent on resurrecting some of the glory of ancient Rome, the kingdom of Italy had set its sights on the Ottoman province to its immediate south. Despite or perhaps because of the fact that Italy was considered to be a lesser European power and had only been unified as recently as 1861, Italian politicians of various stripes were keen to restore lost imperial pride. Encouraged by the Futurists who "worshipped speed and technology" and had issued a 1909 manifesto declaring war to be "the world's only hygiene,"[10] Italy began to clamor for the annexation of Libya, as though the ancient Roman precedent justified current-day rights.

The Italian move on Libya began with a policy of peaceful penetration in the economic and cultural spheres. The Banco di Roma, funded and supported by both the Vatican and the Italian central bank, began to invest heavily in the Ottoman province, especially in real estate.[11] An Italian maritime company backed by the government and financed by the Banco di Roma operated a steamship service between Italian and Libyan ports. Italian educators opened schools in the province. Thus in spite of the fact that there were perhaps only about a thousand Italian citizens in Libya, many of whom were Libyan Jews who had acquired passports of convenience, Italy was increasingly treating the Ottoman province as a zone to which it had special claims.

The Italian pursuit of Libya in the economic and cultural realm was accompanied by a political policy aimed at securing the approval or at least acquiescence of the other European powers. Italian diplomats had been extremely busy in this pursuit and their work paid off. In 1887 Germany had recognized Italian interests in Libya and in 1902 Italy secured agreements from both Britain and France to safeguard Italian interests there. Subsequent agreements with Austria and Russia similarly gave Italy a free hand.[12] The unchecked Italian ambitions in Libya now began to produce an overly ambitious assessment of how their

planned rule of the territory would be accepted by the local population. As a result Rome read too much into some Libyans' criticism of
the Ottoman regime run by the Committee of Union and Progress that
emerged after the 1908 revolution; Italian politicians believed that this
was a rift that they could successfully exploit.[13] The Italians wishfully
believed that the tensions which had begun to appear between Tripoli
and Istanbul meant that they would be welcomed with open arms
when the time came for their triumphal re-entry. They could not have
been more wrong.

Having systematically protected its diplomatic flanks, Italy only
needed an opportunity. In July 1911 Germany sent a warship to
Morocco to test French resolve, triggering the "Agadir crisis," the first
in a series of annual flashpoints that would ultimately ignite World War
I.[14] The confrontation in Agadir was peacefully resolved in favor of the
French position, but the incident worried the Italians who feared that
another power might swoop in to snatch Libya from under their noses
and ruin all their careful preparations. Planning took on an added
urgency.[15] Later the same month the Italians rather outlandishly complained that the Ottoman government was treating it unfairly by allowing Germans to buy land in Libya but preventing Italians from doing so.
Despite Ottoman denials, Italy persisted with its claim and even broad-
ened its argument to demand compensation for the increased French
role in Morocco, brazenly claiming that its interests would be damaged
by the change to the Mediterranean equilibrium. Britain sided with
Italy, declaring that if the Ottomans were indeed treating the Italians
unfairly they would be forced to act and that, in the words of the
British Foreign Minster, "the Turkish government could not expect
anything else."[16] Once again, the Ottomans found that the deck of
European diplomacy was stacked, and not in their favor.

With the European powers closing ranks, the Ottomans did not
stand much of a chance. Italy was bent on taking Libya, and it was all
too clear that the European states were quite willing to allow it. The
Italians now only needed to find a pretext and seem to have been
remarkably untroubled in choosing one that had little basis in fact. As
the British anthropologist-turned-military intelligence officer E. Evans-
Pritchard put it, "all the Italian arguments brought forth post factum to
justify its plan are no more than futile pretexts which Italy would not

have dared to raise in regard to any European state or a region under European rule." The official excuse was that Italians were being mistreated in Tripolitania, but in fact the timing of the ultimatum, and ultimately of the invasion which followed in early October 1911, was dictated by recent events. The Agadir crisis was one such consideration. The Ottoman plans to reorganize its military forces in the province were another, and this belated Ottoman attempt to shore up its garrisons in its province of Tripolitania provided the Italians with the pretext they were seeking.[17] What made the temerity of Rome's ultimatum even more absurd was the fact that the troops belatedly ordered to Libya were merely replacements for Ottoman forces that had earlier been diverted to Yemen to try to cope with an insurrection there. How dare the Ottomans replenish their garrisons in Libya?

The sense of hypocrisy and double standards that the Ottomans faced when attempting to prevent further losses from their empire helps to explain the eagerness with which many in the Ottoman officer corps responded to the Italian aggression. Even though Libya was hardly important in a strategic sense, it was highly symbolic. As the last Ottoman territory in Africa, it embodied the broad imperial reach that seemed to be slipping away with alarming rapidity. Allowing the empire's last African possession to disappear would have an important symbolic significance. Fighting to hold onto its North African province would also be a useful refutation of claims that the Committee of Union and Progress wasn't interested in its Arab population.

Another area of contention that was particularly important for the Young Turks was the empire's military posture. During the preceding reign of Abdülhamid II, the empire had largely managed to avoid armed conflict. Following the disastrous war with Russia (1877–8) during the first years of his rule, the Ottoman strategy had been one of patient rebuilding. The new military alliance with Germany needed to be given time to work. Even when the Ottomans were forced into battle, as was the case in the war against Greece in 1897, they found that what was won on the battlefield was lost at the negotiating table. European "support" seemed to mean that the Ottomans could lose territory, but that regaining it was impossible. While in opposition to Abdülhamid, the Young Turks had been highly critical of what they perceived to be his inability to hold the empire together. They hammered away at his alleged spinelessness in the face of Western pressure. Now that they were in power, the Italian invasion gave them the chance to demonstrate how the empire ought to defend itself against the arrogance and double standards of a European aggressor.

Since Italian naval superiority and British neutrality meant that only a small number of Ottoman officers could make their way to Libya, the confrontation there also gave the Unionist, or "Young Turk," officers a chance to try out the guerrilla tactics that they had grudgingly admired during their experience serving in the Ottoman Third Army. Based in the hotspots of ethnic and national insurrection in Albania, Kosovo, and Macedonia, the Third Army had been forced to defend against guerrilla insurgencies motivated by Greek, Bulgarian, Serbian, Albanian, and Macedonian national feeling. The Third Army was the most important source of recruitment for the clandestine group that came to be known as the Committee of Union and Progress. New members were initiated by swearing loyalty and silence over a revolver and a copy of the Qur'an.[18] Libya represented an opportunity for these Unionist officers to turn the tables and harness these asymmetrical tactics for the sake of the empire.[19] In practice it also gave the Committee of Union and Progress leadership the chance to organize its highly committed "self-sacrificing officers" into branches and test them in the field. These mostly junior officers had cut their teeth in the fighting against the rebellious Macedonian organizations in the first decade of the twentieth century. Even before the Italians invaded, Enver was planning an asymmetrical campaign, to be informed by the experience of Ottoman forces in the Balkans and to be led by his devoted cadre of young officers. Reversing roles, the Ottomans would now form their own resistance network with the aim of harassing the Italian forces and provoking the Libyans to revolt against Italian occupation.[20] Subsequent events would show that the Libyan episode was a crucial phase in the emergence of the Ottoman Special Organization, which was formally constituted (Eşref would later say re-constituted) after the Balkan Wars and which would play a crucial role in the remaining years of the empire's existence, often with dramatic and tragic consequences.

When Enver called them to rally for the sake of defending Ottoman Libya against the Italian aggression, the response of self-sacrificing officers like Eşref was impressive for its enthusiasm. Volunteers from across the length and breadth of the empire quickly declared their willingness to defend Ottoman territory. The Italian–Libyan war provided important experience for key players in the crucial struggles that were to follow: the Balkan Wars, World War I and the Turkish "National Struggle." As we shall see, it was in the faraway deserts of Libya that such men as Enver, Eşref, Fethi, and Mustafa Kemal made the transition from suppressing rebellions to taking on a European power. But in getting there they encountered an array of formidable obstacles in their path, including some from unexpected quarters.

The most obvious of these hurdles was distance, given the remote location of the province. The Mediterranean Sea route, the quickest and most efficient way of getting to Libya for most Ottoman officers, was virtually impossible due to Italian naval superiority. The Italians routinely flaunted their naval advantage during the war by indiscriminately shelling Ottoman ports such as Beirut and Kuşadası. The only way open to Ottoman volunteers was to travel overland. A few made their way to Libya via Tunis, but the vast majority traveled through Egypt. This route was not without its problems. The British wished to remain neutral in the conflict and were under Italian pressure to prevent Ottoman officers from infiltrating to Cyrenaica.[21] This resulted in a number of Ottoman officers being turned back from the border at the first attempt.

But it was not just the Italians and the British who stood in the way of officers who wanted to volunteer in the Libyan campaign. The inherent cautiousness of the Ottoman government in international issues and the specific concerns of the military command concerning its ability to wage a campaign without proper supply lines meant that considerable internal opposition had to be overcome despite the public stance supporting the resistance campaign. Behind the scenes, senior military figures acknowledged that the Ottoman army had virtually no chance of winning the war against Italy.[22] The high command was therefore less than keen to see many of its best officers rush off to participate in what they believed to be a futile exercise. This set up a clash within the Ottoman military itself.

Another development of the Tripolitanian war that would have important repercussions on subsequent conflicts was the mobilization of "the volunteers."[23] This term and the concept behind it operated on two levels in Libya. On the one hand, the Ottomans knew that the logistical obstacles involved made it impossible to send large units of the regular Ottoman army to fight the Italians. The best they could do was to send a small number of officers and hope to train local volunteers, in this case Libyan tribesmen of the Sanusi Sufi order, to provide the manpower necessary for the campaign. On the other hand, the term also applied to a group of Ottoman officers, usually of lower rank, known as the *fedaîs*, a term that can be translated as "volunteers" but with the important connotation of religiously-inspired self-sacrifice. Many of them had gained reputations as *fedaîs* in Macedonia before the "Young Turk" revolution of 1908. Some of these men had taken on, whether individually or in small units, special assignments such as political assassination. But the first concerted, large-scale impact made by this group was in Libya where men like Kuşcubaşı Eşref, Süleyman Askerî, Sapancalı Hakkı, Yakup Cemil, İzmitli Mümtaz, Ali Çetinkaya, and Çerkes Reşid played important roles. They would each develop their own particular historical reputations, some heroic, some decidedly infamous. Together they made a formidable group. All were close to Enver and it was through his initiative that they were mobilized. Later, these volunteers would become institutionalized through the Special Organization, known in Ottoman Turkish as the Teşkilat-i Mahsusa, a covert outfit under the Ministry of War that would take on special assignments directed at what were deemed to be the empire's enemies at home and abroad. Circassians figured heavily in this organization; although little is known about how their networks functioned, they seem clearly to have been a major factor in the constellation of special operations officers like Eşref who circulated in Enver's orbit.

A crucial component in this spirit of volunteerism is what Zürcher has aptly termed "Muslim nationalism."[24] This way of thinking was informed in part by the experience of Muslims as victims of foreign, Christian expansionism or independence movements. It is no coincidence, for example, that many of the key actors in this tendency were themselves from families that had been forced to flee in the face of ethnic violence directed at them as Muslims, whether in the Caucasus or the Balkans.

The idea of defending Ottoman territory by bringing together Muslims from a variety of ethnic and regional backgrounds had both a

4. With fellow volunteers Ali [Çetinkaya] and İzmitli Mümtaz in Libya. (Source: Tunca Örses archive)

practical and symbolic appeal. The pan-Muslim composition of the Ottoman army officers is quite clear, but even more striking is the deployment of notable figures representing a number of Muslim lands. The Libyan campaign would feature Muslim VIPs whose origins lay outside the empire, such as the Tunisian Shaykh Salih (Şeyh Salih) and the Algerian Amir Ali Pasha (Emir Ali Paşa). Future campaigns, for example in World War I, would see units of Muslim volunteers from as far away as Afghanistan. Even within the Ottoman Empire, the range of regional and ethnic affiliation of the key officers was remarkable, and something easily missed due to the normal but rather imprecise use of the term "Turkish" to refer to the Ottomans. For very different reasons, both the Western and the Turkish Republican writers often describe the Ottomans as "Turkish." But the Ottoman officers included Turks, Circassians, Kurds, Arabs, and Albanians and represented a territorial provenance ranging from the Balkans to Anatolia and the Arab provinces of the empire. The pan-Islamic aspect of the Ottoman military cause was something that their German allies would seize on in

World War I. Interestingly, it was often the Germans who were far more keen to pursue this Islamic angle than the Ottoman leadership, as can be seen in early German pressure on Istanbul to declare holy war (*jihad* in Arabic, *cihat* in Turkish) against Britain and France. The Ottomans themselves proved adept at emphasizing the Islamic dimensions of the struggle, such as forming a unit of Mevlevi dervishes (the so-called "whirling" dervishes of Konya) and deploying the religiously inclined poet Mehmet Akif—with whom Eşref Bey spent some time traveling in Arabia—to bolster Ottoman morale. Yet the Ottomans often found that their German allies were overly enthusiastic to "play the Islamic card" and sought to dampen their expectations.[25]

The Libyan war featured a number of Ottoman junior officers from across the empire who would rise to prominence in future years. Mustafa Kemal, the future Atatürk, is the most famous, but other men would make a mark on post-Ottoman national histories, including Sulayman Al-Biruni in Libya, Shakib Arslan in Lebanon, and Nuri al-Said and Ja'far al-Askari in Iraq. Others who featured prominently in Libya would later be forced out of political life, especially in Turkey where the Kemalist leadership would prove particularly skilful in sidelining its rivals. Eşref would be among the first to be so removed.

On the road to Libya

It was at Enver's request that Eşref joined the struggle in Libya. When the Italians declared war on 29 September 1911 (they invaded Libya on 4 October 1911) Eşref was, as we have seen, touring Eastern Anatolia under circumstances that remain unclear. What we do know is that despite his remote location Eşref learned of the Italian declaration of war the next day,[26] demonstrating the reach and reliability of the Ottoman telegraph network—something on which he would depend during his many future campaigns. Hearing the news, Eşref began his long journey back to Istanbul. But the transportation system lagged far behind that of the telegraph. Delayed by illness and the difficult terrain of Eastern Anatolia, it took him several weeks to return to the capital. When he reached Istanbul he was informed, on 31 October 1911, that Enver, well aware of Eşref's experience with Arab tribes, had assigned him to Alexandria.[27] From there he was to organize the operation to guide his fellow volunteers across the Western Desert and infiltrate them into Cyrenaica, or Eastern Libya.

Egypt was the key staging ground for the Ottoman campaign in Libya, the point on which all the volunteers coming from various provinces converged. With the exception of a small group that entered Libya from the western border with Tunisia, all of the Ottoman officers passed through Egypt and thus had to evade British attempts to prevent them from joining the resistance movement. The scene in Egypt is fairly well known. The Egyptian authorities, responding to increasing Italian pressure, presented some difficulties for the Ottoman officers bent on getting to Libya. But there were many in the population who were highly sympathetic, given the strong ties that had developed between Egypt and the empire over centuries of rule. From a practical point of view, Egypt had the transportation links, pro-Ottoman networks and provisions to make it the ideal staging ground for the Libyan campaign, despite the position of the British-dominated Egyptian government.

By the time Süleyman Askerî's group arrived from Iraq, many of the key Ottoman officers had already passed through Egypt. Enver had arrived as early as 19 October 1911. Mustafa Kemal, traveling with his friend Ömer Naci and two Unionist "volunteers," Yakup Cemil and Sapancalı Hakkı (from whom he later attempted to disassociate himself), had come ten days later, on 29 October.[28] After some difficulties at the frontier, Enver had gone ahead to organize the resistance in Derne (Darna). Mustafa Kemal had fallen ill and returned to Alexandria to recover.[29] Eşref arrived in Egypt on 10 November,[30] tasked with organizing the passage across Egypt of a large group, which included İzmitli Mümtaz, Beşiktaşlı Niyazi and Nuri, and two Arab VIPs, Şeyh Salih el-Tunisi and Emir Ali Paşa, the son of the Algerian anti-colonial hero Abd al-Qadir al-Jazairi. Eşref's group set out for Trablusgarp in mid-to-late November, travelling incognito in the garb of Muslim seminary students. They left Mustafa Kemal, who was still unwell, in the hands of a Greek doctor in Alexandria. He would leave for the Libyan border on 1 December, eventually, like Eşref, to take up a position under Enver's command at Derne.

Egypt was also the destination for Süleyman Askerî's small but determined group of young officers stationed in the very easternmost province of the empire in late 1911. The experience of this group in

Baghdad, who enthusiastically volunteered for the Libyan campaign, offers a good example of the battle of wills—and to some extent a clash of ideology and personalities—between the Unionist "volunteers" and the senior military establishment. Given the distance from Iraq to Libya, their story also illustrates the problems of distance and logistics that needed to be overcome.

When the Italians invaded Libya, a number of army and gendarmerie officers serving in Baghdad requested permission to join in the resistance efforts. The key members of this group were Süleyman Askerî, Cemil, Tevfik, and Fehmi Beys. Thanks to the account of one its members, a young officer named Fehmi who wrote his narrative years later at Eşref's request, we can trace the progress of this group against the obstacles of officialdom and geography. The size and composition of the group changed over time, but the clear leader was the brilliant but mercurial Süleyman Askerî, the future leader of the Teşkilat-i Mahsusa. The volunteers applied to Cemal Paşa, then governor of Baghdad, and Ali Rıza Paşa, the army commander, for permission to travel to Trablusgarp. The application went as far as Minister of War Mahmud Şevket Paşa but his response was negative, citing the British request that Ottoman officers be prevented from entering Egypt. But the group did not take "no" for an answer. As Fehmi put it, "Askerî's powers of persuasion were well-known."[31] There followed a bureaucratic tussle between the officers and Istanbul. The former had the strong support of Cemal Paşa, one of the most important leaders of the Committee of Union and Progress. After intervening in a private capacity and agreeing to take personal responsibility, Cemal was eventually able to gain permission for nine officers to leave Baghdad. The high command, perhaps out of spite, refused to provide travel money (harcirah) so the officers resorted to selling their clothing and their swords to raise the necessary funds. According to Fehmi they scraped together 45 gold pieces for the trip.[32]

The group of five army and four gendarmerie officers left Baghdad on New Year's Day 1912. Their route would take them up the Euphrates River via Haditha, Hit, and Dayrizor and eventually on to Aleppo. But even once they were on the road they were not free from Istanbul's intervention. Wherever there was a telegraph office, there seemed to be a message telling them to return to Baghdad. First in Haditha and then in Hit, Süleyman Askerî was called to the telegraph office where he received orders to turn back. The negotiations went back and forth, with the men arguing the case for being allowed to volunteer and the army brass insisting that its officers return; four apparently submitted to this order, but a fifth decided to ignore his superiors and proceed in defiance. When on the fifth day their convoy reached Dayrizor, in what is today eastern Syria, a telegram from Cemal Paşa was waiting. Again Askerî Bey spent hours negotiating over the telegraph wires with Cemal Paşa, who this time informed Süleyman Askerî that he would no longer be able to take personal responsibility for the group and that they would have to return once and for all.

Here Süleyman Askerî demonstrated his stubborn resourcefulness. As Fehmi put it, "Now this time the great patriot Askerî found the solution in the legal statutes."[33] Referring to a provision that granted those stationed in "hot regions" (*sıcak memleketler*) for two years the right either to a transfer or to three months' leave, Askerî Bey asked Cemal Paşa to grant each of them leave. Cemal Paşa liked the idea for two reasons—it relieved him of having to take personal responsibility, and it allowed them to go to Libya as he had wanted all along—and he agreed readily. Thus having solved the problems of bureaucracy, the five proceeded to Aleppo from which they could proceed to Beirut and then by ship to Egypt.

Arriving in Aleppo, the group's first task was to find their contact. The Unionists had an extensive network across the empire and it was mobilized for precisely the kind of operation that the officers from Baghdad were bent on carrying out. In Aleppo their contact was a Muslim cleric and Sufi *shaykh*, a certain Şeyh Ziya Efendi of the Rıfai order whose lodge served as the Committee of Union and Progress's administrative center in the city. They sat down with him and formulated a plan. The group would from now on travel in disguise, adopting the appearance of students of the Islamic religious sciences (*talebe-i ulum*) on their way to study at the famous seminary of Al-Azhar in Cairo. On the journey from Iraq they had not shaved and were already on their way to growing beards. Now each of the officers was to adopt a new identity, passing themselves off as coming from the villages around Aleppo. Şeyh Ziya helped them obtain false identity papers and sent them to the market to buy their costumes: robes (*cübbe*), baggy trousers (*şalvar*), turbans, vests, short-sleeved jackets (*mintan*), slippers (*mes*), galoshes (*lastik*), and saddle bags filled with Arabic books. But while provisioning themselves for their new appearance, they were surprised by a gendarmerie sergeant in the market. This sergeant greeted them, identifying Süleyman Askerî by name, and asked them to visit his divisional commander who had orders for them. Fearing the worst but playing along, Askerî Bey managed to get the sergeant to hand him the order. It said that the group should be arrested and returned to Baghdad. Thinking quickly, Süleyman Askerî promised to comply but said that they first needed to complete their shopping and then would come to visit the commander whom he claimed was an old friend. They shut themselves up in the dervish lodge (*tekke*) and considered their options. Meanwhile they learned with alarm that the fifth member of their group, Kasım, had been arrested and sent back to Baghdad. He was soon replaced by another officer named Sakallı Emin Efendi, who had already been stopped by the British from entering Libya via Egypt but was determined to try again. After a week's stay in the dervish lodge, and believing that the gendarmerie commander had probably assumed that they had disappeared, they boarded the train to Beirut, supplied with food and water by Şeyh Ziya and his men.

The train trip to Beirut allowed them to perfect their new disguises. Yakup Cemil struck up a conversation with any passengers he could find from the area around Ayıntab (Antep) and Kilis, asking after the conditions of life in the *medrese* (Islamic theological college) and learning the names of its teachers, while secretly recording his findings in a notebook concealed beneath his robes. When the train stopped in Baalbek they ordered a meal; Cemil's imitation of a *hoca*, or Muslim cleric—the way he gathered up his robes and washed and dried his hands—sent the others into fits of laughter at the convincing way he played his part.

But their time in Beirut did not begin well. Their train arrived in the middle of the night and they had trouble finding a hotel. Eventually they found an innkeeper who charged them well over the going price for a room that turned out to be occupied. Its inhabitants were abruptly awakened and thrown unceremoniously out into the street so that their still-warm beds could be given to the group of incognito officers. They awoke the next morning to Süleyman Askerî's cry of alarm. The light of day allowed them to see just how dirty the room was: the pillows were filthy and fleas were marching in columns across their beds. They went out into the street to find a meal and a better hotel. They had decided earlier to stay away from high-priced and fancy restaurants lest, as a group of theological students, they attract suspicion. But now Askerî Bey, the son of a Paşa and something of a stickler when it came to food, rebelled: "'Look, guys, I'll sleep wherever you wish, flea-ridden or dirty, but when it comes to food, this I can't do. I definitely want to eat in a good restaurant,' he said, putting his foot down."[34]

Askerî's "rebellion" led to an improbable encounter. Having seen a sign promising a combination casino-restaurant, the five men approached. They saw a crowded but elegant scene with chic customers surrounding the green baize of gambling and billiard tables amid marble columns. Undaunted, they entered and asked for the restaurant. All the gamblers turned and stared in amazement at the unholy sight of these "men of religion" entering the casino. When they had finished their meal and smoked their cigarettes, it was time to pay the bill. None of the men had any money handy so they turned to Fehmi, the youngest of the group, and asked him to pay. In Aleppo they had placed all their gold inside belts that were now covered by their clerical outfits. Poor Fehmi had to unwind his long sash—over 7 meters in length—to extract his pieces of gold from the belt he wore underneath. They paid the bill and left an extravagant tip of 100 para. Immediately the waiters snapped to attention, handing them their umbrellas, holding their robes for them to put on and handing them their turbans as the unlikely group of diners walked out into the Beirut night.

Eventually they made their way, after still more adventures with shipping companies, unscrupulous agents, fly-blown quarantine cordons (third-class passengers were subject to being detained for health reasons, especially cholera) and arms smugglers, to Port Said and Alexandria in Egypt, the staging ground for Ottoman infiltration into Cyrenaica. Given the obstacles they had overcome, reaching Alexandria was a minor victory but still left the group a long way from Libya, let alone the action against the Italians.

From Alexandria, the group moved west. Süleyman Askerî's diary (copied out by Eşref years later) picks up their progress on 7 February 1912 in the town of Delincat (Dalinjat/Dilingat), Egypt. It had taken them five weeks to make their way from Baghdad to their position just west of the Nile delta. They arrived some time after Enver, Mustafa Kemal, Eşref and the other officers and notables mentioned above. Unlike Fehmi Bey's memoir, which was written years after the events he describes, Süleyman Askerî's account appears to be one that he wrote at the time. For this reason and doubtless also due to the different personalities involved, it tends to focus more on the daily aspects of the journey: the frustrations, but also the joys, of what was a difficult trip. It is clear that others making their way to Libya from Egypt joined the original group who had started out from Baghdad. Because the account begins in the middle, there is no explanation of who was travelling with him; eventually we learn that Fehmi and Tevfik Beys were still there; but new travelers included a group of men from Resne in Macedonia and, somewhat confusingly, another person named Süleyman.

The party encountered a new set of problems on their way through the Western Desert. Weather and food featured prominently in Askerî's account. It is hard to know how far Askerî recorded the reality of their trek and how far it reflected his mercurial personality and demanding standards. But whatever the case, they seemed to have a rough trip. Their main obstacles were the winter weather, the lack of a clear route across the desert, the scarcity of food, water, and shelter, and uncertainty about what sort of reception they would meet from the local tribes. This combination of problems could lead the somewhat poetically—and emotionally—inclined Askerî to record some vivid images of their trek west.

Here is an example taken from the night of 8/9 February 1912:

> After such a powerful storm of wind and rain, we couldn't bear this kind of ruinous downpour. All of our covers are wet. Only our underwear stayed dry. There is nothing to spread [on the ground] under us and nothing to cover us. Under these circumstances another night out in the open will be a disaster. Fehmi's situation is very worrisome. We don't know where we are and we don't know where we're going.[35]

They tried to dry out their things when the morning sun appeared, but another storm, this one pelting them with hailstones, caused chaos. Süleyman Askerî describes their camels dispersing in search of shelter as if being whipped and poetically laments the "merciless Schadenfreude" (şemat-i biinsafi) of the hail and the sound of the storm's "thoughtless waterpipe" (lüle-i bişuur).

The officers' ordeal combined the positive and the negative, joyful highs and bitter lows. They faced extreme cold and rain but also bright sunshine and starry nights; guides who were knowledgeable and those whose thieving intentions inspired only anxiety; pleasurable meals and improperly prepared food which led to sickness; and warm Bedouin hospitality as well as mistrust and robbery. On occasion Askerî refers to the Arab tribesmen as "gypsies" (*çingene, kıbti*), ready to strip them of their possessions. Among the officers there were signs of camaraderie but also arguments, especially about whether or not they had managed to pass out of Egyptian territory and cross the border into Libya. Somewhat oddly, days went by without any indication that a military mission lay at the heart of this difficult, nine-week journey. When they eventually heard the sounds of gunfire—both the incoming Italian shells and the Ottoman responses from what the Ottoman men referred to as "Enver's cannon" (*midfa'-i Enver*)—it came as something of a shock.

Perhaps even more incongruous was an episode that caused the group a further delay: the birth of a camel calf. After a particularly cold, wet night—Askerî says that he froze hundreds of times—they were having their tea at dawn. There was some kind of commotion nearby. One of the camels was giving birth. Askerî recorded that, to his surprise, the Arabs paid no attention and left the poor creature to itself. "Seeing us insist that the birthing camel be helped, Hüseyin ripped up his shirt and, wrapping it around the puny legs of the calf that had begun to appear, helped to pull. A lifeless thing fell onto the sand, like a piece of leather." Askerî assumed that it was dead, a still-birth. "But all of a sudden it began to breathe. Its legs and head slowly started to move. We all watched in silent prayer and astonishment and tried to help this poor little thing live. Hüseyin, with a strange insistence and hurrying, tried to get us to mount our camels in order that we leave the young thing in the desert... No chance. We insisted that we would not abandon this calf. He relented a little. Its mother has no milk, he said. Can this be believed?"[36] The birth of a camel had provoked a serious disagreement within the group. In the end, on Askerî's insistence, they placed the camel in a saddlebag and set off. (Interestingly, Enver experienced a similar attachment to the fauna of the North African desert, recording his dismay when his pet gazelle, which he had received as a gift and which followed him everywhere, even sleeping next to his bed, became sick in Libya in June 1912).[37] But after some time they discovered even better news than the survival of this much fussed-over calf: they had crossed the border out of British-controlled Egypt and into Cyrenaica.

Meanwhile, Eşref had smuggled his much larger and more prominent party of VIPs into Libya. Having arrived in Egypt weeks earlier, on 10 November 1911, Eşref had set about organizing their passage across the Western Desert. A photograph taken at Kilometer Three, just west of Alexandria, shows that they, too, had adopted a similar disguise of men of religion. Identifiable in the group are Eşref, Şeyh Salih Şerif, Emir Ali Paşa (son of Abd al-Qadir), his son Abd al-Qadir, İzmitli Mümtaz, Beşiktaşlı Niyazi, and thirteen others. Most of the Ottoman officers were able to make it into Libya, thanks to planning, reliance on smugglers, and travelling inland to avoid British patrols. A few, however, including Resneli Niyazi,[38] one of the heroes of the Young

5. Incognito with VIPs en route to Libya. (Source: Stoddard photographs, author's personal collection)

69

Turk revolution, and Sakallı Emin Efendi, were apprehended. The latter would, as we have seen, join Askerî's group for another attempt to get to Libya.

The details of Eşref's organization for this phase of the journey are sparse but the sheer size of the group and the prominence of some of their number meant that elaborate planning was required. Eşref's diary notes are brief, indicating only that he had made some preparations for the war against Italy while still in Istanbul and that he traveled by steamship via Izmir, where several friends came aboard to meet with him.[39] Eşref arrived in Alexandria on 10 November 1911. Like those coming from Baghdad, Eşref had elected to travel in third class to avoid the scrutiny of the British. This meant that he had to spend a night in quarantine, a fate he would have avoided had he purchased a first- or second-class ticket.[40] Three days later he was at the port to meet several of his "friends," including İzmitli Mümtaz, Nuri [Conker], Şeyh Salih Şerif of Tunisia, and the Algerian Emir Ali Paşa. He accompanied them to the Port Said Hotel. The following day he attended to procuring supplies and general organizational tasks. He mentions that Mustafa Kemal was ill and that he took him to be treated; a few days later he took the future Turkish president to a Greek doctor, a certain Çaçatis. Later in the Libyan campaign Mustafa Kemal would develop a serious eye injury. According to Eşref's family, Eşref was instrumental in arranging for him to see a specialist in Vienna on his way home from the front.

Eşref's group, which included Emir Ali Paşa, İzmitli Mümtaz, Selanikli Nazım, Nuri and Şeyh Salih Şerif, took the train as far as Dab'a (El-Dab'a), which they reached on 19 November. After staying in Cebel Hamam (Jabal Hammam) for four days, they hired a guide to lead them through the backcountry. From then on there would be neither trains nor hotels so they would have to proceed by camel. They stayed in the houses, or more usually tents, of the local Bedouin shaykhs. On 2 December 1911 they passed into Libya inland from the border town of Salloum.

Once they had crossed into Libya, they made for the region of Derne (Darna) where Enver had established his headquarters inland at Ayn al-Mansur, passing through the towns of Defne (Dafna) and Tobruk on the way. Six days after leaving Tobruk they reached Ayn al-Mansur

6. Ottoman officers, including Enver and his father together with Şeyh Salih of Tunisia, while training Sanusi fighters in Libya. (Source: EK papers)

and spent the night. Enver was in the western headquarters, so the next morning they marched for two hours to report to him and learn their assignments.[41]

Derne, the short-lived war

Photographs reveal the calculus behind the Ottoman–Sanusi arrangement for the defense of Libya. Small numbers of Ottoman officers set about training the thousands of Sanusi tribal volunteers. The contrast is unmistakable between the Ottomans with their wool uniforms, imported equipment, which included machine guns, bicycles, command tents, and even a motor car, and the Libyans with their flowing white robes and camels. The Ottomans brought to the bargain the modern military organizational skill and tactics they had learned from the German officers who had been advising the imperial army since the late nineteenth century. The Sanusis contributed the zeal that derives from defending one's own country, the *esprit de corps* inherent in a Sufi order such as the Sanusis that relied on the charisma of its leader, and the vast bulk of their manpower, perhaps as many as 20,000 fighters.[42]

The defense of Libya produced a somewhat unlikely pairing. The rapidly modernizing Ottoman state had invested heavily in Western technology and know-how during its sixth century of existence; the Sanusis were a primitive mystical Islamic brotherhood that was only about eighty years old. Founded by an Algerian scholar who had returned from Mecca in the 1830s, the order prospered in eastern Libya. Fostering a Spartan lifestyle and a dedication to acts of piety, the order grew to the point that it enjoyed a much greater following throughout Libya than that enjoyed by the nominal Ottoman rulers. By the last decades of the nineteenth century the Sanusi leadership had worked out an arrangement with Istanbul that largely left the order in control of eastern Libya.

When faced with the invasion of a hostile Christian power, the sometimes uneasy Ottoman–Sanusi partnership quickly found common ground. The Italians, as might be expected from the arrogance of their approach towards the Ottoman province, expected a cakewalk in Libya. After all, they had brought an expeditionary force of 34,000 men, 6,300 horses, 1,050 wagons, 48 field guns and 24 mountain guns. By contrast, the Ottomans had only about 5,200 men in Libya, but these were poorly equipped and the garrisons were below strength. The Italians would continue to add troops to these already favorable numbers over the course of the conflict, so that by 1914 they had 60,000 men in the country.[43] Given their numerical superiority and their near-total control of the sea, the Italian command naturally expected an easy conquest.

The Italians, to quote Evans-Pritchard again, were therefore:

> surprised, then alarmed, at the resistance they had to overcome. They were dilatory and over-cautious after their main landing at Tripoli, hanging about in the town instead of pushing on into the interior before the Turks had time to organize resistance and attract Arab volunteers. In Cyrenaica also they delayed too long their advance into the interior and gave the Bedouin time to come to the assistance of the Turks and for some adventurous Turkish officers, among them men who were later to make names for themselves in world history, to reach the field from Turkey. The Italians also underestimated the skill and pluck of the Turkish soldiers and they misjudged—the worst of their miscalculations—the attitude of the Arab population of Libya to the war. They believed that the Arabs were so irate with the Turks that they would not assist them and might even turn against

them. Indeed, so confident were the Italians of Bedouin support that, according to local statements, they were themselves supplying them with arms in Cyrenaica for some months before the outbreak of the war.[44]

When the Italian bombardment of Derne began in September 1911, the small Ottoman garrison withdrew out of range of the Italian warships and regrouped. Then, disastrously for the Italian cause, the Sanusi order sprang into action. Its leader Sayyid Ahmad al-Sharif, although far away in the desert to the south, was well informed of the situation and ordered his local leaders to send their tribal forces to join the defense of the territory. Almost immediately the undermanned Ottomans were heartened to receive these tribal reinforcements and set about the welcomed if unwieldy task of integrating them into the Ottoman forces.[45] The delay in the Italian advance gained the Ottomans valuable time and allowed them to blunt the eventual but somewhat cautious Italian attempt to advance into the interior. Critically, the time thus saved allowed the experienced Ottoman officers the opportunity to make their difficult overland journeys to the front. First Aziz Ali, also known as Aziz Ali al-Misri,[46] who had been one of the key activists in Manastır where he had got to know Enver well, appeared to take up the command of the Benghazi front; and then Enver arrived by camel to coordinate the defense in the Derne sector. Mustafa Kemal would later be given command of the Derne front.[47]

The Ottoman officers, grateful for the strong support they were receiving from the Sanusiyya, were careful to include their shaykhs in consultation and planning. This replicated the higher-level demonstrations of affection between the Ottomans and the Sanusiyya, as represented symbolically by the exchange of letters, banners, gifts (Enver was presented with many gifts, including several African women),[48] entertainment, and even the naming of a particular Sanusi *zawiya* after the Ottoman Sultan.[49] This was not just posturing. The banners sent by the Sanusi leader Ahmad Sharif were an important means for him to show the mostly illiterate tribesmen that he supported the Ottoman efforts—and that they should too. Pictures in Eşref's collection show the Sanusi standards, embroidered with Qur'anic verses as well as another important visual symbol of the Ottoman–Sanusi bond: a captured Italian flag. The increased Sanusi support reflected the fact that the nature of the conflict was changing: no longer simply an Italian–

Ottoman war, it was becoming a battle between the Italians and the Sanusiyya, albeit one with an important degree of Ottoman guidance and oversight, and taking the form of an anti-colonial struggle.[50]

In the meantime the Ottoman officers had their work cut out for them. Before they could begin the major logistical challenges of harnessing the Sanusi tribal forces, they had to integrate the Ottoman volunteer officers into the military plan. Süleyman Askerî was assigned to work under the command of Aziz Ali al-Misri but apparently failed to get along with him—rivalries among this group of young, headstrong volunteers were rife—and was allowed to attach himself to the Derne sector. Later, when Enver returned to Istanbul to organize the Ottoman command in the Balkan Wars, Askerî stayed behind along with Aziz Ali, but Askerî gave over the command of Derne to the Egyptian.

Eşref, based in the Ayn al-Mansur headquarters near Derne, was given the crucial tasks of keeping the tribes on side, organizing their military training, and coordinating their attacks within the overall Ottoman command structure. These were assignments to which, given his desert experience and command of Arabic, he was well suited. He "was made responsible for coordination between the army and the local volunteers. In addition to his duties as military commander of the 'Awaqir tribe, Eşref also handled wider coordination, gathering the tribal chiefs, the militia (muhafaziyyah; mufarrizah) commanders and Ottoman officers in 'war councils' in order to discover tribal and Sanusi opinion on current affairs and to plan future moves. Eşref was responsible for the appointment of Ottoman officers who were the senior commanders of the tribal force; he also settled inter-tribal disputes."[51]

None of this was easy. Descriptions of the Bedouin tactics sound eerily familiar to reports of the initial attacks by Libyan rebels against the forces of Muammar Gaddafi in 2011. Exactly one hundred years later, the weapons had changed but the untrained approach to combat remained grimly similar:

> Enthusiastic though they were, the Bedouin who poured into the Turkish [i.e. Ottoman] camps were in no sense soldiers. Full of spirit, courageous to the point of recklessness, their one aim was to charge the enemy, who was armed with the most modern equipment and generally entrenched. They charged on horseback, firing wildly, wherever they might come across him, without any regard to danger, terrain, or odds. The Turkish

officers had great difficulty in the early days of the campaign in restraining these impetuous cavaliers, but Turkish tact, the example of disciplined Turkish troops, and the disastrous results of their own impetuosity soon taught them to act with greater caution, though not with the patience necessary in the professional soldier.[52]

The Ottoman officers, or "Turkish" as Evans-Pritchard called them, thus had their work cut out for them. Photographs preserved in Eşref's collection show the training to which the tribal forces, now organized into militias, were subjected. In private Enver was less than impressed with the tribal forces' discipline, referring to the Arab fighters as acting "like children."[53] Similarly, their marksmanship needed work.[54] More favorable were his impressions of their inherent character that he considered "good and loyal."[55] Time was of the essence and such training as they received was inevitably both brief and rudimentary. In Derne where Enver, Eşref and Mustafa Kemal, as commander of the eastern garrison, were based, there were about 2,000 tribal troops.[56] "Realizing that the war might be protracted, Enver tried to make the Bedouin volunteers feel they were as much part of the army of resistance as the Turkish regulars and to give them some military training, in however random a fashion. He chose 300 young Bedouin of the principal families of the tribal sheikhs from among the volunteers and gave them training at al-Zahir al-Ahmar, some 20 km to the south-west of Darna. They were given arms and uniforms sent from Turkey, were housed in Turkish army tents, and received Turkish pay."[57] Enver later selected 365 boys, mostly sons of the principal tribal chiefs, and had them sent to Istanbul to receive military and administrative training, showing that the Ottoman relationship with the Sanusiyya was not only one of short-term expedience.[58]

The way in which the Ottoman–Sanusi forces interacted can be seen from a single document. A Libyan tribal fighter wrote to Enver requesting money on behalf of a group of nine Libyans, describing them as "fighters in the path of God," emphasizing their extreme poverty and requesting that a missed payment for a week's worth of fighting be made good. The Paşa passed it on to Mustafa Kemal, commander of the Derne sector. The future Atatürk then passed it on to Eşref as commander of the Hasa (i.e. 'Ayn al-Hasa) sector, just south of Derne. Eşref then ordered that the men be given the back pay that they were claiming.[59] The signatures of Enver, Mustafa Kemal, and Eşref on the same petition reflect the close cooperation with which the three men had to work in Libya.[60] Later of course their lives would take sharply divergent paths.

Eşref's first engagement against the Italians took place on 27 January 1912. Eşref was in command of the Awaqir tribe, and they were fighting in the Sayyid Abdullah Mountains in the region of Derne when they

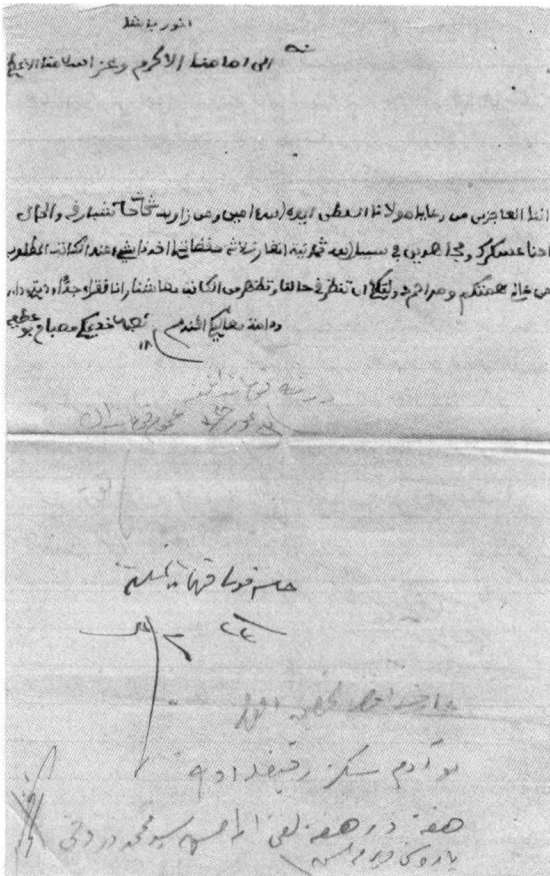

7. Libyan document with the signatures of Enver, Mustafa Kemal and Eşref. (Source: EK papers)

had their first clash with the Italians. As Eşref described it, "With my 300 armed Bedouin we captured two machine guns and a breech-loading cannon and ammunition, locked (*kilitli*) infantry cartridges and 1,500 Italian rifles from the enemy. By way of thanks Enver distributed five gold pieces to the families of those who had died and one gold piece to the wounded. He gave me as part of the plunder an Italian rifle as a present, having carved his name in the rifle butt with his knife, and a photograph."[61] Subsequent days were filled with inspection patrols, along with Mustafa Kemal and Nuri (Conker). A photograph shows Eşref's Ottoman–Sanusi forces displaying a captured Italian flag. Not all missions were so positive; the day after their successful skirmish with the Italians, Eşref's men identified two men from Derne as enemy spies and executed them on the spot.[62]

In the Derne sector, where Enver, Eşref, and Mustafa Kemal were active, the Ottoman forces performed surprisingly well. The Italian war plan for the subjugation of Cyrenaica was to advance two simultaneous columns, one from Benghazi and the other from Derne, in a large-scale pincer movement. On 28 November 1911 the Italians marched out into the suburbs of Benghazi, but quickly found that their superiority only held within the range of their naval guns. They immediately found themselves on the defensive once they moved into the interior. Here the Ottomans had the initiative but made a mistake when they abandoned their more usual defensive strategy and attempted an all-out attack on Benghazi on 12 March 1912. This was a setback for the Ottomans, producing a high number of casualties, although far fewer than the 1,000 that the Italians claimed.[63] Meanwhile, the Italians found the Derne sector even less promising. The terrain there, with its steep incline inland from the town, made it hard to advance and easier for the Ottoman–Sanusi forces to defend. There now began the battle for control of the Wadi Darna, the valley that supplied the town with most of its water. On 11–12 February 1912, Enver was so emboldened by his forces' ability to stop the invaders in their tracks and by the arms and ammunition they had captured that he led an attack on Derne town, but failed to take it. In response the Italians erected defensive works, but Derne remained besieged by an Ottoman–Arab force of over 8,000 men. At this point the situation in the Derne sector was more or less a stalemate. Fighting would flare up from time to time as the Italians sought to increase their strategic position by taking particular strong points in their attempt to control the Wadi Darna. An especially fierce firefight broke out on 17 September at Ras al-Laban. Here the Italians lost ten officers and 174 dead and wounded, while the Ottoman–Sanusi forces lost far more.[64]

The conflict dragged on. Rome was forced to rethink its strategy. General Caneva, the overall Italian commander in Libya, was recalled, replaced by two generals, one in Tripolitania and one in Cyrenaica, reflecting the Italian realization that their earlier optimistic plan needed to be replaced with a much more realistic one. But in the end the stand-off proved to be shorter than it might have been. Timing was decisive. Faced with a much more serious danger closer to home when the First Balkan War broke out in October, Istanbul sued for peace. By the Treaty of Lausanne (Ouchy), signed on 18 October 1912, the Ottomans agreed to withdraw all forces from Libya in return for the Dodecanese Islands that the Italians had seized during the war (a prom-

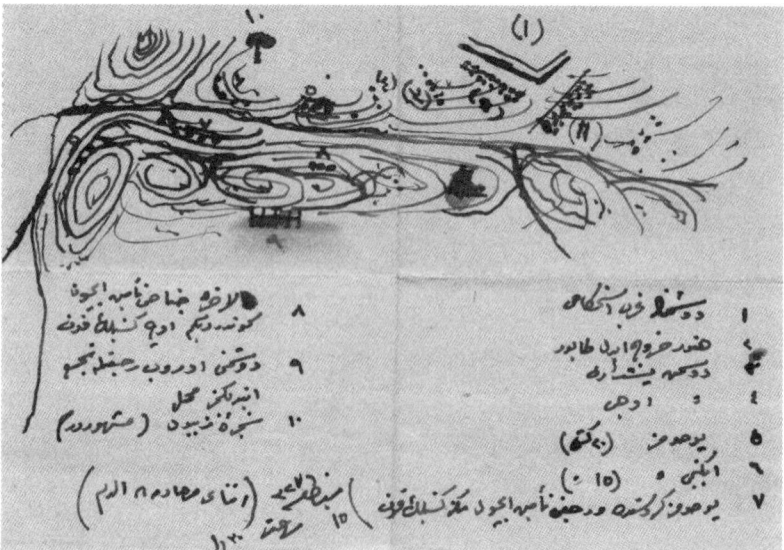

8. Eşref's sketch of the battle of Derne, showing terrain and ambush and attack points. (Source: EK papers)

ise on which the Italians never made good) and the right of the Sultan to be recognized as Caliph in Libya and to maintain a representative there. This concession proved in retrospect to have been a mistake for the Italians who, having promised their populace a quick victory, wanted the Ottomans out. As Evans-Pritchard put it, "The Sultan had gone out by the front door only to return by the back."[65]

Istanbul wanted to soften the blow of having lost its last African possession to a Christian power. A skeletal Ottoman force stayed on in Libya, harassing the Italians and furthering the resistance of the Sanusiyya. Again Evans-Pritchard's appraisal is worth quoting:

> The Turkish soldiers who remained in Cyrenaica were drawn from every part of the empire—Albanians, Kurds, Syrians, Iraqis, Circassians, Anatolians, Macedonians, and Thracians—and were practically mercenaries who lived by the sword. Slovenly though they were, they were fine fighters and frugal as well, being content to campaign on rice, potatoes, bread and an occasional helping of meat; and in Enver they had an inspiring leader. Enver, being a regular soldier, was, however, anxious to return to Turkey to take part in the fighting in the Balkans. Before departing for the Bulgarian front and handing over his command in Cyrenaica to 'Aziz Ali al-Masri he paid a visit to [the Sanusi leader] Sayyid Ahmad al-Sharif at Jaghbub, making a remarkable trip to the oasis in the only motor-car the Turco-Arab forces possessed. Sayyid Ahmad agreed to carry on the struggle in the name of [Ottoman] Sultan Muhammad V and from that point on was more engaged and claimed status of a semi-autonomous state.[66]

Sayyid Ahmad had only recently moved some 700 km north to the oasis of Jaghbub from Kufra, the oasis deep in the Sahara where he had been organizing the Sanusi resistance to French attempts at imperial expansion.

The Italian–Ottoman conflict lasted in one form or another until 1919. Once the Balkan Wars started in 1912, however, the main focus of Ottoman attention was necessarily elsewhere. They withdrew most of their officers, leaving only a skeleton crew to continue to advise and work with the Sanusiyya. Enver's younger brother Nuri [Killigil] was sent back to carry on the fight. But after the outbreak of the Balkan Wars, the conflict in Libya would be even more clearly a fight between the Italians and the Sanusis, one that lasted in Cyrenaica until the early 1930s. The period of intense Ottoman involvement against the Italians in Libya, though brief, was to have important long-term consequences.

First, the Italian seizure of Libya "flashed a green light for the all-out Balkan assault on the Ottoman periphery."[67] Italy's move encouraged Bulgaria, Serbia, and Greece to act more aggressively,[68] thus helping to trigger the Balkan Wars that, in turn, created the immediate background to the start of World War I.

Secondly, it reinforced the Ottoman military's penchant for adopting the new, asymmetrical tactics that they had been developing in Macedonia. The fact that the Ottomans had to abandon the Libyan campaign when it seemed to be succeeding left a powerful, lingering feeling that the strategy of coupling Ottoman command with local forces and pursuing a guerrilla style of war would have produced significant victory against the Italians. The relatively short duration of the conflict and the relative success against a European power—even a second-rate power like Italy—probably gave senior Ottoman military officials a feeling of over-confidence. After all, if a few score Ottoman officers who were hundreds of kilometers away from Istanbul, deprived of proper lines of supply and working in conjunction with tribal forces who had scarcely received any military training could blunt the Italians' overseas adventure, it might well have been argued that the regular Ottoman army would have done much better. Sadly for Istanbul the next conflict would puncture that exuberance and demonstrate the flaws in that argument.

Thirdly, the Libyan campaign was the first major engagement of the network that would coalesce around Enver to form the Special Organization, including some of its future leaders. It was something of a "laboratory" for the campaigns to come, whether in the Balkan Wars, the Great War, or the "National Struggle" that produced the Turkish Republic.[69] The successes that these men inflicted against the Italians undoubtedly encouraged Enver to create this clandestine, special operations organization, a decision that would have dramatic consequences in the years to come. Crucial to this network was Kuşcubaşı Eşref, known for his knowledge of and ties with Bedouin. "Eshref's closeness to Enver (they served together in Libya) led to Enver's decision to appoint him to reorganize Teşkilat-i Mahsusa, and he eventually became its commander."[70] Whether Eşref Bey actually ever commanded the organization is disputed,[71] but it would certainly play a crucial role in the last years of the empire that lay just ahead.

Fourthly, the engagement in Libya symbolized the vision of defending the beleaguered Ottoman Empire by drawing on Muslim "national" unity—in other words, Muslim nationalism. By bringing together what we might refer to as a "Coalition of the Believers" from a diverse group of committed activists from both inside the empire and beyond its borders, the Ottoman command, and Enver in particular, seemed to have hit upon a winning strategy. Whether the Libyan experience generated undue optimism for relying on armed conflict to hold the empire together we may perhaps never know. But it is clear that it was the opening stage for a series of dramatic—and costly—wars to come.

4

THE BALKAN WARS

The outbreak of the Balkan Wars in the autumn of 1912 came as a shock to the Ottoman Empire. The speed with which the armies of a coalition of Balkan states overran Ottoman forces in Rumelia underlined the empire's military deficiencies in brutal fashion. For the officers fighting in the remoteness of Libya it was especially traumatic. Compared with the distant Ottoman–Sanusi engagement against the Italians in North Africa, the outbreak of a conflict against an alliance of Balkan states represented a far more serious threat to Istanbul. As Eşref put it, it killed their joy.[1]

News of the fighting in the Balkans reached Eşref and his men as they were fighting at Barqa. They had been having success against the Italians, keeping them pinned down on the coast while continuing to train and organize the highly motivated Sanusi fighters. But more bad news was soon to follow: Albania, historically a bastion of Ottoman Muslim support in the Balkans, declared its independence on 28 November 1912. Worse still, the Ottoman army was being routed on the battlefield. The alarming prospect of an Ottoman collapse in the Balkans and its enemies menacing Istanbul not only ruined Ottoman plans in Libya, forcing Enver to pull out and leave only a skeleton force behind, but also threatened the very existence of the Ottoman state. The Balkan Wars have aptly been termed "the first phase of the First World War";[2] from this point forward the Ottoman Empire would be fighting for its survival, a fight that would bring dramatic consequences for all involved.

After a final meeting with the Sanusi leadership to discuss tactics, Enver slipped out of Libya and returned to Istanbul. It was not long before he called for Eşref to follow him back to the Ottoman capital. By 20 December 1912, Eşref had gathered together his comrades-in-arms Süleyman Askerî, Yakup Cemil, and Topcu Sadık—each of whom would feature in one way or another in this and subsequent conflicts—and returned to Alexandria en route to the Ottoman capital.

But before Eşref could return to Istanbul he had to carry out a secret mission. Because the sources for this period are limited to the table of contents for his memoirs that no longer exist, the details are unfortunately only extremely sketchy. Here is what he writes: "The upshot of a legally sanctioned confrontation (*mukabele-i meşrua*) was that I had [to carry out] a murderous incident (*bir katl hadisem vardır*). For this reason I secretly returned to Istanbul a few days later."[3] This entry is typically cryptic but confirms the impression that Eşref's career was never far from incident and intrigue. For a Special Operations officer at the sharp end of the action, life was rarely dull.

The returning fighters found the atmosphere in Istanbul considerably changed. The ugly, rapid defeats in the Balkans coupled with the viciousness of the atrocities committed against Muslim civilians in the Balkans had altered life in the Ottoman Empire, perhaps irrevocably. As one scholar put it, it was as if "suddenly, over 500 years of history had come to a screeching halt. More swiftly even than Gladstone could have envisaged in his famous pamphlet, huge slices of European territory ruled by the Ottomans passed into the control of the Christian mini-states in the Balkans."[4] The beleaguered Ottoman capital reflected the changes most acutely. Istanbul was now the scene for public demonstrations, organized meetings and boycotts. The political temperature was rising rapidly. In the background the plaintive creaking of oxcarts and the shuffling of feet reverberated across the city as the seemingly endless procession of abject and traumatized refugees flooded in from the lost Balkan lands. To make matters worse, the refugees were stalked by a dreaded outbreak of cholera which had been initially carried to the Balkans by Ottoman conscripts but soon infected many of the refugees, adding further to their already shocking plight and sending the residents of Istanbul into a panic as the abject arrivals shuffled into the increasingly anxious city.[5] The grimness of the scene was matched by the agitated, desperate tone adopted in the press, reflecting a new direction in political activism occasioned by the shockingly altered geographical and demographic shape of what was left of the empire. A note of political desperation was palpable amid the human misery; narratives of revenge began to gather support.

Simply put, the First Balkan War was a disaster for the Ottoman Empire. Greece, Bulgaria, Serbia, and Montenegro unexpectedly put aside the considerable mutual suspicions and antipathies stemming from their competing claims to Ottoman Macedonia and, encouraged by Russia who wanted a Balkan rapprochement against Austria, formed an anti-Ottoman alliance. Sensing both tacit support from the Great Powers and Ottoman distraction with the distant conflict with Italy, the Balkan alliance attacked the Ottoman Empire in October 1912. In a matter of weeks almost all of the Ottoman territory in the Balkans was lost. Serbian forces pushed south as far as Bitola (Manastır) while the Greeks swept into Salonica, forcing the Ottomans to evacuate the deposed Sultan Abdülhamid II to Istanbul for safety. Meanwhile the Bulgarians, although appalled at the Serbian capture of territory they coveted for themselves, completed a sweeping series of victories over Ottoman forces, whom they expelled from both Western and Eastern Thrace and arrived at the Çatalca lines, a mere 20 km from Istanbul. Only three fortress cities, Scutari in northern Albania, Yanya (Janina) in Epirus, and Edirne (Adrianople) in Thrace, held out against the combined onslaught of the Balkan Allies.[6] Of the three, Edirne, a former Ottoman capital that lay across the road to Istanbul, was the most vital. Battlefield failures during the war resulted in recriminations within the military, most acutely between the leaders of two branches of a failed pincer movement to encircle the Bulgarian army in Thrace: Enver on the one hand and Fethi and Mustafa Kemal on the other. As a result of this failure Edirne was surrounded and eventually forced to surrender. The resentments and recriminations engendered by this inter-officer dispute would have important reverberations in the near future and would directly affect Eşref.

After a prolonged, exhausting siege, Edirne fell to Bulgarian forces on 16 March 1913. This was a bitter blow for the Unionists who in opposition had campaigned aggressively for a liberated Edirne and used this to justify their *coup d'état*, the infamous "Raid on the Sublime Porte" of 23 January 1913, an event that radically changed the pattern of Ottoman politics and ushered in the period of rule by a group of army officers and bureaucrats who would hold power, first in the latter years of the empire and then in the Turkish Republic until after World War II.[7] It is unclear from Eşref's later description of these events whether or not he was there on that fateful and bloody day, but he was well informed about the events. Certainly the cast of characters involved reads like a Who's Who of the inner core of the activist Unionist officers, from Enver and Talat down to the likes of Mümtaz, Sapancalı Hakkı, Filibeli Hilmi, and Yakup Cemil. Eşref writes that the first person to open fire in the raid was his close associate Sapancalı Hakkı who was "well oiled with Cognac."[8]

The senior Ottoman leadership, personified by the Grand Vizier Mahmud Şevket Paşa, was content to accept the loss of Edirne and Western Thrace. The logic behind this position was the strategic consideration that it would be better for Istanbul if Western Thrace were to remain in Bulgarian hands as a buffer zone that would cause friction between Greece and Bulgaria. This would give the Ottomans the opportunity to have "the last word."[9] Following this logic, Istanbul soon sued for peace and by the Treaty of London abandoned its last European territory. But the "self-sacrificing" Unionist officers were unwilling to leave it at that. They considered this unfinished business and soon initiated the plan to take back Western Thrace, forcing the wavering government's hand.[10] Indeed, Eşref's account indicates the level of personal anguish suffered by the activist officers. Enver was "in despair" at the news that the empire had abandoned Edirne by treaty, and the two men "poured their hearts out" over the news. Mümtaz declaimed that if Islam had permitted it they would have been obliged to committed suicide.[11] While the rhetoric may have been strong, it was nevertheless the case that the *fedaî* officers now had the political clout to support such talk with direct action.

To add insult to injury, the Muslim population suffered horribly as the Ottoman Empire's enemies advanced in the Balkans. Atrocities inflicted on the empire's population as its borders contracted were hardly new, but now knowledge about the misfortunes of their compatriots spread quickly and widely in the Ottoman lands. For those who did not witness in person the long lines of bedraggled refugees trudging into Istanbul, the booming press of the period disseminated the news in unmistakably stark, frequently chauvinistic, terms.[12] Reports about the atrocities, including graphic drawings and sometimes even photographs of mutilated Muslim bodies, created an atmosphere of heightened tension and stoked the desire for revenge. But this revenge was not directed towards the Balkan States.[13] With the heavily qualified exception of the Western Thracian episode to which we shall soon turn, the Unionist leadership was forced to accept that the empire's situation precluded further hostilities in the Balkans. The revanchist spirit did, however, inform Unionist policy toward the Greek Orthodox and Armenian population of Anatolia on the eve of and during World War I, with disastrous results. The Unionist leaders, themselves mostly refugees from the lost Balkan lands, "read the situation in Anatolia through the prism of recent events in the Balkans."[14] The spirit of revenge arguably continued to inform popular perceptions about territory and the nation well into the post-war period.[15]

But at the end of the Second Balkan War, all of that lay in the future. Even before Edirne fell, the activist officer group close to Enver were already planning an offensive to recover the lands to the west of the city that had been lost during the war but still contained a sizeable Muslim population. If the Unionist leadership was disproportionately composed of refugees, the "self-sacrificing officers" represented an even more concentrated preserve of refugees or sons of refugees. Almost all of the key actors in the next phase of hostilities, including most prominently Eşref, his brother Selim Sami, and Süleyman Askerî, but also such of their associates as İbrahim Cihangiroğlu, Çerkes Reşid, Sapancalı Hakkı, and "Bulgar" Sadık,[16] were men who had been affected by the shrinking borders of the Ottoman Empire and/or the ethnic cleansing of Muslim lands in the Caucasus. Their overall objective was to defend the empire at all costs. After the disaster of the First Balkan War, their attentions became focused on the region bounded by the Karasu (Mesta) River on the west and the Maritsa (Evros) on the east,[17] the territory of Western Thrace.

When the Balkan allies fell out over how to divide the spoils of the First Balkan War, the inter-Balkan fighting that ensued presented the

Ottomans with the opportunity they were looking for. By the spring of 1913 tensions between the erstwhile allies reached breaking point. Bulgaria was in the most difficult position, particularly when Russian support, previously so strong, seemed to evaporate in a periodic swing away from a pro-Bulgarian and toward a pro-Serbian phase.[18] When the tense stand-off between the Greek and Serbian forces facing each other in Macedonia degenerated into raids and sniper attacks, war seemed imminent. On the night of 29/30 June the Bulgarians attacked, apparently in an ill-advised attempt to bolster their negotiating position.[19] Greece, Serbia, and Romania soon declared war on Bulgaria, initiating the Second Balkan War and presenting the Ottoman state with the possibility of reclaiming some of its lost territory.

It was not long before Eşref was back in the thick of the action. In fact, the Ottoman military had been making plans for an offensive intended to recapture the territorial losses of the First Balkan War well before it was over. Impressed with the possibilities of asymmetrical warfare gained by Ottoman officers on the receiving end of it while serving in Macedonia and recently put into practice in Libya, Enver was instrumental in developing unconventional fighting arrangements. Eşref reports that at the time of the Raid on the Sublime Porte on 23 January 1913 he was acting on Enver's personal instruction by recruiting volunteers in the region around Izmir and Aydın for a mobile volunteer unit. Eşref then gathered them together in Istanbul for military training.[20] A *laissez-passer*, dated 7 February 1913 and signed by Enver, stated that Eşref was in charge of a mobile force of volunteers and had been sent to Izmir to "take care of certain matters."[21] This unit, under Eşref's command and composed of approximately 300 men, many of Caucasian descent but also including Turks and, intriguingly, some Afghans, saw action in the last encounters of the First Balkan War. They were assigned in an irregular capacity to the Xth Corps, commanded by Hurşid Paşa, on the Left Wing of the Ottoman forces in Thrace and thrown into the action of the last-ditch fighting to protect Istanbul. The policy of deploying units of self-sacrificing volunteers alongside regular ones was one that the Unionists had pursued since the 1908 revolution.[22] But it was a policy of which Ahmed İzzet Paşa, the Minister of War during the Balkan Wars, strongly disapproved.[23] The split, vividly illustrated in the different garb of the two types of troops, with the volunteers festooned in bandoliers, was indicative of a fundamental difference in approach that would return with a vengeance in the aftermath of the Balkan Wars when Eşref and his colleagues would establish a rogue state in Western Thrace. Then, as we shall see, it seems clear that the Ottoman force contained both genuine irregular volunteers and regular army troops disguised as either irregulars or locally raised militias.

Details about Eşref's involvement in the later stages of the Balkan Wars are in short supply, but it is clear that it was a tumultuous time. With Istanbul under threat, tensions were running high. Eşref records that at one point he was faced with a mutinous uprising in his own detachment, a mutiny that he duly suppressed, as we shall see shortly.[24] In the latter stages of the First Balkan War, Eşref was stationed at Kallikratia (Kalikratya), a coastal village to the west of Istanbul near Büyük Çekmece, where he was busy taking on new recruits for a guerrilla force of 1,200 men. At times the fighting was bayonet-to-bayonet between the Ottomans and the Bulgarians. Eşref's unit, he says, staged a successful night raid against the enemy.[25] His next recorded action took place in February when the Ottoman forces pushed out to the west from Çatalca and onto the offensive, taking Kartal Tepe,[26] an engagement that left the Ottomans with many wounded, including all three of the Kuşçubaşı brothers, Eşref, Selim Sami, and Ahmed.

This period at Çatalca was a confused, confusing time. In Istanbul political opposition and criticism of the conduct of the war increasingly challenged the Unionists' position. To judge from Eşref's account, the divisions in the capital may have been replicated among the military at the front. An anti-Unionist faction, perhaps an echo of the rival, secret military organization called the Savior Officers (Halaskâr Zâbitân) that had formed with the backing of senior commanders sympathetic with the main oppositional party who had been shunted aside by the Unionist purges,[27] seems to have provoked a confrontation among the Ottoman forces at Çatalca. There, Eşref's writings reveal considerable havoc behind the scenes. On the one hand Eşref was recruiting and training volunteers for his unit of "*mücahidin*," mostly rough mountain men from the Aegean region. On the other hand he was engaged in a fierce rivalry with an officer named Muhiddin who commanded a parallel unit that, like Eşref's, was under the nominal command of Hurşid

Paşa's Xth Army.[28] A quarrel ensued between the units in which one of Eşref's recruits, a mountain man named Çakır Efe from Gönen, was insulted by Muhiddin because he was wearing his brigand's clothes instead of a uniform. Heated words followed and guns were drawn. Muhiddin confronted Eşref at his headquarters but, thanks to Eşref's self-described diplomatic skills and his rising above his rival's "pretentiousness," the case was apparently resolved. But then when Eşref's men returned from a night raid against the Bulgarians, they were fired upon by Muhiddin's forces, despite the fact that Eşref had sent an intermediary to inform them of his movements. Eşref was furious.

Matters were further complicated by the fact that there was a serious rift among the fighting men between those dedicated to the Unionists and those allied with the Liberal Entente, the chief political rival to the Committee of Union and Progress, known as Hürriyet ve İtilâf in Turkish.[29] At one point, fighting broke out between them at their training camp. Eşref's forces marched on a faction of Ententist troops who were threatening to rebel, claiming that they would liberate Edirne on their own. A gunfight ensued which left one dead and three wounded on Eşref's side, and up to ten fatalities and close to thirty wounded on the other. Incidents such as these underscore the problems associated with the Unionist policy of combining regular and irregular forces and the politicization of the military. In the face of a mortal enemy, the Ottoman military were having to cope with a remarkable set of disciplinary problems. Egos and political rivalries did not help the situation.

When things settled down, Eşref took part in the second battle of Çatalca, only 32 km from Istanbul, which took place in March and early April 1913. Here the Ottoman forces showed the positive contribution of the irregular forces since the volunteer units, some thrown into battle after amphibious landings, achieved notable results.[30] This engagement demonstrated impressive levels of Ottoman battlefield coordination and organization. The stiffened Ottoman resistance at Çatalca encouraged the Ottoman command to think about turning defense into offense. Çatalca marked the end of the combat and the beginning of negotiations that would eventually lead to the armistice that brought the First Balkan War to a close.[31] The Ottoman leadership used this breathing period as a time to regroup and make plans for a new campaign. Enver and Eşref had been corresponding in the first weeks of April. Enver wrote that he was pleased to hear that Eşref had recovered from his wounds, sent his regards to Sami, and hoped to see him again soon. Eşref had apparently sent Enver a Qur'an but it had not yet arrived. Enver encouraged Eşref to complete the preparations involved in forming a volunteer force.[32] Thus well before the Treaty of London was signed on 30 May 1913, Enver had already ordered the formation of mobile units. Soon they would be scouting the territory to the west, between the front and Lüleburgaz, more than halfway to Edirne.[33]

When the Ottomans returned to the offensive, Eşref took on the task of spearheading the advance into Bulgarian territory. Soon the Second Balkan War began in earnest, and due to such aggressive thinking the Ottoman military was in a position to take advantage of the inter-allied fighting. The Unionists had seized on the assassination of Grand Vizier Mahmud Şevket Paşa by their opponents on 11 June to consolidate their position in the empire, reinforcing the trend towards an activist stance. Disregarding the admonitions of the Great Powers, the Ottoman army advanced on Edirne.

After the assassination of Mahmud Şevket Paşa, Eşref returned to Istanbul where Cemal Paşa, now Military Governor of the capital, assigned him the task of tracking down the assassins.[34] The list of suspects was remarkably long, reflecting the fact that some in the Committee of Union and Progress wanted to use the plot as an opportunity to eliminate their enemies. Cemal offered Eşref a list and told him out of earshot that Prince Sabahattin, a leading figure in the Young Turk scene, was on the list, meaning that if caught he would be put to death. Cemal told Eşref that he knew that the prince had not really been involved and that he should merely scare him away from Istanbul for a while.[35] Awkwardly for Eşref, however, one of those actually involved in the assassination turned out to be a relative who was hiding in a Circassian village near Izmir.[36] This was an early sign of the ways in which inter-Circassian divisions would complicate and disrupt Eşref's life in the years to come.

On 13 June Eşref was ordered to a house in Beyoğlu where police officers were attempting to arrest a group of the plotters who had been cornered after a fire had been started in the upper storey. Cemal Bey sent Eşref to the scene. He and his crew, which included Mümtaz and

9. Men hanged for their involvement in the assassination of Mahmud Şevket Paşa. (Source: TİTE)

Eşref's brother Hacı Sami, managed to break in through a hole they had opened in the roof and captured the fugitives, one of which was an old associate, fellow Circassian and a member of the "Savior Officers" group named Captain Kâzım.[37] Many of the plotters were publicly hanged soon afterwards. This episode was typical of Eşref's life in those days, complicated, close to the action, and rarely dull.

Eşref soon returned to the front to command his hand-picked unit which began to carry out raids behind enemy lines. Eşref's force captured a Bulgarian battalion in Lüleburgaz, taking them prisoner. This encouraged Enver to be bolder still. He soon gave the order for the formation of a volunteer force of 4,000 men. Interestingly, at least some of the financial support for this unit would be borne directly by the Committee of Union and Progress, another indication of the unusual arrangements being called upon in this time of crisis. On 13 July 1913, two days after Mahmud Şevket Paşa's assassination, Eşref's force made marine landings at two points on the Thracian coast of the Marmara Sea, at Ereğli and Tekirdağ.[38] They spread out in a three-pronged position, with Eşref in the center, his brother Selim

10. Eşref behind enemy lines in Bulgaria, 1913.
(Source: EK papers)

Sami to his right, and İbrahim Cihangiroğlu on his left, a formation they had deployed in the latter days of the First Balkan War.[39]

Their objective was Edirne. Marching inland, they reached Muradlı the same day, taking only light casualties. Eşref now wrote to Sami, spelling out the arrangements he had made to award the volunteers who had demonstrated extraordinary sacrifice and bravery in the liberation of Tekirdağ and Muradlı. Eşref would dispense the sum of 3,000 liras among his force of 300 men, to be provided by the Unionist official Hacı Âdil, who would soon be named Ottoman governor of Edirne.[40] Two days later, on 16 July, they reached the Enez–Midye (Enos–Midiye) line, which had been stipulated as the new Ottoman–

Bulgarian border demarcation in the Treaty of London at the end of May. Here the Ottoman forces paused as their leaders pondered a difficult decision. In the background, momentum was building for an offensive. The Unionist newspapers of Istanbul started a domestic campaign agitating for an attack. This appears to have been coordinated with an international initiative, instigated by Talat, in which an "Edirne Committee" comprised of Muslims, Greek Orthodox, Armenians, and Jews toured the capitals of Western Europe to campaign for liberating Edirne and Thrace from Bulgarian rule.[41] Later Bulgarian nationalists would claim that the Ottomans were carrying out a "chauvinist" campaign, whereas Turkish nationalists pointed to the violence committed against the Muslim population, including the forced conversions of the Bulgarian-speaking Muslim Pomaks, to justify the calls for intervention. The Ottoman leadership was faced with the momentous decision of whether or not to cross the Enez–Midye line.

In favor of prudence was the agreement signed in London. Breaking it would mean risking the wrath of the powers whose support, or at least neutrality, was deemed vital for the survival of the empire, as the First Balkan War had so disastrously emphasized. The British Foreign Secretary Sir Edward Grey threatened that if the Ottomans were to take Edirne they would end up losing Istanbul.[42] An Ottoman advance ran the risk of provoking highly unpredictable consequences. For these reasons a number of high-ranking Ottoman officials, apparently even including the Ottoman Commander-in-Chief, urged caution. In favor of an advance was the fact that Edirne lay tantalizingly close and seemed lightly defended, the Bulgarians having pulled out most of their troops to face the Greeks and the Serbs in the west. Recapturing the former imperial capital would allow Ottoman forces to protect the large Muslim population in the Western Thracian regions of Gümülcine and İskeçe, which had been badly treated during the recent conflict. Securing the territory would have the additional strategic advantage of solidifying the Ottoman military's ability to defend the Straits. Time was also a factor. The Ottomans received the news that the Greeks had landed at Dedeağaç (Alexandroupoli) from which they were proceeding into the interior along the Maritsa River. Although the Greek naval detachment was small, the Ottomans may have thought that it was in a position to threaten Edirne.

The tensions inherent in this decision were palpable. Eşref travelled back to the command center at Çorlu to discuss the situation with Enver and Hafız Hakkı, one of the "freedom heroes" of the 1908 revolution and a classmate of Enver's. Encouraging news continued to arrive. The Ottoman forces had taken 700 Bulgarian troops prisoner and the front was showing signs of breaking up. For the aggressively minded, Edirne was beckoning. Eşref told Enver that the Bulgarian forces had all but disappeared and asked for the order to advance. Enver thus found himself in a very difficult position. The new Ottoman Commander-in-Chief Ahmed İzzet Paşa was against Eşref and his plan. Meanwhile Eşref and his men made an exploratory raid toward Lüleburgaz. According to Eşref's figures, the fighting was remarkably easy: 300 Ottoman forces were able to encircle and trap 1,200 enemy troops. Eşref wanted to bring fourteen captive officers back to the border, but received a firm order to release them. Ominously for Eşref, the Ottoman Commander-in-Chief now wanted him taken prisoner.[43] This generated a heated telephone call between Enver and his superior. The Commander-in-Chief ordered Enver to investigate Eşref's alleged misdeeds and punish him accordingly if warranted. Enver promised to open an investigation and signed off. Things looked grim for Eşref. As he put it, "We had signed away Edirne with the Treaty of London. We were stuck on the Enez–Midye line. What's done was done."[44]

But soon the decision was taken to advance on Edirne. Crossing the Enez–Midye line, the Ottoman forces took the city on 23 July 1913 with relative ease. Eşref was with Enver at the vanguard of a force of 4,000 select Ottoman troops. Enver, acutely aware of the propagandistic opportunity, raced to the city to be there at its "reconquest." He and Eşref were together when the city was taken, a symbolic moment for the empire. Edirne, conquered by the Ottomans in the fourteenth century, had been the second imperial capital and contained some of the finest examples of classical Ottoman architecture. In the context of the early twentieth century, this victory represented a potential turning point away from a series of morale-sapping defeats and retreats and toward a bold, offensive strategy that promised the recapture of lost Ottoman territory and protection for the Muslims who had remained at the mercy of violence and ethnic-cleansing. Whereas only a few months earlier the Bulgarian army had been threatening Istanbul itself, Ottoman forces were now invading Bulgaria.[45]

For Eşref the recapture of Edirne represented a form of personal triumph. After spending the night before the final march on Edirne encamped on a rise overlooking the town, Eşref and his company captured a disoriented Bulgarian. From him they learned that central Edirne was in a panic. Recalling that earlier in his life he had been sent into internal exile in Edirne, Eşref's knowledge of the city was now

11. Eşref's purloined collection of stamps and seals. (Source: EK papers)

aiding their effort to advance on and capture the former capital. He duly reported the situation to Enver.[46] It seems that Eşref took advantage of the confused situation—he recounts a story of a civilian pulling down a Bulgarian flag and then almost comically raising a flag of surrender—to take possession of a set of Bulgarian seals and stamps that might prove useful in forging papers. These remain in his family's possession today.

In the revanchist view of Enver and the Unionist leadership, Edirne was just a start. Having defied the Allies once already, the Ottoman high command decided to push on even further. Subsequent advances would rely on a diplomatic ruse. As in Libya where the Ottoman officers under Enver acted against the official sanction of the Ottoman command, so now in Western Thrace the fighting was to be carried out by volunteers. Officially the Porte informed the powers in a note that it considered the Maritsa River to be the real border and that no Ottoman forces would cross it. After the capture of Edirne, Istanbul would claim that no Ottoman regular units crossed the Maritsa into Western Thrace.[47] But as we shall soon see, a combination of irregular forces associated with the Ottoman Special Organization (Teşkilat-i Mahsusa) under the leadership of Süleyman Askerî and Eşref and some regular Ottoman army troops in disguise would soon cross the Maritsa and commence operations in Western Thrace.

In fact, as soon Edirne was recaptured on 23 July, Eşref and his men were on the move again, raiding into Bulgarian territory. For this task he selected fifteen officers and a hundred fighting men from Hurşid Paşa's army corps with which Eşref, Askerî and the irregulars had been fighting.[48] Among these were many whom Eşref knew well, including his brothers Sami and Ahmed, İbrahim Cihangiroğlu and others, many of Circassian or other exilic descent.[49] Soon Eşref and his personally selected force pushed on behind enemy lines into Western Thrace, setting the stage for a new phase in the interwoven history of Eşref and the final years of the Ottoman Empire.

Western Thrace

The dramatic events that were to take place in the territory of Western Thrace are generally overlooked in the accounts of this period. Passed over in narratives that move quickly from the end of the Balkan Wars to the onset of World War I, this phase in the final years of the Ottoman Empire is rich with significance and merits a closer look. Here again we see, as in Libya, the coming together of the committed Unionist officers close to Enver in what they considered a crucial and patriotic mission. Here again we witness their defiance of an Ottoman hierarchy that was, in the view of Enver and his supporters, more concerned with preserving the empire's standing in the eyes of the Great Powers than protecting its subjects. And here again we observe the core group of committed officers taking matters into their own hands, justified in their view by the need to prevent further atrocities against what was left of the Muslim population of the region. The presumption that the "self-sacrificing officers" of the Unionist stripe knew what was best for the population and should take charge in extraordinary circum-stances—even, as we shall see, to the point of creating a break-away Independent Government of Western Thrace[50]—was one that would be repeated in the years to come, both in the waning years of the empire and, more spectacularly, in the Turkish Republic.

A crucial factor in Western Thrace was the role of information and public opinion. The first Balkan War and the horrors it unleashed were in some senses not entirely new. Gang activity and ethnically- and religiously-motivated violence had been part of the Ottoman Balkan scene for decades. Ottoman Macedonia had become a byword for cycles of transgression and reprisals since at least the 1870s when the "Bulgarian horrors" became part of the Western lexicon regarding "Turkey." All the Ottoman officers who passed through Macedonia—and most of them did at some point—were affected by serving there. What made things different in the period of the Balkan Wars was both the escalation in intensity of such violence and the degree to which knowledge of that violence spread in the Ottoman lands. Thanks to the rapid growth of the periodical press and rising levels of literacy gener-ated by the expanding Ottoman school system, the Ottoman public had achieved an unprecedented awareness of what was happening both on the battlefield and to innocent civilians. The burgeoning Ottoman press took up the case with particular vigor and emotion, especially the pro-Unionist papers such as *Tanin*.[51] Evidence of ethnic cleansing, torture, and mayhem was not limited to textual accounts. Technological innovation allowed the press of the "Young Turk" period to present a range of visual material to its readership. Cartoons, drawn illustrations, and photographs depicted the harsh results that followed the shrinking of the empire's borders. Graphic drawings in some Ottoman publications showed the grisly results of the Bulgarian advance on Ottoman Thrace. One image showed an Ottoman fez-wearing male bound in public with his nose and ears cut off. Photographs of corpses and the seemingly endless trail of refugees made the point for all to see. From this point on, warfare would be an increasingly public phenomenon in which the distinction between the fighting and the home front grew ever more blurred. The graphic accounts of the fighting and violence that appeared in the Ottoman press at the time helped to form the background to the Ottoman counter-offensive in the Second Balkan War.

Another important element informing the episode that was about to unfold in Western Thrace was the fact that "the nationality principle as a method of justifying territorial claims had come of age" during the Balkan Wars.[52] Since the Russo–Ottoman war of 1877–8, territorial claims based on demographic majority had been gaining strength, despite the fundamental incompatibility between such claims and the situation on the ground. But nationalists throughout the region were undeterred. Ethnographic maps were increasingly deployed as a means of demonstrating the right to disputed territory.[53] One potential solution that was being floated by various parties for areas with a mixed population was the creation of zones of regional autonomy, often as a half-measure that would buy time for the respective national actors to achieve their ultimate aims of "national unity." Various proposals had recently been mooted to make regions such as Macedonia, Epirus, and Thrace autonomous. Warfare offered another, far more brutal possibility; it could be waged in such a way as to alter these patterns of settlement themselves. The viciousness of the Balkan Wars and the alternating waves of refugees they created as armies passed back and forth across the landscape were clear indications that the new thinking was having an impact on the military agenda. Historians have noted the connections between the demographic pattern of the conflict in the Balkan Wars and the "ethnic cleansing" practices of World War I and the Turkish War of Independence. The episode of Western Thrace may be seen as further revealing the way in which this process worked, especially given the continuity of some of the key actors involved. It contains many of the elements that would resurface in the subsequent conflicts, including both "ethnic cleansing" carried out on the spot by paramilitary forces and the idea of population exchanges agreed by mutual consent of the governmental representative seated around a negotiating table.

Western Thrace may have supplied a new setting, but many of the key actors were already well known to each other. As in Libya, Enver stood at the top of the pyramid of activist officers. Beneath him came men like Eşref and Süleyman Askerî. Others included Eşref's brother Selim "Hacı" Sami and Cihangiroğlu İbrahim from Kars.[54] All would play important roles in the drama that was to unfold in Western Thrace, a drama that would feature a few short acts: the territorial conquest of the region, the creation of the Provisional Government, the declaration of Independent Government of Western Thrace in defiance of Istanbul and the dissolution of this short-lived entity.

Conquest and occupation

The territory of Western Thrace had a predominantly Muslim population but there were important areas of Greek and Bulgarian settlement. In the period before the Balkan Wars, the area had witnessed concerted attempts at national consciousness-raising, from both Bulgarian and Greek national activists. Its physical proximity to Bulgaria made Western Thrace a natural target for revolutionary activity, but these attempts were plagued with a number of problems, including the fact that the Rhodope Mountains, inhabited overwhelmingly by Muslims, blocked the path for the Bulgarian insurgents trying to enter the territory.[55] When Bulgarian nationalists could reach their target population, they often found them unreceptive to the new concept of national identity. Most people in the region identified themselves by their religious affiliation and local provenance. A further complication for efforts to radicalize the Christian population was the disruptiveness caused by the competition between rival strands of militants. Their efforts frequently ended in chaos.[56] Greek efforts began even later than those of the Bulgarians, but they at least had the advantage of being organized by the Greek foreign ministry. On the whole the Young Turk revolution put a temporary stop to the revolutionary activities, although lingering tensions continued to exist beneath the appearance of calm.[57]

During the First Balkan War the population of Western Thrace suffered heavily as territory changed hands. With the advance of the Bulgarian forces, which included both regular army units and bands of irregulars, the Muslim population was subjected to a range of treatment that we would today associate with the term "ethnic cleansing." Many cases of indiscriminate violence were reported, including killings, forced expulsions and conversions, rape, village burning, mutilations, etc. Once Bulgarian rule was established it was the Pomaks, or Muslim Bulgarian-speakers, who became the focus of efforts to convert them to Christianity. This was a novel approach from a government intent on removing what they considered to be the religious barriers separating a potentially homogenous Slavic population. The Carnegie Report referred to the forced conversion of the Pomaks as being "among the least excusable brutalities of the war."[58] Given all the violence that had transpired, this was no mean statement. Sadly the violence did not end here. As we shall see, when the Second Balkan War presented the Ottomans the chance to reassert control in the region, more killings would follow.

From a military perspective, the seizure of Western Thrace was relatively straightforward, quick even, once Enver gave the Ottoman irregular forces the green light to advance. On 15 August 1913 he sent an all-points bulletin ordering Ottoman units to provide Eşref and Sami's troops with whatever they needed in the way of rations and ammunition.[59] From Edirne, Eşref and his 115 men took Ortaköy, known as Ivaylovgrad in Bulgaria today, the first in a string of conquests in Western Thrace. They left Ortaköy on 15 August, heading west in the direction of Koşukavak (Krumovgrad). Their immediate objective was to track down the Bulgarian bands—Eşref's writings refer to both the enemy's and his own guerrilla bands by the same term, "çete"[60]—responsible for atrocities against the Muslim but also the Greek population.

Eşref sent a field report to Enver describing what he had found:

I have been busy carrying out reconnaissance in the region of Koşukavak. While attempting to gather information about the enemy's position, I learned that a regiment of bandits gathered together by the Bulgarian government and called "soldiers" had attacked the honor, property and lives of the people of the wholly Muslim villages [in the region] of Koşukavak and I even saw with my own eyes the six hundred Muslim corpses with arms bound in a valley near Papasköy. I even heard that the Bulgarian officers together with these Komites collected money from the Muslims by threatening them and announced that these monies would be given to the families of dead Komitacıs. There is no property and not a single virgin left in the villages. The Muslims are living under the constant threat of extinction. Therefore, sir, the aim of occupying Koşukavak was to drive all of these common Bulgarian irregulars (başıbozuks)[61] from the area. Naturally the business turned into skirmishing and the event took on this sort of complexion. I stand ready to carry out any order you care to give…[62]

Eşref blamed these atrocities on a Bulgarian officer named Domuzçiyef.[63] According to Eşref's account, he and his forces encountered Domuzçiyef's gang the next day outside Koşukavak. In a decisive battle Eşref's troops captured a large number of Bulgarians, including Domuzciyef himself and a number of his officers. The rest of this gang of 1,200 Bulgarians seems to have been either scattered or "wiped out" by Eşref's force.[64] The Ottoman casualties were relatively light, at six dead and twelve wounded. With the arms taken from the killed and captured, Eşref indicates that he established a "national regiment" and installed a local Muslim named Kamber Ağa as the head of a provisional local government in Koşukavak.[65] This established the pattern that would be followed throughout Western Thrace whereby the raiding Ottoman volunteers would secure the territory and establish a civilian government headed by a local Muslim notable to administer the liberated district.

After the victory at Koşukavak, Eşref's force pressed on deeper into Bulgarian territory.[66] They first moved south, taking Mestanlı (Momchilgrad) on 18 August without a fight. Then, turning to the north, they captured Kırcaali the next day after a skirmish. Kırcaali was akin to hallowed ground for these men as it was a region that had produced a number of Unionist activists, none more important than Talat Bey, later Paşa, with whom Eşref would be in touch during his time in Western Thrace. In fact, Eşref was relieved to find Talat's uncle Emin Ağa and relatives safe and sound. Soon they were helping to organize a local militia and to appoint local leaders there.[67] Istanbul, nervous about the Great Powers' response to the foray into Western Thrace, wrote to them on 19 August indicating that it would not consider sending a few units into the area in order to protect the Muslim population to be a breach of its international obligations.[68] This was an attempt to finesse an increasingly tricky situation.

Thus in a few days Eşref's small force had secured the districts of Koşukavak, Mestanlı, and Kırcaali. From his description it is clear that the campaign was one of both recovering territory and meting out rough justice. For example, around the time that they took Kırcaali they encountered a Bulgarian cavalry commander who, Eşref says, had threatened to gas the Ottoman troops. "But we punished this commander, who committed atrocities against the population and didn't respect the rules of warfare, not with gas but rather with lead."[69] In fact the body count was beginning to rise as the occupying force dispensed summary justice against those who had committed the atrocities. Some were shot while others were hanged. As we shall see, on occasion the Ottoman forces were themselves guilty of crimes but, in some cases at least, they seem to have reacted quickly and executed the perpetrators amongst their own ranks. At other times the local population and irregular forces took matters into their own hands with predictably grisly results.

Unsurprisingly, Bulgarian sources tell a different side of the story. Many of the salient aspects of the account as told from the Ottoman/Turkish side either do not appear or are rendered very differently by the other side. As we have seen, the name Domuzçiyef, whose band's atrocities play a central role in justifying Eşref's initial advance into the territory, does not feature in the main Bulgarian retelling of the story of Western Thrace. Likewise, events described in Turkish-language accounts as "hard fighting" are treated as civilian massacres in Bulgarian versions.[70] Moreover, the Bulgarian narratives emphasize both the perfidious role of the Greeks in siding with "the Turks" against the Bulgarians: as, for example, when the Greek army "slyly" delayed its hand-over of Dedeağaç to the retreating Bulgarians in coordination with the Ottoman announcement of the autonomous government of Western Thrace;[71] and, of course, the massacres committed against the Bulgarian population by the Muslim forces. These narratives feature accusations of pogroms, indiscriminate killing, and rape.[72] Clearly, this passage of history was one that featured much violence and is therefore invested with a high degree of historiographical contention.[73] The conflicting accounts of both sides agree on the generally brutal nature of the clashes as the borders changed. Eşref's account was not devoid of grisly events, including summary executions, the burning of villages, and violation of Bulgarian women. To be fair to Eşref, he does not appear to disguise these horrible events but actually seems to go out of his way to document them, as we shall see.

Perhaps equally unpalatable to Eşref were signs that high-level Ottoman support for his mission in Western Thrace was starting to crumble. Eşref noted that certain unnamed officials were working to oppose his moves due to their "timidity." What, recalled Eşref, were Talat and Enver to do? But soon it transpired that even the resolve of Enver himself might be wavering. In a telegram to Eşref of 19 August Enver instructed Eşref to go no further than Koşukavak and even to be prepared to withdraw due to the "demands of the present situation."[74] While Enver personally supported the operations in Western Thrace, no doubt encouraged by Eşref's optimistic reports, he was coming under increasing pressure to pull back. By showing such hesitation, Enver was possibly giving Eşref the signal that the door was open for the local commanders to make their own decisions.[75] From now on the story of Western Thrace would take on an independent—and unusual—character.

But if they were to continue with the operation in Western Thrace, Eşref and his men could never be completely independent of Istanbul. For a start they would need more troops and ammunition of the kind that had been arriving from Ottoman territory proper in recent days.[76] Enver recalled Eşref to Ortaköy for discussions. Despite the fact that he was suffering from a boil that had appeared on the nape of his neck and was running a high fever, Eşref went to meet with Enver and his advisors on 22 August. When he arrived, the difficulty of the situation was immediately apparent. Some were voicing the government's position. "I was able to reach an understanding with Enver but only in secret and in snapshot form. Enver's eyes were full of tears but he was under pressure from the Ottoman government. It seemed as though the Russians were squeezing tightly."[77]

Eşref entered into more detailed talks with Hacı Adil, the Unionist Governor of Edirne, Foreign Minister Said Halim Paşa, Talat, and Enver. Eşref describes Enver as undergoing spiritual torment, but that "if it were up to him he would not hesitate to join our side."[78] Eşref made the case for continuing the campaign to seize and occupy Thracian territory. He promised that he would soon be able to retake not only all of Western Thrace but also to push on into Eastern Macedonia. The question was put to him, "Are you capable of occupying it?" Eşref's answer was supremely confident: "My record speaks for itself" (*İş meydanda*). Eşref explains further that "Enver was in support of helping us. Hacı Adil seemed as though he advised for it. Talat would support if he could." After speaking privately and face-to-face with Enver and finding him reluctant, Eşref was apparently able to convince him that the Western Thrace operation should continue.[79] Eşref then asked for a number of men by name. First on the list was Süleyman Askerî. Other names were Lütfi Fatihi, Bandırmalı İlyas, and İskeçeli Arif. These were all Special Organization agents and men on whom he could depend in battle.

They developed a strategy to deal with the reluctant government officials in Istanbul. Eşref would agree to pull his forces back, but they would use the fact that the fighters under the command of Eşref's brother Selim Sami had fanned out across the territory and thus out of the range of communication as an excuse for not being able to withdraw. This would be their trump card. Eşref summoned Süleyman Askerî and they started to plan their activities. On 24 August Eşref sent a telegram to İlyas Bey, a regular army captain, in Ortaköy requesting him to seal the borders between Western and Eastern Thrace, the first indication of the attempt to demarcate the territory of Western Thrace as distinct from the Ottoman Empire proper.

It seems clear that Süleyman Askerî's arrival gave the enterprise a boost. As we shall see, the two friends worked well together, with Askerî's poetic flair complementing Eşref's can-do approach. Meanwhile Enver would neither agree nor disagree to support their energetic efforts, but Eşref sensed that when push came to shove he would back the venture. In fact, Enver promised to send a consignment of Martini-Henry rifles for the Thracian campaign. The upshot of these meetings was that the officers and some of their troops would continue the operations in Western Thrace but in a private, volunteer capacity, with a nudge and a wink from Enver but without the official support of the Ottoman government.[80] In some ways it was like Libya all over again.

Enver and Talat returned to Edirne while Eşref and Askerî headed in the opposite direction, deeper into Western Thrace. They returned to

Koşukavak and welcomed the reinforcements that Eşref had requested. Soon they were moving south towards Gümülcine, or Komotini as it is known in Greece today. At sundown on 31 August 1913, after some brief skirmishes, Eşref and his men entered Gümülcine, which had been handed over by the Greek forces to the Bulgarians only ten days earlier. British reports took the fact that the Ottoman troops who occupied Gümülcine were equipped with Mausers, the rifle supplied to regular Ottoman forces, as a sign of official support; but they could equally well have been supplied to Eşref and Askerî's men from Ottoman military stores.[81] British consular reports were particularly concerned with this question of official or unofficial forces, perhaps understandably so, given the lengths to which the Ottomans had gone to avoid the appearance of official involvement first in Libya and now again in Western Thrace. Either way, it was clear that the occupation of Western Thrace was accomplished with support from the Ottoman War Ministry even if, as we have seen, this support was not universal.

Shortly after capturing the town, the Ottoman officers announced the formation of the Provisional Government of Western Thrace (Garbî Trakya Hükûmet-i Muvakkatesi) with Gümülcine as its capital. A local religious scholar, a Pomak named Hafız Salih, or Salih Hoca Mehmedoğlu as he was also known, was selected as its head.[82] It is clear from various sources, however, that Eşref, Sami, and Askerî Beys were the driving force behind the new mini-state. The three men formed the executive committee and each played a key role: Eşref was Commander of the "National" and the Paramilitary (çete) Bands;[83] Süleyman Askerî was Chief of the General Staff; Selim Sami was Inspector of the "National" and the Paramilitary Bands; Sapancalı Hakkı, Eşref's former school-mate from Edirne, was in charge of the gendarmes.[84] Thus on the Ottoman side the venture involved a civilian government, a paramilitary leadership in Western Thrace and, more tenously, the various actors of the Ottoman government in Istanbul who would intervene from time to time in the project but whose opinions of it ranged from outright support to clear opposition. It was thus hardly a secure foundation on which to build a government, and would soon prove ominous.

At first, however, things went well for the new venture. The government they formed was suprisingly robust. After the capture of Gümülcine, Süleyman Askerî invited the leading members of the

12. Overprint postal stamps for the mini-state in Western Thrace. (Source: EK papers)

Muslim population to a congress with the purpose of running the affairs of the Provisional Government.[85] It managed to raise a militia of perhaps as many as 61,000 volunteers.[86] A parliament, an Executive Committee, a court system, three ministries, a taxation authority, and a coterie of civil servants were all working features of the new would-be state. As if to emphasize its official aspiration, its leaders took pains to provide the official trappings of statehood. Passports were issued, bilingual in Turkish and Greek, and postage stamps were printed (although at least at first these were simply Bulgarian stamps over-printed with Ottoman script). In early September Süleyman Askerî penned a "national" anthem steeped in such patriotic imagery as martyrdom, heroism, freedom, and valor. A sample verse reads:

For the sake of independence we crossed the Meriç and Karasu (Rivers);
Crushing and defeating all the invaders, we reached our aim;
We cleared a path for a glorious republic in the Balkans;
And lit the torch of liberty for the first time.[87]

References to the flag were almost *de rigueur* for such an undertaking, and the symbolically important standard was soon duly produced. There are several overlapping versions of who was directly responsible for designing the flag, but Eşref features heavily in most of them. According to one version of the story, he created a cardboard mock-up of the flag measuring 70 x 100 cm. In another version he had a Greek tailor in Dedeağaç produce the prototype.[88] In any event, the flag was green, white, and black and featured the star and crescent. The crescent

THE CIRCASSIAN

and star represented Turkishness, the green Islam, the black mourning (for the pain and oppression that had been suffered), and the white liberation. The flag flew from official buildings across the territory of the provisional government.

Perhaps surprisingly, given the sectarian violence that had occasioned its creation, the Provisional Government "enjoyed considerable cross-community support and included representatives from the Turkish, Greek, Pomak, Armenian and Jewish communities."[89] Partially patterned on the Ottoman system of multi-ethnic, multi-religious, and multi-linguistic practices and partially on opportunism, the mini-state seems to have drawn strength—and support—from its varied population. It was clearly distinct from the decidedly mono-national model that would emerge with a vengeance in the Turkish Republic. For example, the governors of Dedeağaç and Sofulu were Greek Orthodox; a mixed committee from Western Thrace traveled to Istanbul to meet not only with Talat but also with the Ecumenical Patriarch and the Greek Ambassador; and the Jewish publisher Emmanuel Karaso was tasked with both forming an official Press Agency of Western Thrace and publishing a bilingual Franco-Turkish newspaper called *L'Indépendent / İstiklal*.[90] In certain regions there were clear signs of ethno-religious violence that contradicted this more ecumenical face of the Provisional Government. Nevertheless, because it maintained aspects of the Ottoman communal style of rule, it can hardly be seen as the "Turkish" republic that is often referred to in some Turkish-language accounts.

The Ottoman advance continued, with its combination of skirmishing, accumulating territory, and score-settling. The Ottoman "volunteers" moved westwards, taking İskece (Xanthi) on 1 September 1913, one day after the capture of Gümülcine. British sources noted that the Ottoman force that had taken İskece "was composed of Kurds, Arabs, and Turks, styled volunteers and commanded by Capt Eshref Bey and other officers or ex-officers of the Turkish army."[91] These were troops, they noted, that had been recruited by the Committee of Union and Progress, and thus it was "more than a quibble for the Ottoman Govt to deny that its troops have occupied districts west of the Maritza." Another British account made the connection between the Ottoman "leadership of Eshref Bey, Hajji Sami Bey and Suleiman Bey" and their previous involvement in Libya.[92] Once again the British observers were keen to highlight the fluidity of the distinction between regular and irregular Ottoman troops: "Most of the 'irregulars' under their charge were regulars of the Turkish army who had 'deserted' from the force at the Maritsa to 'volunteer' to aid their co-religionists across the river."

In İskece they again established a temporary form of rule with a local named Niyazi Bey at its head. They soon ambushed a Bulgarian cavalry detachment. Meanwhile, Eşref's brother Sami captured a Bulgarian partisan named Ahmed Ağa and had him executed.[93] In neighboring Eğridere another Bulgarian partisan, curiously named Enver, was accused of treason and oppression and similarly dispatched. His brother, even more curiously named Eşref, was sent to Kırcaali and hanged. Back in İskece a soldier in the "national" forces was hanged for looting.[94] These cases show that the fissures in Western Thrace were not simply defined by religion. Ahmed Ağa was clearly a Muslim who supported the Bulgarians once they had occupied the region. The looter was even a fellow member of the military force that the Ottomans had established in Western Thrace. There were also other cases of Christians and Jews who supported the Ottoman mini-state after it was established.

The dramatic shifts in control during the Balkan Wars and its aftermath, first from Ottoman to Bulgarian rule and then back again, were wreaking havoc with the locals' identities. As Eşref noted, in many cases the Muslim population, especially the Bulgarian-speaking Pomaks, had been forced to convert to Christianity after the Bulgarian troops occupied the region during the First Balkan War, a development noted in the Carnegie Endowment's report on the causes of the conflict.[95] Some of them even seem to have taken part in crimes against their former fellow Muslims. Revenge was quickly taken once the Ottoman forces had secured the territory in question. In Gümülcine several Muslims were hanged shortly after the Ottoman occupation for the crimes of having served the Bulgarians, either as coachmen or as procurers of women for their army.[96] Eşref records that as many as thirty paid with their lives as a result of such identity-shifting. In Eşref's words, "the names of Hacı Ahmeds became Hacı Kostas." To reverse some of the forced conversions from Islam to Christianity that had occurred under Bulgarian rule, the new state sent out teams of officials and imams to restore their Muslim identity, return misappropriated property, and offer aid and support for the victims of oppression.

Amid the score-settling and the rising body count, Eşref recorded a few more grisly scenes. One involved a mother who had witnessed the death of her two sons. As a result she was given some assistance in the form of food. But she protested saying, "You gave more to my daughter-in-law and less to me." Eşref remarked that she seemed more affected by the relative paucity of the aid than by the fact that she had seen her two sons put to death. Eşref expresses astonishment that this is how she responded in her grief: "This, too, was a human being!" (*Bu da insan!*)[97]

After more skirmishes and the capture and punishment of further perpetrators, Eşref recorded another gruesome vignette. Recalling years later that this scene still raised the hairs on his neck, he described five young children unaware of the fact that their father had been executed right next to them. The little ones cried out, "Our father," while painting their bodies with the blood that spurted from his corpse. The man had been shot moments before Eşref and his men arrived, the victim of his neighbor's bullet.

The republic before the Republic, aka "The First Turkish Republic"

From the start the venture to create a state in Western Thrace was marked by a curious mixture of observing legal norms and pure defiance. Amid the violence and recriminations that characterized the region in this period, it might seem odd that the rogue Ottoman venture was so keen to observe all the trappings of statehood. After all, thumbing its collective nose at international consensus, at least insofar as represented by the Great Powers, was inherent in the mission from the start. But the breakaway state went a step further by defying its own military hierarchy, even Enver himself. It was as if those behind the would-be state believed that creating the accoutrements of permanence would be self-fulfilling.

After a relatively successful start, the Provisional Government began to run into problems. The committed, resourceful leadership had overcome most of the many difficulties inherent in setting up and running a new state, but they soon faced problems of a larger magnitude. Over the course of September the prospects of the Provisional Government began to take a turn for the worse. The key difficulty lay in the international arena. When the Provisional Government had been announced in August, the Great Powers had expressed dismay. Britain was particularly worried about the prospect of a strong Russian reaction, including the possibility of another Russian–Ottoman war.[98] The Powers' clear preference was for the Ottoman and Bulgarian governments to come to an agreement over Thrace in which the Ottomans would retain Edirne but cede Western Thrace to Bulgaria. In other words, they were calling for the end of the Provisional Government of Western Thrace. On hearing the news that Russia was on the verge of withdrawing her ambassador from the Ottoman capital, historically an ominous sign, and fearful of straining relations with the Powers any further, Istanbul began to pressure the leadership in Western Thrace to abandon the state they had only recently created.

Meanwhile Greece had grown increasingly worried about the prospect of the territory being returned to Bulgaria. As a result Athens began to cooperate with the Provisional Government in order to thwart Bulgaria's impending control over the region—and its Orthodox inhabitants. We have already seen how Athens timed its withdrawal from Western Thracian territory to allow the Ottoman officers to occupy it in their place. Such tactics were aimed at preventing Bulgarian expansion, and not out of any great fondness for the Ottomans themselves.

In late September a prominent Greek Orthodox bishop went to Gümülcine to discuss the prospect of cooperation with the Provisional Government. In particular they discussed the handover of the southeastern port of Dedeağaç (Alexandroupoli) to the Provisional Government so as to prevent it being taken over by the Bulgarians.[99] Istanbul had previously been more or less content to use the Western Thracian venture as a means to put pressure on Bulgaria, with whom it had not yet signed a peace treaty; but now it became anxious at the prospect of the fate of Western Thrace being decided without its own involvement. Matters were not helped by a flare-up in violence in the south-east of the territory, when a large group of Bulgarian refugees appears to have been set upon by Muslim bands before being partially rescued by Bulgarian volunteers,[100] adding to Istanbul's fears that the autonomous state could turn out to be a major international liability. It was at this point that Istanbul began to pressure the Ottoman leadership in Western Thrace to withdraw altogether.

As the incident involving the refugees indicates, over the course of the month of September the situation on the ground in Western Thrace had begun to deteriorate. The attempt to extend the Provisional Government's control over the rest of the territory created a series of incidents and flashpoints that aggravated tensions in the area. Evidence is piecemeal, but the overall picture is one of further score-settling, deportations, executions, and the appropriation and redistribution of property. Eşref's material indicates that he was called upon to investigate a number of incidents in which order had broken down dramatically and the Ottoman forces had inflicted atrocities on the population.

After what Turkish sources refer to as "fierce fighting" (but what Bulgarian accounts describe as atrocities against the civilian population) in the south-eastern regions of Ferecik (Feres) and Sofulu (Soufli) on 22 and 23 September, Istanbul became even more alarmed. The next day the Greek press reported that a unit under Eşref's command carried out raids on a number of Bulgarian villages and captured about 1,000 *komitacıs* as prisoners. This provoked a response from their Bulgarian comrades who, together with a number of armed villagers, attacked Eşref's forces. In the battles that ensued, eighteen Bulgarian *komitacıs* were killed.[101]

Once the Ottoman–Bulgarian treaty had been signed on 29 September, the Ottoman position shifted still further against the provisional government. With the territorial concession of Edirne having been won, Istanbul now moved to limit its international exposure. Reacting to the foreign pressure that inevitably followed the continued fighting in Western Thrace, the Ottoman high command, including Enver, ordered the Ottoman fighters to return and to accept the terms of the Bucharest Treaty that had ceded Western Thrace to Bulgaria. Predictably, Eşref, Sami, and Askerî Beys reacted angrily to this suggestion and were thus faced with a dilemma.[102] On the one hand, to give up their mission would be to abandon the beleaguered and victimized Muslim population in whose name they were carrying out the mission in the first place. It would also mean discarding what had to be considered in the context of the period a rare victory just as it had been achieved. On the other hand, defying the Ottoman establishment was full of potential pitfalls. Even with the understanding that Eşref and Enver had reached at Ortaköy, defying a direct order would represent a major breach of military protocol. More tangibly it would mean the end of material and logistical support from Istanbul, at least officially. It also meant raising the stakes in the international context. Creating a breakaway state would defy the international consensus and could easily provoke a diplomatic and perhaps even a military crisis.

How long Eşref and his associates deliberated over this decision is unclear. What is certain is that their answer to Istanbul was the unequivocal proclamation of the Independent Government of Western Thrace on 25 September 1913. No longer merely "provisional," the renamed state struck a much more defiant, even truculent stance. They now insisted that anyone wishing to enter the territory from the Ottoman side present a passport in order to insist upon its independence.[103] Eşref and his associates now devoted some time to justifying this change; the reply to the high command in Istanbul and the announcements that Eşref drafted to both the local population and the international community reflect the chief concerns behind the new state. More broadly, the narrative they deployed reveals the mindset of Eşref and his associates at the time.

Eşref's tone was unapologetic, even indignant. It was rooted in a morally based, activist reading of recent events. He opens his letter to Enver and Hurşid Paşa, his former commanding officer,[104] by invoking the spirit of the Raid on the Sublime Porte which had taken place at the beginning of the year. The pretext for that *coup d'état* had been the fate of Edirne, then holding out against a Bulgarian siege. Using the rallying cry of "Free Edirne!" the Unionists had used force to oust their rivals from power.[105] The city eventually fell in late March, much to the consternation of the Committee of Union and Progress, hence the extra motivation to take it back when the opportunity of the Second Balkan War presented itself. Eşref's opening line states, "As is well known, the Bab-ı Âli incident was carried out with the motto 'Don't give up Edirne without a fight' [literally, without blood being shed]." He goes on to say that the cause of holding onto Edirne had prolonged the war. But then, he says, they were shown the Midye–Enez line (which excluded Edirne from Ottoman territory). But, he asks rhetorically, in what cause was the Bab-ı Âli incident carried out, and for what reason was a great commander-in-chief like Nâzım Paşa shot during the putsch and sacrificed? Warming to his theme, Eşref continues:

Now if we had stopped at this line we would not have been able to show the thousand problems and half-planned revolts that allowed us to convince our army corps commander Hurşid Paşa and Enver Bey to break through the enemy's wide open front, take Edirne, ignore the threats that were being made and obtain our goal, even making cavalry raids into the Harmanlı plain [which runs north-west into Bulgaria] before all of a sudden the possibility of Russia's intervention forced us to withdraw.

Eşref claimed that the Bulgarian gangs then took advantage of this withdrawal to return and to intensify their assaults and revenge-taking against the Muslims of Western Thrace. Here Eşref revealed the logic of the semi-official status of the eventual Ottoman campaign in Western Thrace: since the response to the protests against the renewed Bulgarian aggresssion was that the Bulgarian gangs were independent of the Bulgarian army, the Ottomans would adopt the same tactic. Henceforth the Ottomans would play the same game by acting, or at least claiming to act, independently of the official Ottoman chain of command.

With the stage set for action, Eşref explains his role in the campaign. "For my part, selecting the best known raider colleagues, we said 'Bismillah' (In the name of God) and immediately launched our attack with a raid 95 km towards Koşukavak, the center of the Bulgarian gangs who had oppressed Western Thrace." He goes on to describe the raid of his 115 men and their exploits against Domuzciyef and his band who were all either "wiped out" or taken prisoner, tried, and executed. The point of these details and more grisly ones that follow was to establish the rationale for the fact that Eşref and the forces who had fought and established the temporary government of Western Thrace were now morally bound to protect its people. They could not, therefore, accept Istanbul's order to return. Instead they were obliged to cut their material links with the Ottoman state. Eşref's defiant stance extended to rejecting an apparent request for the return to Ottoman custody of a number of officers and fighting men deemed to be criminals. Pointing to the lack of an official agreement between Istanbul and Gümülcine, Eşref rejected any such extradition, insisting on the independence of Western Thrace.

Similarly, in his annoucements to the people of Western Thrace and to the Great Powers, Eşref adopted a characteristically uncompromising attitude. For the diplomatic corps Eşref's approach took on another rhetorical flourish. Accusing the international community of turning a blind eye toward the violence and atrocities committed against the Muslims of Western Thrace, Eşref recounted in graphic detail the hundreds of corpses that resulted from this butchery. Since no one took any notice of these abominable acts, Eşref continued:

> we said, "*Sauve qui peut*," and reluctantly took up our weapons. In order to protect the people of Western Thrace from these atrocities, we armed the population and, trusting in God and His message, from this day forward we have announced the Independent Government of Western Thrace on the condition that it treat Christians, Turks and Bulgarians with the same status. Success comes from God. [106]

Eşref's papers show that he drafted the announcement to be sent to the representatives of the Powers and then passed the text to Süleyman Askerî for him to translate into French. This was yet another example of the teamwork between Eşref and Askerî. But soon attempts to hold onto the increasingly vulnerable status of their state in Western Thrace would require them to split apart.

After the announcement of the creation of the independent government of Western Thrace and as events continued to play out on the international scene, the local situation began to deteriorate further. Eşref was called upon to deal with the repercussions. From time to time, some of the Ottoman forces carried out atrocities against the non-Muslim population and Eşref took on the task of trying to clean up the mess. One incident in particular reveals the breakdown in order. Çerkes Reşid, Eşref's former partner in banditry from their Izmir days, seems to have "gone rogue." Details are scarce but it seems clear that Reşid went on a rampage in the villages of Sıçanlı and Doğan Hisar, two mountain villages to the east of Gümülcine that had held out against both earlier attacks and the efforts of delegations of their fellow Bulgarians to encourage them to flee towards Bulgaria. [107] As Eşref put it, Reşid was serving as a commander of a band (*çete*) of Ottoman forces in Western Thrace and had "cracked." The incident began when Reşid was sent a large number of apparently unarmed and ill-prepared soldiers from Edirne. He responded by writing an angry letter to Askerî, Eşref, and Sami. Using highly intemperate language, he cursed the "criminal officers" who had sent him so many "simpleton, donkey Turks," indicating that they would be useless against the Bulgarians and demanding more weapons. [108] Süleyman Askerî, astonished by the let-

ter, passed it on to Eşref. Commenting on the remarkable overly familiar tone of Reşid's letter, Eşref replied that Reşid must have left his post
and "cracked up" and advised giving him a final warning, indicating that
this was unlikely to have been Reşid's first transgression.

Eşref's answer to Reşid was characteristically blunt. Taking Reşid to
task for displaying an overly familiar and flighty attitude in official correspondence, Eşref upbraided his fellow Circassian, reminding him of
the danger of invoking ethnic divisions at a sensitive time, recalling an
incident when they were fighting together in Libya in which Reşid
had apparently offended the sensibilities of the Sanusis to the point
that they declared him a traitor, and giving his "heedless friend" a final
warning.[109]

But it was not just Reşid's choice of language that was problematic.
Soon Askerî, using his pseudonym of Süleyman Zeynelâbidin, wrote an
extremely urgent letter to Eşref, with a severe warning that anyone
who caused it to be delayed in transit would be held responsible. Askerî
reported that he had been receiving a flurry of telegrams alleging that,
after the attack at Sıçanlı, Reşid had gone out of control, had literally
"taken the bit between his teeth," setting fire to the village and massacring the unarmed refugees. Askerî requested that Eşref go in person
to the area, commandeering a railroad handcar if necessary, seize Reşid
and use force to prevent any more "ugly incidents."[110]

While the public face of the Independent Republic espoused the
brotherhood of all its peoples, what transpired in the countryside was
often shockingly discordant. At midday of 4 October Süleyman Askerî
spoke at a public ceremony in Dedeağaç and, in the eyes of the British
vice-consul, did so eloquently and patriotically, assuring his audience
of the security and fraternity of all the inhabitants of Western Thrace.
Three clarion blows cued a salute to the flag of the autonomous state.[111]
But as Eşref's mission would reveal, matters elsewhere were not in
keeping with such rhetoric.

The aftermath of the Sıçanlı incident proved it to have been ugly
indeed. Eşref went to the region and compiled a report about the
Sıçanlı incident, dated 8 October 1913, indicating that Reşid's forces,[112]
seemingly composed of both regular and irregular (başıbozuk) forces,
had run amok. Eşref's investigation reveals that eight Bulgarian women
had been raped. His report lists the names, ages, fathers' names, mari-

tal status, and villages for each of the victims. They ranged in age from fourteen to forty and came from the villages of Sıçanlı and Doğan Hisar. The report states that the women had been raped at gunpoint and that the perpetrators were eleven members of "our national forces" and the reserve units from Uzunköprü. As a result of the investigation and the verdict of the subsequent trial, all eleven were shot by firing squad.[113] The attention given to the case indicates that the government of Western Thrace seems to have been diligent, or perhaps wanted to appear to be diligent, in this case at least, in investigating the crime and meting out punishment. But the violence had been done. From the time of that atrocity onward, the village of Sıçanlı, later renamed Pontikia by Greece in 1921,[114] has remained eerily unpopulated to this day.

Despite horrible incidents like this, not all the news was bad for the fledgling state. A shift in Greek policy gave the Gümülcine government hope. Reacting to the prospect of an Ottoman–Bulgarian rapprochement, Athens supported the independent Thracian republic. Seeing the breakaway state as a means to sow division between Sofia and Istanbul, the Greeks assisted Gümülcine by handing over Dedeağaç (Alexandroupoli) on 2 October 1913 and entering into talks with the new government. Eşref says that he and his colleagues were engaged in unofficial discussions via local intermediaries.[115] Meanwhile Süleyman Askerî was tasked with conducting direct negotiations with the Bulgarians.[116] It seemed possible that, despite Istanbul's disapproval, the fledgling state might just be able to secure its future by effecting agreements with its Greek and Bulgarian neighbors. In fact, after this episode Ottoman–Bulgarian relations were fairly harmonious. Askerî toured the region with a Bulgarian counterpart in February 1914 and eventually a secret treaty was signed between the two states in August, a prelude to their alliance during the Great War.

The end

Istanbul's position was rather less optimistic. As we have seen, the key Ottoman actors had been divided from the start over the rogue operation in Western Thrace. Many were keen to back the independent republic unofficially in order to defend the Muslim population of Western Thrace; but over time even some of its erstwhile supporters had begun to change their minds. They grew increasingly worried that the breakaway state could land the empire in serious diplomatic, and possibly military, peril.

The European powers kept up their pressure on the Ottoman government. France in particular seems to have pressured Istanbul to conclude an agreement with Bulgaria, dangling a large loan as an incentive.[117] Eventually the Ottoman government decided that the best course of action was to use the territory gained in Western Thrace as a bargaining chip to improve its overall strategic position, especially retaining Edirne. The ensuing negotiations with Bulgaria were led by the key Unionist figure Cemal Bey, who would later write that the off-the-books Ottoman campaign in Western Thrace "brought us substantial political advantages" in the negotiations.[118] Once those negotiations were concluded, the Ottoman government needed to convince Eşref and his colleagues in Western Thrace to abandon their project, and they duly came under heavy pressure from Istanbul. Even Enver, it seems, had finally turned against the mission after the declaration of independence. In any case Enver was soon stricken with appendicitis and required an operation, effectively removing him from the scene.

Eşref was on an inspection assignment in Dedeağaç in early October when Cemal, accompanied by Captain Sabit, previously a supporter of the independent state, came to try to convince them to abandon it. "Vehement," "bitter" discussions ensued.[119] Sabit also took ill seemingly because, as Eşref remarks, he had great affection for him and his men. All the while negotiations between the independent government, the Greeks, and the Bulgarians continued. Eşref reports that they were holding talks with an unofficial emissary from the Greeks named "Monsieur Foti," and that they were making some headway in the negotiations.[120] Meanwhile, Süleyman Askerî was in Sofia negotiating with the Bulgarians. But when Cemal learned that Askerî was in the Bulgarian capital conducting separate negotiations, he apparently "flew into a towering rage" and "went too far." Exactly how far was too far will probably never be known, but it was clear that the writing was on the wall for the Independent Government of Western Thrace.

In the event the Ottoman–Bulgarian negotiations resulted in the Treaty of Istanbul, or Treaty of Constantinople as it is also known, of 29 September 1913. By its terms the Ottoman Empire would retain

Eastern Thrace, including Edirne, Kırklareli, and Demotika,[121] but cede all of Western Thrace to Bulgaria. This amounted to an improvement over the terms of the Treaty of London, which had left only a small area to the west of Istanbul in Ottoman hands. But for those Ottoman officers who had fought for Western Thrace, it amounted to a brutal capitulation. The fate of the short-lived mini-state was sealed.

Eşref was disgusted. This was the same government, he commented, that had previously settled for accepting the Enez–Midye line as the border. Now they were not only satisfied but also "overjoyed" at the prospect of simply keeping Edirne, indifferent to all of the effort expended and the blood shed for the sake of Western Thrace.[122]

Bulgarian forces began to occupy Western Thrace in phases from the middle of October.[123] Shocked and feeling decidedly unsupported, Eşref, Hacı Sami, and Çerkes Reşid all returned to Istanbul. Miffed that his colleagues had returned to the Ottoman capital, Süleyman Askerî broke off his talks in Sofia and returned to Istanbul as well. The founders of the breakaway state left behind a few trusted officers in some of the regions to oversee the handover of power to the Bulgarians and to try to ensure protection for the now effectively abandoned Muslim population.[124] After Bulgarian control was established, these officers, including such figures as Fuat (Balkan), İskeceli Arif, and Sadık, set up an Ottoman consulate and served as conduits with the Western Thrace committee under the leadership of Süleyman Askerî.[125]

By the end of October 1913 Bulgarian forces had occupied all of Western Thrace. The short-lived independent state was over, drawing an emphatic line under the most important effect of the Balkan Wars, namely, the end of an Ottoman Muslim rule in the Balkans and in Europe.

But the story of Ottoman engagement with Western Thrace did not end with the fall of the Independent Government. After World War I the territory would again feature in discussions about how to define what was left of the Ottoman lands once the fighting was over. Along with Mosul in northern Iraq, Aleppo in northern Syria, and Batum in north-eastern Anatolia, Western Thrace formed the source of an important difference in approach. The last Ottoman parliament, sitting in February 1920, produced a manifesto called the Misak-i Millî, usually but awkwardly translated as the National Pact. It claimed a number of territories lying outside the armistice line, including Western Thrace, to be indispensable parts of the Ottoman state.[126] In fact, a faction of Kemalist officers attempted to create yet another independent government in Western Thrace. Confusingly, this proto state was to be called the Provisional State of Western Thrace (Garbî Trakya Hükümet-i Muvakkatesi), and was also sometimes referred to as the Turkish Republic of Western Thrace. Announced on 25 May 1920, its principal actor was Fuat (Balkan) who had been active in the recapture of Western Thrace after the Balkan Wars.[127] But this venture proved to be even more short-lived than its predecessor. It failed to establish any of the trappings of a proper state and instead "soon descended into a guerrilla movement against the Greek army…preoccupied with its campaign in Asia Minor."[128]

The Turkish claim on Western Thrace marked a departure from the stated aims of the nationalists' congresses at Erzurum and Sivas that had taken a more cautious territorial stance. Nationalists like Mustafa Kemal and Kâzım (Karabekir), incidentally a relative of Pervin's by marriage, objected to the more maximalist claims on pragmatic grounds, as Mahmud Şevket Paşa had in 1913, so that when the borders of the Turkish Republic were eventually defined at Lausanne without Western Thrace and the other territories, Ankara downplayed the issue. For example, in Republican versions the National Pact was rendered without reference to the outside territories.[129] The Republican regime did not wish to be seen as having abandoned territories such as Western Thrace in which the majority of the population was Muslim and/or Turkish. The residual population would remain both a diplomatic problem for Turkey and its neighbors and a rallying point for Turkish nationalists for years to come.

More significantly, the ferocity of the ethno-religious violence that occurred during the Balkan Wars and their Thracian aftermath was an unfortunate turn that ramified the trend toward the separation of peoples. Further inflaming the already volatile and emotionally charged atmosphere, these events made violent solutions to what were increasingly seen as "problems" that needed to be "solved" in dramatic fashion. Adding to this drumbeat was the fact that warfare and other acts of violence were, thanks to the newfound reach and appeal of the press, visibly amplified in the public domain.

Perhaps more important in the short run was the radicalizing effect that the Balkan Wars had on the Ottoman leadership. As the coming World War would so dramatically emphasize, it was not a large step from the demographic experience of the campaigns in Western Thrace, on both sides of the ledger, to the ethnic cleansing and such "national" economic policies as boycotts that spelled the end for inter-ethnic trust and cooperation. After the disaster of the First Balkan War and the partially successful second phase, the stage was set for a much greater conflagration. It is perhaps significant that Eşref records that the Special Organization was reorganized at this point, shortly after Eşref was secretly recalled to Istanbul and amid the final negotiations with Bulgaria over Eastern Thrace and Edirne.[130] There has been considerable discussion about exactly when and why this group was formed, so it is interesting to learn from one of its better-known members that he considered it to have been re-formed, as opposed to founded *ab initio*, in late 1913, that is to say on what would prove to be the eve of World War I. For Eşref that imminent conflict would prove especially eventful.

On an individual level the episode of Western Thrace left Eşref with a number of personal experiences, both positive and negative. He had witnessed first-hand some horrific scenes. How much he was involved in perpetrating any is harder to say. There is, however, some evidence to suggest that Eşref and his men benefited personally from their involvement in Western Thrace. His final entries related to this period refer to his having made a gift of a few thousand gold liras to the orphanage in Edirne "from my own behalf, i.e., from my share of the booty."[131] This suggests that the Ottoman paramilitary forces in Western Thrace were benefitting personally from the campaign, as might be expected given the irregular, voluntary nature of their involvement.[132] Indeed, Bulgarian sources document the large flocks seized from the region of Manastır, Sıçanlı, and Doğanhisar where the main livelihood was animal husbandry.[133] Some of the herds were driven to Koşukavak, Ortaköy, and Edirne, while others were taken to Gümülcine.[134]

It bears repeating that Eşref and his men had been mobilized in a special, unofficial capacity in the final fighting of the Second Balkan War when they were attached to Hürşid Paşa's forces. Once they moved into Western Thrace they were acting more or less completely independent of Ottoman military command structure and oversight. It is probable that their service as volunteers would have been secured with the promise of access to booty, a frequent practice in this period. Other evidence corroborates the likelihood that Eşref benefited personally from this irregular situation. One brief but suggestive mention is contained in Eşref's note: he mentions "Eşref's flocks of sheep and the award granted to Eşref in the Ottoman Senate (Meclis-i Âyan)."[135] In a later letter he describes a scenario in which he offered his close friend and Special Organization colleague İzmitli Mümtaz a gift of 1,000 sheep from the larger herds of sheep and cattle that he and Sami had seized during their raids into Bulgaria, presumably at the start of the Western Thrace episode. Eşref relates the anecdote to demonstrate Mümtaz's incorruptibility. As the aide-de-camp to Enver, Eşref implies, a less virtuous man would have had many opportunities to enrich himself. Mümtaz bridled at the offer, saying that as he had not taken part in the raiding, he could expect no share of the booty. Eşref says he later found a legitimate way to give him a gift: when Mümtaz got married, Eşref was able to get him to accept a present in a legitimate and lawful way, and that with Enver's insistence.[136] The raids into Bulgarian territory seem to have enriched Eşref considerably. He mentions 15,000 sheep and 5,000–6,000 head of cattle.

It is therefore interesting to note that Eşref and Sami were heavily critical of their colleague Yakup Cemil's self-serving actions during the Western Thrace campaign. They held that at the time when Eşref and Sami were leading the raid into Bulgarian territory at the start of the campaign, Yakup Cemil, perhaps the most unruly of a generally wilful bunch, was busy rounding up herds of more than 2,000 pigs from the fleeing Christian population.[137] He then arranged for these swine to be driven to Istanbul for sale, a transaction that, Eşref says, earned him several thousand gold lira. Although the money Yakup Cemil gained may have irked Eşref despite his begrudging admiration for what he terms Yakup's "ingenuity"—Eşref claims that when Yakup Cemil was executed he owed him a sum of 1,200 lira—it was rather the fact that Yakup was chasing his own interests when he and Sami were carrying out what they believed to be their patriotic activity. Of course, the dispute could also be seen as a quarrel among thieves. Eşref would probably have defended whatever financial benefit he accrued in the fighting by saying that it was justified by the risk and the fact that as someone outside the normal chain of command he was ineligible for military promotion. More important, the financial advantage seems to have been a by-product of his service and not, as with Yakup Cemil, plunder for its own sake. Nevertheless, it is likely that the Western Thrace episode added to Eşref's experience of command and left him better off financially.

More significantly, the events in Western Thrace reinforced Eşref's role as a key protégé of Enver and it solidified his bond with both his fellow "self-sacrificing officers," Suleyman Askerî in particular, and the men under their command. True, they had felt let down in the final phase of the campaign, but it is noteworthy that Eşref's affection for and allegiance to Enver emerged undiminished. Whether this was due to Enver's absence, through illness, from the final painful denouement is unclear, but whatever the case it is manifestly obvious that Eşref was absolutely devoted to Enver. In fact, the final note in the section of his memoirs dealing with Western Thrace makes mention of his love for and bond with Enver. It seems likely that here Eşref is referring to a four-page essay, preserved separately among his papers, that dwells on his dedication to Enver (and refers frequently to the Western Thrace period).

This episode also gained Eşref a certain degree of what some would see as prominence and others as notoriety. He was now an individual who was well known among the highest echelons of Ottoman officialdom, both civilian and military. He had engaged directly with such Unionist figures as Enver, Cemal, Talat, and Dr Nazım, but had also rubbed shoulders, although not always agreeably, with the likes of Said Halim and Ahmed İzzet Paşas. But it is also clear that his name was increasingly known beyond Ottoman circles. British consular dispatches from the period mention Eşref's involvement throughout the Western Thrace period. When a short time later, at the beginning of a far bigger war, Eşref was making his way toward Egypt, the Russian consul in Mersin reported to Moscow that the Ottoman government was assembling detachments of volunteers of Afghans and Turkish peasants for the campaign against the British in Egypt and that "these people will be put under the command of Eşref, famous from the Balkan Wars."[138] Likewise, British officialdom was aware that the Unionist government had "permitted and even encouraged the sending of emissaries (the Circassian brigand Eshref Bey and others) to Egypt and elsewhere" in order to appease the war faction in their midst.[139] It would not be long before war was declared in earnest. In the course of that global conflict, Eşref's name would become even better known, again in both a positive and a negative light.

5

THE GREAT WAR, PART I

AT HOME AND AT THE FRONT

The Balkan Wars were over. The fighting had been brutal and the Ottoman losses traumatic, but even sterner tests lay ahead both for the Ottoman Empire and for Eşref. The wars had shown both the weaknesses and strengths of the Ottoman Empire's military capabilities, but had also revealed that the empire had not yet lost the will to fight. In fact a new form of Ottoman Muslim patriotism was increasingly evident. Symbolized by the recapture of the former Ottoman capital of Edirne in which Eşref proudly took part, this newly combative spirit increasingly animated public life in the form of writings, public appeals, and demonstrations.

But for Eşref it was time to leave all that behind. After serving his country under difficult conditions, Eşref now planned to return to civilian life. He packed away the collection of stamps and seals that he had used to forge papers in the Balkans and tried to put the briefly exhilarating but ultimately deflating experience of the short-lived Independent Government of Western Thrace behind him. Now a widower, Feride Hanım having died shortly after the birth of their son Feridun, Eşref returned to Western Anatolia and remarried. He had seen his future wife two years earlier and asked her father Hacı Ziya Bey for her hand. He refused, saying that she was too young, and made

125

Eşref wait. Young Pervin was, like Eşref, the descendant of immigrants from the Caucasus whose family had first settled in the Morea (the Peloponnese).[1] At some point her family moved across the Aegean and acquired a large farm in Western Anatolia. After they married, sometime in late February or early March 1914, the newlyweds decided to settle down to run their agricultural estates.[2] Since Eşref's return from Arabian exile, he had assumed control, probably from his father, of a sprawling estate at Salihli in the fertile Gediz valley inland from Izmir. Pervin's family's holding was situated on the rich land near Söke in the valley of the Meander (Büyük Menderes). As Pervin put it, "Whether on his own farm at Salihli or on the farm in Söke that I inherited from my grandfather and father, he was going to turn his attention to improving the land and carrying on the struggle for the homeland using a plough and agricultural implements instead of weapons. That was the decision. With this plan, we built our nest. His service to the nation was finished, or so we thought."[3] These last words were to prove particularly poignant.

Like the peace that followed the Balkan Wars, Eşref and Pervin's rural idyll was short-lived. For one thing, the empire's young leadership harbored a deep-seated desire for revenge that had only been inflamed by the massacres of Muslims as they were driven out of their homes in what would become parts of expanded Montenegro, Bulgaria, Serbia, and Greece. The impulse for decisive Ottoman military action was deeply entrenched in Ottoman society.[4] For another, Eşref was strongly bound to Enver, the leading figure of Ottoman revanchist spirit whose star was rapidly rising. Eşref believed in Enver with a constancy and depth of feeling that was fused in their wartime experiences, first in North Africa and then in the Balkans. Given the extremely volatile situation in Europe, the Ottoman penchant for redressing earlier wrongs, and the strength of Eşref's bond to Enver, it was perhaps only a matter of time before Eşref would again be called into action.

So it proved. After only forty-five days of married life, Eşref received a telegram from Enver, now Minister of War, calling him to Istanbul; Eşref went straight away. It was possibly on this occasion that Eşref received a note from Enver on the back of his calling card. The front of the card was embossed with his new rank and title, brigadier general and War Minister. The handwritten note on the back said: "Eşref,

Welcome. We are grateful for everything you've done. Come to dinner and let's talk freely. Enver."[5] A few days later Pervin had a telegram from her husband saying, "I am going to Europe on official business to sort out some matters there. I'll send you news of my health from the places I visit." Pervin subsequently received telegrams and letters from Belgrade, Vienna, Frankfurt, Paris, Liège, and London, but they gave no clue as to the "matters" to which he was attending.[6] Eşref did not offer any information and Pervin did not ask. Even when he returned after three months, the subject of his business was never broached. As Pervin explains, "I neither feared what it was nor helped him in any way."[7] His travels and comings and goings took place in secrecy that extended as far as his marriage. Pervin suffered in silence, a fate to which she would become sadly accustomed in the years ahead. As she put it, it was as if highway robbers had ambushed their marital path.[8]

In fact, Enver had sent Eşref to meet with potential allies against the British and the French in the conflict that was looming over Europe and the Middle East. The possibility of war had been discussed among high-ranking Ottoman officials since as early as mid-July 1914. Two weeks after the assassination in Sarajevo of the Archduke Franz Ferdinand, heir apparent to the Habsburg throne, Said Halim Paşa, the Ottoman Grand Vizier and Foreign Minister, wrote to Enver from Vienna informing him that war between Austria and Serbia was imminent.[9] The danger for the Ottomans lay in the prospect of a conflict that would widen along the lines of the alliances already laid down by the entanglements of European balance-of-power diplomacy. Among the contacts Eşref met in Europe were members of the Indian revolutionary movement, which was plotting to overthrow British rule in the subcontinent. India, with its large Muslim population, would be a potential weak spot for the British Empire in the event of war. An Islamically-organized revolution would destabilize the Raj and tie down valuable troops that would therefore be unavailable for deployment on other fronts. Eşref's report seems to have convinced Enver to pursue this approach. Similar plans were being drawn up for action to stir up revolts against the French in North Africa using what remained of the Ottoman–Sanusi resistance movement in Libya.

The string of assignments that Eşref received prior to his service in the Great War reflected both the diverse range of problems that the

Ottoman military was trying to cope with on the eve of the conflict and the increasingly unorthodox nature of its response. The range of mobilization efforts meant that Eşref's attempt to settle into the pleasurable tasks of what we would call the gentleman farmer was frequently interrupted by the bolt of the telegraph. One such occasion occurred some time in the early months of 1914. Once again it was Enver calling and once again Eşref answered.

The assignment this time was one of aerial propaganda. The Ottoman military had first encountered the possibilities for using aircraft in 1909, shortly after the "Young Turk" revolution, at a demonstration in Istanbul. Acquiring this and other modern capabilities was one reason that the high command dispatched Ottoman military attachés to Berlin and Paris the following year.[10] The attaché sent to Berlin was the promising young captain Enver, and his counterpart in Paris was Ali Fethi, Enver's main rival within the Committee of Union and Progress. During French maneuvers, the latter was accompanied by another up-and-coming young officer named Mustafa Kemal.[11] All three would figure prominently in the story that would unfold during the empire's final years.

Ottoman forces in Libya had been on the receiving end of some of the first recorded deployments of airborne attacks and, more effectively, aerial surveillance and the dropping of propaganda materials. The Ottoman high command was eager to put this new technology to use and even made some faltering steps to do so before the end of the Libyan campaign. Ottoman aerial capacity increased dramatically during the Balkan Wars. Although initially hampered by a combination of inexperience, mismanagement, and the rapid advance of the empire's enemies, a skeletal Ottoman aviation group made noticeable progress toward the wars' end. Successful reconnaissance flights provided a strategic advantage during the Second Balkan War.[12]

Now, in early 1914, as the possibility of a larger war loomed, demonstrating Ottoman aerial capabilities would also provide a boost to public morale. The War Ministry proposed that Eşref and a certain Fethi Bey, who had gained considerable flight experience during the Balkan Wars, fly a small airplane to Egypt, where it was hoped they would be met with a rapturous reception and so boost pro-Ottoman feeling in that former part of the empire now under British occupation. In those days long-haul flights were impossible so the itinerary involved numerous stops as the plane hopped along over Anatolia and Syria on the way to Cairo; each stop offered a chance to demonstrate the new technology to the population in such important provincial towns as Eskişehir, Konya, Adana, Aleppo, Beirut, Damascus, and Jerusalem. According to Eşref's wife, he was chosen because of his occasional experience with aerial reconnaissance during the Balkan Wars and his knowledge of the terrain in the Levant.[13]

An airborne assignment

Eşref accepted the assignment and, again without a word of explanation to his wife, began to prepare for the mission. For this he returned to Izmir where a pilot named Selim Bey, one of the few Ottoman pilots who had flown missions toward the end of the Balkan Wars, arrived with an airplane called "Edremit," one of several warplanes of that classification to see service in the Ottoman military, some of which later achieved success in defending Gallipoli from the ANZAC assault. Eşref and Selim took practice flights in this small and rather flimsy Blériot XI aircraft, a modified version of the French monoplane that had first crossed the English Channel in 1909. These simple planes were not much more than a tractor engine mounted on a wooden frame with stretched canvas for the wings. In Izmir, Eşref's wife and family members watched from below in nervous excitement. Airplanes had only just been introduced to the Ottoman Empire and naturally were the source of both anxiety and enthusiasm. On the eve of the Great War there were only a handful of aircraft at the empire's disposal, most of which were being used at the military aviation school in Yeşilköy, the future site of Istanbul airport. The appearance of one of these rare planes before the Ottoman public was therefore a novelty. But Eşref characteristically kept Pervin in the dark as to the real reason behind these training flights; she had no idea that the object was a reconnaissance mission to British-held Egypt. As she put it, "Even if I had known, what would have come of it? He didn't take instructions from me but rather from his feelings of patriotism. He was busy preparing to be a volunteer on the orders he received from the seat of government in the name of the state and, yes, as a volunteer in the path of God."[14]

Such was the dynamic between Eşref and Pervin that the state, and more specifically the military command as represented by Enver, seemed almost to represent a third party in their marriage. When Enver called, Pervin tended to lose out. But occasionally she was able to rejoice. Soon after the training flights, Eşref received word that he had been passed over for the Egyptian aerial reconnaissance assignment after all. The reason he had been overlooked on this occasion was the fact that he had recently married. One day Eşref received a letter from his colleague İzmitli Mümtaz who was Enver's *aide-de-camp*. Eşref and Mümtaz were old friends. They had traveled to and fought in Libya together and were both committed members of Enver's group of *fedaîs*. But Mümtaz's letter contained news that displeased Eşref immensely. His face turned red with anger and embarrassment. Pervin asked him if he would like to unburden himself by divulging the contents of the letter. As Pervin remembered it, their conversation went like this:

> Pervin: If it's possible, please enlighten me.
>
> Eşref: By God, I wasn't able to show whether I was pleased or hurt. I was surprised.
>
> Pervin: How so, I ask you?
>
> Eşref: I was given the assignment to Egypt. It required me to take an airplane journey [but] I wasn't able to tell you. Now this letter comes telling me that this time I have been removed from this mission and that Lieutenant Sadık, with whom I fought in Tripolitania, has been appointed in my place.
>
> Pervin: If you have been passed over, then for once I'm thrilled. Don't I have the right to be? What are the separations caused by these various assignments doing to our newly married household? I don't know about you but I'm thrilled...
>
> Eşref: If that's the case, then I'm thrilled too.[15]

But Eşref was far from thrilled. Mümtaz had broached the subject of Eşref's duties with Enver, and like Eşref, Enver himself had recently married, famously to the Ottoman princess Naciye Sultan, giving him the honorific accorded to a royal son-in-law, "Damad," and boosting his popularity even further. In fact, the two weddings had taken place at almost the same time in early 1914.[16] During his conversation with Enver, Mümtaz had underlined the fact that Eşref had been given several dangerous and clandestine assignments, such as the trip to Europe, very shortly after his wedding. Eşref accepted the risky mission to Europe, despite having just married. On his return from Liège he had only narrowly avoided being captured by the French.[17] Mümtaz asked Enver to take all of this into consideration, and Enver appointed Sadık to take Eşref's place in the demonstration flight to Egypt.

The pilots' departure from Istanbul took place amid much ceremony in the presence of Enver, Cemal, and Talat Paşas, the so-called CUP Triumvirate. After taking the Minister of the Navy up for a short demonstration flight, hearing a few words of encouragement from Enver, receiving a bouquet from Princess Hatice Sultan and kissing Enver's hand, Fethi and Sadık took to the skies.[18] Arrangements were in place along the route for newspapers and telegraph offices to record their progress. As it turned out, Fethi and Sadık (Eşref's replacement) never made it to Egypt; after managing to coax their light aircraft over the formidable Toros and Lebanon ranges and into Syria, they ultimately crashed in northern Palestine. Both pilots were killed and their bodies were taken to the Umayyad Mosque in Damascus for burial alongside the great Muslim hero Saladin (Salah ad-Din). The Turkish Republic later commemorated them in a series of postage stamps and in a monument in the Fatih quarter of Istanbul. Although Eşref was furious at being left out of the action for once, he and Pervin had avoided disaster.

Unionist activities in Izmir

More far-ranging assignments lay ahead for Eşref. For now, he was heavily involved in Unionist activity in and around Izmir directed against the Greek (Rum) population. According to one report, Enver had tasked Eşref with establishing a branch of the Special Organization in Izmir as early as January 1914.[19] Another source places Eşref in Izmir in March 1914, not long after his marriage to Pervin, having been sent there by Enver to expel the Rum from strategic locations in the region.[20] It was at that time that the pressure to force the Greeks to leave began. Some considered the fact that Greece had attacked the empire during the First Balkan War as an excuse for revenge. By July 1914, British reports noted that Eşref was a powerful—and feared—figure in the region. The governor had informed the British that Eşref "had arms and armed Cretan retainers in his house at Cordelio but that he could not interfere with him" due to Eşref's strong connections with Enver.[21] Much on the mind of the British was the subject of Unionist harassment and intimidation of the Greek population of the province. Their concerns were heightened by the increasingly menacing stance and, indeed, actions of some Committee of Union and Progress members, particularly in light of the brutality of the Balkan Wars. It was not long before the effects of the violence in the Balkans would spill over into Western Anatolia. The "fragile cosmopolitanism"[22] of the Aegean region was about to be shattered. Approximately 160,000 Greeks would be forced to migrate, and Eşref would be directly involved.

The Unionists' plan was to begin by applying economic pressure that would eventually escalate to violence. During the summer of 1914 the Unionists organized a boycott of non-Muslim businesses and communities. To reinforce the point they also perpetrated atrocities, including murder, against the Greek population in the surrounding territory. The British consul at Izmir identified Eşref, whom he referred to as "the Circassian ex-brigand, the protégé of Enver Pasha," as "the powerful leader in the boycott-movement." In the consul's view, Eşref and his brother Selim Sami were "all powerful here, and the Vali [i.e. the governor, Rahmi Bey] himself dare not go against them openly ... they are hand in glove with Enver Pasha and with the extremist leader Dr Nazim."[23] Rahmi's feeling of helplessness in the face of the hardcore operatives is particularly poignant because he himself was no outsider. A co-founder of the Committee of Union and Progress party in Salonica and activist since 1906, Evrenoszâde Rahmi was an urbane and sophisticated lawyer and Member of Parliament from an established family there. But against the concerted forces of the inner core of Unionist activists, even Rahmi felt outmatched. It was also a measure of how far Eşref and his brother had risen in a short while. Men who had been fugitives from justice as late as 1912 were calling the shots in 1914. The Balkan Wars and the imminence of a larger war had reshuffled the deck. According to the British Consul's informants (including a Greek to whom Eşref had provided protection, first by assigning him "one of his own followers, a brigand, to act as a guard" and then by issuing a letter of safe-conduct), Eşref and Sami could turn the threat to the Greeks on and off as they saw fit.[24]

To understand the situation in the Izmir region during the summer of 1914 we need to take a step back. In May 1914, well before the assassination of Archduke Franz Ferdinand at the end of June, a series of secret meetings took place in the War Ministry in Istanbul that would have far-reaching consequences.[25] Present were Enver, Talat, Eşref and several other important Unionist activists. Secrecy was a priority; many cabinet ministers were excluded from the conversations. Under the strong influence of the impact of the Balkan Wars, with their imprint of bitter territorial losses, ethnic cleansing, and the mounting desire for revenge, these gatherings turned their attention to the western littoral of Anatolia. It is doubtless significant in this connection that following the Western Thrace episode Süleyman Askerî, the first leader of the newly reorganized Special Organization, was selected to be in charge of refugee affairs. When Talat Paşa sought to locate him with a view to bringing him to Istanbul in early July 1914, he wrote to Rahmi Bey, the governor of Aydın (i.e. Izmir), to secure his return.[26] The Special Organization was beginning to focus on the Izmir region, and the networks forged in Libya and Thrace were being called into action once again.

In a section of Eşref's lost memoirs preserved in the autobiography of Celal Bayar, the Unionist boss in Izmir who later became both Prime Minister and President of the Turkish Republic, Eşref describes what Enver and Talat considered to be the most imminent threat to the now greatly reduced Ottoman state: the non-Muslim population. Calling them "ungrateful" despite having been nourished with the bread and favor of the empire, Eşref indicates that the focus of these meetings was squarely on the Aegean coast where the significant concentrations of Rum were now seen to constitute a strategic liability that, coupled with the belief in the imminence of another war, took on the dimension of an existential threat.[27] In the eyes of those taking part in the clandestine meetings, the loyalties of the "Greeks" had been turned by the Megali Idea, the cause of re-creating a Greek state on both shores of the Aegean which had spread its roots during the Hamidian era, to the point where, Eşref reports, the Rum were in a position to rise up and strike the Ottoman army from the rear.[28] From its headquarters on the ground floor of the Meserret, the main hotel for Muslim travelers to Istanbul, located in the Sirkeci quarter of the capital, the Special

Organization had been compiling dossiers on the situation that catalogued the perceived threat of a Hellenizing campaign along the Aegean
coast. One source of worry was the claim that young male Rums were
being conscripted by and undergoing military training in the Greek
army on the nearby islands that had recently been absorbed into the
Greek kingdom; these men were therefore deemed likely to fight for
Greece in the probable event of war. Another was that their population
was concentrated in key strategic locations along the coast and along
the rail lines linking the shore with the Anatolian interior. The rail lines
themselves, Eşref continued, were completely controlled by the Rum,
to the point that Ottoman Muslims could not even get railway jobs.
Moreover, he claimed, there was evidence of a policy to increase the
Greek population through marriage and immigration from mainland
Greece.[29] More alarming was the notion that the Rum had stockpiled
substantial weaponry, including Mauser rifles, machine guns, and hand
grenades.[30] Even worse, says Eşref, was the fact that a number of Greek
Orthodox members of the Ottoman parliament were in on these
activities. As Eşref put it, "The phrase 'Infidel Izmir' was not just a
comparative expression. Not only were we not the masters there but
also not even the guards."[31]

The discussions went on until the morning hours, and their focus
increasingly turned to Izmir and its environs. That brought Eşref to the
fore. Given his experience in and knowledge of the region, Enver
turned to him and, after impressing upon him the gravity of the situation, asked him to carry out an inspection of the region in order to
verify the various reports and information that the Unionists had been
receiving. Tasked with producing a report on the situation, Eşref heard
Talat say, "Eh, Eşref … you are going to love this job. The sun has risen
on you…"[32] Eşref indicates that he devoted considerable time to traveling through the region incognito, making contact neither with
Ottoman officials nor his own personal connections.

In this climate of mistrust and apprehension, the tenor of Eşref's
report was almost a foregone conclusion. It proposed immediate action
to prevent the loss of these strategically vital and "historically Turkish"
lands.[33] Eşref's report is infamous for referring to the traitorous elements among the non-Muslim ethnic minorities as "internal tumors"
that needed to be cleansed.[34] Unsurprisingly therefore it was not long

before the Rum population began to feel the direct effects of this policy; the ethnic cleansing of the Rum was about to begin.

The Special Organization assumed the role of carrying out this fateful task. Eşref's role in the actual process remains unclear. One source indicates that Turkish gangs under his command were carrying out raids around Söke against the Rum population who had strong links with the Greeks on the island of Samos.[35] It is perhaps telling that Rahmi complained to Talat in September 1914 that the "famous" Eşref had received orders and men from Istanbul to drive the Rum out without Rahmi being informed.[36] Using a combination of tactics including economic boycotts, settling the frequently hostile Muslim refugees from the Balkans and Crete in their midst, and finally violent attacks, the Special Organization gangs (*çete*) set to their task of ousting the "enemies within" in the spring and summer of 1914. The Committee of Union and Progress' policy of "organized chaos" was consonant with a strand of nationalist thinking popular at the time in the region. Bulgaria and Greece were also inclined toward population exchanges as a vehicle for securing national unity, a practice to be endorsed by the League of Nations after the war. Nevertheless it seems clear that the Unionists' brutal policy was not universally supported within the Committee of Union and Progress, as several officials are on record as being opposed to it.[37] Still, as at so many crucial junctures in the late Ottoman era, when push came to shove it was the activist, aggressive faction that tended to carry the day. Eşref served as one link in the chain that would effect its violent policies.

On the road again

Hard on the heels of his role in the displacement of the Greek Orthodox population in Western Asia Minor, Eşref accepted an assignment that would involve a trip to a very different part of Asia. In their seventh month of marriage, Eşref was given a role in the mission of the "Five Turks" to Central Asia. They were heading to "Turkistan" to make contact with like-minded Muslim agents, more potential allies for the coming war. The five men in question were Eşref's younger brother Selim "Hacı" Sami, Hüseyin Emrullah (Barkan) (the former police chief of Izmir), Derneli Adil Hikmet, İzmirli Tatar (aka Kırımlı) Hüseyin

(Bay), and Bursalı İbrahim Gürcü (Haklıer). Eşref was to accompany them on their journey, carrying out missions in Oman and Bahrain along the way.

Eşref's brother Sami gathered these men together along with a larger group of committed Muslim nationalists. The top four in Eşref's list of the "Ten Promised Paradise" were all present: Eşref, his brother Selim Sami, Süleyman Askerî, and Yakup Cemil, along with the poet Ömer Naci. They all converged on Eşref and Pervin's house in Izmir. Askerî Bey stayed with the Kuşcubaşıs while the others stayed in the Grand Hotel Kraemer Palace on the Izmir waterfront. The group were to travel on a steamship called the *Kara Deniz* (the Black Sea) as far as the Ottoman port of Basra in the Persian Gulf.[38] From there they would travel onwards to India and ultimately to Central Asia where they were meant to forge links with other Turkist activists. The ship docked in Izmir and the six prepared to go aboard. But before they left the house, Pervin raised the flag of marital revolt. "Eşref Bey," she said, "since you are always going off and leaving me, why ever did you take me in the first place?" To this outcry, Eşref replied, "To stop anyone else from taking you I had to rush things. Did I make a mistake?" According to her account, they both drowned in laughter and tears at the same time.

On 22 July 1914 the *Kara Deniz* sailed. Photos of the group taken on board show these men in unaccustomed poses as they adopted the disguise of traders and government bureaucrats to deflect the attentions of the curious passengers.[39] Eşref appears alternately quite jaunty in a striped sailor's shirt and then rather bemused in his disguise as a merchant from Bukhara.[40] Back home Pervin resolved to suffer through another long wait. The first news she received from the travelers came indirectly from somewhere along the Red Sea coast. Meanwhile, the first blows of the Great War had been struck between Serbia and Austria-Hungary (28 July 1914). In the Ottoman Empire, events moved quickly as the empire shifted to a war footing even though the empire was not yet officially at war. Enver had ordered troop movements almost immediately upon the outbreak of hostilities in the Balkans. Divisions were ordered to the Ottoman borders and reserve units were called up. Enver issued mobilization orders on 1 August and troop movements began two days later.[41] From this point onward, Ottoman trains would no longer accept commercial merchandise; all carriages were given over to military mobilization.

13. Eşref dressed as a sailor and a Bukharan merchant, bound for India. (Source: EK papers)

Meanwhile, after a flurry of last-minute bargaining, Germany and the Ottoman Empire signed a military alliance in early August 1914. The Ottoman government, led by Enver, had come to believe that their survival depended on entering into an alliance with some combination of the European Powers. Istanbul's first choice would have been Britain and/or France, but they snubbed the Ottoman advances.[42] Istanbul then turned to Germany, in many ways a well-suited partner from Istanbul's perspective: German officers had been heavily involved in reorganizing and modernizing the Ottoman military for decades, and the relatively newly formed German state lacked both the imperial baggage or the penchant for snatching Ottoman territory exhibited by

137

the British, the French, and the Russians. The German Kaiser Wilhelm II harbored a "vision of a worldwide Muslim revolution that would be inspired by the Ottoman Sultan-Caliph, orchestrated by Enver Pasha, and staged by the millions of colonized Muslim subjects in the empires of the Entente, from Morocco to India and Central Asia."[43] Turkish matters were followed closely in Berlin where Enver—represented at the popular level by an Enver Bey brand of cigarettes and a bridge named after him in Potsdam—had become a well-known symbol for a revivifying Ottoman Empire.[44] More immediately, the Ottomans brought a large military to the bargain and the strategic possibility of threatening the interests of each of the Entente states. Istanbul and Berlin would soon be discussing the merits of an Ottoman advance on the Suez Canal that would menace Britain's position in Egypt and her vital artery to India; a campaign to hit the Russians in Eastern Anatolia, the Caucasus, and Central Asia; and a plan to subvert the French in North Africa. While some of the German propaganda plans were wildly unrealistic—Eşref and his fellow Special Organization officers found them highly amusing[45]—they were nevertheless part of a larger, well-funded German–Ottoman campaign intended to destabilize the British and French positions in the Middle East. Muslims both inside and out-side the empire responded to the call to arms and men were on the move, arriving in Syria from disparate points to join the campaign.[46] The Ottoman side was unwittingly assisted by the mistaken British perception that the Ottomans were unable to operate independently of German control. As one scholar put it, "Underrating the Ottoman cunning and initiative was probably the most costly error the British made throughout the war in the Middle East."[47]

Throughout this period of frenetic activity, Pervin still had no direct news from the travelers. Then suddenly one day she received a typically cryptic telegram from Eşref in the Hijaz region of Arabia. It read: "I've arrived in Medina. The colleagues are continuing their journey. I'm returning to Izmir soon. I am in good health. Eşref." Indeed, his pres-ence in the Hijaz in August 1914 is confirmed by a telegram from the governor of that province who wrote to Istanbul in mid-late August, asking for instructions about how to treat Eşref and Sami. By reply he was told to provide assistance to the travelers.[48] By 24 August, the brothers had parted ways.[49] Sami and his fellows in the "Five Turks" continued their journey, which took them to Central Asia and then over the Pamir mountains into the Sinjan region of China and ultimately on to Shanghai. After many adventures they eventually escaped the clutches of the British, who were hard on their trail, by way of a Japanese ship that took them to Hamburg, as good an indicator as any of the global dimension of the Great War.[50]

Eşref set out to return to Damascus via Medina. Soon he sent Pervin another telegram, this time from Ma'an in Transjordan, also reporting that he was in good health. Then, silence. Weeks passed and nothing came. Later it became clear that Eşref had been diverted from returning to Izmir by an assignment in the Sinai Peninsula aimed at keeping the Arab tribes loyal to the Ottoman side. Suddenly a telegram came saying that Eşref would arrive at Salihli in a day or two. Pervin and her household rushed to Salihli and there was Eşref.

This time Eşref only stayed at home for three days. Pervin despaired. Her husband was back but seemed to spend less time with her at home than he did at the telegraph office during what turned out to be only another brief stay. Worse still, he spent the nights deep in conversation with his colleagues in the Special Organization. Additional men came from Istanbul; others were gathered from the surrounding region. Off they went again to the Arabian Peninsula, which was proving to be a crucial if largely invisible battleground in the Great War. Pervin wept bitter tears. It was as if her husband was a fleeting, distracted houseguest. Now that war was looming, he only stayed for a few days at a time and even then gathered his colleagues about him at their home to discuss tactics late into the night.

Mobilization had begun, but the empire had not yet declared war. This was part of an Ottoman strategy to avoid outright warfare until the military had completed its lengthy mobilization plans, its allies had demonstrated success on the Western front, and an overland supply route could be opened between Ottoman and Austrian lands. Only then would Istanbul be ready to help its allies.[51] That was the plan, but perhaps inevitably it was overtaken by events. It became even more difficult for the Ottomans to maintain neutrality once they effected the fictitious purchase of the German warships *Goeben* and *Breslau*, which had been chased by the British Mediterranean fleet to the opening of the Dardanelles Straits on 5 August 1914. Once they became Ottoman in name, Istanbul's decision to enter the war drew much closer.

While these momentous developments were taking place in the capital, Pervin was still without word from her husband. Although specific information about Eşref's activities during this period is patchy, it seems that he had been sent on missions aimed at keeping the main tribal leaders in the Arabian Peninsula on the Ottoman side. He met with important tribal leaders such as Ibn al-Rashid, Ibn al-Saud, and Sharif Ali, the son of the Sharif Husayn of Mecca.[52] There is frustratingly little evidence of what transpired in the desert. British intelligence reports dated September 1915 and based on information gleaned from a captured Ottoman staff officer from Aleppo state that "Eshref Bey went sometime ago to Ibn Rashid with £10,000 in gold; it is said to persuade him to attack Ibn Saoud." Here the British intelligence officer interjects some parenthetical background information laced with a strong dose of editorializing: "Eshref Bey—a Circassian—is an old Fedai, who after executing privately in CONSTANTINOPLE for the Committee a number of irreconciliable [sic] politicians, volunteered for the Tripoli War, and showed ability in command of a guerrilla force. His morals are ghastly."[53]

With the major exception of the Hijazi sharifs, Eşref's mission was successful. Sometime during this period he apparently attempted and failed to assassinate Sharif Husayn of Mecca, the future leader of the "Arab revolt." It was a failure that would prove disastrous, both for Eşref personally and for the empire as a whole.

At last Pervin received a telegram from Eşref who had now popped up in the northern reaches of the Sinai Peninsula. Typically he relayed no news about what he was up to in the desert, but Pervin heard rumors that Eşref and Mümtaz had organized their own militias and together with a Bedouin force had crossed the border into British Egypt, establishing a base in the citadel at El-Arish, the most important town in the northern Sinai.

Drive across the desert: the Canal campaign

After the empire took the momentous step to enter the war, military activity intensified even more rapidly. For Eşref much of the war would take place in the empire's Arab lands, for which Syria was the focal point of Ottoman military planning. Cemal Paşa, having been appointed commander of the Ottoman 4th Army and Governor of Syria, arrived in Damascus on 6 December 1914. He established his headquarters in the grand surroundings of the Damascus Palace Hotel. There he contemplated strategy with the German officers Werner von Falkenberg and Friedrich Kress von Kressenstein, the Chiefs of Staff of the Ottoman 4th Army and its 8th Army Corps, respectively. Both men were German officers who might have come straight from central casting.

14. Kress von Kressenstein. (Source: Kress, *Mit den Türken zum Suezkanal*)

This group reviewed the plans that had been drawn up prior to Cemal's arrival. Crucially, they envisioned an attack, either audacious or quixotic, on Britain's lifeline of empire, the Suez Canal.[54]

The decision to attack the Canal served two somewhat conflicting purposes. For the plan's originators in the German General Staff, a thrust toward Egypt made considerable strategic sense. Aimed at the crucial link between Britain, India, and Australasia, an attack on the Suez Canal had obvious advantages. It would also draw Allied troops away from other theaters, both currently, for example alleviating pressure on the Austrian army in Silesia, and in the future. For Istanbul, knocking out the Suez Canal as Britain's imperial artery meant less than reclaiming Egypt for the Ottoman Empire.[55]

To the British, any attack on the Canal represented a mortal threat to empire. "From the beginning of the war, the spectre of an enemy force crossing the Suez Canal had been a key worry among British leaders."[56] Maintaining control over the Canal was not only a strategic imperative but also, practically speaking, crucial to the passage of imperial troops from India, Australia, and New Zealand to the European fronts. Ottoman entry into the war in the fall of 1914 was thus a potential menace to British control over the waterway and Egypt itself. When reports arrived in London of an Ottoman force of 88,000 troops, orders were given to strengthen the British garrison in Egypt. But, given the priority of the Western front, British forces in Egypt were ordered to adopt a defensive position. Living in fear of what might emerge out of the desert,[57] the British pulled their forces back from the Sinai to a defensive perimeter around the Canal, dug in, and waited.

The Ottoman Canal campaign shared similarities with the sort of daring, some would say reckless, strokes that characterized Ottoman planning during the early stages of the war. The operation to cross the Sinai desert was perhaps even more unlikely than the Ottoman campaign to advance over the snowy mountains of Sarıkamış in the dead of winter (an action that, incidentally, came closer to success than is usually realized). However bold the plan was, it is clear that considerable preparations had been made even before Cemal arrived in Syria. They included provisions for demolition work along the Canal, sending a significant detachment, equipped with pontoons, across the desert in order to cross the waterway, and the infiltration of special agents into Egypt to assist the operation and, if possible, instigate a full-blown uprising against British occupation. Eşref was heavily involved. He records that he was given unofficial orders to begin preparation for the Canal campaign as early as 23 August 1914.[58] As we shall see, secret Ottoman correspondence places Eşref in Damascus at some point during the period between late September and early October 1914. He was already overseeing the equipping and arming of a flying detachment in preparation for the Canal campaign, and in communication with Süleyman Askerî at Special Organization headquarters in Istanbul.[59]

In Damascus Cemal Paşa was well aware of the logistical problems that the Ottoman expeditionary force would face in the Sinai desert. After all, it had taken him over two weeks to travel from Istanbul to Syria. His journey had been delayed by major gaps in the main railroad line; construction was ongoing and would not be completed until 1918, another sign of the empire's lack of preparedness for war. At times he had to abandon the rail line and proceed by automobile. In other places, where there was no road, he was forced to traverse by trolley some sections of railroad where the rails "hung suspended over a void of fifteen to twenty meters, and in others were under water."[60] He must have known that any attempt to move men and materiel across the wastes of the Sinai would be extremely difficult.

In fact, by the time he reached Damascus, Cemal was already having second thoughts about the wisdom of the Canal campaign. The situation in Syria and the long list of things he wanted to change there can only have added to his worries. If reversing the plan for the attack was the intention, he made a mistake in confiding his doubts to the German officer cum agent who was Cemal's link with the Germany military leadership. Dr Curt Prüfer, a German intelligence agent, was adamant that the attack should go ahead.[61] He therefore reported Cemal's hesitation to his superior, Max von Oppenheim. The German high command were aware that important sections of the Ottoman elite were less keen on the war and may have been eager to back out of the alliance.[62] As a result of Prüfer's despatch, Berlin put pressure on Istanbul to proceed with the attack at all costs. Soon the order reached Cemal that it should go ahead without delay. Curiously, Prüfer privately expressed doubts about the Canal campaign but he undoubtedly knew how much stock certain sections of the German hierarchy placed in pursuing a policy of *jihad*. As Eşref later remarked, the Germans were always far more enthusiastic about the potential of holy war than the Ottoman officers themselves.

Meanwhile Cemal's territory, the region of Greater Syria including today's Syria, Lebanon, Israel, and Palestine, was about to be hit by a perfect storm of wartime disasters. Over the course of the war perhaps as many as one fifth or even one quarter of its population would perish, mostly due to starvation. Hunger would gnaw at its inhabitants, victims of poor harvests, a pitiless Allied naval blockade, Ottoman military requisitioning of crops and animals, grain hording by powerful merchant syndicates, and even swarms of locusts of Biblical proportions. At various points during the war the situation got so bad that mothers abandoned their babies. Pedestrians found themselves stepping over bodies in the street. Humanitarian workers, many of them American missionaries, found themselves turning callous amid the hunger and starvation. The desperate turned to prostitution and competed with animals for grasses and seeds. The previously inedible and non-potable were routinely consumed. Instances of cannibalism appeared. The normal logic of life in Syria was turned upside down by the war.

It was in this environment that the Ottoman army had to conduct its military campaign. When Cemal Paşa arrived in Syria to oversee the Syria–Palestine front in early December 1914, mobilization was already well underway. The Ottoman 8th Army Corps had been assigned to Syria, with some of its divisions dedicated to the Canal campaign while others were tasked with maintaining security in Syria and Lebanon, regions that were increasingly but not, it was thought, irreparably infected with the spirit of Arab nationalism. Meanwhile key officers were busy with special assignments intended to prepare the ground for the Canal campaign.

The rumors that Pervin had heard were largely correct: Eşref was part of a detachment that had been sent into the Sinai in advance of the larger force that would march towards the Canal.[63] İzmitli Mümtaz had been put in charge of the volunteer Bedouin Arab forces as early as September,[64] while, as we have seen, the Russian consul reported that Eşref was recruiting forces around Mersin in October. An order from Talat Paşa that a prisoner in Tarsus be assigned to "Eşref Bey's gang (*çete*) on the Egyptian border" gives us a sense of the way in which wartime expediency altered the normal rules.[65] Wartime gave prisoners hope. Actually, Talat in Istanbul was not up-to-date with the increasingly fast-paced action in the Sinai. By November the *fedaîs* were fully engaged. Mümtaz's detachment of volunteers had secured El Arish, the northern gateway to the Sinai. Further south Eşref and his "flying force" of volunteer raiders had occupied Qalaat al-Nakhl deep in the interior of the Sinai, carrying out the order he was given on 2 November and taking advantage of the British withdrawal in October.[66] Eşref claims that they had swept the English out of the Sinai interior and even begun to harass shipping traffic in the Canal itself before the war had even been declared.[67]

To provide support for the Canal thrust, an infantry regiment was poised for action at Aqaba and all the desert forces were to be supported by a regiment based in Beersheba in southern Palestine.[68] In some respects the German–Ottoman Canal strategy was already producing results. By Eşref's account, the Ottoman thrust toward the Canal was causing the British the problems intended. The British were obliged to keep 200,000 troops, mostly Indians and Australians, in Egypt to defend against an Ottoman attack. Although the rather ambitious Ottoman hopes of fomenting rebellion in Egypt ultimately came to nothing, the Special Organization did have as many as 600 "agents and agitators" operating in Egypt, including Egyptians, Turks, Germans, and Austrians.[69] Their intelligence and reconnaissance reports, once collected from other sources and analyzed by the Ottoman Second Branch, proved useful in allowing the Ottoman command to have a fairly accurate picture of the deployment of British forces in Egypt. These troops had to be stationed in a variety of places, such as Alexandria and Port Said, and not only along the Canal itself. These were forces that could not therefore be sent to the European theater where the French were desperately calling for British help.[70]

The impending Ottoman advance was making the Egyptian population increasingly edgy. Secret British intelligence reported that rumors were spreading of a massive Ottoman army, perhaps as strong as 750,000 strong, on its way to liberate Egypt. Other stories in circulation talked of an Ottoman force that would divide in two, with one branch retaking the Hijaz and the other, equipped with Zeppelins, conquering Egypt and re-establishing Ottoman rule. According to one report, an Ottoman airplane had bombed British positions on the east bank of the Suez Canal, completely destroying a large fort and killing 3,000 men. Other rumors had the Sharif of Mecca already captured by the Ottomans and incarcerated in Istanbul. The Christian population of Egypt were apparently worried that this was only the initial phase of a larger Ottoman offensive to restore Muslim rule in Egypt and that "the horrors of Belgium are to be re-enacted in Egypt."[71]

The actual Ottoman Canal campaign was far more modest. In many respects it shared important similarities with the Tripolitanian war of three years before. As in Libya, the Ottomans faced superior numbers and a much better equipped enemy. Worse now was the fact that the Ottoman force would have to attack British positions that were well entrenched. In Libya the Ottomans had derived advantage from their essentially defensive posture, their links with local tribesmen who knew the terrain, and the fact that they could choose where and when to fight. But unlike the Italian invaders, the British had been in Egypt since 1882 and knew the area well. Still, many similarities were apparent. As in Libya, the Ottoman campaign against Egypt in the Great War would have to be run as a clandestine operation involving a stealthy advance through the desert; it relied on a combination of irregular Bedouin fighters and Ottoman officers, many of them the committed, volunteer variety; and they deployed relatively small numbers of Ottoman troops, avoiding direct engagement as much as possible and staying away from the coast and thus out of the range of the enemy's superior naval guns. Another parallel lay in the official Ottoman policy of disavowing responsibility for the actions of these mobile forces. In 1911 the British had complained that Ottoman troops were passing through Egypt, a territory that was officially neutral in the conflict between the Italians and the Ottomans, although the British were unofficially very supportive of Italian plans to take Libya. Now, in 1914, it was the British position in Egypt that was under threat. London protested to Istanbul that Ottoman troops were advancing on British Egypt even before war had been officially declared. This tactic reflected Istanbul's desire to avoid an out-and-out conflict with the British while stealing a march on their prospective enemies. In order to maintain this conceit, Istanbul once again sent its officers on their mission, but reserved the right to deny responsibility for their actions.

As in Libya three years earlier, maintaining lines of communications and supply was a major problem. Given the harsh nature of the desert terrain and the great distances involved, the logistical challenges were acute. Sending a force across the Sinai sands in order to cross the Canal, seize and hold positions from the well-supplied and numerically superior British forces was an almost impossible undertaking. Preparing for this campaign caused Cemal Paşa to scratch his head; the numbers and distances involved were staggering. The plan was to establish a chain of outposts stretching from southern Palestine through the wastes of the Sinai all the way to the Canal. The irrepressible Kress von Kressenstein had been tasked with selecting the outposts at intervals of no more than 25–30 km.[72] These stations, though basic, each required considerable work to prepare them for the expedition; artesian wells had to be sunk and dykes constructed to secure them against the flash floods that appeared in the desert with the winter rains.

Each outpost needed to be fitted out with a field hospital and stocked with supplies of water and rations to sustain the expeditionary force. Given the lack of supplies en route, everything would need to be transported ahead of time and stored in depots or carried by the troops themselves. They would have to adopt desert rations, a caloric package grimly calculated to keep the men moving but little more. Each soldier and officer was to be provided with a ration not exceeding one kilo-gram, consisting of biscuits, dates, and olives along with a gourd of water. The plans called for the expeditionary force to survive for only four days on the Egyptian side of the Canal. Within that window of time they would have either to overpower the British position, dig in and defend their positions, or to retreat. According to Dr Curt Prüfer, the German agent who undertook a fact-finding mission to the Arab provinces of the empire in late 1914, the plans for the Suez Canal attack included an even more ambitious goal, one that involved Eşref in particular. Together with his sixty "*komitacis*" Eşref was expected to cross the Canal and join forces with the Ottoman agents of Egyptian origin who had been sent into Egypt to foment rebellion in the wake of Ottoman propaganda leaflets that had been clandestinely distrib-uted.[73] But it is clear that the Ottoman plans did not envision a long stay. Supplies at the nearest outpost to the Canal, some 50 parched kilometers away at İkinci el-Hubra, would scarcely last ten days. After that, as Cemal Paşa later wrote, the troops would be "doomed to distress worse than that of the children of Israel."[74] Unlike the Biblical wanderers, the Ottoman forces had to rely on their own worldly sustenance and protection.

All in all, it was a phenomenally difficult and unlikely operation. The odds were certainly not in the Ottomans' favor, given the British superiority in almost every possible category: numbers, training, terrain, and, as it turned out, intelligence-gathering capabilities. The two advantages the Ottomans could hope to count on were both intangible. One was the fact that the Ottoman soldiers would be fighting a foreign, Christian enemy on Muslim soil. The other, potentially quite effective, advantage was the element of surprise. Indeed, at least initially the British did not expect an attack to come from the Sinai. Ottoman forces in the desert were relatively effective in keeping the British in the dark as to the nature of their advance until fairly close to the attack itself; the British in Cairo assumed the advanced Ottoman troops merely to be engaged in harassment and not a full attack. Although British superiority in resources and intelligence-gathering capability eventually prevailed, for a time the Ottoman counter-intelligence operations, mainly devoted to suppressing the flow of informants moving into Egypt,[75] but aided by some propitious cloud cover that negated airborne reconnaissance,[76] starved the British of an earlier warning than they would otherwise have had. Even when the British began to realise that an Ottoman attack on the Canal was imminent, the campaign's unlikelihood remained in some respects its greatest asset.

Given the bitterness of the recriminations that characterized Arab–Turkish relations after the Great War once the Arab provinces had been separated from Anatolia and "the legends of backstabbing" and repression colored the relationship between the two peoples,[77] it is important to remember that for the most part Arabs and Turks fought well together during the war.[78] Cemal Paşa praised the efforts and heroism of the Ottoman soldiers, noting the spirit of brotherly affection and self-sacrifice that existed between Turkish and Arab soldiers in the force that marched on the Canal. "This first campaign was a brilliant revelation of the fact that the majority of the Arabs stood by the Khalifate with heart and soul."[79] Cemal Paşa was also hoping that the Egyptians would rise up against their British occupiers once they learned of the

Ottoman success along the Canal. In retrospect the plan to capture Ismailiyya, and indeed the entire Suez Canal, looks extraordinarily ambitious, but perhaps, as was the case with another Ottoman against-the-odds decision, Enver's dispatching the Ottoman 3rd Army through the snowy mountains of Sarıkamış in Eastern Anatolia in December 1914, this was a plan that, had it come off, would have been lionized as tactically brilliant.

The Canal campaign was more likely chosen for its capacity to tie down British forces that otherwise could have been deployed either to the Western front or in areas more threatening to the Ottoman Empire, such as the Dardanelles. After the war, Enver said that although many had assumed that his aim was to reconquer Egypt, "that was absurd. With a single caravan route as lines of communication one cannot do that sort of thing in modern warfare... The object of his campaign was to engage and hold a large British force which would otherwise turn the scale on the Western front."[80] Cemal Paşa's memoirs record the details of his meeting with Enver in which Enver asked him to go to Syria and assume command of the Ottoman 4th Army. Cemal's duties there would include both putting a stop to the first stirrings of Arab rebellion and directing the campaign against the British in Egypt.[81] The Canal mission, Enver said, was a top priority for the German high command, and that is why Enver had already sent the Bavarian general Kress von Kressenstein, the real architect of the Suez campaign, to Damascus as German military advisor to the 4th Army. Within a few days Cemal made several appointments to his staff and arranged his departure for Damascus. Organizing a campaign to threaten the British control of the Canal, not to mention crossing and holding it, would prove much more difficult.

Cables, camels, and the Canal

Eşref flung himself into the action. His correspondence, a sheaf of telegrams that he kept among his personal papers until the end of his life, reveals his peripatetic movements in the desert on the way to the Canal—and the variety of problems that the Ottomans faced in the desert. During this period of preparation Eşref crisscrossed Syria, Palestine, and the Sinai. Despite his disparate movements, he was never far from a telegraph connection. For Eşref the flow of information was vital, allowing him both to coordinate his military operations in the desert with colleagues in the Special Organization and the regular chain of command and to keep in touch with his family back in Izmir.

By late October Eşref had reached Jaffa, on the coast of Palestine. From this point the Canal preparations began in earnest. In a series of coded telegrams to Süleyman Askerî, now head of the Special Organization in Istanbul, Eşref raised several operational issues. Men, money, and supplies topped the agenda. Eşref complained that the men Akserî had promised him had not materialized and that he was left with only a ragtag group of Afghan volunteers. He explained that he had used the money that he had received earlier to get this far and to assemble a detachment of thirty men. He was going into "*çete*" or armed militia mode, taking the guise of Bedouins, but he was waiting for money and weapons. Some of the men in his force did not even have shoes, he complained. While he was thus preoccupied with his desert difficulties, Eşref nevertheless also found time to try to coordinate matters far away. For example, he pleaded with Süleyman Askerî to send money to his brother Sami, who had now reached Bombay. Eşref reported that Sami had telegraphed Izmir saying that he had received 100 Ottoman liras but that as he had gone for three months without funding it was impossible for him and his six companions to continue their mission without additional funds.[82]

A week later Eşref was still asking for money and the key to telegraph codes so that he could begin his operations. He signed the telegrams "Ebu Feridun," his *nom de guerre*.[83] By early November 1914 Eşref had made his way to Aleppo in northern Syria. There he received a telegram from Süleyman Askerî, indicating that Eşref had been appointed military commander of Aqaba and its vicinity. Money and the keys to telegraphic codes were waiting in Jaffa for Eşref to collect on the way. Interestingly, Eşref responded by claiming to have arranged to be excused from this posting, preferring to be tasked with a mobile or flying command that allowed him a more central role.[84] His subsequent movements would confirm his penchant for going mobile.

While in Syria, Eşref took part in the first of a series of raids on the sealed French consulates aimed at finding incriminating evidence against local notables who were plotting against the Ottomans with the

French. Eşref and Mümtaz had been organizing Special Organization cells intent on routing out seditious activity, both among the civilian population and among Ottoman officers. We shall return to this operation in the next chapter, but it provides another instance of the ways in which Eşref's brief combined more conventional military duties with unconventional operations.

That mission accomplished, Eşref now moved down the coast toward Egypt. His next area of operations would be further to the west and closer to the action. He was headed for the Sinai, to help pave the way for the Suez Canal campaign. While Mümtaz was meant to carry out initial reconnaissance along a northern line running from Rafa to El Arish to Qantara, Eşref was to do the same along a parallel line to the south running from Aqaba to Nakhl to Suez.[85] In late November he had popped up in Ma'an in Transjordan; from here he fired off a few telegrams, for example to the commandant of the Ottoman fortress in Medina, demanding to know how many troops he was contributing to the Canal campaign. By mid-December he had made his way to El Arish, the center for operations in the northern reaches of the Sinai peninsula. Here Eşref objected to a military order restricting the use of telegraph traffic. For Eşref, this fight over communications was one worth picking with the military command, for he relied heavily on the telegraph network to keep him informed of the military situation—and his family affairs. Ready access to telegraphic communication allowed him to exert his demanding personal style; he was forever sending orders, cajoling funds from his superiors and overseeing his family's affairs, even when he was far away in the desert.

It was along these lines that Eşref contacted Mersinli Cemal Paşa, know in Turkish as "Little" Cemal to distinguish him from the Unionist Triumvir. Little Cemal was the commander of the Ottoman 8th Army Corps which had been tasked with organizing the Canal campaign. Eşref wrote to Little Cemal to protest the prohibition placed on telegraphic communication. Eşref invoked both the operational and personal necessity of keeping lines of communication as open as possible. He argued that it was necessary to send and receive information to carry out his military duties as commander of the volunteers. He also argued that it was vital for him and his volunteers who were "risking their lives in the face of the enemy's bullets" to be able to receive news from the families they had left behind and to keep them informed of their health. Eşref asked the commander to grant his request to send a daily rider with their telegrams, either by camel or horse and rider.[86]

For Eşref, the flow of tactical information was crucial. He was now receiving an almost constant supply of intelligence and scouting reports. Eşref synthesized the disparate pieces of information coming in from his scouts and crafted reports on the overall Canal theater to send to Süleyman Askerî, the head of the Special Organization in Istanbul.

For want of a nail . . .

Written as he faced the world's most powerful empire, Eşref's communications reflect the shortcomings of a stretched but determined Ottoman military. Rations, weapons, ammunition, troops, and mounts— all were in short supply. The problems could seem overwhelming. Eşref was immersed in the minutiae of organizing a largely volunteer operation. His forces were unevenly trained and of highly disparate provenance. Eşref's muster lists included volunteers from all regions of the empire. They had come to fight from Jerusalem and Jaffa in Palestine, from Damascus and Aleppo in Syria, from Baghdad in Iraq and Sana'a in Yemen, from Mardin and Malatya in Anatolia, from Edirne and Drama in Rumelia. And they came from outside the empire as well, from such former possessions as Alexandria and Cairo in Egypt, Benghazi in Libya, or Hanya in Crete. They came from the wider Muslim world, from Daghestan in the Caucasus and from the Sudan. Eşref was the commander of all the volunteer forces. Some of these men were assigned to the detachments led by his subordinates, including İzmirli Haydar and the German officer named Hilgendorf.[87] Remarkably, large numbers of volunteers had come from Afghanistan: forty of these were placed in Eşref's direct control for the march from El Arish to Qal'at al-Nakhl; another seventy-six stayed behind under Haydar and would follow later.[88] All of these men were issued with Ottoman army rifles, either German Mausers or British Martini-Henrys, a rucksack, and a leather water bottle. The Afghans hailed from Kabul, Kandahar, and Herat, from Peshawar, Jalalabad, and Ghazna.[89] Eşref may well have wondered how useful a detachment of Afghan volunteers would prove in the middle of the Sinai desert, but if so his terse notes do not record his doubts.

The task confronting this disparate group was daunting. The supply lines were long and tenuous and it was not as if the terrain, hard in places and sandy in others, was sufficiently bountiful to allow them to live off the land. Eşref found himself constantly having to accost various Ottoman officials for money, food, and transport. For example, on the eve of the final assault on the Canal, one of Eşref's main subordinates, Haydar, wrote to him with a number of concerns. Haydar had sent Eşref a contingent of Arab soldiers who had recently worked for the British, presumably so as to report on the condition of British defences at Suez. Along the way they had had to offer "bakhshish" (bribes) to local Bedouin, for which they would need to be reimbursed. The rations stored in Aqaba consisted solely of hardtack (*peksimet*) so Haydar had been obliged to send a portion of his camel herd off to fetch flour and other rations. In the meantime, Haydar complained, his men had been subsisting solely on hardtack and as a result had grown weak, with many of them taken ill. He asked Eşref to send them some sheep as a matter of urgency. Then, he reported, there were problems with the Afghans. Two of them had broken rifles that needed replacing. They were addicted to tobacco but the tobacco stores were all the way in El Arish and Haydar wanted to know if Eşref could send them some. There was no shortage of problems, large or small.

Transportation was one of the biggest headaches. Back in Syria, Cemal Paşa had been frustrated by the challenge of securing enough camels for the Canal campaign. The plan called for 11,000 camels, and that was simply to supply the two divisions that would move down from Syria. The forces coming from Aqaba would have to bring their own beasts. As Cemal later observed, "It must certainly come as a shock to very many people that in regions such as Syria and the Hedjaz ten to fifteen thousand camels could not be obtained, seeing that hundreds of thousands, or rather millions, of these animals are to be found there. But not all camels can carry burdens."[90] Cemal Paşa was ultimately able to procure the required camels—and photographs of the Ottoman expeditionary force show that there were plenty of them—but not without considerable time, effort, and expense. In some ways the camel problem was easy next to the ultimate test of the desert mission: securing enough water for all these men and animals, a consideration that forced the Ottomans to curtail the plans ultimately adopted to seize the Canal.

15. Ottoman camel corps at Beersheba. (Source: Library of Congress. Licensed under Public Domain via Wikimedia Commons)

Meanwhile problems in the field were becoming acute. In fact, Haydar complained that the shortage of horses was destroying the army. And the horses they did have were coming up lame. Keeping them shod in the desert was proving to be a major challenge. An extract from Haydar's report gives a flavor of the problems bedevilling the Ottoman Canal campaign:

> The artillery horse has thrown a shoe. The other horses' shoes are broken as well. Their hooves have grown out badly. If the horseshoes and nails have arrived in El Arish it is requested that they be sent here urgently in the company of the military blacksmith who is in Mümtaz Bey's vicinity. Because there is nobody here who can shoe a horse and none of the necessary instruments and tools. Under any circumstances, it is requested that Mümtaz Bey be asked to send his blacksmith here quickly.[91]

Eşref was receiving reports from the interior of the Sinai as well. Here the problems were equally formidable. Good sources of food, water, shelter, and transport were scarce. The scouting reports provided precious little in the way of encouragement. In some places, Eşref's subordinates in the field related, the British had dynamited fortifications before they retreated to the Canal. Such was the case at Bi'r Hasna, where the British had blown up the prison; and at Qal'at al-Nakhl, where they exploded the gates of the desert fortress.[92] Securing sufficient sources of potable water for both men and transport animals was difficult in the extreme. In some places where they had expected to find plentiful supplies, there were only pools of water not much deeper than a puddle. In some oases where Eşref's men had hoped to procure supplies of dates, there was simply nothing to be had.[93]

Finding draft and riding animals was, if possible, even more difficult. The Bedouin, when tractable, were adept at driving a hard bargain. Just as Cemal Paşa had found the task of obtaining sufficient numbers of camels for the Canal campaign difficult from his Damascus headquarters, so also did Eşref and his volunteer forces struggle to secure the beasts when they needed to replace or augment their camel trains. The Bedouin were notoriously tough negotiators and were naturally averse to parting with their animals for mere scrip, which the Ottomans, given the general lack of cash, tried to offer. In many places there were simply no Bedouin to be found. One report that Eşref received from one of his detachment commanders spelled out the bleakness of the terrain:

> The country around [Qal'at al-]Nakhl is bone-dry in the full meaning of the term. The English have destroyed the fort and the local population consists of only five or six families. There is nothing resembling Bedouin in the region. The nearest Bedouin are one or two days' distance from here. There is nothing that can be procured from Nakhl or from the Bedouin. There is nothing here.[94]

Elsewhere simply caring for the few camels that could be scared up was proving problematic. Another of Eşref's sub-commanders reported that while he had received fourteen camel-loads of provisions, he had no money with which to pay the camel drivers. As a result he decided to rent the camels and wanted Eşref's advice as to what he should say to the drivers when they returned for their animals. In the meantime, things had become almost comically worse. No one there, he reported, knew anything about taking care of camels or tending the twenty sheep he had at his post. Clearly this had not been part of their Prussian-led military training. What, he asked Eşref, was he supposed to do? In the confusion that reigned, some of the camels had even managed to run away. There seemed no end to the headaches that this adventure in the desert was causing for Eşref.

In spite of all of the operational difficulties that arose from trying to organize both humans and animals, Eşref and his colleagues continued to lay the groundwork for the attack on the Canal. Somehow supplies appeared, telegrams arrived and were despatched, money orders were processed and fighting men reported for duty from a variety of far-flung origins. The fact that the forces under Eşref's command were composed of volunteers doubtless made organizing their affairs more difficult than had they been regular enlisted men. The communications required to track them down, get them properly provisioned, and have them appear at the front seemed almost endless. Eşref was continually having to check on whether the volunteers and their provisions had arrived and to sort out payments and other bureaucratic tasks.

At the same time, Eşref also had to cope with matters back home. The main preoccupations were arranging to have Pervin and the household staff supplied with money and to have Eşref's orders carried out. On occasion Eşref grew very angry over what he perceived as his staff's failure to do as he asked, and his ire was palpable as it came down the telegraph line. One recipient of a particularly harsh telegram was Hasan Ali, one of the staff at the Salihli estate; Eşref accused him of negligence and warned him of the harsh consequences for any continued failure to live up to expectations.[95] When he wanted, Eşref's style could be brutally direct, especially when he was communicating with subordinates.

Meanwhile Eşref's field notebooks were filling up with intelligence on the British positions along the Canal. Reports were coming in thick and fast from all directions, providing information on the quality of the roads—or, more often, desert tracks—among the various camps and temporary bases on the way to the Canal, and the British defences arrayed along the strategic waterway. For instance, two days after Christmas 1914 he received a letter reporting that a large British warship had appeared and was heading down the coast towards El Arish,[96] revealing information about the superiority of British weaponry and defences.

These were formidable. Eşref sent reports to Askerî in Istanbul describing in detail the British positions, force structure, and armaments. Piece by piece the Ottoman forces were putting together a decent picture of the British defences. Combining intelligence gathered by Ottoman agents in the field with information from detailed charts and maps showing the dimensions of the Canal, the Ottoman expeditionary force was filling in the blanks that had existed in their minds when the campaign was first conceived. Somehow Eşref got hold of what appear to be the original survey maps and geographical profiles recorded by the French, including those of Linant de Bellefonds who carried out the surveys of the isthmus of Suez in the mid-1850s; these dated from prior to the construction of the Canal itself, when of course Egypt was still in Ottoman hands. One of these documents ran to almost seven feet in length, and altogether they provided Eşref and his men with a wealth of information about the Canal. They are still in the possession of his descendants today.

This was exactly the type of hard information that the Ottoman high command was hoping to acquire by sending men like Eşref and Mümtaz into the Sinai. "To tell the truth, when we contemplated this first expedition, not a man knew how the Canal was to be crossed. It was *really* necessary to carry out some such reconnaissance," Cemal later wrote.[97] Cemal believed that "it was in expectation of the sequel to our attempt that the English postponed their attack on the Dardanelles, and found themselves compelled to retain not less than 250,000 men permanently in Egypt."[98] This may well have been Cemal's attempt to cast a defeat as a victory, but it is nevertheless true that the aim of tying down British forces in Egypt was an important one in the initial German–Ottoman calculations.

But the difficulties that the Ottoman expeditionary force faced went beyond the already tall task of penetrating the entrenched British positions along the Canal. They also had to protect themselves from active British counter-attacks. These could come out of the clear blue sky at any time, and they arrived with deadly force in the form of aerial bombardment. In the afternoon of New Year's Day 1915 the contingent of Eşref's men stationed at Kale el-Heyl heard the hum of a British plane on the horizon, coming from the direction of Suez.[99] When the Ottoman forces saw the plane approach their position in the fortress of Kale el-Heyl, they opened fire; but because the plane stayed high above them at a distance that Ali Haydar, their commanding officer, estimated to be about 2,000 to 2,500 meters, he ordered them to hold their fire. The aircraft circled the area for a quarter of an hour, continually dropping bombs intended for the fortress. To Ali Haydar's great relief, the bombs missed their target but left craters in the sand that he reckoned to be 1.5 m wide and 35–40 cm deep. He kept a fragment from one of the bombs as a souvenir, indicating perhaps that this was the first time that the men had come under such an aerial attack. A few weeks later, in late January, British spotter planes identified Ottoman units making their way toward the Canal.[100] The element of surprise was proving less of an advantage than the Ottomans had hoped.

Later that month it was the turn of Eşref's Afghan detachment to feel the force of British firepower. On the evening of 27 January 1915 the unit of Afghan volunteers set out towards the Canal from their base on the fringes of the western Sinai. After advancing for six hours they left their baggage train on the bank of the Canal and crossed over towards Madama on the western side of the waterway, just to the north of Suez, in order to carry out some forward reconnaissance. They encountered some problems with their searchlights, but were able to push through the British lines for about 100 m. The terrain was completely flat, so when they began to exchange fire with the enemy, their commander, a certain Mehmet Tevfik, gave the order to retreat. At that moment, chaos erupted. The British opened up with a heavy and constant barrage of artillery fire, but the Ottoman detachment were able to retreat without casualties.[101] Ottoman troops were thus able to carry out reconnaissance missions on the British side of the Canal and remain undetected until they engaged with their adversaries. One week later, the Ottoman forces would return in greater numbers and armed with the intelligence they had gathered on British defences.

A tale of bribery in Egypt

With the insight that we might expect from a Special Organization officer, Eşref reveals that there was more to the story of the Ottoman–British stand-off over the Canal than its purely military dimension. Clandestine operations were afoot, and Eşref's papers contain a fascinating account of what was taking place behind the scenes. While he was raiding in the Sinai, and therefore in the last weeks of 1914, Süleyman Askerî at the Special Organization headquarters in Istanbul was contemplating a covert raid to insert an Ottoman commando force into Egypt. If the expeditionary force were to succeed in crossing the Canal, a band of "heavy" raiders was to be landed on the Egyptian coast. This contingent was to arrive at night by ship from Jaffa. Askerî wrote to Eşref by coded telegram to ask him what this force would need in order to gain the acceptance of the Egyptian people. Eşref responded categorically rejecting the plan on the grounds that the terrain of Egypt offered little shelter for such an operation, with no mountains and hardly a trench for cover. Instead, Eşref recommended infiltrating Ottoman agents who knew Egypt into the country from the naval base at Bodrum via submarine through Libya, taking advantage of the Ottoman contacts with the Sanusi order. This, he reckoned, would be a better way to use Ottoman agents' knowledge of the country to spread propaganda and carry out clandestine operations.[102] In this way, Eşref continued, referring to himself in the third person:

> Our Special Organization men were made to attack in every direction. Among our agents were enlightened figures like the pharmacist Vedad [Yalıntürk] and Aunt Münime. Alas, what a pity. Some time later it seems they were [captured,] interned [by the British], the woman separated and our friend Vedad thrown into a camp. Because the British knew Vedad to be close to Eşref, it is probable that they thought that this woman and Vedad had been sent by Eşref.[103]

Eşref cites a report that Vedad later wrote about an extraordinary proposal that the British made to him while he was their prisoner. The British, it seems, attempted to bribe the key Ottoman commanders to pull out of the war. Vedad's report, as relayed by Eşref, gives an account of this remarkable proposition that is worth citing at length:

> Thinking I was Eşref's friend and a Special Organization man, they imprisoned me. But they didn't get anything out of me. And they knew they wouldn't get anything from me. They weren't able to learn anything from Aunt Münime Hanım either. In time they chose the photographer Arab Kamil, who had been in Libya as part of Eşref's retinue and who was then imprisoned with us [in Egypt], and took him away from us. They sent him to the James restaurant.[104] In the most *luxe* restaurant in Egypt he was handed over to two generals who knew Turkish. Here is the dialogue that passed between Arab Kamil and these generals:
>
> General: Is your name Kamil the Photographer?
>
> Kamil: Yes, sir.

General: From where do you know Enver Paşa and where did you become friends with him?

Kamil: I know Enver Paşa. If he saw me now he might not recognize me. I was a photographer in his army.

General: Do you know Eşref Bey?

Kamil: Very well. Because while I was a photographer [in Libya] he was the commander of the Bedouin, but because he is an amateur with a keen interest in painting and photography, during the war and especially during ceasefires he would take me with him while he took very interesting and aesthetic pictures and because he liked my art and my courage he showed me the kindness of working together in the darkroom tent.

General: We're going to give you an assignment. No one is to hear anything of this. Or else you're finished. Know this well.

Kamil: ——.

General: Listen.

Kamil: Please.

General: We are going to send you to the shore of the Suez where Eşref is. On the other side of the Canal you will find his men and tell them, "Take me to Eşref Bey." And this is what you will say to him: …

The message that poor Kamil was to convey was that the English love the Turks and have no quarrel with their nation. They also wanted to make Eşref an offer. If he were to reassure his friends Enver and Cemal that they need not enter the war, the English would give them 2,000,000 in gold and a loan of 10,000,000 sterling to the Ottoman Empire. If Eşref was unable to convince Enver and company, then they would give him 50,000 in gold to delay his own activities in the Sinai. If Eşref were to agree to this, they would send 50,000 in gold up front to him personally and 3,000 to Kamil. The British officers gave Kamil 100 gold pieces as traveling money and told him that an immediate answer was not necessary because they wanted him to think it over carefully and meet them back at the St James in two days' time.

When he returned forty-eight hours later, we are told that he said to his interlocutors: "My generals, I've thought it over. I've considered Eşref's character. I've studied this proposal carefully and I saw that if I were to make this proposal to Eşref, either I would take a bullet in the head or he would wonder what was behind this business and would turn me over to a court martial which would say that I had come from the enemy in an attempt to deceive us and have me executed. I am the child of a poor family. Don't involve me in these matters." To this, one of the officers replied by asking who else might be available take on the mission. "By God, I don't know," responded Kamil. "The only thing I know is that whoever goes to Eşref in this manner will get a bullet for an answer. To me that's final." The generals then asked him where he would go. If free to go, he said, he would return to his family in Zagazig. He was told that he was free to go but was warned that if word of this got out he would pay with his life. Two hours later he was arrested at the train station on his way home and thrown back in prison.

Although it is not well known, the British government explored several attempts to bribe the Ottoman Empire to quit the war. The first of these was conducted as early as 1915 after the disastrous Ottoman defeat at Sarıkamış. Acting with the approval of the wartime cabinet secretary Sir Maurice Hankey, the British director of naval intelligence Captain Reginald Hall proposed that £4,000,000 be offered to Istanbul. Negotiations took place in April 1915, but the Allied landings at Gallipoli ruined the prospect of any deal.[105] The most spectacular of all such efforts was the secret discussions between November 1917 and August 1918 to induce the Ottoman Empire, and Enver Paşa in particular, to pull out of the war in return for huge sums of money. Figures up to $25,000,000 were discussed over the course of the on-again, off-again negotiations. In brief, Enver was to arrange matters so that Istanbul would open the Straits to British warships and withdraw its troops to the north of the Haifa–Deraa railway line in return for retaining Istanbul and keeping Palestine. This attempt was made through the Ottoman-born Greek arms dealer Basil Zaharoff, who was in communication with the Prime Minister David Lloyd George through Vincent Caillard of the London-based armaments manufacturers Vickers. It was cloak-and-dagger stuff. The central figure of Zaharoff, going by the not terribly impenetrable codename of "ZedZed" (the Prime Minister was referred to as "the chairman"), was a larger-than-life figure who had amassed a fortune selling weapons to a wide number of countries. He approached Enver Paşa on behalf of the British government (codename "money bag") via the Ottoman representative in Switzerland Abdülkerim Bey, who was Enver's uncle.[106] Although initially it seemed that a deal could be arranged, in the end the timing was not right. Russia's withdrawal from the war subsequently emboldened the Ottomans to believe that victory was possible, and the whole affair remained a missed opportunity. Eşref's account adds a new wrinkle to the story. Although unattested in other sources, his account fits with what is known about British policy in the Middle Eastern theater. It must be seen alongside such "out of the box" plans as an attempt to delegitimize the Ottoman claim to the Caliphate and the money and materiel they provided to Sharif Husayn of the Hijaz to instigate the "Arab revolt," a development that would soon have a direct impact on the Ottoman Empire in general and Eşref in particular.

The battle

The British attempt to buy the Ottomans off came to nothing, and the preparations for the assault on the Canal continued in late January and early February of 1915. The Ottoman plan called for a three-pronged attack involving approximately 24,000 men. The flank movements, one to the north opposite Qantarah and another to the south against Suez, were largely diversionary so as to draw British forces away from their stronghold at Ismailiyya and thereby allow the stronger Ottoman central column to break through there. Eşref was put in charge of the left-hand, or southern, column. Eventually Ottoman forces were able to launch their assault on the Canal itself. The Ottoman attack finally took place on 3 February 1915. The pontoons and inflatable rafts that the Ottoman forces had laboriously hauled over the Sinai sands were lowered into position and the battle commenced just to the north of the Great Bitter Lake. The advanced party of Ottoman forces managed to surprise the British near Ismailiyya, but the second wave of troops was delayed, giving the British time to recover from the surprise and bring their superior numbers to bear.[107] To the south, the left-hand flank under Eşref's command focused its attack on the portion of the Canal that ran north from Suez, in the vicinity of Madama and the bridge over the canal at Kubri, or Köprü, which means "bridge" in Turkish. This was the sector where the Ottoman probe in late January had been able to advance across British lines before coming under fire.

Eşref's hand-drawn sketch of the battlefield and the order of battle that he kept in his papers provide a remarkably detailed account of the

Ottoman offensive strategy. Perhaps unsurprisingly, these documents place Eşref at the center of the action. The twelve-step order of battle was his plan and was to be carried out on his orders.[108] The battlefield sketch shows him in a central position, just behind the six forward detachments and in front of three banks of machine gun and two mountain cannon emplacements.[109] He is identified as "Commander of the left Canal wing." The Ottoman troops involved were a combination of regular army (*nizamiye*) detachments and Eşref's irregular units, including the Afghan volunteers, the camel corps infantry, and other units. Eşref's reliable subordinate Haydar appears in command of the three irregular groups. To the rear is the highest-ranking regular army officer, a Colonel Kâzım, placed in front of the reserve units. The orders make it clear that he and his men were placed under Eşref's authority. Eşref's handiwork shows the various lines of British defenses arrayed before the Canal, including a chain of mines in the sand, stretches of barbed wire protecting beachheads on the eastern or Sinai side of the Canal, and a series of fortifications behind the lines. Also visible are a number of British warships and gun batteries floating serenely along the water. The point of attack appears to have been chosen for being out of range of the naval guns that could be concentrated from the Great Bitter Lake to the north and the Gulf of Suez to the south. The battle plans were meticulous. A signalling system was in place to communicate information about troop positions, with green lights for the enemy and red for the Ottoman forces. Kâzım Bey and his commanders were to present themselves to Eşref for consultation and receive their instructions shortly before battle. The forces were to be in position half an hour before sunset on the evening of 3 February when Eşref was to inspect the final preparations before the fighting commenced.

In the end, all of the long hours devoted to planning, provisioning, and marching came to little. With their lines of supply badly overstretched, food and water in short supply, and facing a heavily armed, well-informed, and organized adversary, the Ottoman expeditionary force made little headway. A sandstorm on the previous day meant that the Ottoman plan of attack was delayed. Eventually three pontoons made it across the Canal to the western bank, but they were exposed at daybreak and rendered useless by British gunfire. Soon the pontoons on the eastern side were destroyed by a British torpedo ship.[110] Confusion reigned.

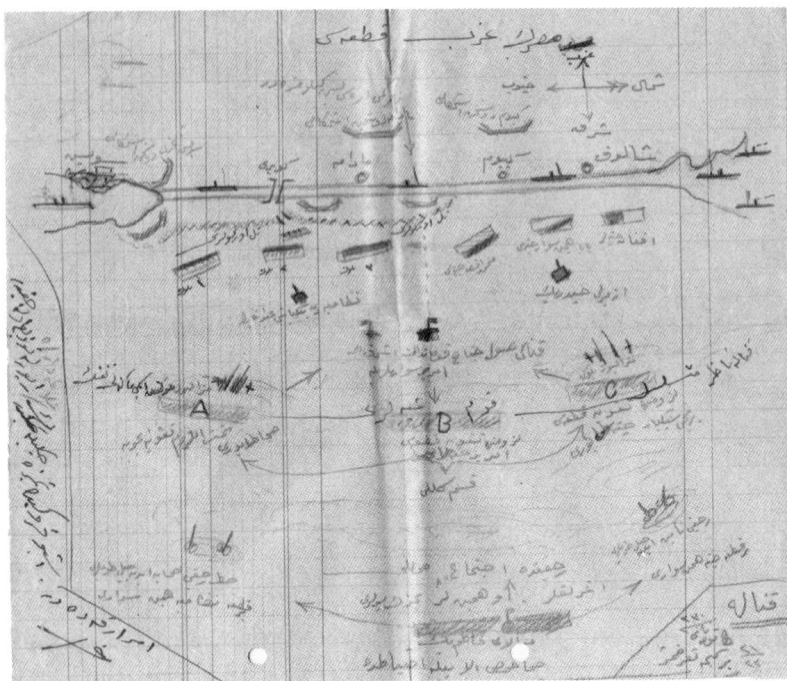

16. Eşref's sketch of the battlefield at the Canal. (Source: EK papers)

Those Ottoman troops who made it onto the waterway in the middle prong of the attack were soon captured or cut down by British fire coming from troops on the land and ships on the Canal itself. What happened on Eşref's flank remains unclear. *The Times* of London's account suggests that, according to British military sources at least, "Eshref Bey's highly irregular force" was mainly intended to "demonstrate" near Suez, analysis consonant with the Ottoman diversionary scheme.[111] It seems clear that neither of the Ottoman flanking operations was successful in drawing British defenders away from the main, central thrust of the attack. On learning of the failed central attack, Cemal Paşa ordered the Ottoman forces to retreat in order to avoid a pitched battle with the larger British force. The Ottoman forces began the disheartening but orderly process of retreating back across the desert. Luckily for them, the British neglected to press their advantage, partly because they had overestimated the size of the Ottoman force and thought a second attack was imminent, and partly because keeping the peace in Egypt proper remained their priority.[112] Both sides would reconsider their options. The British resolved to extend the Canal's defensive perimeter further to the east in order to provide a buffer against any future Ottoman incursions. The Ottomans, having gathered valuable information about the British defenses, resolved to regroup and strengthen their forces with a view to launching another attempt.

News from home

Eşref soon received some news from Pervin that must have cheered him up after the failure to cross the Canal: she had delivered a baby boy. As she put it, "Our round baby boy came into this world. We gave him the name Sencer, Eşref's maternal grandfather's name, and sent our glad tidings to El Arish via the telegraph. Because the telegraph lines to the town of El Arish were even linked with our own telegraph lines!"[113] Eşref kept the telegram among his papers until the end of his life. Dated 14 March 1915 and sent to Eşref Bey in El-Arish from a Captain Adli from the government telegraph office in Izmir, the message reads:

> This evening your son was born and [your brother] Ahmed Bey's operation was successful. Both are in good health. I send my congratulations and kiss your eyes [a greeting of respect].
>
> Captain Adli[114]

This joyous piece of family news must have made Eşref's heart swell, but there was little time to savor the good tidings. Following the defeat at the Canal, the Ottoman forces redoubled their efforts to improve their lines of communication and supply, including building a road from Beersheba into the desert to link up with the supply depots. The Ottoman high command had decided to launch another attack on the Canal.

But not all such domestic news was as positive. Almost two weeks after learning about the birth of his son, news that seems to have induced Eşref to return from the front to Izmir to see the newborn child, Eşref's brother Selim Sami sent a more worrisome message from Istanbul:

To Eşref Bey the Circassian, residing near the station in Karşıyaka, Izmir,
Our father has declined. If you don't come in a few days you won't be able
to see him. Come quickly with Ahmed no matter what happens.

Hacı Sami[115]

Like soldiers everywhere in the Great War, Eşref had to contend
with news from home, both good and bad, that tugged at his emotions.

Meanwhile, away from home the prosecution of the war continued
relentlessly along its many fronts. Although the Ottoman military's
performance during the war exceeded expectations, the war was an
unmitigated disaster for its government and its inhabitants. Despite
poor or non-existent infrastructure such as roads, rail lines, hospitals,
and food distribution and communication networks, the Ottoman military conducted campaigns across a wide swath of territory. In Eastern
Europe they assisted their allies on the Romanian, Macedonian, and
Gallician fronts. At Gallipoli, they famously defended against the Allied
landings and subsequently withstood brutal battles during a campaign
that lasted from early 1915 to early 1916. In Eastern Anatolia Enver's
Sarıkamış campaign nearly encircled the Russian army but ended in
frozen disaster. The attempts to force the Suez Canal, as we have seen,
also failed but were useful in diverting Allied troops away from the
European theaters. In Iraq, the Ottoman army achieved a notable success in capturing an entire British army at Kut. Smaller campaigns in
North Africa, Iran, and Arabia indicated the broad scope of the
Ottoman war effort. The human costs were massive. An estimated
725,000 Ottoman casualties included 325,000 killed and 400,000
injured. Over 200,000 were taken prisoner.[116] Desertion was extremely
high, particularly toward the end of the conflict when only 560,000 of
a total 2,850,000 enlisted men remained in uniform.[117]

The damage to the civilian population was severe. The human cost
of the conflict is almost impossible to calculate, but the effects were
everywhere apparent. No community remained untouched, but by far
the most numerous victims were the Ottoman Armenians. Applying
the same logic that they had used on the Greeks of Western Anatolia,
the Unionist government increasingly viewed the Armenian population
as a strategic threat, especially after the collapse of the eastern front
early in the war. Although most Armenians were not involved, a radicalized minority had joined Armenian revolutionary organizations in

support of the Russian army. The Ottoman authorities resolved to deport the entire population away from the front and into the Syrian desert. Some Special Organization units played a prominent role in the deportations, which were made even worse when the caravans of refugees were attacked and massacred, either immediately after being removed from their places of origin or along the way. The result was the destruction of the Ottoman Armenian way of life.

And here one must consider the question of whether Eşref had any involvement in the Armenian genocide. A number of writers have assumed that as a member of the Special Organization he was guilty either by deed or by association. We have to remember that the Special Organization was a broad organization with operations both inside and outside the empire's borders, for example in Iran, Central Asia, South Asia, and North Africa, and that it was not necessarily the case that all or probably even most of its members were involved in the deportations. Eşref's wartime activities focused on the Arab lands, but when he traveled between Istanbul and the front it is possible that he could perhaps have played a role in the deportations and killings that were taking place in Eastern Anatolia in 1915 and 1916. There are a number of sources that would seem at first to indicate that Eşref might have been involved. Upon closer examination, however, the connections look less probable or at least remain unconfirmed. A number of documents in the Ottoman archives link a man named Eşref to caravans of Armenians being deported to Syria. But these documents turn out to refer to a civil official from Baghdad (Bağdad Mülkiye müfettişi Eşref Bey) who shared the same given name as Kuşçubaşı Eşref.[118] Closer to the bone are accounts that locate Eşref's militia (çete) in the region of Diyarbakır, Harran, and Urfa in late June and July of 1915. They were said to be raiding and plundering villages and even cities in the region. According to Hilmar Kaiser, these were Muslim villages that were being attacked.[119] Enver sent an urgent dispatch to Urfa asking to be sent immediately the "painful details" of the animals that Eşref's unit had taken by force and whatever else they had stirred up. During such incidents the authorities seem caught between trying to keep military communications intact—they were particularly worried about Bedouin attacks on the railway line in that region, for example—and maintaining order. Interestingly, according to the Interior Ministry correspondence Eşref was not with his unit at this time. A group of up to 200 men under the name of Eşref's militia were operating under the command of a man named Rifat in Eşref's absence.[120] Although the Interior Ministry intended to punish Eşref's men for these offences after they were detained in Diyarbakır, Kaiser's research indicates that they ultimately managed to avoid any punitive action.

Once again, tensions between the regular administration and the volunteer units were apparent. After Eşref returned to the scene and produced an order saying that he and his men were meant to join forces with another unit, they were allowed to proceed to the area south of Lake Van.[121] Eşref's involvement in what happened there remains unknown. During the following year there were further instances when officialdom seemed to be having difficulty locating Eşref, in one instance because he had gone to Izmir.[122] Even Enver at the War Ministry was often uncertain as to where Eşref was and what he and his men were up to.[123] Thus it seems that in between his activities in the Arab provinces Eşref and his unit were in the region where atrocities against Armenians are known to have been committed. But apart from information on his men raiding villages in the region—apparently Muslim villages—and his turning up in Diyarbakır and intervening so that his unit avoided recriminations, it is difficult to be more precise. The arrival of volunteer units like Eşref's clearly created problems for the Ottoman bureaucracy who struggled to control them by having them placed, presumably quite loosely, under the control of different armies. Kaiser notes that when, after the war, one of the men in Eşref's unit was brought to trial and shown Interior Ministry communications, he denied all involvement in attacks against civilians.[124] While there is thus no direct evidence linking Eşref to the massacring of Armenians, he is on record, as we have seen, as saying counterfactually that if the Ottoman government had given orders for the massacring of Armenians then none of them would have remained alive by the war's end.

Meanwhile, British intelligence reported on the comings and goings of Eşref's colleagues Süleyman Askerî and İzmitli Mümtaz. As the war dragged on, Enver continued to rely on his trusted disciples. The British traced Mümtaz to Damascus where, if their informants can be believed, Cemal's command was increasingly troubled by rising anti-Turkish sentiment. Cemal's attempts to create a cult around himself, styled as a second Sultan Selim I who had conquered the Arab lands for the Ottoman Empire in the early sixteenth century, were unlikely to quell the rising unrest. Further east, Süleyman Askerî, whom Enver had sent to Iraq to stiffen the resistance against the British advance from the Persian Gulf, had been wounded in the leg. The Ottoman War Ministry sent Kâzım, later known as Kâzım Karabekir, a leader in the Turkish War of Independence and, later still, a rival to Mustafa Kemal, to Baghdad to replace Askerî. The latter, whom the British referred to as "a very rash and impetuous lieut[enant] of Enver's," was having none of it. He refused to yield his command, which left Kâzım "much annoyed" at having to return all the way to Istanbul where he eventually took up a post with the German General Liman von Sanders.[125] Enver's men were fiercely loyal to him, but continued to demonstrate the same quarrelsomeness among themselves that they had displayed in Libya.

In late 1915 Eşref's unit was assigned to a new expeditionary force under Kress von Kressenstein to plan the second assault on the Canal. Taking advantage of the lull in the action before the second Ottoman attack on the Canal, Enver diverted Eşref on a mission to counteract British influence in Arabia. The Ottoman high command was increasingly worried about the deteriorating Ottoman position in the Hijaz, so Enver sent Eşref back to Arabia. According to British intelligence reports, his mission this time was to take £10,000 in gold to Ibn Rashid, the leader of the Jabal Shammar in Northern Arabia, based in Ha'il.[126] Fierce rivals of the Sauds, the Al Rashids were one of the important tribal groupings whose loyalty was crucial to the Ottoman effort to keep Arabia on side during the war. As correspondence captured by the British was later to show, Ibn Rashid was not always best pleased by the treatment he received from the Ottomans and sometimes used his conflict with Ibn Saud as an excuse for not coming to their aid by taking up the fight against the forces of the "Arab revolt." From Istanbul's perspective, his refusal to join in the anti-Ottoman rebellion was an important achievement.

Faced again with superior British organizational and financial power and with inter-tribal rivalries, the Ottoman effort failed to find much traction for a viable anti-British coalition.[127] The "Arab revolt," however overstated its claim to speak for all Arabs, was underway. It proved the exception to the Ottoman pattern of keeping the Arabian tribes on side, thanks to the efforts of Eşref and others. Unfortunately for the

Ottomans, their enticements paled in comparison to the British who, controversially, were promising the Hashemites not only much larger amounts of gold but something that the Ottomans simply couldn't match: a kingdom of the Arabs, however elusive that later turned out to be. In the meantime, the gold and arms supplied to Sharif Husayn's forces proved sufficient to create a real problem for the Ottoman war effort in general and, as we shall soon see, for Eşref in particular.

6

THE GREAT WAR, PART II

BACK TO ARABIA

Consular break-ins in Syria

As the war dragged on, Eşref found himself increasingly drawn back to the Arab provinces of the empire. The knowledge and experience he had gained during his years in Arabian exile were now proving useful for the Ottoman war effort. The outbreak of Sharif Husayn's so-called "Arab revolt" meant that the services of Eşref, ironically himself a former rebel, were increasingly in demand in the Ottoman War Ministry. Given Eşref's paramilitary background and accumulated record, it was perhaps not surprising that he was given a number of unconventional assignments. The first of these called him to Beirut.

This assignment was highly contentious. Enver and Cemal Paşa now sent him back to Syria to help build the case against Syrian nationalists whom the Ottomans suspected, with considerable justification, of collusion with the French.[1] The charges included treason. Throughout the war years the Ottoman administration in Syria and Lebanon had to contend with a series of Allied plots aimed at destabilizing the region. Intercepted communications, a naval blockade, and intrigue with local notables all proved distinctly worrying for the Ottoman war effort. The Ottomans responded by organizing extensive counter-espionage activity, often with German advice. Eşref and Mümtaz were tasked with supervising Special Organization cells to compile dossiers on several Ottoman army officers of Arab origin who were suspected of treason, in particular planning a separate deal with France, proposing to declare Syrian independence, and plotting to murder their Turkish commanding officers.[2] The Ottoman high command made an important distinction between the cases against Arab officers serving in the army and those against civilians. Given the sensitive preparations underway for the Canal campaign, Istanbul generally preferred to reassign the Arab officers away from the region. But it pursued the cases against the Arab notables much more vigorously.

Desperate for evidence to substantiate their strong suspicions of plotting between the French and local Syrians and Lebanese, the Ottomans even went as far as risking their important relations with the United States. First in Aleppo in late 1914, then in Beirut in September 1915, and finally in Damascus in November, Ottoman officials broke into French consulates that had been closed since Ottoman entry into the war.[3] The still neutral Americans had overseen the sealing of the French consulates, thereby taking responsibility for their diplomatic integrity. On 27 September, acting under the instructions of the governor of Beirut, Ottoman agents, including Special Organization officers, broke the seals placed there by the American consulate and took away some thirty-two cases filled with documents left behind by the last French consul François Georges-Picot, despite orders to him to remove or destroy them.[4] Thinking the war would only last a short while, the future partner to the infamous Anglo-French pact known as the Sykes–Picot Agreement had hidden the files behind a false wall in the consulate and entrusted this knowledge to his Maronite dragoman. Unfortunately for the French and their fellow plotters in the region, this dragoman later betrayed the information to the Ottoman authorities in Damascus under threat of deportation to Anatolia. The break-in produced an official protest from the American government, deploring the "infringement of the well-established principles and usages of international law."[5] American indignation, while noted, did nothing to alter the chain of events set in motion by the break-in. The information obtained from the raid on the French consulate in Beirut, in which Eşref took part, would eventually lead to the hanging of a number of Arab nationalists in May 1916.

Undeterred, Enver ordered Eşref and his fellow Special Organization officers to break into the French consulate in Damascus, where they obtained further incriminating evidence. According to information later supplied by Eşref, it was his unit that broke into the consulates and obtained the implicating documents. Eşref and Mümtaz then supervised the compiling of dossiers on several Ottoman army officers of Arab origin who were suspected of intriguing with France.[6] The documents in these files, some of which are reproduced in English translation in Cemal Paşa's memoirs, implicated both Ottoman army officers of Arab descent and civilian Arab notables who had engaged in treasonous dealings with the French.[7] The documents taken from these consulates were so voluminous that the Ottoman administration in Beirut was still working through them in February 1916.[8] The incriminating information the papers contained was used in the military trials that were held later that year, resulting in death sentences for many of the accused. This, together with other aspects of what has been referred to as Cemal Paşa's "massive reign of terror," proved a factor in the alienation of many Syrian Arabs during the war. Cemal Paşa maintained that without the trials the Ottomans would never have been able to maintain order and thereby fend off the British and the French from Syria until the end of the war, such was the extent of connivance between the French and a small but influential group of Arab notables. Cemal's claims, however, overlook the fact that the documents taken referred to pre-war activities, not evidence of wartime treason.[9]

After his work in Syria, Eşref seems to have returned to Izmir. But his activities and whereabouts for this period are typically difficult to pin down. He was thought to be in Izmir by late February when the Istanbul police wrote to the governor to say that one of his men, Hasan Âli the Circassian, was thought to be on his way from Konya to Izmir to meet with Eşref.[10] (In late March 1916 his man Hasan Âli was in Konya trying to procure some railway cars of provisions, for reasons that remain unclear).[11] This may have been the time when a chance encounter with Eşref left a lasting impression on a German medical officer when they met on the train near Söke.[12] Ernst Rodenwaldt, an expert on tropical diseases and later a Nazi official, unwittingly encountered Eşref when he entered Rodenwaldt's train compartment and only later learned his identity. Rodenwaldt described his train companion as an "adventurous character": tall with dark eyes and a dark beard, wearing a grey fur hat and a sealskin coat. He wore a cartridge belt across his chest and a rifle over his shoulder. Two silent but heavily armed associates were at Eşref's side. A language gap existed between the two men, but by gesticulating and exchanging their few words in common they formed a connection. When the three "dark men" alighted at the next station, Rodenwaldt learned from the whispers of an elderly Greek that he was "un homme d'Enver." Rodenwaldt, whose memoir appeared in the 1950s, commented, "Today we would say *Geheime Staatspolizei*," i.e. Gestapo.[13] Their paths crossed again in Izmir where Eşref greeted the German like an old friend and treated him to a dinner and a night's lodging. Later, he says, he learned that Eşref had led a revolutionary movement in Mesopotamia and, better informed, was captured by the British after the war. Soon Eşref was called away on another mission, one that would take him away again from Western Anatolia and back to the deserts of Najd in the middle of Arabia.

The Najd mission

Toward the end of 1915, Istanbul was increasingly worried by British intrigues with the Arabs of the Hijaz. What would later become rather inaccurately known as the "Arab revolt" was the result of an agreement that slowly took shape through an exchange of letters between Husayn, the Sharif of the Hijaz, and Henry McMahon, the British High Commissioner in Egypt, known as the "Husayn–McMahon correspondence." In response, Istanbul began to ponder measures to shore up the allegiance of the other important Arabian rulers, most importantly the Al-Rashids and the Ibn Sauds. One such mission was a delegation that included Eşref, Mümtaz, the poet Mehmed Âkif, and the Tunisian exile leader Shaykh Salih. This project had all the markings of a Special Organization mission to channel Islamic unity toward the Ottoman war effort. Once again it reflected faith in a few motivated individuals to influence the course of events. Mümtaz was, as we have already seen, Enver's trusted aide-de-camp. Mehmed Âkif had toured German POW camps in Germany in 1914 in order to recruit British prisoners of the Muslim faith. Shaykh Salih featured, as we have seen, as one of the Muslim world VIPs acting to rally his co-religionists against the

Italian invasion of Ottoman Libya. He was among those whom Eşref escorted on their way to Libya. This time armed camel caravans would accompany them.

It is hard to glean many hard facts about this mission other than its part in the Ottoman War Ministry's politics of gesture.[14] The only work dedicated to this voyage, based in part on Eşref's recollections, namely, Cemal Kutay's 1963 volume,[15] is remarkably untroubled by dates or citations. Kutay's almost hagiographic account is frustratingly typical of what has accurately been referred to as the "pseudo-journalistic."[16] What seems clear is that the mission made its way to the Najd, conducted discussions with the Rashidi ruler, exchanged elaborate gifts, many of the animal variety, and returned via Medina and Syria. The mission appears to have been successful in that the Al Rashids did not subsequently deviate from their alliance with Istanbul during the war. Mehmed Âkif, who would later compose the national anthem of the Turkish Republic, commemorated the journey in a poem entitled "Necid Çöllerinden Medine'ye" ("From the deserts of Najd to Medina"). The journey was an arduous one, impeded by desert storms and the frequent lack of water. Emotional volatility was supplied by the news that the travelers received from their families back home. Pervin records that a few weeks before the mission entered the desert she had sent Eşref a telegram telling him that their first-born son had died. Little Sencer was only a few months old. Meanwhile, during the trip Mehmed Âkif learned that his wife had given birth to a boy and that she had named him Tahir. As Pervin put it, "While Eşref was congratulating Âkif, the sensitive Âkif with eyes full of tears consoled Eşref. Thus amidst such bitter and sweet news the caravans made their way into the Najd."[17] After such a range of climactic and emotional trials, the travelers eventually emerged from the desert, reaching the Hijaz railway station in the small town of Al-Muazzam, south-east of Tabuk. Eşref immediately set about attempting to get in touch with Enver in Istanbul. Eventually Eşref and the Ottoman commander spoke to each other. Enver gave Eşref the positive news that the Ottomans had successfully defended the Straits of the Dardanelles from Allied attack.[18] The Çanakkale victory, as it is known in Turkish, was joyfully received by Eşref and their party. With their own mission having played its part in keeping two of the key Arabian leaders on the Ottoman side and now receiving the positive news about the Gallipoli defense, the Ottoman travelers had reason to be optimistic about the course the war was taking.

The Yemen mission

By the late summer of 1916, Eşref was in Istanbul where he accepted an invitation to a fateful meeting with Enver.[19] Enver asked his protégé to come to his villa in Kuruçeşme, just north of Ortaköy, overlooking the Bosphorus. Enver intended to ask Eşref to undertake another dangerous assignment, this time to distant Yemen. Enver explained that the Ottoman army in Yemen had been cut off by the revolt in the Hijaz and was in need of gold, orders, and the boost in morale that would come from knowing that they had not been abandoned. According to Eşref's account, he accepted without hesitation and, thinking on his feet, quickly began to explain how he would approach the task.

It may be that this mission had a secondary motivation, namely, to remove Eşref from the fall-out associated with the arrest of his colleague Yakup Cemil. For it was around this time that this infamous individual, who has been referred to as the wildest, most unpredictable of all the self-sacrificing officers, was arrested on charges of conspiracy to overthrow the Unionist government. Yakup Cemil had begun to think that the government was beholden to him for having shot the Minister of War Nazım Paşa during the raid on the Sublime Porte. He was further frustrated by not being granted the independent command that he thought he deserved.[20] This time, it seems, Yakup Cemil had simply gone too far and now even Enver was unable to save this notorious assassin.

According to Pervin, Eşref was implicated in this affair, perhaps by association, a matter that added to her growing anxiety.[21] Eşref was apparently also under investigation. One day a telegram arrived at Salihli from his colleague Sapancalı Hakkı accusing Eşref of having sent some goods, possibly the ones procured by Hasan Âli, that were found to be inappropriate for the market. Eşref went to Istanbul along with his friend Hüsrev Sami who was also one of Mustafa Kemal's oldest friends.[22] Pervin, increasingly anxious, did her best to piece together the story from the various reports and rumors provided by those coming from the capital who alighted from the Bandırma train. Eventually

she heard that both Eşref and Hüsrev Sami were among the large number said to be arrested and brought before a military tribunal as the
investigation into the plot widened. Weeks passed but there was still no
word from Eşref. Eventually Pervin heard that although her husband
had indeed been arrested and then released, his case was still before a
court martial. Finally she received a brief telegram saying that he
would be back at Salihli that evening. The household was thrilled, and
Pervin especially relieved.

But that evening, before Eşref even entered their house on his
return to Salihli, Pervin's brother saw the news in the paper. He
showed it to Eşref as they climbed the front steps. The news, which
the men were still keeping from Pervin, left them stunned: Yakup
Cemil had been shot by a firing squad. On hearing it, Eşref exclaimed,
"No! This verdict is too much. It should have been restricted to what
was required by law. But this is ugly." Slowly the men's anger abated,
and they referred to their companion as a "poor" and "silly friend."
Finally Pervin learned what had happened from her brother. Was this,
she wondered, the same Yakup Cemil who had been a guest in their
Izmir home only a month before?[23]

Yes, her brother explained, it was that Yakup Cemil. He had been
executed for an attempted coup against the very Unionist government
whose power he had helped to consolidate. Under interrogation, he
apparently named Mustafa Kemal as the person he wanted to replace
Enver.[24] Others in their circle were also affected. Talat Paşa sensed an
opportunity to use the affair to pressure Enver to restrict the influence
of the self-sacrificing officers.[25] As a result, a number of Enver's key
acolytes had to leave Istanbul. Those banished included Mümtaz,
Sapancalı Hakkı, Hüsrev Sami, and Yenibahçeli Nail.

According to Pervin, Eşref was also included in this number. She
explicitly links his being handed the mission to Yemen to the aftermath
of the Yakup Cemil episode. She later learned, she says, that Eşref was
to be spirited away from Istanbul through being given an assignment to
travel secretly to Yemen via a desert route.[26] The network that linked
Enver with Eşref and the rest of the "self-sacrificing officers" showed
once again—as it had for Mustafa Kemal en route to Libya—both its
close-knit and its unsavory sides.

Regardless of the precise reasons behind Eşref's being handed this
mission, it was a dangerous one. Its chief aim was to deliver a shipment

of gold and orders to the Ottoman forces in Yemen. In the course of late Ottoman history the province of Yemen had become a byword for a lost cause. To be assigned there was considered akin to a death sentence, given the province's remoteness and the ferocity of its rebellions. But the so-called "Arab revolt" had rendered the situation even more desperate. British gold and promises of an Arab kingdom after the war had turned the head of the formerly loyal Sharif of Mecca, Husayn ibn Ali. For a time Husayn had played a double game. While it was unclear which way the war was going, Husayn promised but then delayed sending troops for the Ottoman assault on the Suez Canal, hoping to win some autonomy from Istanbul.[27] At the same time he entered into secret negotiations with the British through the infamous Husayn–McMahon correspondence, which was concluded by the beginning of 1916. In return for the promise of an independent Arab state, something the Ottomans could never offer, Husayn pledged support for the Anglo-French war effort.

Thus by the time Eşref began to plan his mission to Yemen Husayn's well-financed rebellion in the name of the Arab people was well advanced. Husayn had been gaining strength to match his outsized ambition—he proclaimed himself King of Arabia in November 1916 despite the fact that he was only one of many important local rulers—and threatening to burst out of the Hijaz and destabilize Ottoman control of southern Syria. Although the extent to which the revolt represented a real threat to Ottoman wartime rule remains a subject of historical debate, the developing nature of the revolt added a degree of unpredictability to Eşref's mission that he scarcely needed. Planning the mission had to allow for considerable flexibility. For example, when Enver asked Eşref how he would handle the mission, Eşref replied that he would take his expeditionary force overland to Damascus and then southwards to a port on the Red Sea from which they would proceed by boat. Indeed, much of the planning and subsequent delays would turn on the procurement, transport, and deployment of a marine engine that was to be fitted into a small, lateen-rigged coastal sailing vessel called a *zambugh*. This, Eşref suggested, would allow the party to avoid British detection as they maneuvered along the coastal reefs and shoals of the Red Sea. But the evolving success of the Sharifian revolt meant that Eşref could not be sure which parts of the Red Sea coast remained in Ottoman hands and which had fallen to the rebels.

Although Eşref's account provides a verbatim record of his meeting with Enver, including Enver's specific questions and Eşref's equally precise answers, it seems clear that the entire mission was marked with a remarkable degree of precariousness and unpredictability. According to Eşref, he came up with the plan on the spot. This hastily concocted plan involved assembling a team of commandos, a naval officer with experience of navigating the reef-lined coast of the Red Sea and a marine engineer, as well as all the supplies and ammunition, including a machine gun, which they would need on their long journey. This would be complicated enough, but the need to plan both a land-based route through the Arabian interior and an alternative nautical route down the Red Sea coastline added a highly problematic dimension to the preparations.

Enver had chosen Eşref because of Eşref's considerable experience among the tribes of Arabia, and because Eşref had proved his loyalty and usefulness to his commander over a period of many years, dating at least as far back as 1908 when Eşref was carrying out assignments for Enver in the Balkans. Enver now assured Eşref that he would have all the funds and powers he would need to carry out the mission. "Do everything that you can and take as much money as you need."[28] Promising that Eşref's men would be rewarded on their safe return, Enver gave him God's blessing and drew the meeting to a close. "As I turned to go," Eşref recalls, "that clean-cut face of his smiled. He had the graciousness to accept my hand in those of his that do not know how to do anything unjust, and when he said a prayer for the success of my mission his eyes filled with tears."[29] Eşref's faith in Enver was remarkably strong, a mixture of shared history and a strong personal bond, fused with a commitment to a mutual religio-patriotic ideal.

Preparations

Eşref set to the task of organizing the expedition. The day after his meeting with Enver, Eşref went first to the War Ministry in Beyazid Square to obtain his official orders, and then to the Finance Ministry to take possession of the large sum of money intended for the army in Yemen. Eşref indicates that this amounted to over a third of a million gold liras, or the equivalent of approximately $1,500,000 in 1917 terms. In connection with such a large amount of money, Eşref felt obliged to comment on his disputed character. "Such large sums as this would occasionally come my way in the course of my duties. There was no hesitation in entrusting so much money to me, a man who has struck many blows against injustice, but who is called by some a bandit. Could not this (opportunity) be called a 'gift from God'?" It would give Eşref the chance to prove his critics wrong. Here was Eşref in microcosm: confidently presenting himself as ready and capable for the most challenging of assignments for his country, while defiant—but painfully aware—of his checkered reputation.

With the money held for safekeeping in the War Ministry, Eşref soon absorbed himself in the practical details of the preparations. He went to see the Ottoman Quartermaster General, İsmail Hakkı Paşa, to begin the process of obtaining the supplies he would need. Among the most important of these were a machine gun and the crew of five trained men under the command of Afyonlu Ethem Efendi who would be in charge of it. Eşref told them to be ready to leave as soon as possible. He then returned to the War Ministry and oversaw the money being packed in crates labeled "EXPLOSIVES" for disguise.[30] His next stop was a visit to his good friend and fellow Circassian Rauf [Orbay] at the Ministry of Marine. Rauf Bey was the captain of the cruiser *Hamidiye*; we have seen how he had become a national hero for his ability to run the Greek embargo during the Balkan Wars. Rauf Bey offered Eşref advice on the Red Sea and recommended two naval officers to be seconded to Eşref's mission. The first of these was Lieutenant Commander Mudanyalı Asım, who had considerable experience of running patrol boats along the Arabian coast. The second was "Tatar" Ali Efendi, a marine engineer and experienced mechanic.[31] Preparations for the sea route were well in hand, and Eşref sent the men in charge of the money and the marine detachment off on the long, slow train journey to Pozantı, a town north-west of Adana astride the rail line running between Anatolia and Syria.

But the question mark that hung over the viability of the final stretch of the Red Sea route to Yemen meant that Eşref had to account for the land route as well. With this in mind he added to his growing force the Istanbul-based representatives of the Yemeni leader Imam Yahya: a man named Shaykh Mazighir, and his companion "Bearded" Ahmet Mücahit (the Holy Warrior). Also considered useful for the prospect of a trek through the desert were a certain Lieutenant Behçet and Eşref's old comrade-in-arms "Gazinocu" (or Casino-keeper) Necati. As usual Eşref's imposing orderly, "Arab" Musa, was an indispensable companion. As he had demonstrated in Western Thrace, Eşref firmly believed in hand-picking his fighting men in preparation for a conflict.

The British, whose path Eşref would soon cross, took note of his activities in the Ottoman capital. The Arab Bureau in Cairo, the outfit responsible for inciting Sharif Husayn's revolt against the Ottoman Empire and keeping it well supplied with guns and gold, noted Eşref's appearance in Istanbul, indicating that, "The brigand Eshref Bey of Salihli, Enver's protégé, has recently been to Constantinople, and has been deputed to enlist a body of irregulars to proceed to Arabia."[32]

When his Istanbul preparations were complete, Eşref returned to Salihli. There he recruited a further thirteen fighters to fill out the ranks of his expeditionary force. He also completed his own personal preparations. These Pervin observed with a mixture of curiosity and dismay. Although he had not told her about his next mission, Pervin could tell from Eşref's provisioning that he was headed back to the desert. He was busy cleaning camel saddles, examining special apparatus for extracting water from desert wells, repairing tents, and selecting a number of his own valuable Arab horses and the fastest riding camels. She understood that the trip he was planning was not simply intended for a change of weather or a flight to summer pasturage but rather a "hard and deadly journey."[33]

Despite her misgivings she raised no outward objection, knowing it would be futile and predicting the response it would provoke: "I knew that he would silence me with words like, 'It's service for the fatherland. I don't want to see you in despair. On the contrary I expect encouragement from you,'" phrases he had used on similar situations to forestall her protests. Once again, they said their farewells.

Not long after their departure from Salihli, things started to go wrong. The first problem was a delay in the delivery of the marine engine. Eşref decided to wait at Karahisar with his core companions. When learning that the engine's arrival would be further delayed, Eşref instructed one of his men to stay behind and wait for it. Eşref and the others proceeded by a combination of rail and automobile to Aleppo.

Arriving at the famous Hotel Baron, Eşref learned that they had narrowly missed his advance party that had just left for Damascus. Two days later Eşref caught up with the rest of his group and they gathered in the Syrian city that as the home of the 4th Army was the center of all Ottoman military operations during the Great War and, it seems, a degree of intrigue.

While lodged in the Damascus Palace hotel, Eşref received an unusual visitor. A Lebanese woman wanted to see him, but Eşref turned her away in irritation because he was caught up in his preparations. The woman insisted that he visit her the following day at the hotel where she said she was staying. Ultimately unable to resist his curiosity, Eşref called on her at her hotel and met with her in the lounge where he was regaled with a tale of woe, including a recently dead husband and the wrongful seizure of all her money. Eşref curtly informed her that she should apply to the Ottoman authorities to help her obtain restitution of her money. When she pleaded that she lacked the proper connections, Eşref offered to intervene on her behalf. Two days later the woman showed up again, but her tone was now very different. She volunteered that she had a lovely singing voice, could play the piano and knew some girls with whom she wanted to give a private party for Eşref in a garden outside the city. Increasingly suspicious, Eşref declined her invitation, citing pressing official business. But the story did not end there. The woman reappeared the next day at Eşref's hotel and affected an accidental meeting, claiming she was there to visit some other people. She asked Eşref to introduce her to the important Ottoman officers, ostensibly to help her recover her lost assets. "Suddenly, I started to suspect the woman," Eşref recalls:

> First she had talked about her affairs… Then she had dropped all of her important affairs and had started to talk about throwing parties for me, about the beauty of her voice… And she had implied that I had time for feasting and debauchery. I thought it all over; I recalled the lessons of history. I remembered that always in time of war such women have been used for espionage.[34]

Deciding to play along in order to look into the matter, Eşref changed his tune and asked her to come to see him the following day. When they met as arranged, she began to speak about Cemal Paşa, the Ottoman commander at Damascus. How many men, she asked, did he command? How many other pashas were serving under him? How many large guns were there in the Ottoman arsenal, etc.? His suspicions confirmed, Eşref changed tack. Saying he had changed his mind and now wanted to prolong his stay in Damascus for a few months, he asked the woman if she would be able to help him find a house. The woman took the bait, volunteering to rent a villa for him and to spare no expense in furnishing it for him, promising to come there with her friends to entertain him. When Eşref asked her about the initial matter of recovering her lost money, she showed little interest, indicating that it could wait until after the war. "Thus this dim-witted woman was postponing until after the war matters which two days before she claimed to be of life or death... I was certain that the woman was a spy in the pay of France" and he informed the local gendarmerie officer.[35] When Eşref left Damascus he heard that she was still being questioned by the police.

He had more pressing matters on his mind. Despite over a week's stay in Damascus, the marine engine had still failed to materialize. Ironically, an even worse prospect was the possibility that they would not need it after all. Eşref heard rumors that the forces of the Sharifian revolt were about to capture the length of the Red Sea coast, which would mean that the expedition would have no port from which to embark on the naval leg of their journey. To keep both options open, Eşref left orders for the troublesome engine to be forwarded on to them as soon as it arrived, and set out with his party from Damascus for the southern Syrian town of Darʻah en route to Medina.

The expeditionary force pressed on. Overcoming distance, bouts of illness, and a thicket of Ottoman red tape, Eşref and his men finally reached the Hijaz. Eşref met with Fahri Paşa (Ömer Fahrettin) at a military outpost outside Medina on 8 October 1916. Fahri Paşa, who had arrived there at the end of May, would prove to be a legendary figure in the waning years of the empire.[36] His defiant defense of Medina against the Sharifian forces, the British, and even orders from Istanbul continued long after both the withdrawal of the Ottoman army from Syria and the signing of the armistice that ended Istanbul's participation in the war. But in 1916 they discussed instead the aims and details of Eşref's Yemen mission. Fahri Paşa was struggling to defend Medina against the encroachments of the revolt and the longer-

standing tradition of Arab tribal raids. He was responsible for considerable successes but simply did not have the forces to keep Medina both
safe and well supplied with such basics as food and fuel for the railway.
Although Eşref's mission was a risky one, Fahri Paşa doubtless saw the
possibilities for improving the Ottoman position in the Hijaz. If the
Ottoman army in Yemen could be revitalized, it might be able to relieve
the pressure on Medina.

Despite the strictures of their surroundings, Eşref continued his
preparations. Firing off telegrams to Damascus, Aleppo, and Pozantı,
Eşref tried again to track the ill-fated marine engine. As we've seen,
Eşref could be a ferocious telegraph writer when he wanted to be. He
was finally able to track down the engine and its crew, receiving word
that they had arrived in Damascus on 10 October. But as soon as one
problem appeared to have been solved, another popped up. The cans
containing the fuel and oil for the pesky engine were discovered to
have been leaking. The Damascus party would have to spend a few
more days sourcing replacements amid the wartime scarcities.
Meanwhile, other headaches appeared. Only one of the two and a half
railway cars needed to transport Eşref's men and equipment from
Damascus to Medina were available. This caused Eşref to take "very
forceful measures," and the detachment arrived on 21 October.
Characteristically, Eşref did not leave it at that but took time to investigate the matter thoroughly, an investigation that uncovered an ener-
vating litany of logistical and bureaucratic shortcomings. The Ottoman
war effort in Syria was, as Cemal Paşa had discovered even before he
arrived in Damascus, hampered by terrible infrastructural and organizational inadequacies.

Finally, the various troubles were overcome. The engine, the fuel,
and the oil were all ready. But a larger problem surfaced: they "no
longer had a coastline from which to embark."[37] The rumors that Eşref
had heard while still in Damascus proved correct: Sharif Husayn's
forces had occupied the coastline. There was nothing for it but to abandon, once and for all, the plan to proceed by sea. Eşref sent Asım Bey,
the naval commander, and "Tatar" Ali, the marine engineer, all the way
back to Istanbul. He could now devote all his attention to the overland,
desert route.

The situation in Medina was increasingly desperate. Fahri Paşa had
succeeded in pushing back the Bedouin forces loyal to Sharif Husayn

that had been closing in on the city, but it seemed as though any ground gained was almost as quickly lost. The Hijaz railroad was short of coal, and the resulting drop in regular service meant that the population was facing shortages of food and basic supplies. They were increasingly isolated from the surrounding territory. Amid these straitened circumstances, Eşref had somehow to prepare his men for an arduous journey into increasingly hostile territory. His plan was to prepare and equip a caravan of sixty men. Because they had a surfeit of rifle grenades but no training in how to use them, Eşref asked for and received permission from Fahri Paşa to allow his men to practice with these weapons. Meanwhile, Eşref added to his numbers by recruiting to his force some men he had known from his previous years in the Hijaz as well as some Yemenis living in Medina.[38] One particular addition to Eşref's force was a shaykh from the Awali tribe who had previously served in Sharif Husayn's entourage but was now imprisoned in Medina. Obtaining Fahri Paşa's permission, Eşref had the man released from jail on the strength of his promise to fight for Eşref. This was a risky proposition because, as Eşref knew well, loyalties in the region could easily shift.

Eşref continued to train the men. Each of the new recruits was given a late-model Mauser rifle, the best available to Ottoman forces at the time. Eşref had had to call in a favor from one of Cemal Paşa's officers in Damascus to take possession of the new Mausers, rifles that were particularly scarce at the time. Those recruited only as camel drivers were given much older versions.

While the men grew accustomed to their weapons, Eşref turned his attention to how he would organize the final stage of the expedition. The plan he came up with was to divide the group into two separate caravans. The idea was for them to keep close enough together to be able to help each other if they got into trouble and to avoid being a larger group that would be more easily seen. The smaller of the two detachments was to be led by the Yemeni Shaykh Muhammad Mazighir, with Sakallı Ahmed assisting him. This force was composed of thirty-six men, of whom twenty were the camel corps troops. This caravan assumed responsibility for the money, which was entrusted to Lieutenant Yusuf Efendi and Eşref's personal orderly, Arap Musa. The money was disguised as ammunition and Eşref had kept its real identity hidden even from his own men. Eşref assumed command of the second, larger caravan, a force of seventy-eight, of whom forty-nine were soldiers. This group contained the machine gun detail.

Just as they were about to depart, Eşref received an order from Cemal Paşa indicating that they should not set off until a certain shaykh from Ibn Saud's men joined them. What was more, almost every military or bureaucratic officer of note in the Hijaz appeared to be against Eşref's mission, thinking it unfeasible and perhaps even impossible. Then came word that Husayn's son Abdallah had left Mecca for the north at the head of a column of 10–15,000 men with the intention of cutting the rail line north of Medina. Eşref drew up a new plan. This envisioned the larger of the two expeditionary caravans leaving Medina before Abdallah's army arrived, feinting in one direction and loitering there in order to draw away the Sharifian scouts. This would enable the second caravan to slip out of Medina undetected. Once it was safely on its way, Eşref's caravan would then turn to the north, towards the oasis of Khaybar, in order to convince the enemy that he was on his way back to the territory of Ibn al-Rashid. Once that second feint was carried out, Eşref would turn south to meet up with the smaller caravan en route to Yemen. A key consideration in this plan was to reduce the risk to the smaller caravan. Eşref's thinking was that as it was composed mostly of Yemenis, it would arouse less suspicion. Letters from Eşref and from Fahri Paşa to Ibn al-Saud were prepared, indicating that they were a group of travelers on their way to Yemen and asking for safe passage. Eşref's caravan, composed largely of Turks, would be in greater danger. As a result, Eşref says, "I decided to turn most of the gold over to Shaykh Mazighir, taking with me only 20,000 liras. This included 5,000 liras of my own money."[39]

Finally, both caravans left Medina in the direction of Jabal Uhud. The smaller caravan slipped away and Eşref set up his camp in a valley between Jabal Uhud and Jabal Sah. They were under the constant watch of the Bedouin and the Sharifian scouts. Eşref's plan seemed to be working: the larger force was attracting all the attention and was reported to be staying put in its camp. They were surrounded on three sides, leaving only a northerly route open. But Eşref's caravan now had to wait for the arrival of Ibn al-Saud's supporter, a certain Abd al-Aziz, as Cemal Paşa had requested. Moreover, Cemal wanted Eşref's detachment to visit Riyadh, the Saudi stronghold, on the way to Yemen. They changed the location of their camp and hunkered down in Bir Uthman to wait. The wait was a long one. Finally after 42 days, Abd al-Aziz arrived with a note from Cemal Paşa. Eşref thought the new arrival was acting suspiciously and that he would offer little benefit to the mission. Abd al-Aziz said he would have to leave secretly after three or four days, and then began criticizing Fahri Paşa, saying that the Paşa had not respected him and did not know anything. Eşref started to make his own investigations and learned that the man was a former adherent of Ibn al-Rashid who had been turned away for some incident and taken up with the main rival to the Rashidis, Ibn al-Saud. As Eşref himself had only recently gone on a mission to Ibn al-Rashid, he wondered how it would appear if he were now seen traveling in the company of one of his enemy's men. The more Eşref thought it through, the worse it looked. So he decided to go it alone.

> Besides, there was another reason for not making a long detour through Riyadh. Because we had spent so much time around Medina my camels had grown weak from lack of good pasturage. I would therefore carry on with my original plan, marching north-east in the direction of Ibn al-Rashid's territory, then turning south-east to the Khaybar oasis.[40]

Eşref only needed to find a pretext to get rid of the unwanted Abd al-Aziz. He announced that he had suddenly been recalled to Istanbul and that they were sending all their supplies north by rail, which did the trick.

Finally, they were on their way. Fahri Paşa sent a telegram to Istanbul on 14 January 1917 indicating that Eşref was on his way to Yemen.[41] But a few days later, when they arrived at the garrison of Abu al-Naam, between Medina and Khaybar, Eşref was forced to hesitate. For Cemal Paşa had sent a telegram to Fahri Paşa suggesting that if Eşref had not yet left Medina, he should leave the treasure there and return to Istanbul. Fahri's covering note indicated that he thought the situation to be dangerous and the distance great but that he should "try to do what is necessary." If Fahri really thought that Eşref would turn back, he was mistaken. "To tell the truth, the idea of turning back in the face of danger did not sit well with me. And besides, I was now well beyond the enemy lines surrounding Medina. My situation was not too perilous. I was convinced that I could perform my duty without too great a risk."[42] Eşref wrote to the Paşa that he was already on his way and that henceforth he would be incommunicado in order to maintain secrecy. For once he was probably glad to be away from the reach of the telegraph lines. There was now no turning back.

The next day they left Abu al-Naam, the last Ottoman outpost, and headed out into the desert. The officer at the fort gave them a camel corps escort on their way out of town. Just as they were about to take their leave, the news came that the Sharifian forces were advancing on Medina. The officer in charge of the outpost said, "God willing, you will succeed. But if I could I would force you to turn back."

It was almost as ominous a sign as the dream Eşref had the same night. After a laborious day's march in the direction of Khaybar, during which the caravan encountered a stretch of terrain too steep for their camels to pass, a "difficult operation" ensued in which the men had to unburden the beasts and pull and drag them up the escarpment. The Bedouin guide kept responding to the Ottoman forces who accomplished what to him seemed an outlandish feat by telling Eşref, "May God be my witness, your men are devils." They spent the night in the shelter of a hill that offered cover to the rear. As a precaution against a surprise attack, Eşref ordered the machine gun to be hauled up to the top of the hill so that that they could sleep under its protection.

But Eşref's sleep was fitful. He finally awoke about two hours before dawn on 12 January 1917 and contemplated his unpleasant but unspecified dream. He gazed out at his men still asleep on the ground and considered their fate and his responsibilities to them and to his mission:

> Leaving their children and loved ones behind in their homeland, they had followed me here to perform their duty to their Fatherland. Now they were sleeping in the empty spaces around Khaybar, an ancient battlefield where the Caliph Ali, the son-in-law and a successor of our prophet Muhammad, had once fought. Who knows what their dreams were, whether they were sad or gay. As they awakened, I could not help wondering how my men had spent their last night.[43]

Several of them had been similarly troubled during the night. Although Eşref claimed that he put no faith in the traditional practice of dream interpretation, many of his men clearly did. One of them was so upset by his nocturnal premonition that he was convinced he would die in service. He thus entrusted Eşref with the upbringing of his children. Another, the Circassian cavalryman Eyüp Berzenc, was equally convinced of the prophecy of his dreams. They foretold an imminent battle. He also told Eşref that he would have to be responsible for raising and educating his child. Eşref felt "an uneasiness and a sadness" in his heart but dismissed such talk as silliness in order to boost the morale of his men.

This proved a difficult task. They were short of water and had to forgo cooking a proper meal. Eşref ordered them to be given tea and hardtack instead. The machine gun had become coated in dust and sand after being exposed all night and now needed to be disassembled and cleaned. Eşref noticed that the Arab guide "was sitting on the ground making strange signs with his finger in the desert sand." When Eşref asked him what he was doing, he averred that he would not be going any farther than their present location because he had consulted the sand and it said that they should stop there. Eşref grew livid. "I don't believe in soothsayers and dreams," which only served to allow the enemy to gain time. "The days when lives were wasted away by soothsaying have long gone. Whatever God has written will happen," he replied and told the guide to be on his way.[44]

The caravan was soon on its way though the men had not had a hot meal or, for many, a sound sleep. Their destination was the oasis of Khaybar. This town is famous in early Islamic history as the site of a battle in 629 in which the Muslim forces defeated its Jewish inhabitants, eventually displacing them and taking over its rich date palm production. Before that it was known as the place where the Prophet's grandfather went to consult a sorceress to ask whether or not he should sacrifice his youngest and favorite son Abdallah, the Prophet's father.[45] Because they were now in enemy territory, Eşref ordered that they adopt "maximum-security measures." So as not to affect their morale, he told them that this was only intended as an exercise, but he knew that this was territory well known for raiding and ambushing by local tribes. He set off in the vanguard while flank guards took up positions on either side of the main caravan. Soon they would leave the cover of the valley through which they were riding. Eşref ordered that horses be brought up from the rear to allow him and his scouts to reconnoiter the terrain ahead.

But soon one of the Bedouin scouts stopped dead in his tracks and signaled the caravan to halt. Running back to Eşref, he said that he had spotted a caravan far ahead in the distance. It was, he reported, a huge caravan, with a host of men that appeared "like locusts."

Eşref asked for the machine gun and all of the camel corps to be brought forward. Climbing a mound, he was able to see the large force at a distance of about 1.5 kilometers, moving from south to north. From their loose formation it appeared that they had not noticed the Ottoman force, which was at that point heading from west to east, and thus on a collision course. The identity and hence the loyalty of this large force was unclear. It could have been forces loyal to either the Sharifian or the Ottoman cause. Eşref took steps to conceal his caravan behind the rock formations and they lay prone in the folds of the terrain. Unfortunately for them, two of the Bedouin now broke off from the main group and advanced towards the hill where Eyüp Berzenc and ten men had deployed to Eşref's right. Eşref's forces were under order not to fire unless absolutely necessary, so as not to reveal their presence. The two outliers eventually stumbled onto Eyüp Bey's men who grabbed one without firing a shot while the other escaped. Shortly Eşref received the British rifle of the captured rider; they were clearly on the side of enemy, well supplied by the British.

Since the escapee would soon alert the main column, Eşref abandoned the caution they had been observing up to that point. He sent a scout to get as much information about the caravan as he could and to report back. The local guides disputed the identity of the large force, but Eşref knew that they had to be part of the "Arab revolt." The size and proximity of the enemy force together with the accidental exposure of his own much smaller group left Eşref feeling sick to his stomach. Soon it became clear that the main force had paused so as to send a force of about 2,000 men to investigate. The battle prophesied in his men's dreams was now imminent.

The battle

When the Meccan cavalry force was about 1 kilometer away, it started its charge. Its 2,000 camels and their riders swept down on the Ottoman expedition. Eşref had organized three small detachments—those of Eşref in the center, the ten-man unit headed by Çallı Hüseyin to the left, and Eyüp Berzenc's ten men ahead and to the right—to take up defensive positions with the main caravan hidden in the ravine to their rear. When the Sharifian cavalry came within 700 meters, Eşref ordered the machine gunners to open fire to immediate effect. But at that moment Eşref detected another attacking formation, this one composed of horse-mounted cavalry bearing down on the Ottoman center from the left. Çallı Hüseyin's men had not opened fire, thinking to let them pass and then to fire on them from behind. But the terrain obstructed the machine gun's firing field, allowing the horse cavalry to bear down unimpeded. Since it was too late to alter the position of the machine gun, Eşref and four men moved out to an exposed mound from where they could direct rifle fire on the onrushing cavalry. Soon Çallı Hüseyin's detachment opened fire. The concentrated fire spread confusion among the charging Arabs. This turned to panic when one of Hüseyin's men launched a rifle grenade. The attacking force broke up, but unwittingly fled to an area that effectively blocked the Ottoman line of retreat. Just when the Ottoman force sought to take advantage of the chaos they had instigated, the machine gun jammed. This allowed the Arab forces to retreat, reorganize in an orderly fashion and resume their frontal attack.[46] Their second advance was more cautious so that when the machine gun was repaired and firing again the Arab cavalry wisely stopped, thus depriving the Ottoman machine gun of a decisive role.

Now the main Sharifian force regrouped in order to encircle the Ottoman detachment. As they began a wide flanking movement, Eşref realized that the only way to survive against such a superior force was to break out before they were surrounded. But their escape route was blocked. Eşref and his aide-de-camp left their advanced position and went back to oversee the retreat of the main caravan. Now they came under a barrage of small arms fire from a group of Meccan cavalrymen who had descended and approached to within 300–400 meters. Finally reaching the main cavalry, Eşref instructed them to attempt a retreat up a parallel valley, avoiding the one by which they had arrived which was now blocked. Ordering that the money they were carrying be buried in the floor of the valley, Eşref began to orchestrate his improvised plans for an orderly retreat. He wanted Eyüp Berzenc's group to retreat first and then cover the retreat of both Çallı Hüseyin's men and the machine gun detachment.

Meanwhile the enemy kept tightening their encirclement. Eşref's aide came rushing up with the news that the valley up which they were hoping to retreat had turned out to be a dead end after only 500 meters. Eşref ordered to have the camels squat in the gorge while the men climbed to positions on the ridgeline to defend the main group. Eşref was hoping to be able to withdraw the machine gun to that gorge, followed by the rest of the men. They would then adopt defensive positions and hope to be able to hold out until nightfall, when they could use the cover of darkness to attempt to break away from the tightening noose. When the machine gun squad began to retreat, the enemy intensified its attack. Despite taking several casualties, referred to by Eşref as "martyrs," they were able to pull back into a tighter defensive position, which one of them defiantly referred to as "fortress Khaybar."[47] Now another hail of rifle fire announced another enemy charge. This was only stopped 50 meters from the Ottoman position by a barrage of rifle and grenade fire. The Sharifian forces were closing in. To the right and front the fighting turned toe to toe, bayonet to bayonet, and dagger to dagger until it resembled, in Eşref's words, "a football match with one team outnumbered a hundred to one."

Time elapsed rapidly. The battle had begun in the morning and already it was afternoon. Eşref and his men could feel the exhaustion gradually overtaking them. They became wooden and reeled like punch-drunk fighters trying to stay on their feet. By now almost all the Ottoman force had been wounded in one way or another. Eşref grabbed the barrel of the machine gun and with the help of another man tried to lift it up to higher ground, but the ridge was quickly taken by the Bedouin. It was now every man for himself.

Eşref could no longer hear any signs of resistance from the direction of Çallı Hüseyin to his left or Eyüp Berzenç to his right. The situation was extremely bleak. Eşref could only take a modicum of pride in the fact that his men had died without surrendering. Only a few were now left alive. These were scattered across the battlefield, holding on wherever possible in groups of two or three. Eşref finally managed to seize a ridge with one or two of the remaining Ottoman soldiers, but the Arab onslaught continued. He suddenly caught sight of one of his men still fighting, firing his rifle from behind a rock and lunging at the approaching enemy with his bayonet. In a rare moment's break he saw Eşref and urged him to mount his horse and make a break for it, promising to cover him with supporting fire. On the other side, Eşref was

17. Eşref's painting of the Khaybar battle. (Source: Eşref's family collection)

urged to do the same thing by another of his men. "My Bey," he said, "mount your horse and save yourself, for God's sake. Don't let these rascals get you!" Eşref saw his horse below, still somehow being held by one of his men. Just then a shout went out: "Sir, they have found the treasure." Eşref looked over and saw a mass of Bedouin swarming on the buried money. The remaining Ottomans fired on the teeming crowd. "Every bullet that smacked into that mound of humanity pierced several bodies. Yet none of them took any notice. Although the corpses were piling up, nothing could stop the looters."[48]

Elsewhere the scenes were equally grim. Eşref heard that one of his men had been disemboweled. Another was hit by a bullet and tumbled headlong from the rocks and fell 5 meters to his death. Eşref and the small group that still surrounded him saw his skull crack open from 50 meters away. Another comrade was so exhausted that he was unable to reload his rifle. He started to foam at the mouth while his eyes rolled from side to side. When Eşref approached to find out why he seemed unable to respond to commands, he found out why. His body had been riddled with bullets and his eyes were glazing over.

Amid the carnage Eşref attempted to summon up one last effort. He ordered his men to try to take a rocky peak and establish a position from which to concentrate fire on the onrushing Bedouin. A lieutenant from the machine gun corps joined them but was hit while trying to carry out Eşref's order. Eşref grabbed the gun and started up the hill himself. But then he noticed that the tripod and the ammunition were missing. Those responsible for carrying them were either dead or missing. Sensing the futility of the situation, Eşref ordered the gun to be destroyed and buried. Increasingly desperate, Eşref tried to move along a goat path with the few men around him. But they again came under heavy fire. One of the men behind him was hit. Another lay writhing on the ground while others tried to bind his wound. Trying to move forward with two remaining comrades, Eşref felt an intense pain in his groin and rolled on the ground.

> The pain in my groin took my breath away. Something was pressing down on my chest. I was blacking out. For a moment I couldn't see around me. I was going stupid and must have fainted.[49]

When he came to, his ears were ringing and he felt nauseated by the pain in his kidney and groin. He tried to summon the strength to move on but could only fire on the looters, rekindling the battle that had begun to die out. Eventually the fighting subsided again when it was almost sunset. Eşref was hit again while trying to move, and he was urged to flee again from their pursuers. Finally they managed to reach a ridge but Eşref was hit yet again and fell to the ground. His thoughts turned to his wife, child, and family. His subordinate İzzet propped him up behind a rock and Eşref tried to keep firing on the enemy. Presently a Meccan Sharif stood over him, urging him to surrender and thus be spared. The Sharif insisted, spurning Eşref's order to flee, and the two men shook hands. İzzet pointed his revolver at the Sharif's head and offered to blow his brains out. Eşref pushed the revolver away, saying that his handshake meant that he had promised to surrender without further struggle.

Aftermath

The battle was over and all they could do was survey the battlefield, looking out for the wounded and fallen. The Bedouin had stripped naked the bodies of many of the dead. Eşref commiserated with the wounded. Suddenly the pain of his wound took over and he had to lie down. One of his men cleared the ground and bound his wounded leg. Lying on the ground, Eşref tried to compose a battlefield report; but finding that his pencil had gone missing during the battle, he gave an oral version to İzzet, instructing him to find his way back to Abu al-Naam and deliver it to the Ottoman forces there. Finally, Eşref agreed to be taken peacefully into the custody of the forces of the revolt. After being allowed to recite a tearful prayer for his fallen men, Eşref was taken by camel to Amir Abdullah's tent. There he was laid out on the ground, seen by a doctor, and given some nourishment. He was treated respectfully but also subjected to some ribbing as to why he had bothered to fight in an Arab country and for the Committee of Union and Progress. He recognized some faces familiar from his earlier years in Arabia under the old regime, when he was known as the Shaykh of the Birds. The next day Eşref and a small detachment, including the doctor who had treated him after the battle, were on the move, with his camel's jerky movements exacerbating the pain of his wounds. They were headed for a place called Waid Ays.

For the forces of the "Arab revolt," Eşref's capture was cause for celebration. On 19 January 1917 T. E. Lawrence was traveling with a large group of Arabs that included Emir Faysal. After dinner he noticed a commotion:

> A breathless slave thrust his head under the flap crying, 'News! news! Sherif Bey is taken'... Feisal was radiant, his eyes swollen with joy, as he jumped up and shouted to me through the voices, 'Abdullah has captured Eshref Bey'. Then I knew how big and good the event was.[50]

For the man who would become known as "Lawrence of Arabia" and to whom Eşref would often be compared, Eşref's capture represented a turning point in the campaign against the Ottomans in Arabia. The camp's inhabitants celebrated until the early hours of the morning.

In Egypt, the British officers in the Arab Bureau were equally enthusiastic. Eşref was a known figure among the Arab Bureau staff. They considered him a formidable if unscrupulous adversary. It should be remembered that one of the key figures in Cairo was Wyndham Deedes, who had faced off against Eşref and his brother Selim Sami during his secondment to the Ottoman gendarmerie in Izmir during 1912–13.

Eşref's capture was the first piece of news in the weekly summary provided by the *Arab Bulletin* in late January 1917. "Sidi Abdullah, on the 13th of the month, surprised an armed convoy under the notorious Turkish bravo, Eshref Bey of Salihli somewhere near Kheibar."[51]

The information that they gleaned from interrogating some of Eşref's men confirms the main details of his account. For example, the fact that he traveled from Abu al-Naam, that his smaller caravan was carrying 20,000 liras, and that a machine gun had been captured among other smaller arms were all included in the British intelligence summary. Cairo also believed that the capture of Eşref and his men was a sign that the tide was turning against the Ottomans. The second news item was that Ottoman forces were pulling back from more offensive positions. It was clear that British military intelligence in Cairo believed the two events to be related, as cause and effect. In other words, the failure of Eşref's mission meant that the Ottoman forces stranded in the south would be unable to assist in putting pressure on the rebels, leaving them free to concentrate of their offensive to the north without having to worry about an attack from the rear.

Back in Arabia, Eşref's capture emboldened the Arab revolt. Abdallah posted a triumphant report of the attack on the railway to embarrass Fahri Paşa and sent Eşref's ornate gold Meccan dagger as a trophy to Faysal, who in turn gave it to Colonel C. E. Wilson, the British agent at Jeddah.[52] Eşref himself was also considered as a kind of living trophy. Soon he would be handed over to the financiers and weapons suppliers of the revolt, the British military delegation in Egypt.

Overlooked amid the aftermath of the battle at Khaybar and its significance for the revolt was the fact that the other, smaller caravan apparently did make it all the way to Yemen. The British accounts focus on the 20,000 Ottoman liras but, as we have seen, Eşref had sent the much larger share of the treasure with the smaller detachment when they separated on leaving Medina. According to Eşref, this larger amount, which had been entrusted to Lieutenant Yusuf and Eşref's orderly "Arap" Musa, was successfully delivered to Yemen, thanks in part to the protection offered by Ibn al-Saud, a rival to the Meccan rebels. When Musa handed the gold to the Ottoman commander in Yemen, Ali Said Paşa, Musa had tears in his eyes, saying, "Thank God we have succeeded and delivered the treasure. But we have allowed Eşref Bey to fall into the hands of the enemy!"[53]

7

PRISONER OF WAR

For a restless and combative character like Eşref, captivity was hard to bear. Surrender meant the loss of his freedom of maneuver, forced inactivity, and the countless indignities that came with becoming the prisoner of his former enemies. First in Arabia, then in Cairo, and finally on Malta where he would remain a Prisoner of War for almost three years, Eşref would struggle with an uncharacteristically long period of inactivity. This would allow his wounds to heal but would require that he take up a range of pursuits to pass the time. Yet even in forced idleness, Eşref was affected by the Great War's international reach.

The global dimension of the Great War and the advent of total war were reflected in its regimes of captivity. An estimated 6.6 to 8.4 million men were imprisoned during the conflict.[1] Prisoners taken into custody by the Allies in such remote places as Indonesia, East Africa and, in Eşref's case, the deserts of Arabia found themselves incarcerated in what were to them equally remote locations such as the Isle of Man, New South Wales, British Columbia, Barbados, Trinidad, Burma, India, Egypt, and Malta.[2] On the opposite side of the conflict, captives from North Africa, India, Canada, the United States, France, the British Isles, Russia, etc. were concentrated in over 300 camps across Germany. The juxtapositions that these prisons produced are one of the more fascinating but little studied dimensions of the war. The mixing of nationalities, political ideologies, ethnicities, relations, languages, cus-

toms, and social classes that ensued was mind-boggling. While it is difficult to determine how this globalizing experience affected Eşref in
specific detail, it seems clear that it simultanesously opened his hori-
zons and gave him occasion to reflect on his own country and his role
in its history.

Eşref's period of captivity began on 13 January 1917. In the days after
his capture at Khaybar, Eşref would be led from place to place around the
Hijaz as he tried to make sense of his newly diminished status. At first he
could think of little beyond the searing pain of his wounds. Sharif
Husayn's son Amir Abdullah sent a detachment to collect Eşref and the
few men who remained in his unit. They delivered Abdullah's greetings
and placed Eşref on a camel. The physical movement required in mounting the animal caused his pain to spike. Worse for his spirit was the fact
that the raised position afforded him a better view of the battlefield carnage. "To the right and left of the ridges behind us lay our dead. All had
been completely stripped. The Arabs had removed even their under-
wear."[3] Eşref asked that their departure be delayed so that he could recite
the Fatihah, the first *surah* of the Qur'an, for the souls of his dead comrades. The Bedouin partially restored their status in Eşref's eyes by joining in the prayer "as if they were not the ones who had killed my comrades" and by praising their bravery.

After a few tearful words for the fallen men, the traveling party
moved on to Abdullah's headquarters where the "Shaykh of the Birds"
received a hearty welcome. In the midst of a conversation in which
Abdullah questioned Eşref about his contacts in Arabia and the reason
why he had come to fight there, and in which the Amir attempted a
somewhat disingenuous distinction between the revolt's animosity
towards the Committee of Union and Progress and their loyalty to the
Ottoman government, Eşref was given medical treatment. A doctor
named Isa tended his wounds while a slave cradled his head between
his knees. He was given butter and honey to restore his strength and a
burnoose to replace his torn and bloody uniform, the only item that
was left of his scavenged wardrobe.

The next day they moved on to a place named Hadiyah. The necessary full day's ride on a jerky camel caused Eşref's wounds to flare up
again. Initially treated in the desert under less than optimal conditions,
they were now becoming seriously inflamed. Dr Isa produced first one

and then a second shot of morphine to try to help Eşref sleep that night, but he was in too much pain. By the next morning his leg had swollen dangerously "to twice its normal size and was like a chunk of wood from the hip down."[4] His thigh had turned black, and purple patches had appeared on his calf. Unluckily for him they had two further days of travel ahead of them. Abdullah tried to help by seeing that Eşref was well attended to, but there was little that could be done where they were. Meanwhile the Amir informed Eşref that he was going to post a note on a telegraph pole to announce that Eşref was his "guest." Word would then spread of Eşref's captivity. This induced Eşref to request to write to Fahri Paşa in Medina, informing him of the battle and his subsequent capture and asking him to notify Eşref's family that he had been wounded and captured.[5] As we shall see, it would take a while for the news to reach Pervin and the rest of their family.

Meanwhile the party carried on with their journey. At one point Eşref's pain was so intense that he fainted when dismounting from his camel. The doctor tried to change his bandages, causing Eşref to strike out at him because of the searing pain.

Throughout this ordeal, Eşref was predictably keen to defend his sense of honor. When one of the Bedouin in the escort party showed him a sign of disrespect, Eşref was quick to put him in his place. Abdullah reassured Eşref that he would punish any of his men who attempted to abuse him, even ordering the doctor to shoot anyone who showed him the least discourtesy.[6] But it was Eşref's leg that was the greater concern. Abdullah himself inspected the wound. Increasingly worried that he would need it amputated to save his life, Eşref asked Abdullah to send for an Ottoman military surgeon to perform the operation. Abdullah advised patience, arguing that all the travel had made the wound worse and that it would soon start to heal. The next day Abdullah ordered that a kind of couch be rigged up on top of Eşref's camel so that he could lie flat as they continued their journey. This reduced the jarring effect of the camel's pitching movement, as it kept the weight off of his leg. As they proceeded, Abdullah lamented Eşref's wound and the battle that inflicted it. Why had he not surrendered his much smaller force without a shot, the Amir asked. Eşref responded with the soldierly line that he could easily have done so but that would have left him with an "eternal wound" stemming from his failure to do his duty. Then, amazingly, Adbullah offered to turn his army over to Eşref's command if he would join the revolt. Predictably, Eşref declined, explaining:

> Abdullah Bey, I am a Muslim. I do not criticize your nationalist movement because it is not something that concerns me. But above everything else, I have a profession. I am a soldier. Even though I have been captured, how can I command an army today that I fought against yesterday? I came here as an enemy, and I want to leave as an enemy. Please realize this. Even if I were convinced that you were in the right, I could not accept your offer because I would not want to stain my profession. I really am very much chagrinned by your offer.[7]

Embarrassed, Abdullah apologized and galloped off. In the coming days Eşref would re-encounter a number of his former colleagues of Arab origin who had decided to throw in their lot with the rebels. These would prove uncomfortable reunions.

More discussion about the state of Eşref's leg followed. All who had seen it agreed that it would need to be amputated. Abdullah eventually relented and agreed to allow Eşref to write to Medina to summon the Ottoman military surgeon to perform the operation. But at this point a practitioner of local medical practice appeared. This Bedouin "doctor," as Eşref pointedly and skeptically refers to him in his account, which often seems to channel the spirit of "Ottoman Orientalism" in its disdain for the tribesmen,[8] tried to examine the reluctant patient. But "because of his filthy fingernails and the strange object of undetermined purpose that he was holding in his hand," Eşref refused, informing Abdullah that he had no confidence in this man. The Amir demurred. Just then another tribal commander named Sharif Shakir, the Amir of Taif, arrived on the scene. During the battle he had led the cavalry charge against Eşref's men. Now he inspected his wound and offered to treat it himself, promising to stop the procedure if Eşref felt no relief from the pain within five minutes. Sharif Shakir also pledged not to use any drugs or touch, much less poke around in, the suppurating wound. Mystified but clearly intrigued, Eşref asked for an explanation. Sharif Shakir indicated that he would treat Eşref's leg with heat. He had dug a large hole in the ground, about 9 inches deep, which would serve as a kind of miniature sweat lodge or desert sauna. They would build a fire and heat some large stones. These would be placed under Eşref's leg, which would be covered by a blanket. They would then pour water over the heated stones, generating steam that would penetrate the wounded limb. Shakir promised that several applications of this technique would result in immediate relief.

Eşref somewhat reluctantly agreed. When he was stripped from the waist down and positioned over the hole, Sharif Shakir personally directed the operation. Within five minutes, Eşref felt his leg begin to soften and the blood begin to flow. "For the first time in days the sweet sleep that I had yearned for gradually overwhelmed me." Eventually he asked that the procedure be expanded so as to treat his whole leg. The hole was duly enlarged and filled with the heated rocks. Within half an hour Eşref found that he was pain-free. The leg was perspiring and the wound emitting "an astonishing flow of yellowish-purple pus." After the procedure Eşref slept for fourteen hours straight.[9]

When he came to, he found himself hungry for the first time in days. Thanks to the local cure he had escaped the surgeon's knife and was on the mend. That had the dubious merit of meaning that he was better able to deal with the reality of his situation. Problems large and small were readily apparent. For instance, some of Eşref's freed slaves had been taken as booty by the Bedouin and were now in jeopardy of being re-enslaved. These men, of Sudanese origin, had seemingly joined Eşref's men when he was gathering together his expedition in Medina. Four of six survived the battle, one with heavy wounds to his chest. After their status became known, their wounds were treated and they were grateful to be reunited with Eşref, whom they considered their benefactor. Looking after his remaining men took Eşref's mind off his own troubles and seemed to restore his sense of purpose and duty.

After a number of other incidents, conversations about the battle, and interactions with the Bedouin, the caravan moved on. Eventually, it was time for Eşref to be sent on his way to the British. Abdullah wrote a letter to the British urging them to take good care of Eşref, and pledging to pay for his stay at a comfortable house in Cairo. Abdullah organized a caravan to escort Eşref to the Red Sea port of Yanbu, where he would be handed over to the British. They reached Yanbu on 28 January 1917, but soon learned that the plans had changed. Sharif Husayn had sent word to his governor at Yanbu that Eşref should be sent instead to Jiddah and then on to Mecca, advising him of Eşref's reputation for escape but ordering them to take good care of this "important person."

They were put on board a British ship at Yanbu and taken to Rabigh, a port town to the south that had become a headquarters for Sharif Husayn's forces. Colonel Cyril Wilson, the British representative in the Hijaz, was there, as were a number of former Ottoman officers of Arab origin who had joined the revolt: men such as Nuri Bey, who had fought with Eşref at Derne in Libya but would become better known as Nuri al-Said, the future Prime Minister of Iraq; and the former Ottoman Special Operations officer Aziz Ali Bey al-Masri, a Circassian who would go on to play a prominent role in the Egyptian military.

When Eşref's ship called at Rabigh, Colonel Wilson and Aziz Ali Bey came on board to call on Eşref; but the reunion with Aziz Ali was an awkward one. The two men had fought together in Libya against the Italians but now found themselves on opposing sides of a much larger conflict. Aziz Ali had been court martialed for allegedly deserting his command in Libya after most of the Ottoman officers had pulled out to fight in the Balkan Wars, and for appropriating funds from the Ottoman military. Although at first condemned to death, his sentence was commuted, probably because Istanbul feared making a martyr out of a popular and experienced Arab officer.

As soon as Aziz Ali saw Eşref, he embraced him affectionately and wished him a speedy recovery. Eşref recoiled: "I was astounded and saddened by the spectacle. Yesterday Aziz Ali Bey was serving in our army to defend our country. Today he was fighting on the opposite side. Amazing!"[10] Eşref found himself alone with Aziz Ali, now promoted to the rank of "Paşa" and "Minister of War" for forces of Husayn's revolt, and lamenting the circumstances of their meeting. He said that he feared that Eşref considered him a traitor but that he was still ready to shed tears of blood for the Turkish nation. In light of Eşref's subsequent experience of changing sides during the subsequent "National Forces" period, it is interesting to see how harshly Eşref judged his former colleague's switch from Ottoman officer to rebel "Paşa."

Word then came from Sharif Husayn that Eşref was to be sent on by ship to Jiddah. Coming ashore at this bustling port, Eşref was given something close to a hero's welcome, complete with a delegation of notables and military honors. After a meal, a courtesy call from Husayn himself, and a chance to order new clothes, Eşref and his men were sent on their way to Mecca.[11] Little did he know that the tone of his reception would change for the worse when he reached the birthplace of Islam. Outside the city the the travelers were met by a detachment that included Husayn's aide-de-camp, named Rauf al-Kubaysi. He also was a former Ottoman army officer and erstwhile classmate of Eşref's at the Military Academy, where, Eşref remembers, he was "notorious for his shabby appearance." Now they met on a very different footing. "I had thought that this dirty creature was there to welcome me. But it turned out that he had come only to give me a taste of the stupid and shameful treatment I was to receive at the hands of the Sharif."[12]

Ever sensitive to being slighted or shown any sign of disrespect, Eşref would now have considerable cause for complaint. For starters he considered the Kurdish mercenaries sent to guard him an affront to his dignity. He compared "these characterless mercenary scoundrels" most unfavorably with their countrymen who had fought with the Ottoman army against the British or against the Russians in Iran. Then they tried to separate Eşref and his men but, Eşref proudly declares, the latter refused to go anywhere "without our Bey."

Worse treatment was to come. When they arrived in Mecca they were paraded through the town. Eşref knew of the degrading treatment given to some Ottoman officers taken to Mecca in the past, some only a few days earlier, but began to fear the worst when asked to remove the robe that he had been given in the name of Sharif Husayn. He was about to be paraded around the town, but what really irked Eşref was that he and his men were being humiliated in front of the women and children of Mecca:

> The last pathetic survivors of a detachment that had fought against 15,000 men, we passed in front of them to stimulate their national pride and to proclaim the royal greatness of the Sharif. I was sure that humanity was crying over that spectacle as I wept in my mind and heart.[13]

After many more indignities, some attempts to placate him, two audiences with Sharif Husayn, and an attempted roadside ambush, Eşref was taken back to Jiddah. Arriving in the city on 16 February 1917, Eşref appeared before a certain Colonel Watson whose behavior, he thought, was "as cold as his face, his manners nonexistent."[14] For Eşref this meeting marked the beginning of a long and frequently unpleasant encounter with British military authority. Watson kept Eşref standing to attention, pretending not to know who he was or where he had been and questioning him in a stand-offish manner that Eşref considered beneath his dignity. Eşref responded by replicating the rudeness and arrogance shown to him. In this small way Eşref managed to show a little of his old fighting spirit before he limped out of the colonel's office.

Two days later he was put on board the armored British troop ship *Hardinge*, a vessel that like Eşref himself had seen service in the Suez Canal,[15] and had been riding at anchor in the Jiddah harbor. Cue more rude behavior from the commanding officer and another furious reaction from Eşref when he was unceremoniously thrown into the ship's storeroom beside a few other imprisoned Ottoman officers. Under the watchful gaze of an armed guard with fixed bayonets, Eşref fumed. Then he lost control, insulting and gesturing at the guards. He was placed in solitary confinement near the galley, and photographed from various angles by "every Englishman who had a camera." Eşref the erstwhile photographer had become the object of British souvenir-seekers. He objected strenuously to being presented as a trophy before his enemies.

Finally the ship sailed and made its way to Rabigh, where all prisoners were transferred to HMS *Lama*. On this armed boarding steamer, a converted civilian liner,[16] Eşref was confined in a tiny cell, but the intervention of Aziz Ali "Paşa" allowed him the freedom of the ship if he promised not to cause trouble or try to escape. With his dignity thus at least partially restored, Eşref whiled away the hours talking with Aziz Ali as the ship proceeded to Suez. Shown the courtesy of an escort when disembarking, Eşref was transferred to a train which took them to a desert encampment where the prisoners' wounds were treated during a week's stay in a hastily erected and poorly equipped field hospital; he was then sent on to Cairo, which he reached on 2 March.

Cairo

Eşref's stay in the Egyptian capital intensified his contacts with British officialdom. These encounters undermined his admiration of Britain and its empire. Poor food, more signs of disrespect and "scandalous treatment," including being granted no privacy when going to the toilet, caused him to reconsider:[17]

We used to think of the English as having the greatest respect for laws and tradition. Yet I have come across many individual Englishmen who have punched and kicked the law in such a manner that I am now convinced that their respect for law and their vaunted humanity are pretty flimsy and useful only for show. I swear by God that after the treatment I had received at their hands, my love for the British turned to hatred.[18]

Eşref's brushes with the British military bureaucracy continued. He defiantly registered his complaints about the treatment he and his men had received at various stages since his capture at Khaybar. Presently he was questioned about his own activities at the time of the Armenian massacres of 1915–16, which had by now become well-known outside the empire. Asked where he was during the massacres, Eşref replied that that was not the business of his interrogator but rather an internal Ottoman affair. "But," he added, "I will tell you one thing. I am a member of the armed forces, and I fight against other armed forces. Even in the smoke of battle I am a servant of humanity, and I serve it with all my energy." To this the offical asked Eşref if he simply carried out the orders he was given. Eşref responded that his interlocutor had the wrong idea. "Still," he added chillingly, "if our government had given orders for the massacre of the Armenians, not one of them would remain alive today in Istanbul or in all of Anatolia."[19] He followed this up with an argument that would be taken up again and again in future polemics: "Why are there incidents in Zeytun, Urfa or Van [areas with a large Armenian population before the war], while nothing happens in Konya, Izmir and Bursa where there are also Armenians?" It was, Eşref added, only in areas "where Armenians have fired at us that they have had to face the consequences of their actions."

The British interrogator also pumped Eşref for information about his friend and colleague Mümtaz and Eşref's brother Selim Sami. British intelligence seems to have believed, incorrectly, that Mümtaz had a sister who lived in Egypt, but in asking about those two they were on the right track in the sense that they were both, along with Eşref, key figures in Enver Paşa's special forces network.

Eşref the prisoner showed more signs of irritability, and his wounds were causing him difficulty sleeping. One night his sleep was interrupted by the sounds of a concert. The booming drum particularly disturbed him. He abandoned his attempt to sleep and instead "got out of bed in a great temper and started to curse the whole world." The contrast between those like him who had suffered as a result of the war and were still suffering and those who were blithely undisturbed by the conflict was especially irksome. "These rascals safe at the rear were enjoying life… A curse on such people… I was trying to find something to vent my anger on, but with four walls around me, I was like an animal in a cage at a fair."[20] The theme of Eşref as a captive beast seems to have struck a particularly emotive chord. "I felt like a lion or a tiger whose lady tamer cracks her whip from outside the cage. Those people were out there enjoying life and I was stuck here, eating my heart out." Revenge was not far from his thoughts: "I could not help thinking what those poor lions and tigers might do if they encountered one of those whip-wielding lady animal trainers out in the desert or in the jungle. Wouldn't they pounce on her [literally 'wet her bare thighs'] and show her a thing or two!" After a lot of pacing back and forth in his cell and uncharacteristically resorting to chain smoking to relieve his suffering, Eşref eventually thought of his family and gradually forgot his plight.

More interactions with British officialdom followed, some of which Eşref found insulting and some he deemed courteous, showing him the respect and "chivalrous treatment" he felt he deserved. He learned that he was due to be sent to the British POW camp on Malta. Then he learned that his departure was inexplicably going to be delayed. At one point he admitted to be suffering from nerves and depression; at another he says that he even comtemplated suicide more than once. He was singled out for worse treatment than his fellow prisoners and resented the special treatment intensely.

Among the many meetings he had during this low period, one encounter stands out. After several years Eşref now came face to face with Wyndham Deedes, the British officer who had chased Eşref and Sami when they were brigands in the Izmir region before the war. Now, in Cairo, he entered Eşref's cell as part of a group of officers allegedly investigating Eşref's complaints about his treatment. Eşref didn't recognize him at first, but took note of his excellent Turkish and his position as a staff officer and a major. After clearing up a misunderstanding, Eşref complained that he had been more honorably treated by the Bedouin of the Hijaz than by the British. He asked to know why he was being treated differently from his fellow Ottoman prisoners.

Deedes, still anonymous in Eşref's eyes, laughed and said, "But, Eşref Bey, are you the same as they are?" Eşref asked him what he meant, to which Deedes replied, "There aren't ten Eşref Beys in Turkey. There is only one, and because he is unique we have to treat him in a special way." Again Eşref asked for an explanation, saying that he did not understand this kind of talk, although doubtless his *amour propre* was not displeased with the recognition. Deedes responded that he knew Eşref very well by reputation. Startled, Eşref asked him what he knew. Deedes said, "I have lived in the province of Izmir and have heard about you. I also know about your brother Sami Bey. You rebelled against the government and took to arms. I have had some dealings with you in the past." When prompted, Deedes added that he believed he and Eşref had clashed. Eşref was astounded. How, he wondered, could he have tangled with a British officer? Eşref became defensive, saying that he did not want to talk about long-ago incidents and that since 1908 he had worked within the law, adding grandly: "Service and self-sacrifice for its sake constitute my duty now."

Deedes countered by saying that he had served with the Ottoman gendarmes and remembered incidents that took place after the Constitution had been restored. Deedes said he knew that Eşref had clashed with government forces in the region of Sarayköy and had been responsible for incidents in Ödemiş as well. Eşref explained that these had been Sami's doing and a result of family feuds. Sami, he added, had since been pardoned and was now serving his country. Eşref clearly respected Deedes and even admitted that he liked the man. Deedes put Eşref's mind at ease by telling him that he could stay in Cairo for three more weeks. Eşref asked for some improvement in his treatment, namely that his door be allowed to remain open so he could get some air, and that his guards treat him with respect. Deedes promised those things and volunteered to help Eşref with any letters he wanted sent. Eşref thanked him for this and asked for a cable to be sent to the War Ministry in Istanbul informing them that he was a prisoner of war. Again Deedes agreed to send it via the auspices of the still neutral Americans. They parted on good terms, with Deedes even offering to make Eşref's cell more comfortable. Eşref was so pleased with the newly courteous treatment that he asked for Deedes' address so that one day he could return the favor and send a present to him in England.

Seeing Deedes' name, Eşref recognized him at last. His view of the English had been positively revised. The favors duly materialized and Eşref, though still a prisoner, felt better about the world. Coming face to face with Deedes had made a big difference for Eşref, in terms of both his treatment and his peace of mind.

On 14 April 1917 he and a fellow prisoner, an Egyptian who rather comically refused to believe he was actually being taken away from Cairo, were escorted under armed guard, again with fixed bayonets, to the Cairo station where they boarded a train for Alexandria. They were then taken by ambulance to the port where they boarded the Egyptian steamship *Abbasia*. On deck Eşref watched with amusement as his fellow passengers inflated life-preservers in case German submarines penetrated the protection of the British destroyers that were guarding the liner and hit it with a torpedo. Characteristically he defied instructions to put on, much less inflate, the safety device, saying that he would have plenty of time if the ship were attacked. The threat from the U-boats was real enough but, despite one or two alarms and with a naval escort for the last segment of the passage, the ship reached Malta on 18 April.

Malta, way station of empire

Although the island had once unsuccessfully been besieged by the Ottomans in 1565, they had never managed to capture it. The island had been a British possession since 1800, when the Napoleonic forces who had seized it on their way to Egypt surrendered in the face of Lord Nelson's blockade. With the opening of the Suez Canal the island, and particularly its accommodating harbors and dockyards, grew in importance to Britain, eventually becoming the headquarters of the empire's Mediterranean fleet. Ships, both civilian and military, traveling through the Canal frequently stopped at Malta to refuel. During the First World War the island became known as the "nurse of the Mediterranean" to the British, due to its military hospital. Its strategic importance was reflected in the men chosen to serve as its governor. For almost all the war years that man was Paul Methuen.

Methuen, or Field Marshal Paul Sanford Methuen, 3rd Baron Methuen, GCB, GCMB, GCVO, DL to give him his full nomenclatural due, was a living embodiment of the British Empire. With his moustache and erect bearing he might have rivaled Lord Kitchener for his place on the famous wartime recruiting poster. An Eton graduate, he rose quickly in the British army, seeing action in Africa during the Third Anglo-Ashanti war in what would later become Ghana, followed by postings to Ireland and Berlin as military attaché. He was in Egypt during the battle of Tel el-Kebir, which was the turning point in the British suppression of the Urabi Rebellion of 1882 and the eventual colonization of Egypt. He commanded a division during the Boer Wars, where he was captured after his horse fell on him. Promoted to field marshal in 1911, he was involved in training British forces to fight on the western front in the Great War. In 1915, at the age of seventy and already retired, he accepted the post of governor and commander-in-chief of Malta. By the war's end he would have transformed British operations on the island, with priority given to expanding its hospital capacity.[21] He was also in charge of running the POW camps on Malta. It was into Methuen's domain that Eşref now entered.

On arriving on the Malta quayside Eşref asked if there would be any fellow Ottomans where he was headed. He was glad to hear that there were. He was less pleased when he saw the imposing fortress to which he was taken. Looking up, he saw a sprawling complex dominating the Cottonera hill across the Grand Harbor from Valetta. The defensive complex incorporated the Verdala Barracks and the ramparts of the St Clement Retrenchment, massive fortifications dating back in part to the seventeenth century but modernized by the British in the 1880s. The British had first used the island to intern POWs during the Boer Wars when they infamously invented the concentration camp, and the practice was revived during World War I when it accommodated German, Austrian, Italian, Egyptian, and Ottoman prisoners in a vast camp. The large fortress complex proved particularly conducive to the highly secretive POW operation. Even the arrow slits had recently been boarded up, a result of the British discovery that certain German prisoners were recording the movements of the British navy from the fortress's vantage point and inexplicably relaying the information back to Germany. The forbidding appearance of the fort gave Eşref a foreboding sense of the confinement in store for him. If he had known then that it would last for three years, he would have been even more distressed.

But life as a prisoner on Malta was much better for officers than enlisted men. Class distinctions ensured that the latter were mostly kept in row after row of canvas tents. According to one observer, these were just about tolerable in fair weather (although they must have been very hot in the baking summer sun) but were disastrous in the frequent wind storms when the tents had a habit of breaking loose. During rainy periods the tents were often flooded with ankle-deep water.[22] The officers lived in much better conditions: the more important officers, Eşref included, were housed in the Verdala Barracks.

Eşref's fellow prisoners made a fascinating and diverse cast of characters. A mix of military men and civilian internees, old and young—one Ottoman prisoner was only twelve years old[23]—and coming from an almost dizzying variety of professional, religious, and class backgrounds, these men found themselves brought together by the war. They included Germans, Austrians, Swiss, Hungarians, Italians, Greeks, Bulgarians, and Ottomans. The Ottoman contingent alone comprised a great many ethnic backgrounds, including Turks, Greeks, Armenians, Circassians, and Arabs. The Egyptians were particularly well represented, given the strength of their national movement, spurred on by the strong British military presence in their country.

The Maltese prisoners were a particularly polyglot group: among their number a German prince rubbed shoulders with an Italian artist, a Triestan composer, a South Tyrolean photographer, a ship surgeon, a German chemist, several Arab nationalists, mainly Egyptians,[24] including Saad Zaghlul, and Ottomans of various stripe,[25] including both a member of the Ottoman dynasty and the CUP activist and later Turkish MP Eyüb Sabri (Akgöl).[26] The German officers were the more famous and included Franz Joseph Prince von Hohenzollern, Karl Dönitz, who arrived after Eşref in 1918 and who conceived of the idea of the German navy "wolf packs" while on Malta and later briefly succeeded Hitler at the end of World War II, and Karl Friedrich Max von Müller, captain of the mythical German raider *Emden* which torpedoed many Allied ships before finally being captured off the coast of Indonesia.[27] There was also a contingent of German prisoners from East Africa. It is hard to know how close Eşref became with the Germans, but a watercolor portrait of the prince, first cousin of the Kaiser, remains in the family of Eşref's descendants to this day.

Life in camp

Despite the forced inactivity and isolation, many aspects of prison life on Malta were quite comfortable, even cushy, at least for the officers. Reports on the conditions differ considerably, depending on the source. The German prince found it mostly "tolerable,"[28] while a report prepared by the Swedish consul for the Ottoman government gives a more favorable view of the conditions of the "Turkish" prisoners during the period when Eşref was among them. There were a little over 300 Ottoman POWs on the island, the vast majority civilians and only forty-two officers. Most of these were accommodated in the barracks, while almost a third lived under canvas. They were either given "ample space for promenade and sport," frequently being allowed to take excursions outside the walls, or they were crammed together in their tents. In the summer they were taken to the sea to swim.[29] Their lodgings were deemed to be comfortable, with each man—there were no female prisoners—given an iron trestle bed with two horsehair mattresses, cushions, sheets, blankets, a washstand, and a chair. The prisoners had access to recreation rooms for reading, writing, and games, and had their own mosque where the Imam of the Ottoman consulate in Malta, also an internee, conducted services.

Conditions had apparently improved during the course of the war in response to prisoner complaints. Prince Franz Joseph complained bitterly about the state of the camp after his arrival in late 1914. At that time the inmates had little room to exercise, the post was badly delayed, and the state of the latrines was "scandalous."[30] A manifesto that catalogued the various injustices the prisoners faced was presented to the authorities, and things appear to have improved as a result. For example, a fort was demolished to open space for "gardens, huts and green things." As we shall see, Eşref benefited from these new features of prison life and was somehow given the run of a cabin in the newly opened green areas in the St Clement's camp.

One interesting provision in the camp arrangements concerned labor. The report says that "Servants, waiters, cooks, etc., are selected by the prisoners from the lower class of fellow prisoners and are paid by the employers by agreement." The "employers" were the upper class of prisoners. This division and the labor relations that both reflected and underpinned it were the source of many problems, some involving Eşref, as we shall see. But he certainly seems to have benefited from the system and had at least one servant during his stay. Otherwise, the conditions were quite amenable. The prisoners were not required to carry out manual labor, only to keep their quarters clean and tidy. The consul deemed the sanitary arrangments to be "perfect" and health care to be "excellent" and free of charge, with medics on staff day and night.

Clothing was provided and food rations were ample—although the Germans had registered earlier complaints. Prisoners could expect an allotment of sugar, rice, tea, salt, pepper, marmalade, cheese, milk, meat, bread, fresh vegetables, lentils, and beans, all of the "best quality." Beer, wine, and spirits were made available. Prisoners could supplement their diet from camp stores. Ten per cent of the takings of the stores were returned to the prisoners for spending money, to buy beer (up to two pints per day) and tobacco, for example. Wine and spirits were also available as long as the privilege was not abused.

Access to the outside world, always an important consideration for Eşref, was possible through the POW mail system. Special stationery was provided to the prisoners who knew that their correspondence would be monitored by military censors. Limits were placed on the quantity of outgoing post—two letters of 200 words or six postcards per week—but incoming mail was unlimited. They were not allowed to receive newspapers through the post but were permitted those supplied by the camp authorities. The camp library offered books in French, Italian, and German but none in Arabic or Turkish. The prisoners were allowed to receive money from overseas as well as parcels of clothing and food. The consul's remarkably favorable report concluded by saying that apart from some complaints "of no importance," the prisoners were satisfied with their treatment in the camp.[31]

Other views of camp life differed. The Hohenzollern prince severely criticized some of the British officers tasked with distributing the money sent to the prisoners from overseas, accusing them of charging exorbitant commissions and cheating on the rate of exchange. Elsewhere he condemned the Maltese guards for extracting bribes from the inmates.[32] He found the delays in the post caused by censorship highly ennervating. He only wanted to write to his sister, the Queen of Portugal. Eşref and Pervin would also encounter friction due to the long delays to their letters, as we shall see. Others were more positive. One Arab prisoner remembered his internee days very fondly, saying that "The best days of my unfortunate days were the days of my imprisonment. One meets with all types of people, but the British know how to treat people." An Istanbul Greek was more equivocal, revealing perhaps his Anglophile leanings: "Paradox: to be held prisoner and to love the ones who hold you captive."[33]

Whatever they thought of their treatment, it is clear that the prisoners managed to form strong bonds of affection during their confinement. They had access to a Gestetner printing device and published a largely satrical camp newspaper called Camp *Nachrichten*. They also formed groups who worked together to produce theatrical evenings and musical entertainment—the crew of the *Emden* was particularly well represented. Perhaps because of the presence of a number of photographers and artists in their number, the prisoners prepared books to commemorate their time together on Malta.[34] Eşref's collection contains a large number of photographs of the many individuals and the groups they formed in captivity, produced as souvenirs to mark their time together.[35] One gets the clear impression that individually and collectively the men had decided to make the best of a bad situation. Looking at camp life in the round it is clear that it was on the whole not a miserable experience for most of the prisoners interned there, particularly once conditions had improved. Unlike their fellow POWs in the British internment camp in Ahmednagar, India, for example, those on Malta appear to have been untroubled by rats and the bubonic plague they carried. It was certainly not a gulag.

How Eşref fit into the camp's regime is not always clear, but it seems that he soon asserted himself as the leader of the Ottoman prisoners. As we shall see, this may have produced some disgruntlement among the others. He was certainly among the better treated of the inmates.[36] Photographs show him lounging in what look like tennis whites with a newspaper in his hand. One shows him fitted out in a British military uniform to replace his lost Ottoman garb. His room in the Verdala Barracks was furnished with a carpet on the floor and a bed that was covered by an ample mosquito netting descending from a carved wooden fixture emblazoned with the Ottoman star and crescent, an arrangement far more elaborate than the standard steel-framed bed mentioned in the report. His room appears to have benefited from a balcony on which he kept plants and an aquarium and watched and fed the birds.

When Eşref got up from that bed in the morning he had quite a few options to pass his time, most of them pleasurable. He would often go to what he referred to as his "*köşk*," a one-storey hut or summerhouse in the recently improved St Clement's camp. This was a simple but comfortable building set amid trees and fitted with all the modern conveniences, even a bath. A photograph shows it to be surrounded by plants and covered in vines, with Eşref's attendant standing in the foreground.[37] "I would go there every day at 9.00 and would pass the time relaxing and conversing with my friends." Sometimes he would converse with a religious figure named Mevlana Mahmud Hüseyni. These religious and political discus-

18. Eşref's room on Malta. (Source: EK papers)

sions helped keep his mind off things. At other times Eşref and his companions would play the gramophone and Eşref would either make music, practice carpentry, or draw. Eşref used his time on Malta to work on his memoirs—there is a picture of him seated while working on them, surrounded by large volumes—and to learn to paint. His teacher was an Italian painter, possibly of the post-Scapigliatura school, named either Litta or Ditta Dellastora.[38] He taught Eşref in both watercolor and oil painting technique; there are photographs showing them out sketching and socializing together during their Malta days. Some of his teacher's paintings remain in his family's possession today, including the large oil painting of the battle at Khaybar.

Prison stories

Like prisoners everywhere, Eşref wrote extensively while imprisoned on Malta. Many of the sections of his memoir that survive from this period are fairly long and contain detailed and at times rambling stories. In the activities they describe and in the way they are written they reflect the abundance of time he had at his disposal. They are thus in direct contrast with the short, telegraphic mode of much of Eşref's earlier writing, especially when he was at the front. With a few exceptions these stories serve to paint Eşref in a positive light. His concern with his own status, strength, eloquence, or wisdom is again paramount.

One such story turns on his physical strength. As he recuperated, Eşref began to busy himself with sport. Fitting perhaps for Eşref's sometime pugilistic personality, one of his prison pastimes was boxing. When he recovered his strength, he devoted himself to training. One day he received a visit from his fellow prisoner Kazım the Pharmacist. Kazım was a Turk who had practiced his profession for many years in Cairo but had been sent to Malta after the outbreak of the war because he was considered a Unionist and an Ottoman agent. Kazım dropped by when Eşref was working out and he took an interest in Eşref's boxing gloves.[39] He thought the swollen gloves were like puff pastry, so padded that they could not possibly deliver a painful strike. Eşref told him that they did not prevent a powerful blow. Kazım then told Eşref to punch him. Eşref at first refused, saying it was going to hurt. Eventually he obliged, but only with the slowest of blows. Then Kazım

215

asked for a harder, faster punch. Again Eşref delivered. Finally, Kazım asked for his hardest shot. Eşref hit him with all of his considerable force on the fleshy part of his shoulder. The blow left Kazım stuttering and reeling until he keeled over on the bed, holding his arm. Eşref ran to his side. They wondered if Kazım had suffered a broken bone. German prisoners came running and asked if they should call an ambulance. Kazım shook his head to indicate no. A German pharmacist examined the arm and confirmed that nothing had been broken. Kazım explained that it was all his fault; he had, he said, expected a punch like puff pastry but got a sledgehammer instead. Eşref referred to the incident as unforgettable, no doubt taking pride in the power of his punch and relief that it had all ended without lasting damage.

Not all aspects of camp life were so jovial, however. Occasionally there were real fights between the prisoners. Eşref recalls a grisly story of one conflict that ended in murder,[40] and an incident which, Eşref writes, brought shame on all the Ottoman prisoners.

Another incident reflected the broader ethnic tensions of the empire itself. This event occurred during Eşref's early days on the island. Eşref had become friendly with an Ottoman Greek from Alaşehir named Yanko. Since Alaşehir was very close to Salihli, Yanko considered that he and Eşref shared a place of origin, an important link in the Ottoman world. When Yanko suddenly died of a heart attack, Eşref helped with plans for the funeral, arranging for his body to be enbalmed and paying for the casket.[41] He attended the funeral at the head of a group of about ten Muslim prisoners, joined by many of the approximately thirty Greek inmates and members of the local Maltese Greek community. The priest was a member of the latter group. Eşref mentions that there were tensions among the Greeks, separating those who were loyal to the Ottoman government and those who were inclined toward the nationalist Venizelist camp and therefore pro-British. The prisoners who were allowed to attend the funeral were under strict orders not to socialize with members of the local Greek community, a restriction which angered the priest.

During the ceremony Eşref was astonished to see that some of the Greek inmates were starting to chuckle and then laugh while prayers were being recited. Eşref turned to the man standing next to him, who was from Crete, and asked him what was so funny. He was told that if he knew, he would be laughing too, so he thought it might be because some of the Greeks from the prison seemed to be out of synch with the liturgical Greek the priest was chanting. Soon Eşref realized what was going on and start to chuckle. From his time in Izmir he knew enough Greek to make out that the inmates were using the cover of the liturgical chanting to communicate with the priest, complaining of the conditions in the camp. "They squeeeeezed ussssss intooo tennnts," they chanted to the singsong rhythm of the service and asked him to intercede on their behalf with the Ottoman government. While swinging his censer so as to send plumes of incense among the mourners, the priest responded in kind, singing, "If Gooood willlllls, donnnnn't worrrry at allllll." He indicated that he would write to the government by the first available post. The chuckling continued but the mourners left the graveyard with tears in their eyes.

The next day Eşref was called to the camp commander's office and asked what had happened at the funeral. One of those present had apparently informed on the fraternization cum chanting and the commander wanted to ask Eşref as a neutral observer for his take on what had transpired. Interestingly, Eşref responded by giving very little away. He claimed that he did not know Greek but told the commander that it had seemed to him that the Greek inmates were laughing at the inability of one of their number's attempts to assist the priest. A week later Eşref learned that the British had expelled the priest from the island.[42] Considering that Eşref had played a role in expelling some of the Greeks' co-religionists from the region around Izmir, he maintained surprisingly close relations with those imprisoned on Malta, perhaps because he felt they were on the same side in the conflict.

The same cannot be said of an episode involving Eşref, two fellow Muslim internees, and an Armenian prisoner, an incident that ended with all four men being hauled before a court martial. In Eşref's telling, the incident happened like this. This Armenian somehow ended up on Malta and was housed as part of a group that was segregated from the other prison camps and prohibited from visiting them. One day when Eşref was walking along he noticed a group of such prisoners standing in the road. When one of them—who turned out to be the Armenian—saw Eşref, he started cursing the Ottoman sultan and Islam. Eşref presumed the man was crazy and stopped. Eşref noticed two of "his" Muslim Ottoman officers, one called "Blond" Mustafa and the other "Crazy" Hasan,[43] standing nearby and asked them who the man was. They told Eşref that he was always acting like this. He had, they said, painted curses against the sultan on his tent (which the British had erased) and was always yelling. The swearing continued and Eşref asked the man angrily what he was saying.

At this point, things took a turn toward violence. The two Muslim officers asked Eşref what they should do. Eşref replied by saying, "Hit the scoundrel." Later the court martial would turn on the signifcance of these words, especially the word "hit" which carries a wide semantic range in Turkish. Acting on their interpretation of Eşref's order, the men promptly drew their knives and started to stab the Armenian. Heedless to commands to stop, they inflicted much harm.

In the ensuing investigation a British guard testified that from a distance he had seen Eşref stop and speak violently to the two Turkish officers who then drew their knives and attacked the man. The Armenian was taken to hospital and only emerged twenty days later. The action proceeded to the military tribunal where a case was opened against Eşref and the two assailants. The day of the trial came and the men were brought before the military judge, a British general. Eşref sat apart from the other two men and refused a lawyer, saying that he was was not on trial for the crime itself but only at the trial because he was an accessory to the crime (*Davada ancak kasıt olabilirim*). He said he therefore had no need of a lawyer but would answer questions on his own. The other two indicated that Eşref would serve as their representative. Here Eşref indicates that before the Armenian was brought in he asked the judge to beware that the "somewhat crazy" victim was liable to act provocatively. Since Eşref and the others were angry, he told the judge that he did not want to be provoked into losing control and acting disrespectfully before the court. The judge ordered that respect be shown all around. (In Eşref's account, he naturally depicts himself as being in charge of the whole scene, including the judge!)

Soon they got down to proceedings. The Armenian claimant was brought in, gave his greetings to the court and then turned to greet Eşref, literally offering his peace. Eşref responded by saying, "And peace be upon you, my son." The judge immediately turned to the translator and asked him what Eşref had said, making notes of the answer he received. The questioning proceeded. In a rather longwinded declamation, Eşref asked the judge to consider how he would feel if a soldier from, say, India or anywhere else insulted his king and his religion and even made "textual assaults" (referring to the slogans painted on the Amenian's tent). "Wouldn't that drive you mad," Eşref posited, "and wouldn't you be unable to remain calm in the face of such provocation, especially after the pain and wrecked nerves of years of war? I don't deny it," he continued. "I'm speaking the truth. When I said 'Hit him,' I certainly didn't mean for him to be stabbed with a knife." Here Eşref described the full range of meanings that could be implied in the term "hit," particularly in military terms. It could mean to punch, hit with a stick, a dagger, a bullet, a sword, or even an artillery shell. He was ready to accept the sentence of the court, however heavy or light, whether he was to be imprisoned for a matter or days, weeks, or months; but he would do the same thing again on the day of his release, if similarly provoked. To do otherwise would be cowardly, he declaimed, and banged his fist defiantly on the courtroom table, causing it to tremble. Seeing the judge calmly move to keep the inkwell from spilling, Eşref realized that he had breached the decorum of the court. He then launched into a speech about the differences in temperament between those who lived in northern and southern climes, contrasting the inherent difference between the "ice-like" English and the "volcano-like" Mediterraneans. Interestingly, he included a sketch of his arm coming down on the table in the notebook where he recorded his account of this incident, even recording the measurements of the court table and indicating the seating plan.

Eventually the Armenian got his chance to speak. He referred to the death of his parents at the hands of "these Turks" during the war, and said that at Zeytun 40–50,000 Armenians had been killed. He said that the British had brought him to Malta and asked, "What else was I supposed to do? Certainly I was going to take my revenge by swearing."

The Armenian, who is never named, repeated the charge that these Turks had killed his parents. The judge wanted clarification: was it these very men sitting in the courtroom who had done it? The Armenian responded by saying, "Is there any distinction between this one and that one? Turks killed them, Turks. That means that these ones killed them." Eşref couldn't contain himself. Without being given the floor, he interjected that this was nonsense, the man was either ignorant of what he was saying or crazy. The judge reprimanded him for speaking out of turn and urged patience. The judge asked the victim how could it be that on Malta an Ottoman officer like Eşref could treat him so respectfully, greeting him properly and calling him "my son." The judge concluded the proceedings and asked Eşref to step outside.

Soon the court reached its verdict. The judge said that the court believed Eşref's words to have incited the unfortunate events; but taking into consideration his senior position and his being a gentleman, the court had reduced his sentence to a two-month period of being confined to barracks (although he would cotinue to be able to bathe in the sea) with no access to correspondence. Meanwhile the perpetrators Mustafa and Hasan were each given fourteen days' confinement in the military prison. As for the Armenian, he was to be transferred to a paid-work unit with British forces on the French front.

As we might expect, Eşref took exception to being cut off from postal connection to the outside world. He protested that this would victimize his innocent family. Why, he asked, should they be punished? The judge indicated that he would be able to write to them to explain that he would be out of touch for the two-month period. Eşref objected, asking how he could possibly explain that he was going to be doubly imprisoned when his family already knew he was incarcerated on Malta and thought he was being well looked after. He asked that he be confined to barracks for six months if necessary, but not to be cut off from news from his family. Eşref officially registered his protest and says that the papers went all the way to Lord Methuen. Finally he was absolved of all complicity in the crime. The perpetrators had their sentences reduced to one week in the military prison. Eşref drew the lesson that his banging his fist on the table was crucial to explaining the difference in temperament between "northern" and "southern" climes and that this explanation was vital, in his eyes at least, to making sure that justice was done.

Eşref's role in the Malta prison camp may have had another shady aspect. He was accused of misappropriating a sum of money that had been sent for the Ottoman prisoners by the Ottoman Red Crescent Society in 1918.[44] This allegation was made by some of the prisoners and reported to the Ottoman Foreign Ministry by the Swiss Embassy.

(The Swiss had taken over from the Americans as the neutral diplomatic liaison once the US entered the war.) We have no other details about his accusation, the identities of those who made it or, more importantly, whether or not there was any truth to the matter, but at the very least it suggests that there may have been discontent with Eşref's position at the forefront of the Ottoman POWs. It is possible that his more recent arrival and his strong personality caused tensions among the Ottoman prisoners. If so, such problems are not visible in the photographs that show the Ottoman internees in the island's Muslim cemetery at Marsa. Eşref was responsible for repairing an older Ottoman cemetery and for erecting a monument in memory of the Ottoman soldiers who died in captivity during the Great War. A plaque on the site today refers to Eşref as the "Commander of the Muslim warriors on Malta" and to the fallen Ottomans as martyrs (şehid).[45] Later on, Eşref's daughters would visit the island and pay a visit to the monument. He kept photographs of the monument in his papers until the end of his life.[46]

Letters from home

While Eşref grew accustomed to life on Malta, back in Salihli Pervin had yet to hear about her husband's fate. Eşref's earlier attempts to send word of his capture had proved fruitless. She now got the news in the worst possible manner. One day she heard the harsh voice of Çerkes Reşid,[47] whom she loathed, interrupting the calm of the walled surroundings of their Salihli estate. Up the road leading to the main house from one of the lower buildings came a man screaming at the top of his lungs. The harsh voice, which Pervin likened to the screeching of an owl, was calling out for Eşref's mother. When Pervin heard it she thought he sounded almost gleeful.[48] The news he conveyed was that Eşref was alive but had been wounded in four places, captured, treated, and sent by the English to the island of Malta. Pervin was too stunned to respond, but Eşref's mother delivered a stern rebuke to Reşid, asking him if he was reveling in their misfortune and wanted to give them apoplexy. Reşid, oblivious to this censure, carried on, explaining what Malta was and how the Boers had been imprisoned there as POWs for as long as twenty years. Pervin's mother-in-law finally cut him off, saying "Curse your tongue. You have truly gone crazy, you ungrateful man. May God punish you. Get away from here." Pervin, almost paralyzed with fear, simply fainted. She would never forgive Reşid for his behavior that day, not to mention a long list of other sins.[49]

Soon, however, she began to come to terms with her husband's captivity. One of the ways she coped with his absence was through her correspondence with Eşref. He and Pervin wrote to each other regularly, although there were occasionally gaps of as long as two or three months between letters, seemingly due to the military censorship and the problems associated with delivering mail between empires at war. At times the resulting gaps in correspondence caused them anxiety. At one point when Eşref had waited a long time for a letter, his tone got rather sharp. "It's been two months. I haven't received a single letter. Above all, I can't accept that I haven't received a letter or any news from Feridun. What is this? In the letters you sent before you began by speaking of Feridun. Now it seems you have forgotten. Don't forget!"[50] Their letters reflect the trials of a difficult period, one that truly tested their relationship. The letters are full of the ups and downs of daily life—their health, Feridun's cleverness, the relatives visiting Pervin's family, problems with the post, etc.—but were occasionally punctuated by more momentous events.

At first Pervin was able to remain almost unfailingly positive, despite her husband's internment. Although from time to time the letters she wrote to Eşref on Malta contained news that would worry any mother, as for example when Feridun required medical attention, Pervin was determined to put the most positive face on things. She frequently reassured Eşref by saying that he need not worry about them back in Salihli. She also encouraged young Feridun to write to his father, and these are some of the most touching aspects of the family's correspondence. For example, Feridun wrote to thank his father for a present that Eşref had sent. The child described his excitement at opening the box by the light of a lamp, finding three riding whips inside, showing them to everyone in the room and even dreaming about them at night.[51] For her part, Pervin promised to follow Eşref's advice that she be patient—he had told her that he might be in Malta for as long as a year, a considerable underestimate, as it turned out. She vowed to develop a heart as strong as that of a man's.[52]

But maintaining such stoicism proved difficult for Pervin, especially as she had to keep up a brave front to the others in their family. Sometimes she described the beautiful scenery around Salihli for Eşref, as she did in late summer of 1918 when she wrote of the red and green mountains across the way from the nearby natural springs. She described how she and her relatives had gone bathing for four days and reported that they were enjoying wonderful weather. Yet such pleasant scenes seemed only to magnify the misfortune of their separation. The fact that he was not there to share it with her, she said, made her painfully sad.[53]

She took consolation wherever she could find it. She received support from Enver in the form of reports on Eşref's health, and was eternally grateful that the empire's highest-ranking officer found time to think of her and her family in the midst of running the war. She also says that Enver offered to send her 4,000 gold lira to compensate for Eşref's absence. She thanked him but said that instead of money all she wanted was Eşref's safe return.[54] The years of Eşref's captivity passed slowly for Pervin. She took solace in religion, praying continually for Eşref's safety, giving alms and asking for God's intercession by reciting special verses of the Qur'an.

Still, Pervin longed for the end of the war and Eşref's return. In her letters she returned again and again to the theme of their joyous reunion. But days and months passed without any sign of that happy event drawing closer. Occasionally she heard reports that the Ottoman prisoners on Malta were being allowed to return home, but these proved premature. In April of 1919 she wrote to Eşref that she had read in the newspapers that peace had been agreed and that the prospect that she would soon "embrace her happiness once again" caused her endless joy. She expressed the hope that he would be home by Ramadan, which coincided with June that year.[55] Actually, hostilities had ended with the Mudros Armistice, signed at the end of October 1918. Pervin seems to be referring to the prospect of a peace treaty. This was famously delayed and eventually overtaken by events. The Treaty of Sèvres was signed in August 1920 but soon rendered obsolete by two simultaneous events, the Greek invasion of Izmir on 19 May 1919 and Mustafa Kemal's landing in Samsun to organize resistance in the Anatolian interior. The conflict that would come about between the

Greek army and the Muslim "nationalist" forces would end with a Turkish victory and the establishment of the Turkish Republic, fundamentally reshaping the region. It would completely upend Eşref and Pervin's life all over again.

Meanwhile, the longer the political situation remained unresolved and her husband remained on Malta, the more it proved difficult for Pervin to maintain her brave stance. Even though she had learned to live with his disappearances before this, the worry and anxiety caused by Eşref's extended absence gradually began to take its toll. In February she mentions that she is grieving and that the disappointment of having her hopes raised by the prospect of his return led her to stop writing for a while. In April she was again optimistic about his swift return from Malta. But two weeks later Eşref received a letter from a female relative named Seza Hanım explaining that Pervin had been unwell to the point of not being able to leave her room. She said that Pervin could not live without him and hoped that all of this would be forgotten when he returned. She enclosed a brief note from Pervin in which she said that she was unwell and unable to write more than a few words, and those only in a shaky hand, saying, "I kiss a million times your sweet eyes which I love and to which I have devoted myself for years."[56] By August she said that she had been to see a specialist doctor about her nerves and been prescribed medicine and exercise.[57] In November she adopted a more business-like tone, but still mentioned that she was suffering from nerves and sleeplessness.

As time went on, the unsettled political situation began to shape Pervin's letters. She treated the Allied occupation of Istanbul as a catastrophe, but worse was to come. After the Greek occupation of Izmir, she heard about atrocities being carried out against the Muslim population. In June 1919 Istanbul received reports that a Greek gang had raided Eşref's Salihli estate and stolen valuable animals.[58] Eventually, as we shall see, Pervin and her household would go to stay with relatives in Istanbul to avoid the increasingly difficult circumstances in the countryside. Pervin wrote that she felt like a nightingale in a golden cage that pines for its home. At some points Pervin in Istanbul was not even able to communicate with her family; she was cut off from Salihli, Söke, and Bandırma. Meanwhile, to make matters worse, the political and military situation was changing. She did not know it at the time but eventually things would get much worse for Pervin and her family.

Signs of the coming trauma are easier to identify in retrospect. Even relatively early in the course of the war, the Ottoman high command began to make preparations for defeat and a resistance campaign against a likely Allied occupation of the remaining Ottoman lands. A key aspect of this planning was the stockpiling of weapons in secret locations. Unsurprisingly, given Eşref's links with Enver and the "self-sacrificing officers," his farm at Salihili was chosen as one such spot.[59] Once the Greeks invaded, efforts to turn these plans into reality began in earnest. As the menfolk began to turn their estate at Salihli into a center of resistance, Pervin made plans to leave. Her mother-in-law suggested that they go first to Bandırma on the coast to stay with her father. From there they could more easily move on to Istanbul, where they could stay with her brother or Eşref's uncle Hacı Murad. They quickly prepared their departure. Escorted by an armed guard that included Eşref's younger brothers Ahmed and Mekkî, they made their way to Akhisar. On the road they met Eşref's friend and colleague Rauf (Orbay) who was heading to Salihli to establish his headquarters. In fact, he was in such a hurry to make preparations that he suggested a quicker route for the travelers to take. He wanted Eşref's brothers to return as soon as possible. When they returned he would ask Eşref's younger brother Ahmed, aged only sixteen, to hand over to Çerkes Edhem the arms and money that had been hidden there.[60] These supplies were plentiful; Eşref's estate had been turned into a secret military depot stocked with rifles, machine guns (both heavy and light), cartridges, German and British bombs, military clothing, sidearms, canteens—in short, enough to kit out two divisions from head to toe.[61] This equipment, together with a substantial amount of gold, would be instrumental in the furnishing of Edhem's Mobile Forces,[62] a body that would play a crucial role in the subsequent period both for and against the "nationalists."

A kidnapping

But even before the war was over and while Eşref was still on Malta, his involvement with Edhem and his brother Reşid took an ominous turn. An event occurred in Izmir that served as a reminder of Eşref's outlaw connections, links that would complicate his future. On

12 February 1919 a carriage containing four armed Circassians drove up in front of Miss Florence's school in Izmir just as the children were getting out for the afternoon.[63] The men beckoned to one of the children, the son of Governor Rahmi. Young Alparslan climbed into the carriage and was driven away at speed. The kidnappers had horses waiting for them outside town. There they abandoned the carriage for their mounts and rode away up into the mountains, eventually taking the child to Eşref's farm at Salihli.[64] The kidnappers, with Reşid in the lead, demanded the huge ransom of 250,000 gold liras.[65]

Eşref's role in the affair is, perhaps predictably, somewhat curious. As we have seen, Eşref and Rahmi were two men with strong CUP connections but rather different approaches, for example toward the Greek Orthodox population around Izmir (although at least one British official thought that Rahmi was playing a double game). Edhem and Reşid apparently saw the kidnapping as a way of exacting revenge on their rival Rahmi, who had thwarted their band's attempt to extract a large sum from a Dutch expatriate family in the province.[66] Eşref says that while he was initially in favor of the ransom idea, he changed his mind at the time of the armistice, preferring to postpone the plot. With the armistice and the government in Istanbul weak because of Allied occupation, he said that all patriotic Ottomans would need to band together to protect the Izmir region, particularly in light of mainland Greece's designs on it. Eşref preferred to blame the kidnapping on Edhem's older brother Reşid, accusing him of having run wild in Eşref's absence and, as he described him during the episode when he "cracked up" in Western Thrace, likening him to an unbridled mule that had broken loose and galloped away out of control.[67]

By chance Pervin learned about the kidnapping and tried to take matters into her own hands. Pervin was well disposed to Rahmi because he had passed her news about Eşref during the war. As a mother, she was immediately sympathetic to Rahmi's wife, Nimet Hanım. Luckily, the child was unharmed. He was induced to write a note to his family to indicate that he was in good health. He wrote it in English, perhaps to prove that it was not forged. The note was poorly transliterated and read, "I am gut will but you imalet saend the mainey" (I am good but will you immediately send the money).[68] Pervin demanded that the child be brought to her so that she could take him to his tearful mother. Nimet had gone to plead with Reşid for his return, abjectly throwing herself at his feet. Reşid haughtily rebuffed her, saying that Rahmi should come instead and blaming the kidnapping on his brother Edhem. Edhem, who was always depicted much more favorably in Eşref and Pervin's accounts, was going to bring the child to Pervin. Reşid got wind of this plan, however, and spirited the boy away to another hiding place. Pervin then announced that she would pay the ransom and managed to reduce the fee from 250,000 to 50,000 liras, which she paid out of her own money simply to put an end to the terrible ordeal.[69]

Despite the fact that Eşref was in Malta, he knew that his name was mixed up in this sordid affair. He blamed Reşid first and foremost for his generally good-for-nothing behavior and for fanning the flames by provoking the incident when Eşref wanted it postponed. Interestingly, he also criticized Pervin for getting involved. He said that unlike women of later times—he was writing in the early 1960s—the women of those days did not have the experience to deal with such a situation. Pervin was only twenty-three years old at the time, he said, and should not have spoken out so openly.[70] Edhem was subsequently protected from prosecution over his role in the kidnapping when his brother Reşid intervened with Rauf (Orbay).

Getting back to the action

With events in the now-defeated Ottoman Empire gathering pace, Eşref was keen to return. But his position as the leader of the Ottoman POWs on Malta meant that he would have to wait until his colleagues were repatriated. This was a slow process. It certainly seemed that way to Pervin, who found it difficult to wait out his last few months of captivity. Pervin says that the Ottoman government of Damat Ferid Paşa requested that Eşref be repatriated sooner for political reasons. But the British refused on the grounds that Eşref had been an active combatant captured in battle and the established repatriation practice would have to be followed. Worse still, he would be returned as an internee to be handed over to the Ottoman authorities. The government had changed since the armistice and the new government, under Allied occupation, was busy arresting CUP activists. It seemed that

Eşref would be unable to walk free when he returned to Ottoman soil. With this uncertainty hanging over her husband's repatriation, Pervin finally received the news that Eşref was coming home. A hospital ship was bringing him to Istanbul. British records indicate that he was released from his Maltese confinement on 2 January 1920. They also state that he was released in error and that he was "a most dangerous and criminal propagandist."[71]

8

RETURN, "NATIONAL STRUGGLE," AND EXILE

Escape on the quayside

As Eşref's ship approached Istanbul harbor, Pervin joyfully prepared for their long-awaited reunion. But on board the hospital transport carrying him from Malta, Eşref got wind of the fact that on arrival he would simply be transferred to Ottoman control and remain a prisoner. On the eve of their disembarkation he learned that the prisoners would be counted off one by one and taken into custody. It would be a heavily controlled operation under armed guard. His fellow passenger Blond Mustafa, with whom he had been in the court martial on Malta for the stabbing of the Armenian, informed Eşref that he was under surveillance. The time came to disembark. With Blond Mustafa acting as a look-out and a heavy rainstorm reducing visibility and creating confusion on deck, Eşref waited for the moment when he would be out of sight of the guards. He then slipped through a side door and made his way toward the ship's bow. Finding the deck empty, Eşref seized his chance. Sliding along one of the thick hawsers that tied the ship to the shore, Eşref flung himself onto the quay. The rain had forced everyone from the quayside to the awnings of the wharf buildings or to pack themselves into a coffeehouse. Eşref tried to blend into this crowd, but a bystander asked him why he had risked his life by coming down the hawser. "It's a shortcut," he joked and headed out into the streets of Karaköy.[1]

Soaked to his skin, Eşref eventually made his way to Pervin and the other relatives who had waited so long for his return. They spent a joyfully sleepless night in celebration. But like so many others before it, this reunion was to be short-lived. In the morning Eşref realized that he would not be able to stay long. After what Pervin referred to as his quayside "gymnastics," Eşref knew that the authorities would be looking for him. He would have to leave the house of his relatives, where the law could easily find him, and move quickly. He set off to find Yenibahçeli Şükrü and was soon in contact with him and other leading members of an organization called Karakol (The Guard) that carried on the line of clandestine operations begun by the "self-sacrificing officers" of the Special Organization. The Karakol was only the latest incarnation of this paramilitary genealogy. Pervin records that Eşref met up with various members of this underground Karakol organization in clandestine night-time gatherings in various locations around the city, almost right under the nose of the government and the Allies.

The Istanbul to which Eşref returned in early 1920 was a very different city from the one he had left when he embarked on the ill-fated mission to Arabia. Indeed, the Great War had inflicted momentous changes on the Ottoman Empire as a whole. Stripped of all of its provinces in the Arab lands, the empire retained only Anatolia, Istanbul, and part of Thrace. The Paris peace talks dragged on, but the lines of a post-war settlement were largely clear: the Allies had divided Anatolia into spheres of influence, leaving very little in Ottoman Muslim control, despite Istanbul's objections. The victors were increasingly visible in the capital, even before their full military occupation occurred in March 1920. Given the devastation of the war—the Ottoman Empire had experienced levels of mortality due to fighting, disease, and dislocation that made what the Western participants experienced seem almost like child's play—there was little appetite for renewed hostilities. And yet a growing proportion of the Muslim population felt increasing despair about the new dispensation.

The period following the armistice of late October 1918 was one of great uncertainty in Istanbul. The departure in early November of the main Unionist leaders, including Enver, Cemal, Talat, Dr Nazım, and Bahaddin Şakir, on a German submarine bound for the Crimea en route to Odessa and Berlin created a power vacuum.[2] As in the other defeated empires of Austria–Hungary and Germany, a search for a new form of political legitimacy now took place in the remaining Ottoman lands.[3] As the nationalists consolidated power in Anatolia, the political scene in Istanbul comprised various factions, including the Palace, the Liberals, the Allied powers, and the remaining Unionists who, despite being tainted by their wartime actions, still represented a formidable force. With Sultan Mehmed VI (Vahdettin) attempting to reassert lost sultanic authority by appeasing the Allies, the Liberals trying to reorganize under Damad Ferid Paşa, and the Unionists determined to hold on to their power base against Liberal-inspired purges, it was a tumultuous period. The last Ottoman parliament met in January 1920, reflecting the power of the nationalists in Anatolia where, in the absence of Enver and the senior Unionist leadership, Mustafa Kemal was quickly consolidating his control;[4] they adopted the Misak-i Millî (the so-called "National" Pact), a manifesto aimed at protecting the interests of the Ottoman Muslims. The gap between this strong assertion of Muslim sovereignty and the de facto Allied control of key strategic points coupled with the palace's policy of appeasement produced considerable unease amongst the Muslim population.

The Allied-sanctioned Greek invasion of Western Anatolia in May 1919 changed the situation dramatically. The disquiet among the Muslim population quickly turned to anger. In Istanbul demonstrations against the occupation took place almost immediately.[5] But the plans for what would happen next had been laid long ago. Behind the scenes the Unionists began to carry out the worst-case scenario plans that had been drawn up during the war. Back in late 1915 and early 1916, when the Allied campaign to force the Dardanelles had threatened the Ottoman capital, Enver had, as we have seen, made contingency preparations to retreat and to wage a "resistance" campaign from the interior of Anatolia.[6] In reaction to the Greek invasion, these Unionist networks now mobilized, guerrilla cells were formed, or in many cases either re-formed or were re-named, and the arms that had been cached in Anatolia were distributed. As the Greeks pushed inland from the Aegean coast, these forces began to mount resistance, with Çerkes Edhem playing a prominent role. Edhem's Mobile Forces, using the weapons hidden at Eşref's estate in Salihli, formed "the only effective nationalist force in Western Anatolia in 1919–1920."[7]

19. Çerkes Edhem with Mustafa Kemal and fellow members of the "National" Forces in November, 1920. (Source: TİTE)

In Istanbul the secretive Unionist Karakol underground network took over many of the functions of the now defunct Special Organization and served as a conduit for sending men, arms, and intelligence reports to the forces organizing resistance in the interior.[8] Eşref's long-standing associates and fellow Enverist *fedaîs* Yenibahçeli Şükrü, Kel Ali (Çetinkaya), and Çerkes Reşid were among its important members. Yenibahçeli Şükrü used his position as director of the Ottoman Artillery School at Maltepe to take charge of Karakol's escape routes, along which various members of the resistance fled from British-occupied Istanbul to Anatolia. This was the volatile situation into which Eşref entered in the early days of 1920.

Eşref's imprisonment on Malta meant that he was late in joining the movement that came to be called the National Forces, or Independence, War. By comparison, his comrades in the country already had established roles in the movement. For example, many had joined Karakol in the capital, as we have just seen, and others, such as Edhem, had been using their regional origins and contacts to build up a military presence in the provinces. As Eşref had been out of the country and not had a regional base of his own, he would have to take what he was offered. Still, his contacts were in place and it did not take him long to be in touch with his former Special Organization colleagues who were now at the forefront of the resistance movement.

Back in action

On the evening of 22 January 1920, Eşref had a decisive meeting with his friend and fellow Circassian Rauf (Orbay) who had achieved fame as a naval hero in the Balkan Wars. Now an MP and confidant of Mustafa Kemal who still had access to the War Ministry, Rauf was secretly acting as a conduit between Ankara and the resistance groups in Istanbul. In a coded telegram to Ankara, Rauf reported that Eşref had returned from Malta and accepted with pleasure a command in the "National Forces."[9] Following the death two weeks earlier of Yahya Kaptan, a Karakol agent of Albanian origin with a Special Organization background who had been working under the aegis of Ankara,[10] Eşref was being named commander for the region of Kartal, İzmit, and Adapazarı. This area to the east of the capital lay astride the road to Ankara and thus was crucial for the fledgling National Forces organization. The next day Mustafa Kemal sent a telegram to Eşref, informing him that he had been appointed to the position of Kuva-yı Milliye Commander for Bolu, Adapazarı, İzmit, and Kartal and that he would report to the Representative Committee in Ankara, essentially to Mustafa Kemal himself.[11] Kemal informed him in no uncertain terms that he would need to coordinate his efforts with Rüşdü Bey, the commander of the First Division, and to demonstrate the same degree of zeal and cooperation as this colleague. It was perhaps an indirect way of warning Eşref not to act on his own.

Pervin's version of the story is slightly different. In her account it is her husband who proposes the idea that he establish a clear route between Ankara and Istanbul to Mustafa Kemal. Mustafa Kemal responded that this was "very fitting" (*pek yerinde*). Eşref subsequently received a telegram from the nationalist leader to the effect that he was appointing Eşref commander of the "national" organization (*millî teşkilat*) in Kartal, Adapazarı, and Bolu and that he should come to Ankara for consultations.[12]

There is also an intriguing third version of this story, which if true might help explain the second. According to Hüsameddin Ertürk, a key Special Organization officer, the decision to send Eşref to Adapazarı was made by none other than Enver Paşa.[13] Although absent from the scene after his departure from Istanbul, Enver still maintained the allegiance of his key supporters, particularly with those on the leftist side of the national movement.[14] Eşref was, as we have seen, personally dedicated to Enver, a factor that at least partly explains the tensions that would develop between him and Ankara. Eşref's brother Sami remained fighting with Enver until his death, in early August 1922, at the hands of the Bolsheviks in what is now Tajikistan. In fact, Enver's last known letter to his wife Princess Naciye indicates that he had asked Hacı Sami to come to his location in the Pamir Mountains.[15] The Enverist connections would, as we shall see, continue to haunt the nationalists in Ankara who went to great lengths to exclude Enver, who outranked all the nationalist officers, from the movement they were forming in Anatolia.

Whether the idea originated with Mustafa Kemal, Enver, or Eşref himself, it is clear that Eşref was handed this important assignment soon after his return from Malta. Both his connections and his appetite for taking on difficult missions were still intact, despite his years out of circulation. The fact that he was now reporting to Mustafa Kemal and not Enver would, however, be an important difference, and one that would have dramatic consequences.

It is also apparent that the strategy behind sending Eşref to Adapazarı had a clear ethnic dimension, even if the way in which such affinities worked in practice was confused—and confusing. The nationalist movement seems to have been using officers of various ethnic backgrounds to recruit members and win the allegiance of areas whose inhabitants corresponded to their own ethnicity. Sending Eşref to Adapazarı with its important if perhaps only dimly understood North Caucasian population was part of such a strategy. A complicating factor may have been that Eşref had some connections in the region with those who were considered servile (*köle*) in the Circassian social hierarchy and with some of his former slaves in İzmit.[16] As we shall soon see, Eşref in turn adopted his own version of an ethnic policy when he got to the region.

Eşref's re-engagement with a clandestine military operation had direct consequences for Pervin that went beyond rekindling old anxieties about losing her husband to another fight. During the period after Eşref's return from Malta, she had to contend with the social consequences of her husband's frenzied preparations. Among her group of friends was a woman named Şerife Hanım who was the mother of the Sapancalı brothers Hakkı and Baki. According to Pervin, Şerife loved Eşref and Sami like her own sons and was aggrieved that Eşref had failed to ask after her or pay her a visit on his return from exile.[17] During a visit to Pervin, Şerife complained about this perceived social slight. Pervin informed Eşref and they organized a visit to the Sapancalı family in Tarabya, far up the Bosphorus, to repair relations between the families. Because of the preparations he was making to join the resistance movement, Eşref's time was short. To save time he arranged for them to be driven in a motor car supplied by one of Eşref's comrades from the Canal campaign named "Paşa" Kazım and driven by a cousin of Eşref's named Ali.

Time was of the essence, because they had to fit the social visit around Eşref's meeting with Bulgar Sadik's Karakol gang. As the car sped along the road leading north from Istanbul over the ridge overlooking the Bosphorus, the passengers were laughing along with the comic patter of "Paşa" Kazım. But the happy outing quickly turned tragic. Due to the speed of the car and condition of the road, Pervin miscarried the tiny foetus she carried inside her. As soon as they arrived in Trabya they called a doctor. Pervin was told that she might need to have an operation. Eşref was obliged to meet up with his colleagues and so would have to leave Pervin on the operating table. A small consolation was that her relatives, including Seza Hanım (Polar), were there to take care of her once again. Before Eşref left, Pervin offered him all the money she had with her, a sum of 3,500 lira in banknotes. Eşref made her keep 500 but took the rest because, as she says, such a sum could cover the expenses of an armed band of fourteen men. Pervin's rushed narrative, combining the family visit, her miscarriage, personal finances mixed up with expenditure for the "national" cause, and another painful parting, reveals once again the extent to which the personal and the paramilitary were intertwined in Eşref and Pervin's marriage.

Pervin had a warning for Eşref as he left. This is how she remembered their parting conversation:

Pervin: Eşref, in my view, when you go to meet Mustafa Kemal Paşa, don't do so at the head of a military force or go armed.

Eşref: Why?

Pervin: Because your brother and Enver are now outside the country. If you, inside the country, are to go at the head of an armed force, you will give Mustafa Kemal justifiable reason to be suspicious of you.

Eşref: Who whispered this to you?

Pervin: On my honor I assure you, I see it this way myself. You are taking on a heavy task. You've undertaken to go to the region but you should absolutely not go armed.

Eşref: On such a day, such an idea can never be in question. I am neither Enver's backbiter nor Mustafa Kemal's eulogizer. I am a son of the nation. I'll be respectful but I'll never be bound to any individual if it goes against my character (*akidem dışı*). Be calm.[18]

And so Eşref departed, undeterred but, despite Pervin's plea, not unarmed. Pervin was left in the caring hands of her relatives but with much to worry about over her operation and national events beyond her control. Although she could not have known it at the time, the warning she had given her husband would prove ominously prophetic.

Regional commander

After that less-than-ideal parting with Pervin, Eşref quickly found himself thrown into the maelstrom of what would come to be called the "National Forces" period. This resistance network was increasingly powerful in Anatolia, but the change of government and the Allied occupation made its work in Istanbul and the environs much trickier. A glaring problem was the lack of an effective resistance set-up in the regions to the east of Istanbul, a deficiency that made the communications and transportation of men and materiel on which the movement depended extremely difficult. As we have seen, the areas assigned to Eşref were crucial to the resistance movement because of their geographical position. The towns of İzmit, Adapazarı, and Bolu were key points in the "land bridge" connecting Istanbul with Ankara.

Despite the strategic importance of the region east of İzmit, it was not a natural heartland for the resistance. For one thing, its population was extremely varied, reflecting complicated patterns of settlement. Before the war it been home to Albanians, Greeks (Rum), Armenians, Circassians, as well as Turks who themselves reflected considerable diversity. It was an area that since antiquity had been inhabited by many layers of migrants.[19] A large share of the population, both Muslim and non-Muslim, were fairly recent immigrants. Circassians featured heavily among the more recent arrivals. The districts of İzmit, Adapazarı, and Bolu had experienced an influx of close to 75,000 immigrants from the North Caucasus since the late 1870s.[20] The allegiances of the Circassian population of the region added another level of complexity. Notoriously difficult for outsiders to discern, the affinities of the immigrant populations from the North Caucasus depended on kinship, class, and region of origin. How these allegiances mapped onto the existing Ottoman socio-political scene depended to some extent on relations with the Ottoman palace. The long-standing tradition of Circassian women entering the imperial harem and Circassian men being recruited into the armed forces not only continued but was heavily strengthened in the period after the great exodus of the Circassians from their homelands.

In the Adapazarı region this tradition continued to thrive well into the twentieth century. Adapazarı in particular had an important link with the Ottoman palace: an extraordinary number of its daughters had married Ottoman sultans. During the reign of Abdülhamid II it was the daughters of the Maan clan, immigrants to the empire after the Russo-Ottoman war of 1877–8, who became imperial brides. But after the 1908 revolution while the trend of Adapazarı brides continued, none of them belonged to the Maan family. Something had changed in the relations between Adapazarı and the Ottoman establishment.[21] The Circassian notable families in the region were close to the palace and suspicious of the Unionists, whom they saw as representing a drastic departure from the order of the old regime. A rebellion had flared up in Adapazarı as recently as October 1919 when, according to Mustafa Kemal, they asserted, "We do not accept Mustafa Kemal in the Sultan's place."[22] As Eşref would soon discover on his own, a welcoming reception from Adapazarı and its large Circassian population could not be taken for granted.

During the war years, instability in the region had increased dramatically. Armenians and Rums were harrassed as part of Unionist intimidation efforts; great numbers of Armenians were deported in 1915–16.[23] Meanwhile the Muslim population, although not directly victimized by Young Turk policies, had neverthless been adversely affected by the war. As the army dug deeper into its potential stock of recruits and poverty bit, desertion became a major factor. Many deserters joined bandit gangs in the region, adding a level of insecurity to the already volatile mix. Armed bands openly roamed in the region around Adapazarı.[24] Friction between Albanian and Circassian bands was another facet of the regional picture. There were also armed gangs comprising Armenians and Greeks operating in the region. After the war, many Greek and Armenian refugees returned to try to pick up the pieces of their shattered lives, a turn of events that played on the guilt of those who had taken part in or benefited from the deportations and served as a grim—and to some a provocative—reminder of the Ottoman wartime defeat.[25]

In short, the region to which Eşref was being sent as a commander of the resistance forces was one where the combination of ethnic diversity, demographic change, and political instability made for a highly unsettled mix. To some extent the ground was prepared for Eşref's arrival by the activities of Special Organization officers turned Karakol operatives such as Yenibahçeli Şükrü and "Bulgar" Sadık (aka Sadık Baba). In İzmit, for example, three of the paramilitary officers in charge had previously served with either Eşref or Süleyman Askerî.[26] Also, as we have seen, Eşref may have had connections to some elements of Circassian society in the area. On the other hand, Eşref may have felt anxious about the volatility of the region, and in particular the untested nature of the reception that he would receive from the local Circassian population due to his lack of a strong personal connection to the area. These factors probably explain his hesitancy in setting out to take up his new command.

The subsequent problems that Eşref experienced in Adapazarı stand in contrast to the success that, for example, Edhem and Reşid enjoyed in recruiting in the Bandırma region where they had a direct personal connection and where their family were landowners.[27] One contemporary observer of this period claims that the fundamental reason for the opposition to Eşref among the population of Adapazarı, despite their shared Circassian origins, was the problem of his social standing, but no other source mentions this.[28] If true, it is nevertheless probable that this played less of a role than the problems inherent in Eşref's initial conduct toward the notables in Adapazarı.[29]

Whatever the reason, it is clear that Eşref took his time before moving to the region. Rauf had informed Ankara that Eşref would travel to the Adapazarı region on the morning following their meeting, that is the morning of 23 January. But ten days later he had still not taken up his post. Mustafa Kemal wrote to Rauf to request particularly that Eşref move to the region.[30] Eight days after that, on 11 February, Rauf responded that he thought Eşref might depart that day. On 14 February the director of the intelligence bureau on the western front wrote to Eşref via Ankara to ask pointedly if there was something preventing him from coming to Eskişehir, the major town between Istanbul and Ankara.[31] As we have seen, when Mustafa Kemal appointed Eşref to his position he had emphasized the necessity for Eşref to be bound to Ankara and to coordinate his actions with his fellow commanders. But now, even at an early stage in his involvement with the "national" forces,[32] signs of trouble were beginning to appear.

Eventually on 24 February Eşref was reported to be on the move, but the news was picked up by the other side. The Ottoman Interior Ministry, which considered the Kuva-yı Milliye (National Forces) illegitimate, received a report from the district governor of İzmit informing him that an armed group of sixteen men, twelve on horseback and four on foot, had spent the night in a village outside Kandıra, to the north of İzmit. Their commander was Eşref and they were heading for Adapazarı. Their mission was apparently to ensure that no incidents took place in the region of İzmit, Bolu, and Adapazarı. They were also said to be carrying out persecutions in the name of the National Forces and to be carrying bombs and Mauser rifles.[33]

Although Eşref was reportedly heading toward Adapazarı, his arrival seems to have been inexplicably delayed. Ankara sent telegrams to a number of Kuva-yı Milliye officials asking for information about Eşref's movements during this period.[34] Finally on 27 February Eşref wrote to Mustafa Kemal to say that he was outside Adapazarı. Now signing his telegram as a Kuva-yı Milliye Commander, Eşref reported that he had a small detachment of fighters and that he was awaiting Mustafa Kemal's orders.[35] Two days later, on 29 February (it was a leap year), he wrote to say that he had arrived in Adapazarı.[36] But curiously one of Mustafa Kemal's informants, the Albanian Abdurrahman, wrote to Ankara saying Eşref's arrival in the town, although expected, had yet to take place.[37] Eşref's involvement was not getting off to the best of starts.

Finally on 1 March Eşref reported to Mustafa Kemal that he had reached Adapazarı. But even then he said that his detachment had remained outside the town.[38] What was causing Eşref's rather uncharacteristic hesitation was undoubtedly the prospect of the reception he would receive in Adapazarı. The region had only recently felt the reverberations of the second of three uprisings, or "rebellion," led by Ahmed Anzavur, a Circassian gendarme officer loyal to the Ottoman government. This uprising had begun on 16 February and would not be suppressed until mid-April. The region south of the Marmara Sea was undergoing something akin to civil war as the Circassian communities in the wider region found themselves torn between loyalty to Istanbul and Ankara. Eşref was probably right to proceed cautiously to Adapazarı.

Eşref's key contact in the Adapazarı region was Maan Şirin, a former Special Organization officer who had had served under Eşref in Macedonia and Bulgaria and fought on the eastern front during the war; there he was taken prisoner by the Russians and sent to Siberia. He escaped and returned to Adapazarı in 1918.[39] As a member of the notable Circassian Maan family whose marital ties to the palace have already been noted,[40] Maan Şirin was exactly the kind of respected local contact that Eşref needed in Adapazarı. Initially Maan Şirin vouched for Eşref before the local Circassian notables, who were generally suspicious of the CUP leadership with Balkan experience.[41] They undoubtedly associated the Balkan lands with being the stronghold of the CUP. As immigrants from the Caucasus, they were naturally aligned with the Palace and saw the sultan as their benefactor, a relationship that had been further strengthened by marital links to the Ottoman royal family. Siding with the nationalists went against their natural instincts.

After reaching Adapazarı, Eşref engaged in a flurry of planning and correspondence with Ankara. In an upbeat report he indicated that he had been recruiting amongst the population and that his men were brave and eager to join the resistance. He said that he was hopeful of completing the preparations for assembling forces of advanced troops and rifle-men very soon.[42] Interestingly, Eşref seems to have been operating an ethnic policy of his own. He mentioned, perhaps optimistically, that his contacts with the Circassian leadership were facilitating things. He also reported that his assigning Laz officers had helped organize the Laz forces in the region and that he had assigned an officer of Georgian origin named Yusuf to liaise with the Georgian population of Sapanca. With respect to Düzce and its environs, he summoned the brother of Rüşdü Bey, presumably his man in the area. According to another account, Eşref also sent Dr Fahri Can to Gebze, where he organized local resistance into what became the Kara Aslan Çetesi, which was led by former Special Operations officers who had carried out guerrilla raids during the Balkan Wars.[43] Despite his optimistic assessment that "I don't see any difficulty here,"[44] it is likely that Eşref was getting a clearer sense of the problems inherent in his new assignment.

Certainly the wish list he presented to Ankara indicated that he was preparing to go into armed "*çete*" mode. Although he gave Mustafa Kemal the welcome news that the Anzavur rising was essentially over ("Those who were Anzavurists yesterday have today bowed their heads in humility and become examples for the others," he said),[45] the sup-plies he was asking for suggested that further hostilities lay ahead. His list included money (he wanted 2,000 or 3,000 liras to be sent straight away—presumably Pervin's money was running out), food supplies, and equipment sufficient for a company-sized force and thirty head of riding horses (for the officers who would carry out inspections and correspondence). He also wanted to know how, from where, and what kind of weapons and ammunition could be quickly procured, and asked for telegraphic codes and special instructions to be sent to him urgently. Once the things that he was asking for had been procured, he said, he would be able to call the region to arms. If bringing in an armed force from outside the region were needed, however, that would cost considerably more.[46] Financing the operation was one of Eşref's preoccupations. Eşref estimated that it would cost him about 12,000 liras to acquire the necessary provisions, excluding the weapons and ammunition, and that he would personally meet any costs that went beyond that amount.

Mustafa Kemal's response reflected Ankara's broader concerns. He was more exercised about strategic issues, such as the need to concentrate Kuva-yı Milliye forces to prevent "foreign" i.e. British forces from repairing the railway running down the İzmit peninsula, and the immediate need to destroy what he referred to as "reactionary movements"[47] i.e. those loyal to Istanbul, in Eşref's region. In response to Eşref's specific requests, Mustafa Kemal told him that commissary and equipment supplies would be provided by the First Division and that arms and ammunition could be secured from the XXth Army Corps. As for the specific funding request that Eşref had made, the future Atatürk said that Ankara had no budget for the expenses of the various regions and that as a result he would need to approach the committee in his area. With respect to areas having a large non-Muslim population, Mustafa Kemal ordered Eşref to make arrangements to prevent attacks on the Muslim population.[48]

On the vexing question of finance, Mustafa Kemal told Eşref that if the divisional commander were unable to cover the full amount of his expenses, Eşref should obtain funding from the "patriotic" people (*eshab-i hamiyet*) in his region and that Eşref should do so "in person."[49] Eşref may have been somewhat over-zealous in pursuing this suggestion. According to local sources, Eşref's practice of extracting high "taxes" from the notable families of the region—one family alone was apparently convinced to part with 100,000 liras—was turning them against his command.[50] It also seems likely that Eşref either did not receive or ignored a report about the conditions in Adapazarı, and the extent to which its Circassian population were making known their discontent with the Kuva-yı Milliye, in particular the way it pressed them for money.[51] Whatever advantage Maan Şirin's support of Eşref had initially given him among the Circassian elites was now wearing thin. Soon Mustafa Kemal was writing to Eşref to ask him politely but firmly to come to Ankara at the first opportunity to speak in person.[52] Ominously for Eşref, Mustafa Kemal had first addressed the telegram to "Eşref Bey the Kuva-yı Milliye commander in Düzce," but then crossed out the words "Kuva-yı Milliye."

The Adapazarı debacle

To recap the situation in Adapazarı, things had not gone well from the beginning. First Eşref hesitated in approaching the town, probably aware that as a Kuva-yı Milliye commander he could expect at best a lukewarm welcome despite his Circassian roots. When he finally entered it he left his troops outside, no doubt fearing the reaction their presence might provoke. But instead of mollifying the already delicate situation, Eşref's pressing the local notables for money had exacerbated it. Another factor adding to the negative reception Eşref met in Adapazarı was his recruitment of men from among what a local Ottoman official referred to as "the vulgar elements" of the population and his stirring up of local tensions.[53] Adding fuel to the fire, or perhaps providing a pretext to justify their dissension, was the claim, mentioned above, that it was Eşref's servile (köle) origins that had caused the Circassians of Adapazarı to revolt against him.[54]

The notables eventually came to view the presence of National Forces in the town as something like an occupation. When Eşref first arrived, the introduction he received from Maan Şirin had helped to assuage local concerns. But objections were soon raised. The main figure to put himself forward as an alternative was Karzeg Sait, a Circassian notable from Adapazarı. His position was that the Kuva-yı Milliye was not needed in the town because the locals were fully capable of doing their own organizing. He was worried that if Eşref were left to continue with his extortionate behavior, he would pillage the region. He therefore declared that Eşref be asked to leave for Ankara.[55] By the middle of April they had had enough and formed a committee to try to effect his removal from the area.[56] Meanwhile they began to raise their own militia. British intelligence sources link the opposition against Eşref in particular and the Kuva-yı Milliye in Adapazarı and elsewhere in the region to the broader anti-nationalist movement associated with Ahmed Aznavur. The British viewed Ankara's forces as rebels and were positively inclined toward the anti-nationalists. They saw evidence of a "popular" movement and pointed to other instances of local resistance to nationalist organization.[57]

Faced with this opposition, Eşref hoped to negotiate and refused to leave. But for Sait this was out of the question because he considered Eşref to be a mere activist (komitacı) and not his social equal. It was at this point that Eşref opened the prison in order to increase his numbers in preparation for a conflict. But he was too late; Circassian cavalry had surrounded Adapazarı. It was only through the intervention of the district governor that Eşref, who had been warned about the growing danger of the situation, was allowed to leave the town.[58]

The speed with which the situation in Adapazarı had deteriorated presented Ankara with a big problem. Instead of securing a vital region linking Istanbul with Anatolia for the resistance movement, Eşref's actions there seem to have inflamed the situation alarmingly. Reports soon reached Ankara that the local Circassian leadership had not only rejected the Kuva-yı Milliye presence but also asked Anzavur's forces for help, thus possibly rekindling an important uprising directed against Ankara just when it appeared to be dying out.[59] At the same time, other Kuva-yı Milliye officers were expressing their doubts about Eşref's suitability for the task to which he had been assigned in Adapazarı. An officer based in İzmit wrote to Ankara to indicate that Eşref had not passed through İzmit and that he doubted that Eşref would be able to do anything in Adapazarı on his own. It would require sending a clever official who would be able to understand the situation.[60] Clearly, in this man's view, Eşref was not such a man.

During the early and middle days of March, further signs of Ankara's growing mistrust of Eşref appeared. Since pulling his forces out of Adapazarı he had moved east. On 12 March he arrived in Düzce en route to Bolu in the company of a force of thirteen fighting men, three mounted and ten on foot.[61] From Düzce he wrote to Ankara that he was minded to advance against British lines in the west,[62] but Ankara had other ideas. Disagreement over a number of operational issues created further problems between Eşref and Ankara. None of these issues was by itself of particularly great importance. They included, for example, whether or not the assignment of distributing materiel being transported from the capital be given to Eşref and whether or not a certain gendarmes officer could be trusted. But in each case they were settled by Ankara against Eşref, reflecting Ankara's increasing wariness toward a regional commander in a particularly sensitive region. In one case Colonel İsmet (İnönü) had weighed in categorically against Eşref.[63] İsmet's intervention reflected his suspicion that Eşref might not be trusted to hold certain information in confidence. İsmet's view was that they had already given Eşref many assignments and that as this one depended on cooperating with other officers and a fair degree of discretion, it would be better to give it to the commander of the 1st

Division. Mustafa Kemal took İsmet's advice—and an increasingly suspicious view of Eşref.

As time went by, Mustafa Kemal began to take a sterner tone with Eşref. After Eşref wrote to Ankara on 12 March from Düzce to ask once again about the reliability of the gendarmes commander Kemal Paşa, literally what "color" he was, Mustafa Kemal responded curtly the next day. Again dropping the words "Kuva-yı Milliye" before "Commander" in the address of his telegram, Mustafa Kemal made two points. First, he told Eşref that the matter of the gendarmes commander, whom Eşref had suggested could be trusted and Ankara insisted could not, was very important. Secondly, Mustafa Kemal asked Eşref directly whether or not he had received his summons to appear in person in Ankara. In closing he informed Eşref that he was expecting him to travel to Ankara at the earliest possibility.[64] Ankara was calling its troublesome officer in for face-to-face discussions. Eşref duly set out for Ankara, reporting his departure from Bolu on 14 March.[65] Trabzonlu Rauf, writing from Adapazarı where he was acting as deputy commander of the Kuva-yı Milliye, confirmed that Eşref was on his way.[66]

Whether or not Eşref went to Ankara is unclear. According to Pervin, Eşref led a raid on the Maltepe depot on the same day that he was supposed to be heading to Ankara.[67] This was the same date that the Allied occupation of Istanbul commenced in practice, with the occupation of the telegraph office. The next day British officers began to arrest those suspected of supporting the Ankara movement. Many of them would be sent to Malta, but Eşref was keen to avoid a second stay at His Majesty's pleasure. The Maltepe raid led to the "recovery" of weapons and military equipment for the Kuva-yı Milliye. According to Pervin, the haul was large: 93 oxcarts and 150 pack animals were used to carry away the weapons and ammunition to the Anatolian resistance. This was just in time, because over the course of the following days the British occupying forces strengthened their positions, taking over the key points of control in the capital.

For Eşref, the consolidated Allied occupation and his involvement in the raid meant that it was also time for Pervin and his family members to leave Istanbul. He sent word to his younger brother Ahmed and a certain Captain Hasan Adli to go to Istanbul and collect Pervin and other family members. Ahmed was continuing the involvement with the Kuva-yı Milliye that he had begun when Eşref was still in Malta. It will be recalled that in the spring of 1919 Ahmed had supplied Edhem's forces with the arms and money that had been pre-positioned at Salihli. Now, roughly a year later, he was still involved.

Pervin had taken along her adopted son Feridun, Eşref's son from his first marriage, and a Circassian girl of a similar age named Yektal. Captain Adli's wife and family joined the group of travelers. They made their way in secret to Samandıra, to the east of Istanbul. Ahmed and Adli were travelling incognito, adopting the guise of merchants to hide the real purpose of their journey. But their presence was betrayed and their whereabouts became known. A cry went up in the Samandıra guard station that Eşref's family and children were among the "traitors who were fleeing to Anatolia."[68] The troops from the guard station quickly surrounded the travelers. The women and children were taken to the house of the local head man (*muhtar*) where they would be kept for ten days, while Ahmed and Adli were arrested and taken to the guard station. Later they would be turned over to military authorities in Istanbul and incarcerated in the notorious Bekir Ağa prison.[69] Ottoman government sources refer to Ahmed as the brother of the "notorious *çete* commander Eşref." The officials believed the real purpose behind the secret journey was to transfer money and information to the Kuva-yı Milliye.[70]

Pervin's group was taken under armed guard to Üsküdar. Eventually they were able to escape and make another attempt to reach Anatolia. This time, aided by Eşref's relative Abdurrahman Bey, the man who had been wanted in association with the plot against Mahmud Şevket Paşa, they were successful. Giving false names so as to avoid the tight controls in place, they boarded a ferry that allowed them to make their way to Bursa. There they were safe. The governor of Bursa at the time was Hacim Muhittin (Çarıklı) and the military commander was Bekir Sami (Günsav), both Circassians and allies of Eşref. They settled the traveling party in the Selvinaz Hotel in Çekirge, the spa region just outside the town. They informed Eşref that they had arrived and he made arrangements for them to travel to İnegöl, where he came to meet them. As Pervin put it, "Now we were safe in Anatolia among those participating in the National Struggle. We were in a happy environment."[71] Ahmed and Adli were not so fortunate. They spent eight months in prison, but were released thanks to the intercession of Eşref's relative Hacı Nazmi Paşa, who was a neighbor of "Kurdish" Nemrut Mustafa Paşa (Yamulki) and in charge of the Ottoman Military Court.[72]

Meanwhile Ankara had responded to the problems Eşref experienced in Adapazarı by sending another officer to the region to serve alongside Eşref. Interestingly the man selected, whose name was Mahmud Bey, was also a Circassian. This appointment rankled Eşref who, as we have seen, was used to having a free rein in conducting his operations. Mahmud was sent in to ameliorate the situation in early April. He held talks with the disaffected Circassian notables on 4 April. Eşref immediately wrote to Ankara to complain about Mahmud's presence. He conceded that Mahmud was his superior in rank, a member of the General Staff and a good soldier, but he objected to the interference Mahmud's presence would represent in his operations. He promised to be completely obedient to the orders he would receive as long as he knew that he had individual responsibility, and requested immediate confirmation that no one else would interfere in his area of responsibility and command.[73] But Eşref would receive no such confirmation.

Instead, Mahmud's reports had the effect of deepening Ankara's mistrust of Eşref. His initial strategy seems to have been to try to get Eşref out of the area. On 2 April he wrote to the commander in Bursa that Eşref would send units toward Kandıra and İzmit, conduct inspections, and destroy bridges between İzmit and Sapanca.[74] On the night of 7 April Mahmud sent an urgent telegram to Ankara in which he described the magnitude of the problems that, in his view, Eşref's presence in Adapazarı had provoked. Claiming that he had only with difficulty prevented things from escalating further, Mahmud described the bubbling up of rage (*galeyan*) that Eşref's presence had produced.[75] In response to the negative reaction he received, Eşref had freed all the prisoners in the local jail. Things had reached the point where Mahmud expected the locals to mount an attack. The only solution was to remove Eşref from the area. Indicating that he had spoken with Eşref, Mahmud requested Ankara's order to send Eşref to Ankara to be investigated for having freed the prisoners in contravention of the law.[76] British intelligence reports indicate that Eşref and thirty of his men had been driven out of Adapazarı on 9 April, with those unable to flee being beaten and imprisoned by the inhabitants, with the Circassians playing a prominent role in the attacks.[77]

Sensing that he was in trouble, Eşref wrote to Ankara to explain his actions. Faced with an armed gathering that had been incited by "scoundrels" who had been influenced by the power of British money and were intent on setting the region on fire and on murder, Eşref said that had been obliged to free the prisoners.[78] There were twenty who had been condemned and thirty who were suspected but not condemned. Eşref said that he had been obliged to free them, and did so in the presence of Muslim and Christian clerics. His opponents had been planning a massacre and, he argued, had he not freed the prisoners, the enemy would certainly have carried out their plan. It was a decision he had had to make on the spot. Moreover, the prisoners had not been completely freed but remained under Kuva-yı Milliye observation in barracks.

Mustafa Kemal's response was swift. He wrote an urgent message the next day, to be hand-delivered to Eşref. Interestingly the original text indicated that all of Eşref's activities would now have to be coordinated with Mahmud Bey. But those lines were then crossed out and the surviving text simply indicated that Mustafa Kemal requested the honor of his presence in Ankara to discuss his situation.[79] In the event, Mustafa Kemal sent Mahmud Bey to suppress a loyalist uprising in Düzce, but he was killed on 22 April in the fighting that broke out as his unit approached the town.[80] The Adapazarı incident was only one of many flashpoints in the region to the east and south of the Marmara Sea, caught between forces loyal to Ankara and Istanbul.

Mustafa Kemal's decision to summon Eşref to Ankara was clearly influenced by İsmet, who presented his view in characteristically blunt terms. Eşref's forceful actions in Adapazarı, İsmet declared, had produced an uprising of 200 armed Circassians and Laz. Mahmud Bey had been sent in to resolve the situation peacefully, but Eşref had given the order to open the prison. İsmet therefore advised that Eşref be summoned to Ankara.[81] Interestingly Eşref's own writings preserve part of a late-night conversation he had had with Mustafa Kemal in Ankara that focused on the way in which Eşref should approach Adapazarı. In an undated notebook in which he recorded various events, chronologies, and clippings, he wrote that Mustafa Kemal had warned him to treat the Circassians of Adapazarı carefully. They were, he counseled, in a difficult position, on the border between "us" and Istanbul. It was our duty to gain their friendship. "Don't use excessive force," Mustafa

Kemal finished by saying. Tellingly perhaps, Eşref responded by asking, "Have there been complaints?"[82]

If Eşref had wanted to test the resolve of Mustafa Kemal and his supporters in Ankara, he had chosen a bad time. Late March and early April 1920 saw Mustafa Kemal win a number of important tussles and consolidate his leadership over the resistance or "national" movement. In this he was at least partially if inadvertently served by the Ottoman government in Istanbul and the Allied Powers. The former, in choosing Damad Ferid as Grand Vizier, the arch-enemy of the nationalists, convinced a number of key but wavering army officers to side with Ankara.[83] The latter, in attempting to impose what one British official referred to as "drastic peace terms," drove a number of "many soi-disant Anglophiles into the Nationalists' ranks."[84] This was also the period when Mustafa Kemal asserted his authority against the Karakol, who had hitherto largely operated independently of Ankara.[85] This new-found security and lingering doubts about Eşref's behavior seem to have encouraged Ankara to take a harder line with him.

Meanwhile the Circassians of Adapazarı had been mobilizing. Mahmud had reported to Ankara that Eşref was solely responsible for the breakdown in relations and the setback to the "national" cause. In his view, Eşref had created a mess in Adapazarı, both by his actions and by his inability either to comprehend the situation or to control his nerves. Mahmud reported on 8 April that a general committee of the Circassians and Abkhazians of the region had already met to take action against Eşref.[86] These were the gatherings led by Karzeg Sait Bey who was able to rely on a network inherited from his father, a prominent Circassian figure in the region.[87] Mahmud reported that he had forced Eşref and several of his officers to leave Adapazarı on the evening of 8 April. (British sources state that the Circassians chased Eşref out of town on 9 April.)[88] Soon, however, Mahmud filed a much less alarmist report to Ankara. On 10 April he wrote that the situation in Adapazarı would calm down upon Eşref's return and that there had been a misunderstanding among the Circassian leadership about a perceived threat to the Caliphate. In his telling, Mahmud had resolved matters satisfactorily for the Kuva-yı Milliye. Despite Mahmud's positive change of tone, an official in Ankara, probably Mustafa Kemal himself, made the following marginal note: "Let's put all these matters pertaining to Eşref

---

---

on one piece of paper."[89] Ankara was increasingly viewing Eşref as something of a liability and now decided to open a file on him. Instead of settling the situation in Adapazarı, he seemed to be inflaming it to the point where Ankara had to send in someone else to resolve the crisis.

By contrast, Eşref's associate Edhem was demonstrating remarkable success in rallying men to his side in the region around Bandırma. Edhem's local roots and family connections, together with his personal charisma and apparent fearlessness, resulted in a string of military successes that were crucial to saving the Ankara movement at various times over the course of 1920. Later on, after his defection from the Kuva-yı Milliye, the Kemalists would criticize Edhem for acting out of personal rather than national interests; but at the time they depended heavily on his connections and his military prowess.[90]

Eşref's subsequent movements are somewhat difficult to follow. Presumably Eşref went to Ankara to meet with Mustafa Kemal, but there is no direct evidence of this. In fact, whereas Mustafa Kemal had summoned Eşref on 9 April, on 11 April he was still in the vicinity of Adapazarı. Mahmud reported to Ankara that Eşref had not gone to Ankara, with the implication that he had been expected to do so, but had instead spent the night of 9 April in the region.[91] Mahmud also noted that reports were circulating to the effect that Eşref had remained near Adapazarı and that his aide-de-camp and some of his key officers had been seen in the town, sightings that had enraged the local population once again. According to a local official it was obligatory that Eşref and his men be sent to the region of Karaçam, south of town. On 19 April Ali Fuad Paşa (Cebesoy) wrote to Ankara that complaints were being raised by the people of Kandıra, to the north of İzmit, that Eşref was extracting "salaries and other things" by force. He was worried that Eşref's actions would cause incomparable damage and urged that he be transferred to the region of Bolu.[92] By contast, Mahmud's region was reported to be calm.

Four months earlier Pervin had warned Eşref about how he conducted his relations with Ankara. This may have been the kind of problem she had hoped to avoid. If so she was unsuccessful. Meanwhile Mustafa Kemal's power was on the rise. Eşref later wrote that Pervin came to Anatolia, presumably to their property at Salihli, a few days after 23 April 1920, the date of the opening of the Grand National

Assembly in Ankara.[93] It was at this gathering that Mustafa Kemal took another step toward concentrating power in his hands. He was elected both speaker of this new parliament and its president.[94] According to Eşref's descendants, Mustafa Kemal asked Eşref to become a member of this parliament but Eşref declined, indicating that he was a soldier and not a politician. If true, this may have aroused further suspicion in Mustafa Kemal toward Eşref. It was certainly the case that in this period the future Atatürk was extending many such invitations. Establishing a parliament at Ankara, now emphatically his political domain, was an effective tool in his consolidation of power.

Whatever did or did not transpire in Ankara, it was not long before Eşref was back in military action against the Greek army. On 28 April 1920 Eşref was reported to be in charge of a unit of 150 men, one of several groups of fighters who had been scattered by Mahmud but were now being brought back together in the region of Geyve where Ali Fuad Paşa, a key Kuva-yı Milliye general, was organizing the suppression of a rebellion there.[95] By 2 May 1920 Eşref had taken the town of Göynük, to the south-east of Adapazarı, after a fight.[96] The next day Eşref's detachment had occupied the town of Mudurnu, to the east of Göynük.[97] The "rebels" had been put to flight and the Kuva-yı Milliye forces were pursuing them as they retreated. Ali Fuad Paşa, who had been reporting on the development in this sector of the front, was optimistic about Ankara's prospects of overcoming the opposition.

Uşak

For a while thereafter, Eşref's trail goes cold. Toward the end of June he appears in the role of commander of a cavalry detachment at Salihli. Although this was his territory, he was operating under the command of a Major Cevdet.[98] In early July he sent an urgent request, written on a reused tobacco register, to Ali Fuad Paşa requesting that the twelve-man cavalry unit of Mehmed Arnavud Pehlivan and Rıza Bey be sent to where he was, possibly İlyas near Burdur, as soon as possible.[99] At some point in the spring or summer of 1920 Eşref seems to have been based outside Uşak, about 100 kilometers east of Salihli. According to memoirs written considerably after the period by a veteran of the Kuva-yı Milliye period named Şükrü Nail (Soysal), Eşref and his detachment of roughly 150 fighters were headquartered in the village of Kalfa Köyü, on the eastern fringes of Uşak.[100] They were well supplied with choice mounts, arms, and men. What Eşref lacked, according to Şükrü Nail, was the trust of the local population. In his view, that had been broken by Eşref's intimidating behavior, which allegedly included beating men until they fainted in full view of the population of the town, robbing the wealthy men in the region, and even extra-judicial killings. For this reason, the account continues, a second headquarters had to be set up nearby,[101] a situation with clear echoes of Eşref's Adapazarı disaster.

In Şükrü Nail's telling, Eşref's behavior in Uşak went from bad to worse. He relates one incident in which Eşref sent a detachment of ten fighters under the command one of his men named Güllülü Ali Efe to plunder the town of Ortaköy, further to the east of Uşak. This force began to sack the town in broad daylight and without restraint. An altercation broke out between Ali Efe's band and the villagers which ended in the death of Ali Efe. Soon the news reached Eşref and all hell broke loose in Ortaköy. Eşref mobilized his entire unit and by sundown they had the town surrounded. As no one attempted to resist, they poured into the town and rounded up a number of old and young who had been unable to flee. Meanwhile the men set about looting and burning the conspicuous houses of the town. At the time when the men were allegedly going to shoot the captured inhabitants whom they had lined up for this purpose, a voice cried out, "An Arab would never burn Arabia; let's separate those in the right from those in the wrong." The words came from the commander of a local police station, a man named Talip, who had been trying to put out the fires started earlier. Shocked to hear a voice questioning his authority, Eşref apparently then rounded up his men and moved them to the village from which the station chief had come. Arriving late, Eşref immediately sent a party of eight to ten men to capture Talip and had him shot. Şükrü Naili concludes this grisly story by explaining that Talip was a Kemalist whose personal sacrifice saved many others from being killed at the hands of Eşref who, realizing that the population was against him, withdrew.[102] The story is told in starkly partisan terms and Eşref emerges as a kind of stock villain. Nevertheless, from what we know of Eşref's behavior in Adapazarı, the piece would seem to have at least a whiff of verisimilitude about it.

Exactly when Eşref went to Uşak is unclear, but he was apparently there in late June. Stationed in the town of Güney Köy, between Uşak and Denizli,[103] he was receiving messages from İzzeddin Bey (Çalışlar), the commander of the 23rd Division. The Greeks were advancing in two parallel eastward thrusts. Their northern march had advanced as far as the western outskirts of Alaşehir, to the south-east of Salihli, while their more southerly advance was approaching Nazilli from the direction of Aydın. But as far as İzzeddin could tell, the Greeks had yet to occupy either town.[104] In fact their precise positions were unknown to the Kuva-yı Milliye forces at this stage. In Güney, due east of Alaşehir, Eşref was in a critical position to gather intelligence on the Greek positions. İzzeddin Bey therefore asked him to send a search party north towards İnegöl and another west towards Alaşehir, in order to fix the locations of the Greek headquarters and to determine whether or not trains were operating between Salihli and Alaşehir.

But there was a problem: the Kuva-yı Milliye units were experiencing shortages of ammunition. Eşref had presumably been asking for fresh supplies because on 28 June İzzeddin Bey wrote to Eşref to say that bullets and machine guns were on their way.[105] He also asked Eşref to send the cannon that had been saved in a particular battle on to Uşak where he was planning the defense of the town. He also requested that Eşref encourage and embolden the men in his unit with positive words so that they would advance and force the enemy to retreat, and to spread such an example to the other units in his vicinity.[106] In the event the Greek forces occupied Alaşehir briefly but were pushed out in early July when Ankara's forces were able to retake the town.

Eşref was still or perhaps again in the region at the end of August when the Greek advance pushed east toward Uşak. On 21 and 22 August Eşref's volunteer forces and the Uşak battalion changed places,[107] perhaps to relieve those who had been defending the town. Greek forces occupied the town on 29 August 1920. The next day, Eşref and his cavalry forces arrived in Ankara.[108] Heavily involved in the action though he was, it is clear that Eşref was operating in a relatively minor role. He was no longer a Kuva-yı Milliye commander, but rather merely a leader of an armed battalion.

In late October the Greeks renewed their advance into the interior of Anatolia in an attempt to try to pressure Ankara to sign the Treaty of

Sèvres.[109] Eşref was back in action in the region near Uşak. On 26 October Ali Fuad, the commander of the western front, reported that Eşref's unit had been in action, first making a raid on the Greek position in Uşak from the south-west and then opening a front to the east of the town in the vicinity of Çarık and Karlık where the villagers were reported to be inclined toward him.[110] Perhaps Eşref had changed his tactics toward the local inhabitants. If so, it was a change that probably came too late, because Eşref's engagements near Uşak are the last of his documented activities for the Kuva-yı Milliye.

During 1920 Mustafa Kemal had been able to extend his control over the previously more independent group of actors who comprised the resistance movement. Apart from some political maneuvers, Kemal's main move was his attempt to crush the combination of anti-Western, Islamic, and corporatist elements that had coalesced around Çerkes Edhem. Ankara had relied heavily, perhaps existentially, on Edhem's victories to quell revolts in both western and central Anatolia. But when Edhem joined the Green Army, a political organization intended to offset the sultan's rallying of forces under the aegis of the Caliphate, shortly after it was founded—with Mustafa Kemal's approval—in May of 1920, it became "a force to be reckoned with and a serious threat."[111] In time it developed into rather too great a force for Mustafa Kemal, who declared Edhem a traitor at the end of December. After Ankara's victory at the first battle of İnönü on 11 January 1921 had halted the Greek advance and reduced Ankara's reliance on Edhem, Mustafa Kemal turned against the Green Army. First he ordered Edhem to disband his troops in January 1921. Edhem refused but then Ankara sent its forces against Edhem's, taking many of them prisoner. Edhem's threat to Ankara was quickly ended. By the middle of January his Mobile Forces had ceased to exist.[112] Edhem fled, crossing over to the occupied Greek zone. Eşref followed shortly thereafter, entering into a new phase of exile.

The break

Precisely how and why Eşref changed sides is less than fully clear, but a number of clues point to a combination of factors. As we have seen, at a time when Mustafa Kemal was consolidating his control over the "national" movement, those whose loyalty was considered suspect were being supplanted. Eşref's role in the Kuva-yı Milliye had become limited as Ankara viewed him with increasing suspicion. He had been downgraded from a regional commander to a mere unit leader. Ankara had been receiving intelligence that Eşref had been participating in "treason" with Edhem and his brothers since as early as September 1920. The same source also indicated something quite interesting, namely that Eşref had been invited to the Greek zone of occupation by the top Greek Orthodox prelate in Izmir, Metropolitan Chrisostomos.[113] Despite his earlier involvement in the clearing of the Rum population of Western Anatolia, Eşref had seemingly managed to maintain contacts with the Rum establishment, who perhaps saw him as a useful Muslim ally against the Ankara movement.

From Eşref's perspective, Ankara was not affording him the independence of movement—and probably the respect—that he had come to expect. An underlying factor was undoubtedly Eşref's unequivocal loyalty to Enver. Although Enver was now in distant Central Asia fighting the Bolsheviks, he remained a powerful potential alternative to Mustafa Kemal. The fact that Eşref's brother Selim Sami was with Enver—he was in Taşkent by mid-November 1920[114]—was probably taken by Ankara as casting further doubt over Eşref.

The growing rift between Eşref and Ankara came to a head in late 1920. In Pervin's telling, a string of unfortunate developments took place that allowed those around Mustafa Kemal to poison relations between the two former comrades-in-arms. First came an incident involving a crop of opium. During the period when they had moved to Eskişehir from Bursa, Pervin says, Eşref received a brusque telegram from Mustafa Kemal in Ankara. The message ordered Eşref to send immediately to Ankara a crop of opium that was in his possession. Several months before, Eşref's unit had confiscated 1,500 kilos of opium from a "rebellious" (i.e. loyalist) merchant in a skirmish. Eşref had sent the crop to the district governor of Eskişehir and the head of the local nationalist committee, Ülvi Bey (Aykurt). Now, out of the blue, Ankara was insisting that Eşref had kept the crop and demanding it be sent to Ankara. Eşref was much aggrieved by the telegram, and in particular the suggestion that he was harboring the goods. He wrote to Mustafa Kemal to explain that there was no such opium in his possession as he had had the crop delivered to the local officials three months ago. He said that in exchange for the crop, which he valued at 100,000 liras, he had only received a shipment of 300 boots for his fighters. He suggested that it must be some hypocrites or backbiters (*münafık*) who had provided the Paşa with this out-of-date information. He asked Mustafa Kemal to trust him to carry out his duties and maintain his ties and respect for the Ankara leader. Eşref showed the telegram to his friend Atıf Bey (Kamçıl), who was one of Mustafa Kemal's commanders, and asked him to intercede. Atıf tried to prevent a break with Mustafa Kemal by vouching for Eşref, but it semed clear to Pervin that the hypocrites were trying to sow trouble between the two men.

The second and perhaps fatal incident occurred when Eşref apparently declined Mustafa Kemal's offer to serve as a representative in its newly established alternative parliament, called the Grand National Assembly. After the establishment of the Ankara legislature, Mustafa Kemal sent out invitations to a number of military officers. It was a useful test of loyalties and also a means of control. Pervin's account makes it quite clear that Eşref was offered the role of MP for Manisa, the provincial capital of the region that included Salihli. After she and her relatives had moved to Anatolia with the assistance of Eşref's brother Ahmed, had subsequently been captives and had escaped to settle temporarily in Eskişehir, Eşref received a visit from a representative of Mustafa Kemal. Known to Pervin only as "H," this man relayed the proposal that Eşref move to Ankara to represent Manisa in the parliament.[115] Pervin was pleased with the offer, but Eşref hesitated. He told "H" that "This business isn't my kind of business." (*Bu iş benim işim değildir.*) He explained that in times such as these when unity was essential, he was not the kind of person to curry favor. He was, he said, not adroit at politics and it would be better if he did not join them in Ankara. "H" asked him to clarify his position. Eşref, demonstrating the very lack of political adroitness to which he had just confessed, proceeded to explain. "Decisions will be taken outside parliament," he said. There would not be long discussions, but rather actions taken according to commands coming from above. In such a situation, he asked, what business would Eşref or people like him have in parliament? "H" restated things in the clearest possible way: "His excellency the Paşa [i.e. Mustafa Kemal] thought it proper for you to take the

Manisa seat. Can you really be refusing it?" (*Kabul etmemeniz doğru bir şey olurmu?*) Eşref replied by presenting his respect to Mustafa Kemal, but said that the best work for him was that which he was already doing, i.e. military and not political business.[116] In another account, Pervin says that Eşref congratulated the Paşa on the founding of the assembly but respectfully declined the offer, citing his wish to resign from duty and to retire in peace, given the presence of many newly arrived men to take his place.[117] Pervin lamented his decision, ruing his penchant for speaking freely and for giving occasion for a lot of "loose talk" and for opportunists (*ayyam adamları*) in Ankara to assign false motivation to Eşref's refusal. She said it gave the "parasites" (*tufeyliler*) surrounding Mustafa Kemal ample ammunition to ruin the otherwise good relations between her husband and their leader in Ankara. "No matter what," she said, "it wasn't good. It had produced a bad mark (*kırık numara*) on Eşref's report card."

Two aspects of the affair made Pervin particularly bitter, beyond the general point that Eşref had sacrificed heavily for his homeland, an issue on which she could be quite eloquent. The first was that Eşref had earlier been approached by unmamed individuals, including a representative in the assembly, who were keen on agitating against Mustafa Kemal but had turned them down. The implication was that if he had really wanted to move against Mustafa Kemal, he had had a clear opportunity but had firmly rejected the advance. The second was that the people she suspected of turning Mustafa Kemal against her husband had been guests in their own home. In Pervin's vivew, the close mix between professional and personal had now turned against them.

She was so disheartened by the latest turn of events that she convinced Eşref to withdraw from the scene completely and to move to Söke in Western Anatolia. This was where Pervin had been born and raised and, she thought, it would allow them to escape the gossips of Ankara.[118] But what may have appeared to Pervin to be a solution to Eşref's problems probably multiplied them significantly. Going to Söke entailed more than simply moving house. Söke was in the Greek zone of occupation. Moving there meant changing sides in a still unresolved war for the future of Anatolia. By following Edhem to the other side of the conflict, Eşref similarly lay himself open to claims of treason. Ankara was quick to affix the labels of traitor (*hain*) and rebel (*asi*) on

Eşref. It was a charge that would, despite his defiance, follow him across his years of exile and would weigh heavily on his family. Pervin writes that she is unconcerned with political issues—"I am not one to wrap myself up in studying the affair's political aspects"—but the apparent lack of awareness of the consequences of crossing over to the other side is particularly striking. It is almost as stark an omission as the yawning gap that appears in Eşref's biographical synopsis, accompanying his published volume on his activities in Arabia. But that story belongs to another chapter.

9

AFTERMATH

A LIFE IN FRAGMENTS

In the post-Ottoman era, the many lives that did not follow the nationalist script present both a challenge and an opportunity for historians. For a variety of reasons, both voluntary and not, large numbers of inhabitants of the core Ottoman territories did not become citizens of the Turkish Republic. Some looked at the unfolding political, religious, and cultural developments and voted with their feet. Others, especially non-Muslims, were either reduced by wartime extermination or forced to leave with population exchanges organized along rather crude religio-national lines. Even among the Muslim Ottomans, many departed for more specific political reasons. Eşref belonged to the latter category, but some aspects of his post-imperial existence reflect the broader fate of those who departed from the expectations of the newly created national states predicated on the "un-mixing" of nationalities. For many Muslims the move from a broadly inclusive Ottoman sense of belonging to a more rigidly policed Turkish identity proved uncomfortable. Most of those lives are understandably lost to historical record. Eşref tried to remain relevant, first through an ultimately unsuccessful attempt to unseat the Ankara government and then to establish his place in history.

After his split with Ankara, Eşref's story becomes much more difficult to follow. This phase of his life, beginning with a flurry of resistance efforts aimed at the Ankara movement for which he had until recently fought, turned into a lengthy period of exile, first in Greece and then in Egypt before his eventual "return" to Turkey as an old man; it is obscured both by gaps in the available sources and by attempts to infuse it with historical "spin." As a result this chapter is necessarily rather more provisional and speculative, attempting only to highlight some of his activities immediately after he broke with Ankara and entered the Greek zone of occupation before going on to consider his exile and his larger place in history. Given the lack of available but seemingly crucial sources from the Greek archives for this period, the result is inevitably spotty. Still, the broad outlines of Eşref's activities are apparent, at least for the early period. When he begins his exile proper, first in mainland Greece, then in Crete and finally in Egypt, his movements become much more difficult to trace. A thorough account of Eşref's long exile is beyond the scope of this book, which is intended to be an episodic biography, dwelling on those phases of his life that were both historically important and supported by documentation. In my opinion the period of his life from 1920 until his death in 1964 is not unimportant. He was part of the broader, largely unstudied phenomenon of the post-Ottoman diaspora which saw people from a wide variety of backgrounds leave their homes for political, cultural, social, and economic reasons. Eşref's story in this period is also not without pathos or excitement. His and Pervin's first child was born in 1922, just as he was beginning what would prove to be an extremely long period of separation from his family. According to his descendants, Eşref apparently was sometimes able to slip back secretly at night into what had become the Turkish Republic to see his wife and to look at his children as they slept. He avoided seeing them when they were awake lest they reveal his presence to those outside the family. But Eşref's story in this period is filled with gaps even larger than those relating to his more active years. There were also many silences, some of them deafening. Eşref seems not to have been keen to discuss his exilic phases, particularly the early stages when he took up arms against the nationalist movement. The chapter ends with a discussion of Eşref's relationship to history, both as a lived phenomenon and as perceived in retrospect.

As we saw in the last chapter, the increasingly uneasy relationship between Eşref and Ankara finally broke in late 1920. After Edhem signed a protocol with the Greek forces in early January 1921, Eşref followed him across the front into what was now the Greek zone of occupation. By this point the line of Greek advance into Anatolia had encompassed both Söke, where Pervin's family had their property, and Eşref's estate at Salihli, so it was perhaps natural that Eşref would soon be spotted in both places. More broadly, the changed status of his two geographical bases combined with his problems with Ankara and Edhem's defection militated in favor of Eşref's westward shift. Changing sides, however, was a high-stakes move. Eşref and Pervin perhaps saw it as returning home, but Ankara saw it in a very different light.

In early February, Ankara's informants on the Greek side reported that Eşref had arrived in Izmir. Together with some of his relatives from Manyas, Eşref had crossed over into Greek-occupied territory by night and had slipped into Izmir. Since the days of Edhem's revolt, Eşref had apparently been secretly fortifying his properties with barbed-wire fencing and machine gun installations. He was also assembling a fighting force from Edhem's men. Intriguingly, the same report also indicates that Eşref had been engaged in negotiations with the Christian authorities in Izmir.[1] Another report one week later confirmed the main lines of Eşref's activities, but added a few other interesting details. Using heavily partisan language, Refet (Bele) described "the rebel" Edhem and his brother Reşid "surrendering" to the Greeks and claimed that documents they had acquired showed that Eşref had engaged in "treason" with Edhem since September 1920.[2] It also claimed that the three men had "fled" to the Greek zone and that Eşref had secretly been invited to move in that direction following negotiations (supposedly facilitated by an unidentified Englishman) between Eşref and Chrisostomos, the Greek Orthodox Metropolitan of Izmir and an individual who appears at several points in Eşref's writings. (Chrisostomos was the main opponent of the Greek High Commissioner Stergiadis, and the prelate may have been trying to effect a rapprochement with the anti-Kemalist forces in order to strengthen his position vis-à-vis Stergiadis, especially after the defeat of his supporter Venizelos in the 1920 Greek elections, but without recourse to the Greek sources it is difficult to say more.[3] He died a grisly death after Izmir was captured by Ankara's forces.) Finally, the report claimed that Eşref had recently arrived in Söke.

Thereafter Eşref seems to have gone back and forth between Söke and Salihli. In June he was spotted at his estate there and was said to have subsequently brought eighteen men to Izmir.[4] In July Eşref's younger brothers Ahmed and Mekkî were arrested with some other Circassians who had been among Edhem's forces and charged with making propaganda for Edhem's "revolt." They were held for a period of time in Konya until they were released on their own recognisance after the Ankara cabinet, including Mustafa Kemal, signed a decree to that effect.[5]

Eşref, Edhem, and Reşid were soon working together again, now with at least the tacit approval of the Greek military, to carry on the fight against Ankara. In the early days of this new phase of activity the prospect of Enver's return was still a possibility. Throughout the spring of 1921 there had been considerable unrest within the "national" movement. This was partly due to fears about what concessions might be made during the peace talks taking place in London. It was also provoked by Ankara's removal of several key officers in the east whose loyalty to Ankara was considered untrustworthy. A concentration of officers suspected of being in Enver's camp coalesced in the towns along the eastern Black Sea coast. Enver's uncle Halil Paşa (Kut) had moved to Trabzon in February, but was told that he would not be allowed to remain in the country. Meanwhile the Greek offensive had gathered pace, taking the towns of Eskişehir and Kutahya in July and raising anxieties among the movement.[6] In June rumors had circulated that Enver's supporters, including Halil Paşa and "Kücük" Talat Paşa (Muşkara), had attempted a coup against Mustafa Kemal's leadership. In July, when the Greek army was advancing, many were calling for Enver's return.[7] Mustafa Kemal responded by tightening his control of the assembly, provoking the creation of an opposition group called the Second Group, who were worried that Mustafa Kemal was taking on dictatorial powers. Several of the opposition group represented Black Sea constituencies.

Enver had gone from Berlin to Moscow in order to try to obtain Soviet support for his plans to create a pan-Islamic state. He was hoping that the anti-imperialist element in his agenda would be sufficient to attract Moscow's backing. But he also had an eye on Anatolia. In late July Enver left Moscow for the Black Sea port of Batum on the Turkish border with the intention of returning to Anatolia. Returning to the city he had captured in April 1918,[8] Enver met with his uncle Halil, "Küçük" Talat, and Dr Nazım, the *éminence grise* of the Committee of Union and Progress. Importantly for our story, Eşref's brother Selim Sami would soon join them. After his adventures in India and the Far East, Sami had gone to Berlin after the war and met with Enver whom he followed to Moscow. While in Batum Enver and his followers were in constant contact with their allies in Trabzon and also received visitors from loyalists in other parts of Anatolia.[9] In early September they discussed plans to enter the country and head to the front to fight the Greeks, a pointed reminder of Ankara's current military shortcomings. They also held a conference under the name of the old Committee of Union and Progress. An attempt at an Enverist political revival was clearly on the cards.

While the pressure on Ankara was at its height and Kemalist forces were on full alert, Ankara was given another reason to worry. In early September Ankara's agents spotted Selim Sami and "Küçük" Talat in the Black Sea port of Giresun, to the west of Trabzon. They had come by ship from Istanbul bearing Italian passports and claiming to be businessmen. They were said to be en route to Batum where Enver was staying, but ultimately headed to Central Asia.[10] The news was quickly related to Ankara in a telegram labeled "Important and extremely urgent." Three days later an intelligence report reached Ankara from Trabzon stating that the travelers had reached Batum after their ship had called in Trabzon. They were said to have been making important plans while aboard ship and were bent on making contact with Halil Paşa. When the ship docked in Trabzon, they engaged in a two-hour conversation with the militia leader Yahya Kahya, described as an extremely stubborn and influential figure in Trabzon. Yahya Kahya had previously met with Enver's uncle Halil when he had stayed in Trabzon for three months from late February.[11] It was clear, the report continued, that they planned to make Trabzon their base of operations.[12]

But a combination of missed timing and Ankara's preparations prevented the Enverists from capitalizing on their position. Acutely aware that Enver continued to enjoy the loyalty of many key military figures, Ankara moved to check his advance. Enver and his men were refused at the border. Mustafa Kemal also benefited from a fortuitous change of fortunes on the military front. The brutal Battle of Sakarya lasted for three weeks in August and September, ending on 13 September. When finally the fighting turned in Ankara's favor, Mustafa Kemal was given a huge reprieve.

Interestingly, Eşref seems to have played no part in the major political development among Ottoman Circassians in this period. On 24 November 1921 a group of prominent leaders of the communities with historic ties to the North Caucasus met in Izmir, then under Greek occupation. Calling themselves the Association for the Strengthening of Near Eastern Circassian Rights, the group issued a manifesto calling for the Great Powers to recognize their rights and their wish for autonomy under Greek rule. Eşref's colleagues Edhem and Reşid took part, as did Maan Şirin, Eşref's erstwhile supporter in Adapazarı.[13] But Eşref's name does not appear among the participants.[14] Why he did not take part is perhaps impossible to know: Efe wonders if his non-participation was due to the Circassian class system, but he generally was not one to engage in political discourse, favoring direct action and the *fait accompli* to political parleys and platforms. Perhaps, as he later wrote, he felt himself an Ottoman and not an ethnic separatist. Like the rest of his fellow self-sacrificing officers, Eşref had dedicated his career to keeping the state together. As he later reflected, "I was an Ottoman, a Turkish-speaking Muslim, and not a Circassian dreaming of Daghestan…"[15]

While Eşref steered clear of the Circassian conference, Enver and Selim Sami eventually made their way to Central Asia where they took part in the final stages of the Basmachi movement that fought the Red Army. When Enver was killed in action during a cavalry charge in the summer of 1922 in what is today Tajikistan, Sami briefly became the movement's leader before it soon collapsed and he fled to Afghanistan. In Tajik history he is referred to as "Selim Pasha" as a result. He would soon return to play a role, ultimately fatal for him, in the resistance movement against Mustafa Kemal and his government in Ankara.

Meanwhile Eşref and Pervin's first child, a daughter named Cuyap (Persian for flowing water), was born in February 1922. During this period Eşref appears to have continued to work with Edhem and Reşid in the fight against Ankara. By April 1922 Eşref was reported to be organizing for this group in Thrace, where a number of Ottoman Muslims who were aligned against Ankara had gathered, while Edhem was similarly engaged in his native Bandırma and in Izmir. Ankara's intelligence sources thought that the Greek government was engaged in plans to unite the opposition if they would cut their ties with Ankara.[16] In late July Eşref arrived in Istanbul on a Greek ship together with Reşid. They were staying in Kadıköy where the police were keeping tabs on them.[17]

The broader situation in Western Anatolia was about to change dramatically. The Greco-Turkish War, known in Turkey alternatively as the War of Turkish Independence or the War of National Liberation, was about to enter its final phase. After spending most of the spring on the defensive, Ankara's forces had rallied. Soon the Greek army was in retreat as Ankara launched the "Great Offensive" in late August. The Greeks were decisively defeated at Dumlupınar, a battle that was to result in roughly half the Greek forces being either captured or killed and their general taken prisoner. It would prove to be the last major battle of the war. Soon Ankara's army was driving toward the Mediterranean. Izmir was captured and soon was in flames; and the Greek army was expelled from Anatolia by the middle of September.

The capture of Izmir by Ankara's forces did not put an end to the fighting in Western Anatolia.[18] Seeing which way the war for Anatolia was going, Eşref, Edhem, and Reşid moved their operations to Mytilene (Midilli in Turkish), the large Greek island off the Anatolian coast to the north of Izmir that had been in Ottoman hands until 1912. The island was the site of a refugee camp for those who had fled the mainland during the Greek collapse, Circassians in particular. Edhem, Reşid, and Eşref engaged in training a guerrilla force, largely of Circassian composition, possibly with the intention of an invasion or a coup. Called the Anatolian Revolutionary Committee (Anadolu İhtilal Komitesi),[19] this group was engaged in training troops on Mytilene and in Western Thrace with the aim of eliminating the Kemalist leadership. Warily watched—and sometimes bombed from the air—by Ankara, this force organized raids against the Anatolian mainland but never constituted a serious threat to Kemalist rule, which vigilantly monitored those it deemed to oppose Mustafa Kemal's growing authority. With time Ankara would use a combination of emergency decrees, purges, banning orders, and sending those it suspected into exile ruthlessly to impose the era of centralized control known euphemistically as the "single-party period" in Turkish history. Soviet influence was strong, as evidenced in five-year plans, state control of key industries, and even in public art and sloganeering. Dissent was often dealt with harshly.

Eşref and Edhem went to Germany in June 1923. Ostensibly this trip was arranged so that Edhem could undergo an operation, but other motives have been surmised. German security officials believed that the pair were using the trip in order "to make their net" and suspected that their voyage was financed by the Entente states. The German authorities were keen for them to leave. Eşref was known to be back in Greece via Italy by August, whereas Edhem had moved to Leipzig.[20] Efe suspects that the trip was timed in order to attempt an assassination of İsmet and the other Ankara representatives taking part in the negotiations for Turkey's future at Lausanne, but credible proof is lacking.[21] What was really happening remains obscure.

The Anatolian Revolutionary Committee, founded by Eşref, Edhem, and Reşid, was naturally high on the list of groups under Ankara's surveillance. Possibly the first outlawed political body of the Turkish Republican era, this group seems to have been bent on overthrowing Mustafa Kemal. It proceeded on the assumption that large swathes of people in Anatolia were against the nationalist leader.[22] Details are sketchy, but it is clear that it was in operation before the Turkish Republic was founded in October 1923 and probably received support from the Greek military. The British, although knowing that the movement was unlikely to succeed and violated the armistice, nevertheless gave their consent.[23] Eşref was its commanding officer.[24] It appealed in rather vague terms to military officers and soldiers in Anatolia.[25] Proclaiming themselves to be fighting in God's victorious cause for the restitution of the legitimate rights of the nation, they made mention of the injustices, deprivations, and contemptuous behavior they perceived to have been perpetrated by the scoundrels, presumably in Ankara, against those whom they were addressing. Referring to the widows and orphans of the martyrs whose lives needed to be avenged, it urged its audience to continue their fight. The Anatolian Revolutionary Committee would fight against the (undefined) "internal enemy," while the fighters to whom it appealed would continue to wage war against the external enemy, presumably the British, the French, and the Italians. In response, Ankara scattered propaganda leaflets directed against the Committee, calling it a "plaything" of the Greek enemy, identifying Edhem, Eşref, and "Hacı" Sami as the key agents and urging the "patriotic" population to kill them.[26]

Practically speaking, the organization trained its men on Mytilene with a view to infiltrating them into the Turkish mainland. According to British sources, as many as 1,400 Circassians and others including Armenians and Rum formed its ranks. Its incursions onto the Anatolian mainland seem to have begun in April 1923 and were said to include as many as 1,700 men.[27] A smaller incursion was reported to have taken place in August 1923 when a force of thirty-two men including both Greeks and Circassians came ashore between Söke and Kuşadası. The Ankara government, intent on wiping out these groups, saw the hand of Athens behind such raids, indicating that the organization was operating under the protection of the Greek government. İsmet Paşa (İnönü), now Ankara's Foreign Minister, therefore wrote to the Entente Powers in Istanbul so that they could "forcefully" bring it to the attention of the Greek government.[28] But Ankara perceived that it was Edhem and Eşref who represented the force behind this movement, and warned its cadres to be on alert.[29] As Gingeras has noted, the biographical synopsis supplied in the sole published volume of Eşref's memoirs makes no mention of this period. Likewise it is absent from the other, scattered accounts that he wrote. Perhaps he hoped to gloss over what Gingeras calls "this brief, but desperate, campaign."

Little was heard from the Anatolian Revolutionary Committee in subsequent years. But in 1927 Eşref's brothers Sami and Ahmed took part in another raid in the same region. Coming ashore near Kuşadası as part of a larger group, they were engaged by Republican forces. The encounter left both brothers dead. According to Ankara's version of the story, the brothers were killed in a skirmish. According to the family, when they knew they would be captured Sami decided not be taken alive. He shot his younger brother and then turned his gun on himself. A witness to the incident later approached the family because, they say, he wanted them to know the truth of the matter. Like much in Eşref's story, an element of dispute and mystery perhaps inevitably remains.

Out-takes from the exile years

In exile, Eşref's life went on. Four years later, in March 1931, he was said by Ankara to have belonged to a Circassian exile organization called Vahdet (Unity) which was being founded in France under the leadership of Rauf (Orbay) with the intention of inciting Circassians in Turkey against the Republic.[30] What happened to this organization is unknown, but after ten years of exile in Europe Rauf later made his peace with Ankara and served as Turkish ambassador to London during World War II. Almost a year later, ten years after the birth of their first child, Eşref and Pervin's second child was born. They gave the baby girl the almost certainly unique name of Diktam. The choice was drawn from a flower known as Burning Bush or Dittany, scientific name *dictamnus albus fraxinella*, which grows only on Crete and is known for its powers of healing. Eşref's Cretan exile was thus given a living testimonial. The cost it exacted from his family is more difficult to discern as these must have been difficult years for them, not only because of the long periods of separation and the problems inherent in Pervin's having to raise three children on her own, but also because of the stigma associated with Eşref's name in Kemalist Turkey. Income from the Söke property seems to have been crucial to supporting not only Pervin and the children but also Eşref, who showed little sign of earning any income in exile.[31] Later, when Diktam went to England, Ambassador Orbay acted as her guardian and remains a revered figured among Eşref's family to this day.

In July 1935 he sat for a photographer's portrait, signed the result and sent it to his elder daughter Cuyap. Taken in Candia (Heraklion), it shows Eşref looking aged. His hair is almost completely gone. His gaze is direct and he looks somber, almost severe. Exile seems to have taken its toll; but he was fashionably dressed, with a tie-pin on his white tie, a dress shirt with a loose-fitting collar, and a light-colored suit jacket with wide lapels. His signature, now in the Latin script, is large and finished with an elaborate flourish. Although diminished in circumstance and unable to return to his family, he appears to have lost none of his sense of self. At some point in this period Eşref apparently fell out with Edhem, probably after one of Edhem's men named "Bald" Kadri shot and wounded him in the hand.[32] Little by little Eşref's old life had fallen away. In 1936 he wrote to Mustafa Kemal asking for forgiveness.[33] It was not forthcoming.

Despite this snub, it is noteworthy that on learning of Mustafa Kemal (Atatürk)'s death in 1938, Eşref wrote to his daughter Cuyap, praising his

20. Eşref in exile on Crete. (Source: EK papers)

former comrade—"my school friend, my comrade in Trablusgarb, my beloved confidant, my commander in the War of Independence, and the father of the nation"—in a moving personal tribute. Despite their difficulties, Eşref clearly remained fond of Kemal to the point of reverence and lamented that circumstances had prevented them from meeting again. "If only," he closed his letter to his daughter with a final word about Mustafa Kemal, "we had been able to meet in a state of forgiveness and making amends for one minute before his death. In the name of the nation I send you condolences, my dear."[34]

Eşref's day-to-day life in exile was lived in marked contrast to that of his more celebrated former colleague. Eşref remained in Greece until some time in the early 1940s. Although the "150" were pardoned in 1938, Eşref refused to return, defiantly arguing that he had done

nothing wrong so could not accept a pardon. The circumstances surrounding his move to Egypt are unclear. In the 1920s Ottoman exiles
in Greece had been supported by successive Greek governments who
viewed them as useful enemies of Ankara. This attitude changed after
Venizelos returned to power in 1928. The Ottoman exiles were subsequently encouraged to leave in order to enable the new policy of rapprochement between Greece and Turkey. After 1936 the Metaxas dic-
tatorship more or less continued the same policy.[35] So how and why
Eşref stayed so long in the country is somewhat puzzling. Nevertheless,
Eşref soon found himself in Egypt once again, an exile but no longer a
prisoner as he had been when he last "visited" the country during the
war. Staying mostly in Alexandria and in Cairo with relatives, he also
traveled quite a bit, including one trip up the Nile into Upper Egypt
and the Sudan by *falucca*, the lateen-rigged sailboat of the Nile. He
camped along the way but always slept away from his tent, hidden from
view. Wary of attack, the old militiaman still maintained his vigilance.
At other times Eşref seems to have passed his time in exile by painting,
taking photographs, and writing his memoirs. With this last goal in
mind, he engaged in lengthy correspondence with former colleagues
and popular historians in both Greece and Egypt. The former group
included a Greek general and the Turkish Islamist thinker Mehmet
Âkif,[36] with whom Eşref had traveled to the desert of Najd during the
Great War.

In later years, even after his "return" to Turkey in the early 1950s, he
would continue to write his massive memoirs. Dividing his time
between Izmir and Söke, Eşref stepped up his correspondence with
various friends and former colleagues. One such interlocutor was
Cihangiroğlu Hasan from Kars, with whom Eşref had fought in Western
Thrace, along with his brother Cihangiroğlu İbrahim. İbrahim had gone
on to preside over another similar mini-state called the Provisional
Government of South-Western Caucasia, established in Kars in 1919.[37]

Eşref also seems to have made many trips to see the men with whom
he had fought over the years. In one case he apparently made the arduous journey to Eastern Anatolia to visit a Kurdish comrade, riding for
long hours in the back of a truck despite his advanced years. In many
cases the men he knew had died but he visited their widows and children, helping to provide for them when he could, according to his

family. Increasingly he found that he had outlived many of his comrades-in-arms. Apart from his lawsuit against the Turkish government aimed at restitution for his seized property in Salihli, he seems to have avoided any further political activity.

Even if Eşref had wanted to get involved, his close associates were now gone. He had broken with Çerkes Edhem and Reşid and both brothers died in the early 1950s. The "ten promised paradise" were all but extinct. Selim Sami (number 2) had died in 1927, as we have just seen. Süleyman Askerî (3) had committed suicide in Iraq in 1915 on the Mesopotamian front. Yakup Cemil (4) had been executed after his failed coup attempt the following year. Sapancalı Hakkı (5) was the member who had traveled to Egypt with Mustafa Kemal and Yakup Cemil in 1911 and played a part in the raid on the Sublime Porte of 1913. He had been brought to trial in Allied-occupied Istanbul for unlawful economic activity along the way, but was acquitted in 1919.[38] Suspected also by Ankara, he was prosecuted after the Izmir assassination attempt in 1927 but released again. He stayed out of politics thereafter and died in 1937.[39] Çanakkaleli Atıf (Kamcıl) (6) served as an MP under the Republic and died in 1947. Abdülkadir Antepli (7), the former governor of Ankara, was caught trying to flee to Greece in 1926 and was hanged. Topçu İhsan (Eryavuz) (8), Eşref's friend from Kuleli military school, served as Minister of the Navy and was at the center of the "Havuz-Yavuz" kickback scandal in 1928; he died in 1947. Filibeli Hilmi (9) served briefly as an MP in the Turkish Republic but was convicted and sentenced to death in 1926 by the Independence Tribunal investigating the Izmir plot to assassinate Mustafa Kemal. İzmitli Mümtaz (10), Enver's aide-de-camp, uniquely managed to live a quiet life after the war and died in 1936. Therefore, Eşref was the sole member of the list to remain alive at the time when he returned to Anatolia. Being a member of the innermost group of the activist officers did not promote longevity.

The personal matrix of activist military officers who served Enver, so crucial to Eşref's story, had been broken up by the events of World War I, the "National Forces" period, and the early Turkish Republic. Personal networks, of course, revolve around personalities. Normally these remain fairly hidden from the historical record. In Eşref's case, thanks to his penchant for saving a variety of source materials, the astute and detailed observations of his wife Pervin, and other existing accounts, we have been able to catch occasional glimpses of this crucial but elusive dimension. They have shown Eşref's personality to be clearly energetic, restless, stubborn, proud, and combative.

Even as an old man, Eşref did not shy away from physical confrontation. Philip Stoddard, who went to interview Eşref in the early 1960s for his PhD dissertation, reported a telling incident. After having arranged to meet Eşref at the Söke farm, Stoddard arrived to find him absent. He was told that Eşref was in court in Izmir. Stoddard retraced his steps and proceeded to the courthouse where he found the old combatant in the dock, charged with assault. The plaintiff was a phaeton driver who claimed that Eşref had gravely wounded him. Eşref, "mad as hops," was putting up a lively defense. He explained that the plaintiff, whom he described as a pipsqueak and harem hanger-on, had made fun of the crocheted cap that Eşref had been wearing at the time of the incident: which involved Eşref pulling him from his vehicle in response to the taunt. Eşref asked the judge: "Could I help it if he passed out when he hit the ground?" The judge dismissed the case.[40] On another occasion Eşref took umbrage at the treatment he received from a much younger construction worker who was building one of the new boulevards in Izmir. Words were exchanged and in an instant Eşref had knocked the man into the ditch that ran along the side of the new road. Eşref was on him in a flash, raining blows upon him, and had to be persuaded by onlookers to leave the unfortunate man alone. As he told his son-in-law, he always preferred to take pre-emptive action.

Eşref was, like most of us perhaps, paradoxical. Vilified as a traitor to his nation, he was also clearly also highly loyal, especially to Enver. Stubbornly, it seems, he refused to throw in his lot with the new power base being constructed at Ankara by Mustafa Kemal when it would have been in his best interests to do so. Like a few others, including Çerkes Edhem, Eşref rejected the new post-Enver dispensation and voted with his feet. Perhaps he was thinking that, as had happened in his youth during the reign of Abdülhamid II, he would always be given another chance. Sadly for him that chance only came when he was an old man. He "returned" to his country only in the 1950s after the party that Mustafa Kemal had founded was swept from power in Turkey's first elections. By then most of his former comrades were dead and his prized estate at Salihli had been confiscated. He devoted his considerable energies to writing his memoirs, corresponding with and visiting his former colleagues whom, it seems, he considered in some respects as much as his own flesh and blood as his family members.

Back to Eşref's trunk

It is perhaps appropriate to end this story where it began, with Eşref's trunk. It kindly offered up many leads—more in fact than I could ever trace—names, facts, documents, images, and memorabilia. Amid the likes of Eşref's sheaf of telegrams from the Sinai front, his Malta souvenirs, Pervin's memoir, various photographs, there were also a few items that speak to the physicality of the archive and the materiality of some of its sources. These serve as useful reminders that the papers, for all of their importance as texts, can only tell us part of the story. When I first visited one of Eşref's descendants, she showed me a green pouch. As I watched, she poured out its contents: rubber stamps, all in Bulgarian, that Eşref had picked up somewhere, probably in Edirne or Western Thrace. Presumably he had used these to forge documents when he and his men were working behind enemy lines after the recapture of Edirne. In the trunk itself I also found Eşref's Egyptian gun permit, showing that he had registered his 0.37 gauge automatic revolver, a weapon with an eight-shot capacity and the serial number 34749, every year between 1946 and 1950. During the last phase of his exile, this most famous (or infamous) of what Stoddard called the "tough guys," a man the British referred to as a "notorious brigand," and who referred to himself as someone with nothing to lose, had registered his handgun year after year as a law-abiding civilian.

In a story of many ironies, there is one last one. A final list from Eşref's trunk shows a list of his signatures as they changed over time. It sheds some light on the way Eşref regarded himself in the light of history. We have already seen, through the title of his ill-fated memoir, *My Lessons for History*, and the list of the "Ten Promised Paradise", indications that Eşref positioned himself squarely on the historical stage. Let us now consider a table he compiled to track his changing signatures over the years. This document reveals his strong sense of historical consciousness. It seems specifically intended to help any future histo-

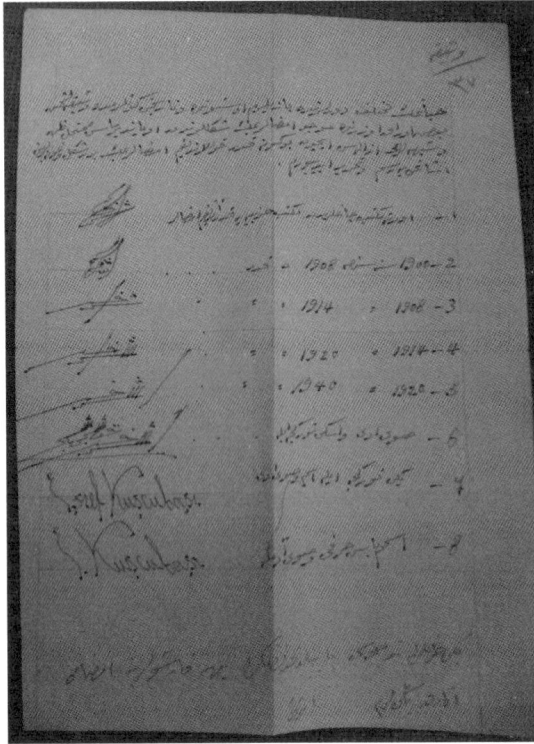

21. Eşref's changing signatures. (Source: EK papers)

rian who might, or even, Eşref must have thought (correctly, it turns out), would certainly come along to investigate his life. In the accompanying annotation he indicates that he has written this document in order to remove any supposition or doubt over the signatures he affixed to the documents he wrote during the "historical days" of his life. But it also raises a curious irony: how could it be that someone so self-consciously interested in his place in the historical record as to compose this guide for posterity could write a multiple-volume memoir that failed to see the light of day?

This is but one of many unsolved riddles presented by the case of Eşref Bey and his trunk, a reminder perhaps of both the enduring and fleeting nature of history, of both its heavy hand and its often mercurial and elusive character.

NOTES

1. INTRODUCTION: TALES FROM THE TRUNK

1. The best overviews of this period are to be found in M. Şükrü Hanioğlu, *A Brief History of the Late Ottoman Empire* (Princeton: Princeton University Press, 2008); and Erik Jan Zürcher, *Turkey: A Modern History*, 3rd edn (London: I. B. Tauris, 2004).

2. On the relationship between the historian and the archive, see Arlette Farge, *The Allure of the Archives* (New Haven: Yale University Press, 2013).

3. Ahmet Efe, *Efsaneden Gerçeğe Kuşcubaşı Eşref* (Istanbul: Bengi, 2007).

4. Hakan Kağan, *İmparatorluğun Son Akşamı* (Istanbul: Timas, 2008).

5. See, for example, www.gazetevatan.com/turk-istihbaratinin-kurucusu-bir-vatan-haini-miydi—152286-gundem and www.yenidenergenekon.com/15-tarihin-en-buyuk-casusu-ve-gerillasi-esref-sencer-kuscubasi (accessed 7 November 2014).

6. On this organization, see Polat Safi, "History in the Trench: The Ottoman Special Organization—Teşkilat-ı Mahsusa Literature," *Middle Eastern Studies* 48:1 (2012), 89–106; Ahmet Tetik, *Teşkilat-ı Mahsusa (Umûr-u Şarkiye Dairesi) Tarihi Cilt I: 1914–1916* (Istanbul: Turkiye İş Bankası Yayınları, 2014); Philip Hendrick Stoddard, "The Ottoman Government and the Arabs, 1911 to 1918: A Preliminary Study of the Teşkilât-ı Mahsusa" (unpublished PhD dissertation, Princeton University, 1963).

7. Taner Akcam, *A Shameful Act: The Armenian Genocide and the Question of Turkish Responsibility* (New York: Macmillan, 2006).

8. The controversy is many-layered. An article by Vahakn Dadrian entiled "Ottoman Archives and Denial of the Armenian Genocide" in Richard G. Hovannisian, ed., *The Armenian Genocide* (pp. 300–01) claimed that Eşref, erroneously referred to by all parties as the head of the Special Organization, had effectively admitted to being involved in the killing of Armenians during the war in passages attributed to him in Cemal Kutay's book on the Special Organization in World War I (*Birinci Dünya Harbinde Teşkilat-ı Mahsusa ve Hayber'de Türk Cengi* (Istanbul: Tarih Yayınları, 1962). The writer Guenter Lewy subsequently published a book called *Armenian Massacres in Ottoman Turkey: A Disputed Genocide* (Salt Lake City: University of Utah Press,

2007) in which he criticized Dadrian's interpretation of some of Eşref's comments, indicating that, in his view, Dadrian had manipulated the comments (in part by interpolating phrases in brackets) to put words in Eşref's mouth that he never would have said. When this book was favorably reviewed in *IJMES* 38 (2006: 598–601), his colleagues Keith Watenpaugh and Joseph Kéchichian wrote highly critical responses in which they questioned the suitability of the reviewer and called his scholarly credentials into question. In his piece Kéchichian calls Eşref's statement a "confession of his involvement in the wholesale elimination of Armenians" (IJMES 39:3 (2007: 510)). Looking at the original text makes it clear that Eşref's words had been manipulated to make it appear as though he had admitted to involvement in crimes against the Armenians when actually he was discussing Sait Halim Paşa, the wartime Grand Vizier subsequently assassinated by an Armenian agent for his alleged role in the genocide. Without wanting to delve any further into the stratigraphy of this dispute, it seems important to point out that Eşref was not the head of the Special Organization (as Polat Safi's work has clearly demonstrated) and that what he is alleged to have said, at least in Dadrian's rather creative reconstruction, is possibly at odds with what he himself wrote about an exchange he had with British officials in Egypt before he was sent to Malta, as we shall see in Chapter 6. It is, however, also possible that Eşref's statement was intended as a kind of rationalization of the treatment of the Armenians.

9. Selim Sami has been viewed as possibly an even more legendary character than his brother. He is the subject of another novel, Ekrem Hayri Peker's *Teşkilat-ı Mahsusa'dan Kuşçubaşı Hacı Sami Bey* (Istanbul: Kastaş, 2012), and also has "his" own Twitter account.

10. Bülent Bilmez, "A Nationalist Discourse of Heroism and Treason: The Construction of an 'Official' Image of Çerkes Ethem (1886–1948) in Turkish Historiography, and Recent Challenges," in Amy Singer, Christoph K. Neumann and Selçuk Akşin Somel, eds., *Untold Histories of the Middle East: Recovering Voices from the 19th and 20th Centuries* (London: Routledge, 2011), 106.

11. Ann Laura Stoler, *Along the Archival Grain: Epistemic Anxieties and Colonial Commonsense* (Princeton: Princeton University Press, 2009), 47.

12. Nicole and Hugh Pope, *Turkey Unveiled: Atatürk and After* (London: John Murray, 1997), 53–4.

13. Eşref Kuşçubası, *The Turkish Battle at Khaybar*, eds. Philip Stoddard and H. Basri Danışman (Istanbul: Arba, 1997); Eşref Kuşçubası, *Hayber'de Türk Cengi* (Istanbul: Arba, 1997).

14. Christine M Philliou, *Biography of an Empire: Governing Ottomans in an Age of Revolution* (Berkeley: University of California Press, 2011).

15. Andrew Mango, *Atatürk* (London: John Murray, 1999); M Şükrü Hanioğlu, *Atatürk: An Intellectual Biography* (Princeton: Princeton University Press, 2011), to name only two of the many biographies of Mustafa Kemal. Michael Reynolds' eagerly awaited study of Enver Paşa will undoubtedly make a major contribution.

16. Eşref Kuşcubaşı, *Kanuna, aklıselime ve hukuk devleti devri iddialarına rağmen devam halindeki bir zülmün acı hikayesi* (Istanbul: Tan, 1953).

17. Private papers of Eşref Kuşcubaşı. Pervin Sencer'in haltercümesi. I hope to publish this memoir in due course.

18. Nadir Özbek, "Policing the Countryside: Gendarmes of the Late 19th-Century Ottoman Empire (1876–1908)," *IJMES* 40:1 (2008: 56).

19. Zeynel Abidin Besleney, *The Circassian Diaspora in Turkey: A Political History* (London: Routledge, 2013), 53.

20. Justin McCarthy, *Death and Exile: The Ethnic Cleansing of Ottoman Muslims, 1821–1922* (Princeton: Darwin Press, 1995), 34–6. For an assessment of alternative estimates of the demographic changes, see Besleney, 49.

21. On the question of the use of the term "Circassian" in the context of Ottoman exile, see Besleney, 54.

22. For the connections between Ottoman debt and the Circassian crisis, see Nazan Çiçek, "'Talihsiz Çerkesleri İngiliz Peksimeti': İngiliz Arşiv Belgelerinde Büyük Çerkes Göçü (Şubat 1864–Mayıs 1865)," *Ankara Üniversitesi Siyasal Bilimler Fakültesi Dergisi* 64:1 (2009), 57–88.

23. Muhittin Ünal, *Kurtuluş Savaşında Çerkeslerin Rölü* (Ankara: Kafkas Derneği Yayınları, 2000); Sefer E. Berzeg, *Çerkes—Vubıhlar: Soçi'nin İnsanları (Portreler)* (Ankara: Kuban, 2013); Ryan Gingeras, *Sorrowful Shores: Violence, Ethnicity, and the End of the Ottoman Empire, 1912–1923* (New York: Oxford University Press, 2009).

24. Edward J Erickson, *Ottomans and Armenians: A Study in Counterinsurgency* (New York: Palgrave Macmillan, 2013).

25. "Diaghilev and the Golden Age of the Ballets Russes, 1909–1929," an exhibition at the Victoria & Albert Museum, 25 September 2010—9 January 2011.

26. Reşat Kasaba, *A Moveable Empire: Ottoman Nomads, Migrants and Refugees* (Seattle: University of Washington Press, 2009).

27. Antonio Giustozzi, *The Art of Coercion: The Primitive Accumulation and Management of Coercive Power* (London: Hurst & Co., 2011), 51.

28. Erik Jan Zürcher, "Macedonians in Anatolia: The Importance of the Macedonian Roots of the Unionists for their Policies in Anatolia after 1914," *Middle Eastern Studies* 50:6 (2014), 964.

29. Ibid.

30. Erik Jan Zürcher, *The Unionist Factor: The Role of the Committee of Union and Progress in the Turkish National Movement* (Leiden: Brill, 1984), 50.

31. Zürcher, *The Young Turk Legacy and Nation Building: From the Ottoman Empire to Atatürk's Turkey* (London: I. B. Tauris, 2010), 134.

32. As cited in Stoddard and Danışman, *Turkish Battle at Khaybar*, 174.

2. FROM PALACE TO REBEL AND BACK AGAIN

1. Aléxandre Toumarkine, "Entre Empire Ottoman et État-Nation Turc: Les Immigrés Musulmans de Caucase et des Balkans du Milieu du XIXe Siècle à Nos Jours"

(unpublished PhD thesis, University of Paris IV—Sorbonne, 2000), 519. My thanks to Dr Toumarkine for kindly granting me access to this important work at the Orient Institut in Istanbul and for his valuable advice. Perhaps symptomatic of the fact that the family did not establish strong roots in the region, another source gives Kızıksa, a village in the same region, as the place they first settled. Sefer E. Berzeg, *Çerkes—Vubıhlar: Soçi'in İnsanları* (Ankara: Kurban, 2013), 298.

2. Philip Hendrick Stoddard, "The Ottoman Government and the Arabs, 1911 to 1918: A Preliminary Study of the Teşkilât-ı Mahsusa" (unpublished PhD dissertation, Princeton University, 1963), 161.

3. Among the few scraps of information currently available about Mustafa Nuri is one archival document indicating that his position was vacant as of 22 January 1894. Başbakanlık Osmanlı Arşivi (BOA) İ.HUS 20/36. The paucity of sources was not confined to the Ottoman archives. Eşref would later lament that the only picture he possessed of his father was destroyed in a house fire in Karşıyaka, Izmir in 1917. Şehir Üniversitesi Kütüphanesi Taha Toros Arşivi (TT) DSC00251, Eşref to Âsaf Bey, 17 September 1962, 4.

4. For an evocative, if at times somewhat romanticized, account of this Circassian family's trials and tribulations, see Aydın Osman Erkan, *Turn My Head to the Caucasus: The Biography of Osman Ferid Pasha* (Istanbul: Çitlembik, 2009).

5. Stoddard, "The Ottoman Government and the Arabs."

6. T C Nüfus Kayıtı Örneğı, kindness of İrem Toner.

7. Scarlet fever killed his sister Ayşe when she was fourteen years old. The same disease spared the life of Eşref's brother Yusuf, but left him deaf and needing many years of hospitalization and special care.

8. "Selim Sam Istanbullu ve Beşiktaşlıdır." EK, "Selim Sami hal tercümesi," 4.

9. On educational trajectories in this period, see Benjamin C. Fortna, *Learning to Read in the Late Ottoman Empire and the Early Turkish Republic* (London: Palgrave Macmillan, 2010).

10. Taha Toros papers (TT) DSC00244, EK to Âsaf Bey, 17 June 1962 (reading 1893 for 1983).

11. "Selim Sami hal tercümesi," 5.

12. Ryan Gingeras, *Sorrowful Shores: Violence, Ethnicity, and the End of the Ottoman Empire, 1912–1923* (New York: Oxford University Press, 2009), 60–63. Toumarkine indicates that Eşref never graduated from Harbiye because he was sent into exile in the Hijaz during his final year, due to his links with the political opposition to Sultan Abdülhamid. Toumarkine, 519.

13. Gingeras, *Sorrowful Shores*, 14–15.

14. Gingeras, *Sorrowful Shores*, 63.

15. TT DSC00244, EK (İzmir) to Âsaf Bey, 17 June 1962, 1. Topcu "Artilleryman" İhsan (Eryavuz) would go on to be a member of the Teşkilat-ı Mahsusa and the Karakol and became the head of the "Independence Tribunals" in the early 1920s as well as an MP and Minister of the Navy. While serving in the last post he was

involved in one of the largest scandals of the early Republic, the "Havuz–Yavuz" corruption case.

16. TT DSC00247, EK to Âsaf Bey, 17 June 1962, 4.
17. Nurettin Şimşek, *Teşkilât-ı Mahsusa'nın Reisi Süleyman Askerî Bey: Hayatı, Siyasi ve Askeri Faaliyetleri* (Istanbul: IQ Kültür Sanat Yayıncılık, 2008), 28; Celal Bayar, *Ben de Yazdım: Millî Mücadele'ye Gidiş* IV (Istanbul: Baha, 1967), 1289.
18. On the significance of this group, which usually goes unnoticed in most accounts of the period, see M. Naim Turfan, *Rise of the Young Turks: Politics, the Military and Ottoman Collapse* (London: I. B. Tauris, 2000), 346.
19. For a chart indicating the importance of a Harbiye education in the creation of the factions of the tumultuous "National Forces" period, see Toumarkine, 917 ff.
20. Şerif Mardin, *Religion and Social Change in Modern Turkey: The Case of Bediüzzaman Said Nursi* (Albany, NY: State Universitiy of New York Press, 1989), 78.
21. Hulusi Turgut, "Nur cemaatinin Türkiye'de 20 bin medresesi var," *Sabah*, 19 January 1997 (http://arsiv.sabah.com.tr/1997/01/19/f05.html), accessed 19 June 2014.
22. Mardin, 82–3.
23. Personal communication, DA, 4 July 2010.
24. BOA DH.ŞFR 357/72.
25. Cemal Kutay, *Türkiye İstiklâl ve Hürriyet Mücadeleri Tarihi*, vol. X (Istanbul: Nurgök Tarih Matbaası, 1957), 5755.
26. Eşref Kuşçubaşı, *Kanuna, aklıselime ve hukuk devleti devri iddialarına rağmen devam halindeki bir zulmün acı hikayesi* (Istanbul: Tan Matbaası, 1953), 1.
27. TT DSC00242, 16 April 1962.
28. TT DSC00249, 250, EK (Söke) to Âsaf [Tugay], 17 September 1962, 2–3.
29. TT DSC00249, EK (Söke) to Âsaf [Tugay], 17 September 1962, 2.
30. Eşref K, *Kanuna*, 2.
31. Stoddard, 162.
32. Eşref K, *Kanuna*, 1.
33. "Selim Sami hal tercümesi," 9.
34. Martin Strohmeier, "Fakhri (Fahrettin) Paşa and the end of Ottoman rule in Medina," *Turkish Historical Review* 4 (2013), 194.
35. Stoddard and Danışman, "The Life of Eşref Sencer Kuşçubaşızade" in EK, *Turkish Battle*, 227.
36. T. E. Lawrence, *Seven Pillars of Wisdom: A Triumph* (New York: Penguin Books, 1962), 159–60.
37. BOA BEO TFR.I.M 9/863.
38. BOA DH.ŞFR 357/72.
39. These estates were huge, the result of Abdülhamid II's policy of expanding them from the early years of his reign, partly for strategic reasons and partly to spur agricultural development. It is estimated that the sultan's income amounted to 6–10 per cent of state revenues.

40. Zeynel Abidin Besleney, *The Circassian Diaspora in Turkey: A Political History* (London: Routledge, 2014), 62.

41. Sabri Yetkin, *Ege'de Eşkiyalar* (Istanbul: Tarih Vakfı, 2003), 133.

42. TT DSC00306-DSC00307.

43. EK2, Scan 6.

44. TT DSC00309.

45. TT DSC00307, EK (Kuşadası) to Âsaf Bey, 22 August 1962, 2. "Zayif ve oldukca bozgun ve düşkünümüz günlerde."

46. M. Şükrü Hanioğlu, *Preparation for a Revolution: The Young Turks, 1902–1908* (New York: Oxford University Press, 2001), 226–7; Nader Sohrabi, *Revolution and Constitutionalism in the Ottoman Empire and Iran* (Cambridge: Cambridge University Press, 2011), 126.

47. BOA HSD.TFR1 1/70, Kosova Kaymakamı Tahsin (Kosova) to Enver (Manastır), 8 January 1908, referring to "jandarma mülazımı Eşref Efendi."

48. Toumarkine, 517.

49. Gingeras, *Sorrowful Shores*, 62, citing Stoddard, 166.

50. This information comes from a relative of Feride Hanım: personal communication İrem Toner, 22 June 2014. The lack of information about Feride contrasts dramatically, as we shall see, with that pertaining to Eşref's second wife, Pervin Hanım. Particularly since Pervin's writings survive, both in the form of letters and a memoir, our knowledge of his life improves dramatically once she comes into the picture on the eve of World War I.

51. TT DSC 00256. Interestingly, Eşref says that although he had registered the property in the name of Çerkes Edhem, it was coveted by an uncle of Rahmi Bey called Hıfzı Bey, who was the Governor of Izmir. While Eşref was imprisoned on Malta, this man took the opportunity to appropriate it from Edhem. Clearly these property transactions were far from straightforward or by the book, a further reflection of the unsettled period.

52. Eşref Kuşçubaşı, *Kanuna, aklıselime ve hukuk devleti devri iddialarına rağmen devam halindeki bir zulmün acı hikayesi* (Istanbul: Tan Matbaası, 1953), 7. When Eşref returned in the early 1950s, he initiated a legal challenge to the confiscation of his property and won a relatively small monetary amount by way of compensation. This indicates that he was able to prove legal ownership prior to his exile.

53. Sened-i hakanî 13/82/74, 29/82/46, and 14/82/75 (23 Rebiülevvel 1336). My thanks to Sedat Aktay for kindly sending me these documents. These deeds show that Eşref was purchasing land from both Muslims and non-Muslims, including a woman listed as "Meryam, the daughter of Mustafa" and a man named "Leonidi the son of Apostol."

54. Hervé Georgelin, *La fin de Smyrne* (Paris: CNRS, 2006), 179.

55. EK2, Picture 012.

56. Sohrabi, *Revolution and Constitutionalism*, 252.

57. EK2, Picture 012.

58. John Presland (pseudonym of Mrs Gladys Skelton), *Deedes Bey: A Study of Sir Wyndham Deedes, 1883–1923* (London: Macmillan, 1942), 87.
59. Middle East Centre Archives (MEC), St Antony's College, Oxford Archives. Deedes Papers, 4/18, 23 April 1912.
60. Deedes would later become a social worker and a fervent Zionist, but in 1915 he wrote a report entitled "Plan for the Retention of the Ottoman Empire" and presented it to Kitchener. He was with Allenby when he entered Jerusalem in December 1917 and eventually served as Secretary to the High Commissioner of British Palestine.
61. MEC. Deedes Papers, 5/76 (n.d., 1914).
62. Whoever later typed up Deedes' original pen-and-ink letters and diary entries rendered this name as "Sauri," but the similarity between Sauri and Sami, particularly in English script, the timing of the event, and the presence of a great many other errors in transcription—the typed versions contain errors that someone with Deedes' knowledge of Turkish would never have made—make Sami the logical subject of an incident that Deedes reports from 1912. Also pointing in this direction is the mention made of Sami in the *Arab Bulletin* a few years later in Cairo, as we shall see. Some further errors seem to have been added by "John Presland," the pseudonym of of Mrs Gladys Skelton/Bendit, née Williams, the author of *Deedes Bey: A Study of Sir Wyndham Deedes, 1883–1923* (London: Macmillan, 1942). For example, s/he renders the van Lenneps as the "van Hempsters."
63. Yetkin, 166.
64. Ibid. Interestingly, the CUP organizer Dr Nazım had tried to recruit the bandit Çakırcalı Mehmet Efe for its cause before the 1908 revolution. Hanioğlu, *Preparation*, 226–7.
65. Yetkin, 166.
66. MEC. Deedes Papers GB165–0079 4/13, 1 March 1912.
67. BOA DH.H 40/8/4, 25 June 1912.
68. BOA DH.H 40/8/6, 21 June 1912.
69. BOA DH.H 40/8/28, 27 July 1913.
70. BOA DH.KMS 1/28, 27 October 1913.
71. *The Arab Bulletin* I, 361–2.
72. Nader Sohrabi, "Global Waves, Local Actors: What the Young Turks Knew About Other Revolutions and Why It Mattered," *Comparative Studies in Society and History* 44/1 (2002), 57.
73. Fatma Müge Göçek, "What is the Meaning of the 1908 Young Turk Revolution? A Critical Historical Assessment in 2008," *İstanbul Üniversitesi Siyasal Bilgiler Fakültesi Dergisi* 38 (2008), 199.

3. VOLUNTEERS IN THE DESERT: THE OTTOMAN–ITALIAN WAR FOR LIBYA

1. EK, Scan 252.

2. EK, Scan 248.
3. Feridun was later adopted by Eşref's second wife, Pervin.
4. Bayar, *Ben de Yazdım*, 1289.
5. While many have claimed that Eşref was the leader of the Special Organization, it seems clear that he served as a field officer and that Askerî acted as its first director under the overall leadership of Enver. For the details, see P. Safi, "History in the Trench: The Ottoman Special Organization—Teşkilat-ı Mahsusa Literature," *Middle Eastern Studies* 48:1, 98.
6. EK2, Scan 13–14.
7. "Gidipte iş görmeden dönen kahramanlar yazılıdır." EK2 Resim 015.
8. Mesut Uyar, personal communication, 16 October 2012.
9. İlber Ortaylı, *İmparatorluğun En Üzün Yüzyılı* (Istanbul: Timas, 2008).
10. David Gilmour, "He Dared the Undarable," *New York Review of Books* LXI: 4 (6–19 March 2014), 22.
11. Rachel Simon, *Libya between Ottomanism and Nationalism: The Ottoman Involvement in Libya during the War with Italy (1911–1919)* (Berlin: Klaus Schwarz Verlag, 1987), 49.
12. Simon, 53–4.
13. E. E. Evans-Pritchard, *The Sanusi of Cyrenaica* (Oxford: Oxford University Press, 1949), 100.
14. Barbara W. Tuchman, *The Guns of August* (New York: Macmillan, 1962) (repr. Ballantine), 50, 53.
15. Simon, 55.
16. Simon, 55.
17. Evans-Pritchard, 107.
18. Zürcher, *The Young Turk Legacy and Nation Building*, 115.
19. Ibid., 114–15.
20. Safi, "Ottoman Special Organization: An Inquiry," 94, citing Enver's letter of 4 September 1911.
21. Fehmi, 10.
22. Simon, 93.
23. Zürcher, 102.
24. Zürcher, 195–6.
25. Tilman Lüdke, *Jihad Made in Germany: Ottoman and German Propaganda and Intelligence Operations in the First World War* (Münster: Lit Verlag, 2005).
26. EK, Scan 248.
27. EK, Scan 239.
28. Andrew Mango, *Atatürk* (London: John Murray, 1999), 104; Zürcher, 127.
29. Stoddard, 80.
30. EK, Scan 234.
31. "Askerî'nin ikna' kuvveti malum." EK Fehmi, 11.
32. Fehmi, 11.

33. "İşte bu defa büyük vatanperver Askerî, işi ve kurtuluşu kanunda buldu." Fehmi, 13.

34. "Ha bakın çocuklar. Yatmak için nerede isterseniz yatarım. Bitli, pislikli fakat yemek işine gelince bunu yapamam. Mutlaka iyi bir lokantada yemek yemek isterim, dedi ve ayak diredi." Fehmi, 22.

35. EK S Askerî, 2.

36. S Askerî, 4.

37. Enver Pascha, *Um Tripolis: Feld-Ausgabe* (München: Hugo Bruckmann Verlag, 1918), 33, 36.

38. Simon, 115.

39. EK, Scan 236.

40. EK, Scan 238.

41. EK Resim 044.

42. Simon, 144.

43. Evans-Pritchard, 107–8.

44. Ibid., 108.

45. Ibid., 110.

46. Aziz Ali was of Circassian descent but culturally Arab as his cognomen "The Egyptian" indicates. He had been a key CUP activist in Manastır before the 1908 revolution, when he got to know Enver well. He appears again in Eşref's story. After the Libyan war he founded a secret Arab organization in Istanbul called *Al-Ahd* ("The Covenant"), an important vehicle in the spread of Arab nationalism among Ottoman military officers. Hasan Kayalı, *Arabs and Young Turks: Ottomanism, Arabism, and Islamism in the Ottoman Empire, 1908–1918* (Berkeley: University of California Press, 1997), 178, 186–7. Eşref would encounter him again in Arabia in 1917, by which time Aziz Ali had joined the "Arab Revolt" against the Ottoman Empire.

47. George Gawrych, *The Young Atatürk: From Ottoman Soldier to Statesman of Turkey* (London: I. B. Tauris, 2013), 25.

48. Slavery was still somewhat common in Libya during this period.

49. Simon, 244.

50. Evans-Pritchard, 110.

51. Simon, 144.

52. Evans-Pritchard, 110–11.

53. M Şükrü Hanioğlu, ed., *Kendi Mektuplarında Enver Paşa* (Istanbul: Der, 1989), 101.

54. EK2, Scan 615.

55. Hanioğlu, ed., *Kendi Mektuplarında Enver Paşa*, 108.

56. Mustafa Kemal reported the much higher number of 7,742 tribal fighters at Derne. Gawrych, 25.

57. Evans-Pritchard, 110–11.

58. Ibid., 112.

59. EK2, Scan 578.

60. Although its precise origins are unclear, the period in Libya produced the first signs of a rift between Enver and Mustafa Kemal. Kemal seemingly resented what he considered to be Enver's high-handedness and glory-seeking. But Enver outranked him and Mustafa Kemal had to make the best of it. Still, word of the friction reached the high command in Istanbul. Mango, *Atatürk*, 105.
61. EK Resim 045.
62. EK Resim 045.
63. Evans-Pritchard, 112.
64. Ibid., 112–13.
65. Ibid., 114.
66. Ibid., 115.
67. Christopher Clark, *The Sleepwalkers: How Europe Went to War in 1914* (London: Penguin Books, 2013), 244.
68. Richard Norton-Taylor, "First world war abridged," *Guardian*, 13 August 2013, 28.
69. Zürcher, *Turkey: A Modern History*, 114.
70. Simon, 127.
71. Safi, "History in the Trench," 98.

4. THE BALKAN WARS

1. EK2, Scan 273. This chapter draws in part on an extended, annotated table of contents of the portion pertaining to the Balkan Wars and the episode of Western Thrace corresponding to Eşref's now lost multi-volume work that was to have been called *Tarihe Benden Haberler*. The table of contents is at times remarkably detailed but clearly represents only a small proportion of the larger work.
2. Richard C. Hall, *The Balkan Wars, 1912–1913: Prelude to the First World War* (London: Routledge, 2000), 132.
3. EK2, Scan 273.
4. Syed Tanvir Wasti, "The 1912–13 Balkan Wars and the Siege of Edirne," *Middle Eastern Studies* 40:4 (2004), 60.
5. Oya Dağlar Macar, "Epidemic Diseases on the Thracian Front of the Ottoman Empire during the Balkan Wars," in H. Yavuz and I. Blumi, eds., *War and Nationalism: The Balkan Wars, 1912–1913, and their Sociopolitical Implications* (Salt Lake City: Utah University Press, 2013), 275 ff.; Erol Baykal, "Istanbul During the Balkan Wars (1912–1913): Cholera, Medicine and the Press," *Turkish Historical Review* 5:2 (2014), 141–64.
6. M. Şükrü Hanioğlu, *A Brief History of the Late Ottoman Empire* (Princeton: Princeton University Press, 2008), 171.
7. Yakup Cemil, who had travelled with Mustafa Kemal en route to Libya and who had fought with Eşref against the Italians, was the triggerman who shot Nazım Paşa, the Minister of War. Enver was appointed in his place.

8. TT DSC00250. The tone of Eşref's account suggests that he was not physically present.

9. Mahmut Şevket Paşa, *Sadrazâm ve Harbiye Nazırı Mahmut Şevket Paşa'nın Günlüğü* (Isanbul: Arba, 1988), 171–2; Vemund Aarbakke, "The Muslim Minority of Greek Thrace" (unpublished PhD dissertation, University of Bergen, 2000), vol. 1, 22.

10. Erik Jan Zürcher, *The Unionist Factor: The Role of the Committee of Union and Progress in the Turkish National Movement* (Leiden: Brill, 1984), 50, 56.

11. EK2, Scan 276. In fact, as we shall see, Süleyman Askerî would take his own life in Iraq during World War I after failing to prevent the British advance up through Mesopotamia.

12. Eyal Ginio, "Paving the Way for Ethnic Cleansing: Eastern Thrace during the Balkan Wars (1912–1913) and their Aftermath," in Omer Bartov and Eric D. Weitz, eds., *Shatterzone of Empires: Coexistence and Violence in the German, Hapsburg, Russian and Ottoman Borderlands* (Bloomington: Indiana University Press, 2013), 287; Y. Doğan Çetinsaya, "Atrocity Propaganda and the Nationalization of the Masses in the Ottoman Empire during the Balkan Wars (1912–13)," *IJMES* 46:4 (2014), 759–78.

13. Erik Jan Zürcher, "The Balkan Wars and the Refugee Leadership of the Early Turkish Republic," in H. Yavuz and I. Blumi, eds., *War and Nationalism: The Balkan Wars, 1912–1913, and their Sociopolitical Implications* (Salt Lake City: University of Utah Press, 2013), 673–4.

14. Ibid., 674.

15. The geographical impact is seen through the production of "revenge maps" in Ottoman school textbooks from 1912 onwards. Behlül Özkan, *From the Abode of Islam to the Turkish Vatan: The Making of a National Homeland in Turkey* (New Haven, CT: Yale University Press, 2012), 114–15. The narration of the Balkan Wars would continue to have a large impact in inculcating state-driven policies in the Turkish Republic. For an analysis of the ways in which Turkish republican history texts told the story in line with desiderata of the nation state, see Nazan Çiçek, "More History Than They Can Consume?" in M. H. Yavuz and I. Blumi, eds., *War and Nationalism: The Balkan Wars, 1912–1913, and their Sociopolitical Implications* (Salt Lake City: University of Utah Press, 2013), 777–804.

16. Bulgar Sadık was somewhat anomalous in that he was apparently an ethnic Bulgarian originally named Stoyan Dimitriev who had converted to Islam. Active as a *çeteci* in the Balkan Wars, Western Thrace, and the Greco-Turkish War, he later became the subject of a 1954 film called *Bulgar Sadık* ("Flee, the Turks are coming").

17. Some definitions of the region included areas west of the Karasu that are usually considered part of Eastern Macedonia, another region with a large Muslim population.

18. Clark, *Sleepwalkers*, 275. On Russia's hot-and-cold Bulgarian policy, see 263 ff.

19. Hall, 105.

20. EK2, Scan 273; Tevfik Bıyıklıoğlu, *Trakya'da Millî Mücadele* (Ankara: Türk Tarih Kurumu, 1955), vol. 1, 69 n.
21. Stoddard documents, II.
22. M. Şükrü Hanioğlu, "The Second Constitutional Period, 1908–1918," in Reşat Kasaba, ed., *The Cambridge History of Turkey*, vol. 4: *Turkey in the Modern World* (Cambridge: Cambridge University Press, 2008), 81.
23. Cemal Kutay, *1913 de Garbî Trakya'da İlk Türk Cumhuriyeti* (Istanbul: Tarih Yayınları, 1962), 116.
24. EK2, Scan 273–4.
25. EK2, Scan 172, 274. Kallikratia is today known as Mimarsinan, a neighborhood in Kücükçekmece. Thanks to Paraskevas Konortas for this information.
26. Edward J. Erickson, *Defeat in Detail: The Ottoman Army in the Balkans, 1912–1913* (Westport, CT: Praeger, 2003), 274.
27. Hanioğlu, "The Second Constitutional Period, 1908–1918," 72.
28. "Balkan harbinde Çatalca mudafaa hattında vukua gelen iki hadise, 1912," TT DSC00332 ff.
29. Eşref doesn't use the term but it is highly likely that these men represented former members of the Savior Officers.
30. Erickson, *Defeat in Detail*, 289.
31. Ibid., 290.
32. Stoddard documents III, Enver to Eşref, 2 Nisan 1329 (15 April 1913), author's personal collection.
33. Ahmet Efe, *Efsaneden Gerçeğe Kuşçubaşı Eşref*, 75–6.
34. This position was created in response to the emergency situation of the Balkan Wars. Thanks to Mesut Uyar for this information.
35. Celâl Bayar, *Ben de Yazdım: Millî Mücadele'ye Gidiş*, vol. 4 (Istanbul, 1967), 1232–3. Celâl Bayar, both a Prime Minister during the single-party era and President of Turkey during the Democrat Party era, had been an important figure for the CUP in Izmir. He indicates (vol. 4, 1229) that Eşref shared some of his writings with him. Bayar also played a role in Eşref's return to Turkey in the 1950s.
36. Eşref Kuşçubaşı, *The Turkish Battle at Khaybar*, trans. and ed. Philip H. Stoddard and H. Basri Danışman (Istanbul: Arba, 1997), 30–31. The relative was "Şöför Abdurrahman," the driver involved in the plot, who was the son of Eşref's maternal uncle Hacı Nazmi Paşa. Bayar, vol. 4, 1230–31.
37. Bayar, vol. 4, 1238, 1242; Togay Seçkin Birbudak, "Osmanlı Basınında Mahmud Şevket Paşa Suikastı," *Bilig* 65 (Bahar, 2013), 79.
38. Nevzat Gündağ, *1913 Garbî Trakya Hükûmet-i Müstakîlesi* (Ankara: Kültür ve Turizm Bakanlığı, 1987), 106; Efe, 76, citing Bıyıklıoğlu, 161; EK2, Scan 276.
39. Kutay, *1913 de*, 110–11, 115.
40. Kutay, *1913 de*, 116–17.
41. Bıyıklıoğlu, 71.
42. Taha Akyol, *Rumeli'ye Elveda: 100 Yılında Balkan Bozgunu* (Istanbul: Doğan Kitap, 2013), 180.

43. EK2, Scan 277.
44. "Olan olmuş biten bitmiş." EK2, Scan 277.
45. Hall, 119.
46. EK2, Scan 277.
47. In fact, some regular Ottoman forces had apparently already crossed the Maritsa to seize and defend the pocket of territory to the south and west of Edirne. Vemund Aarbakke, Georgios Niarchos, and Vassilis Koutsoukos, "The Independent Republic of Gumuldjina (1913)—A New Test for Young Turk Policy Makers," in Dimitris Stamatapoulos, ed., *Balkan Nationalism(s) and Ottoman Empire*, vol. 3 (Istanbul: Isis Press: 2015), 10, citing Bulgarian sources. But Cemal Paşa later wrote that he considered not having gone further to have been a "political mistake," given the need to protect the hinterland of Edirne; he deemed controlling both banks of the river to be necessary and that it was a "sacred duty" to attempt to regain control over the regions of Western Thrace where the Muslim population was in the clear majority. Djemal Pasha, *Memories of a Turkish Statesman, 1913–1919* (New York: Arno, 1973), 47.
48. Süleyman Askerî had been serving as a staff officer in the Tenth Army Corps under Enver. Zürcher, *Unionist Factor*, 48.
49. For a list, see Bıyıklıoğlu I, 74, n 103.
50. It is important to note that the impetus for the autonomous state may have come from Greek sources. Miletich describes the combined efforts of Greek officers, clerics, and civilians to make propaganda against the Bulgarians, even distributing weapons to the Muslim population so as to form armed bands and encouraging them to ask Istanbul to send soldiers to declare autonomy. L. Miletich, *Istoriyata na Giumiurdjinskata avtonomiya* (Sofia, 1914), 9–11. My thanks to Vemund Aarbakke for kindly providing me with his own translation of Miletich's work.
51. Vemund Aarbakke, "The Independent Republic of Gumuldjina (1913)—What do the sources tell us?" 3.
52. Aarbakke et al., "A New Test", 1.
53. Ibid.
54. Cihangiroğlu İbrahim Bey would go on to play an important role in another provisional government after World War I when he became the president of the Provisional National Government of the Southwestern Caucasus, based in Kars, until its territory was occupied by British troops and he was captured and sent to Malta as a POW. On the connections between these two provisional governments, see İbrahim Şirin, "İki Hükümet Bir Teşkilat: Garbî Trakya Hükümet-i Muvakkatesi'nden Cenub-î Garbî Kafkas Hükümeti Muvakkate-î Milliyesi'ne," *History Studies* 6:2 (2014), 125–42.
55. Vemund Aarbakke, "Uneven nation formation and the disruptive effect of the Balkan Wars," in Dimitris Stamatapoulos, ed., *Balkan Nationalism(s) and Ottoman Empire*, vol. 2 (Istanbul: Isis Press: 2015), 5.
56. Ibid., 6–7.

57. Ibid., 8.
58. As cited in Aarbakke, 12.
59. For the original circular, see Bıyıklıoğlu II, document 9.
60. The Bulgarian term for such an irregular armed band is *cheta* and its members are called *chetniks*.
61. Bulgarians would only have used this pejorative term for Muslims.
62. ATASE 1-A/64/148/115/5–20, as reproduced in *Askeri Tarih Belgeler Dergisi* 89 (Kasım, 1989), 82–3.
63. Domuzçiyef/Domuschiev does not appear in the main Bulgarian sources, which tend not to dwell on the events of the Second Balkan War. Miletich's account does mention Bulgarian atrocities in Papasköy, including against unarmed Muslim civilians, but does not name Domuschiev. Dr Vemund Aarbakke has, however, uncovered an account recorded among Bulgarian testimonies from the period that places Domuschiev in the region during the summer of 1913. The testimony of a man from Papasköy (Popsko) records that he and his compatriots abandoned their village in the wake of attacks by Ottoman soldiers and başıbozuks. They went to Koşukovak (Krumovgrad) where Major Domuschiev, whose battalion was garrisoned in the town, welcomed them and gave them bread and shoes. According to this account, "After a few days Krumovgrad/Koşukavak was attacked and surrounded by Turkish soldiers and başıbozuks. They killed the battalion of Domuschiev and he himself and some of this soldiers were taken prisoner." Thus Eşref's account is largely substantiated, although it remains unclear whether Domuschiev was actually responsible for the atrocities at Papasköy and how large his battalion was. Vemund Aarbakke, personal communication, 18 February 2014.
64. EK2, Scan 283. Elsewhere Eşref says that 83 Bulgarians were taken prisoner, tried and executed. Gündağ, *1913*, EK1, 181.
65. Gündağ, *1913*, 121; EK2, Scan 283.
66. This territory had only recently been Bulgarian, having been won during the First Balkan War.
67. EK2, Scan 283; Gündağ, *1913*, 122.
68. Bıyıklıoğlu I, 73.
69. EK2, Scan 283.
70. Vemund Aarbakke, "The Independent Republic of Gumurdjina (1913)—What do the sources tell us?" unpublished conference paper. Bulgarian accounts depict this episode as a national disaster and trauma. Miletich's account is called "The Destruction of the Thracian Bulgarians in 1913."
71. In reality, the Greek move was intended to disrupt the rapprochement between Sophia and Istanbul by encouraging the creation of an independent Western Thrace, an entity whose border Athens respected. Venizelos' government even went so far as to promise a supply of arms for the fledgling state. Şimşek, 79–80.
72. For one prominent example, see Lyubomir Miletich, *Istoriyata na Giumiurdjinskata avtonomiya* (Sofia, 1914). Miletich, a Bulgarian ethnologist, visited Western Thrace

\ת

soon after the withdrawal of Ottoman forces and the end of the Independent Republic of Western Thrace. I am extremely grateful to Dr Vemund Aarbakke for sharing his translation of the relevant passages of this work.

73. On the historiographical dimension, see Aarbakke, "The Independent Republic," 14 ff.
74. Bıyıklıoğlu I, 75.
75. Gündağ, 123, citing Bıyıklıoğlu I, 75; Şimşek, 71.
76. TNA FO 195/2454, 28, 24 September 1913.
77. EK2, 283.
78. EK2, 283.
79. Bıyıklıoğlu II, Vesika 10.
80. Bıyıklıoğlu I, 75. In fact, veterans like Ahmed İzzet Paşa were clearly disturbed. A few days later a (false) rumor was reported that Selim Sami had been killed and a number of his companions had crossed the border into Western Thrace, presumably to exact revenge; to which Ahmed İzzet noted his disdain. BOA DH.KMS 63/10 (27 August 1913).
81. TNA FO 195/2454, 59, 10 September 1913.
82. Hafız Salih later felt betrayed by Istanbul for failing to support the independent government and went on to collaborate with both the Bulgarians and the Greeks, serving twice as an MP in Greece.
83. The term "*millî*" is almost always translated as "national," but this is problematic in two respects. First, it fails to convey the religious/confessional sense implied in its Ottoman usage, reflecting a collapsing of religious (Muslim) and ethnic (various, including both Turkic and other) categories. Secondly, it serves the ahistorical narrative of the post-Ottoman nation-states, including the Turkish Republic, which sought to impose ethnic uniformity on a population that was distinctly heterogeneous on the Muslim side alone. But alternatives are clumsy, so I render the term in quotation marks.
84. Iliya Slavkov and Boryana Dimitrova, *Sachanli—Historical and ethnographic study* (Sofia, 1989), 106. Thanks to Vemund Aarbakke for providing me with an English translation of this work.
85. Şimşek, 75–6.
86. Gündağ, 143.
87. Şimşek, 195. For clarity's sake the Karasu River was the western border, and the Ottomans did not cross it.
88. For variants of the flag creation story, see Şimşek, 82, n 230.
89. Kevin Featherstone et al., *The Last Ottomans: The Muslim Minority of Greece, 1940–1949* (London: Palgrave Macmillan, 2011), 28.
90. The publication seems perhaps not to have been realized despite intentions.
91. TNA FO 195/2454, 59 ff., 10 September 1913.
92. TNA FO 195/2454, 30 ff., 18 September 1913, Morgan (Salonica) to Marling (Constantinople).

93. EK2, Scan 284.

94. Miletich ascribes this to posturing designed to put forth a civlized façade. Miletich, 1918, 214–15.

95. Taha Akyol, *Rumeli'ye Elveda*, 178.

96. TNA FO 195/2454, 49–50, 9 October 1913, Badetti (Dédéagatch) to Eyres (Constantinople).

97. EK2, Scan 285.

98. Gündağ, 128.

99. Aarbakke, "The Independent Republic," 17.

100. Carnegie Endowment for International Peace, *Report of the International Commission to Inquire into the Causes and Conduct of the Balkan Wars* (Washington, DC: Carnegie Endowment for International Peace, 1914), 135.

101. Nilüfer Erdem, "1913 Yılının Temmuz—Ekim Ayları Batı Trakya Türkleri ile ilgili Gelişmelerin Yunan Basınındaki Yansımaları," *History Studies* 6:2 (February 2014), 111.

102. Bıyıklıoğlu I, 78; Featherstone et al., 29.

103. Aarbakke et al., "A New Test," 13.

104. Text supplied in Gündağ, 180–83.

105. Hanioğlu, *A Brief History*, 173.

106. Bıyıklıoğlu II, Vesika 14.

107. This seems to be corroborated by the Bulgarian account of Miletich, mentioned above, who says that the village of Sıçanlı was threatened by 2,000 irregular forces of the Gümülcine Republic (i.e. the Independent Government of Western Thrace) in September 1913. Miletitch indicates that the forces were under the control of Süleyman Bey, presumably Süleyman Akserî, although it is unclear whether he says this because of Askerî's general role or if he was there on the spot. In any case, he reports that after the Bulgarian population fled, the "Turks" burned the village to the ground. Lyubomir Miletich, *Istoriyata na Giumiurdjinskata avtonomiya* ("The History of the Giumurdjina Republic") (Sofia, 1914) 14 ff.; and L. Miletich, *Razorenieto na trakiiskite Bǎlgari prez 1913 godina* ("The Destruction of the Thracian Bulgarians in 1913") (Sofia, 1918), 220–21. Another Bulgarian account claims that the Turkish force numbered 4,000, that some victims were "killed on the spot with large knives," probably bayonets, and that the survivors formed a long train of refugees whose subsequent liberation becomes a heroic episode in Bulgarian national historiography. Slavkov and Dimitrova, *Sachanli*, 124 ff.

108. Bıyıklıoğlu II, Vesika 17.

109. Bıyıklıoğlu II, Vesika 18.

110. EK2, Scan 298.

111. TNA FO 195/2454, 5 October 1913, Biletti (Dédéagatch) to Eyres (Constantinople).

112. The accounts of Bulgarian survivors from Sıçanlı refer to the attackers as "the

bashibozuks of Kushchubashı Eshref Bey and the hordes of major Süleyman Askerî Bey." Slavkov and Dimitrova, *Sachanli*, 126. The final attack on Sıçanlı took place on the night of 4/5 September.

113. EK2, Scan 301.
114. Paraskevas Konortas, personal communication, March 2013.
115. EK2, Scan 286.
116. This was undoubtedly difficult. Eşref says that when his colleague "Bulgar" Sadık had earlier attempted a similar mission on Talat's orders, he had been captured and they had had to work to secure his release. EK2, Scan 285.
117. Gündağ, 162, citing Bıyıklıoğlu I, 86; also Bayur II, kıs 3, s 4.
118. Djemal Pasha, *Memories*, 50.
119. EK2, Scan 285–6.
120. Foti, perhaps Foti Stefanopoulos, is another mysterious figure in this story. Several Turkish accounts identify him as either the Metropolitan of Gümülcine or of Dedeağaç. But there is also a photograph taken of him in a suit and tie, which, according to Aarbakke, would be quite unlikely for an ecclesiastical figure in this period. Aarbakke, "Independent Republic," 8–9. Eşref writes that he was in negotiations with "Monsieur Foti" in his capacity as an unofficial representative of Greek state during the last days of the independent state.
121. The Demotika region would be ceded to Bulgaria in 1915 as part of forming the Ottoman–Bulgarian alliance in World War I.
122. EK2, Scan 286.
123. Gündağ, 162, citing Bıyıklıoğlu I, 87.
124. One source cited by Erickson says that Eşref, Süleyman Askerî, and others continued to fight and harass the Greeks and Bulgarians after the Ottoman withdrawal. Erickson, 112.
125. Gündağ, 163.
126. Özkan, 87.
127. Berzeg, 40.
128. Firestone et al., 32–3.
129. Özkan, 87.
130. EK2, Scan 286. His brief comments are limited to the table of contents for his now missing memoir. He writes, "The Special Organization is created *de novo* (*yeniden kurulluyor*). A comparison between the old Special Organization and the new one and some information." A few lines later he writes, "Full explanation about the Second Special Organization." Frustratingly, that is all that remains.
131. This orphanage seems to have been run under the auspices of the Special Organization, perhaps as a source of future members. Personal communication, Vemund Aarbakke, 30 January 2014.
132. The practice of Ottoman volunteers living off the land through the "donations" (*iane*) of the local population was to become standard practice during World

War I. This was especially the case for the armed bands organized by the Special Organization. Mehmet Beşikçi, "Mobilizing Military Labor in the Age of Total War: Ottoman Conscription during the Great War," in Erik Jan Zürcher, ed., *Fighting for a Living: A Comparative History of Military Labor 1500–2000* (Amsterdam: Amsterdam University Press, 2013), 561–3. As we shall see, it was a practice that would engender considerable resentment during the "National Forces" period when Ankara would receive complaints that Eşref and his band were exacting onerous "taxes" on the population in the Marmara region, one of the factors that appear to have led to the rift between Eşref and Mustafa Kemal.

133. Slavkov and Dimitrova, *Sachanli*.
134. Miletich, 1918, 220–21.
135. EK2, Scan 286. Livestock was the usual form of booty to be taken. Beşikçi, 563. Some of the areas where fighting and/or violence and massacres against the civilian population had taken place, including Sıçanlı, were known to be regions of plentiful flocks. Personal communication from Vemund Aarbakke, 30 January 2014.
136. TT DSC00315.
137. EK, "Yakup Cemil'e ait bazı notlar." EK2, Scan 468–70.
138. Secret telegram of Russian Ambassador M. N. Girs in Istanbul, 13/26 October 1914, No. 1577. My thanks to Erman Şahin for finding and translating this document.
139. TNA FO 195/2459, 399, Heathcote-Smith (Smyrna) to Mallet (London), 12 October 1914, a confidential report based on an interview with Governor Rahmi. In a subsequent interview Rahmi noted that he had been asked to assist, presumably financially, the emissaries bound for Egypt (and others for Macedonia) and had done so despite telling them that their work would do no good lest he lay himself open to the reproach of the "war party." TNA FO 195/2459, 394, 17 October 1914.

5. THE GREAT WAR, PART I: AT HOME AND AT THE FRONT

1. Pervin's arrival on the scene would greatly add to our understanding of Eşref's life and, more broadly, the life of Ottoman women during this war-torn period. Her memoirs and letters, preserved among Eşref's papers, provide a level of domestic detail not available up to this point.
2. Pervin's account says that their wedding took place in the same month as that of Enver and Princess Naciye, the granddaughter of Sultan Abdülmecid, which happened on 5 March 1914.
3. Pervin, 4
4. Mustafa Aksakal, *The Ottoman Road to War in 1914: The Ottoman Empire and the First World War* (Cambridge: Cambridge University Press, 2008), 14–15.
5. Stoddard documents IV. This is one of several photographs very kindly given to me by Dr Stoddard.

6. Eşref wrote to his brother Selim Sami as he was moving from Vienna en route to Liège before he continued on to London. This undated letter is reproduced in facsimile form in Cemal Kutay, *Ana-Vatan'da Son Beş Osmanlı Türk'ü* (Istanbul: Bahadır Matbaası, 1962), 31. Liège may have been on the itinerary because it was the home of the arms manufacturer Fabrique Nationale, but that is speculation.

7. Pervin, 5.

8. Pervin, 5.

9. Aksakal, 10–11.

10. Bülent Yılmazer, "Ottoman Aviation, Prelude to Military Use of Aircraft," Appendix A in Edward J. Erickson, *Defeat in Detail, The Ottoman Army in the Balkans, 1912–1913* (Westport, CT: Praeger, 2003), 347.

11. Ibid., 347–8.

12. Ibid., 356 ff.

13. Pervin, 6.

14. Pervin, 7.

15. Pervin, 8.

16. Enver's marriage to Naciye Sultan took place on 5 March 1914 (M. Naim Turfan, *Rise of the Young Turks*, 417); the date of Eşref and Pervin's marriage is unknown, but several sources indicate that it occurred at around the same time.

17. Precisely how risky this was is unclear, as are details of the mission, but Eşref's and Pervin's accounts stress the danger inherent in the assigment.

18. www.gezgindergi.com/fatih-te-hava-sehitleri-aniti, accessed 16 December 2014.

19. Raymond Kevorkian, *The Armenian Genocide: A Complete History* (London: I. B. Tauris, 2011), 180.

20. Mihail Rodas, *Almanya Turkiye'deki Rumları Nasıl Mahvetti* (Istanbul: Belge Yayınları, 2011), 99.

21. TNA FO 195–2458, Acting Consul General Heathcote Smith, Smyrna, to Mallet, London, 8 July 1914, 460.

22. Emre Erol, "Preparing for the First World War: Forced Migration as a Tool of 'Demographic Warfare' in the Pre-War Western Anatolia," paper presented to the international conference "Not All Quiet on the Ottoman Fronts: Neglected Perspectives on a Global War, 1914–1918," Istanbul, April 2014.

23. TNA, FO 195–2458, Acting Consul General Heathcote Smith (Smyrna) to Mallet (London), 27 July 1914.

24. Ibid.

25. Uğur Ümit Üngör, "'Turkey for the Turks': Demographic Engineering in Eastern Anatolia, 1914–1945," in R. G. Suny, F. M. Göçek and N. M. Naimark, eds., *A Question of Genocide: Armenians and Turks at the End of the Ottoman Empire* (New York: Oxford University Press, 2011), 295. Üngör indicates that these meetings discussed "the elimination of the non-Turkish masses." Curiously, he also claims that Eşref died in 1922.

26. BOA DH.ŞFR 42/184 19 Haziran 1330 (2 July 1914).

27. Bayar V, 1573.

28. Bayar V, 1574.

29. Emre Erol, "Organised Chaos as Diplomatic Ruse and Demographic Weapon: The Expulsion of the Ottoman Greeks (*Rum*) from Foça, 1914," *Tijdschrift voor Sociale en Economische Geschiedenis* 10:4 (2013), 90.

30. Bayar V, 1574.

31. Bayar V, 1574.

32. Bayar V, 1575.

33. Emre Erol, "Organised Chaos," 91.

34. Bayar V, 1578.

35. Nurdoğan Taçalan, *Ege'de Kurtuluş Savaşı Başlarken* (Istanbul: Hur Yayınları, 1981), 57.

36. BOA DH.ŞFR 442/46, 28 July 1914. Rahmi also mentions that men fresh from taking Bulgarian land had recently arrived in the Izmir region, further underscoring the connection between the end of the Balkan Wars and the shift in focus to the Aegean littoral.

37. Emre Erol, "Organised Chaos," 93.

38. This ship, not be confused with a later Turkish liner of the same name, was later confiscated by the British in Bombay. Pervin, 10.

39. Adil Hikmet Bey, *Asya'da Beş Türk*, Yusuf Gedikli, ed. (Istanbul: Ötuken, 1998), 52.

40. EK Resim, 25.

41. Aksakal, 104; TNA FO 195/2459, 284, 3 August 1914, Amat (Ismidt) to Eyres (Constantinople).

42. Kayalı, *Arabs and Young Turks*, 185–6.

43. Aksakal, 101.

44. Stefan Ihrig, *Atatürk in the Nazi Imagination* (Cambridge, MA: Belknap Press, 2014), 2.

45. Stoddard, 67.

46. Ibid., 67–8.

47. Tilman Lüdke, *Jihad Made in Germany*, 82.

48. BOA DH.ŞFR 44/90, 25 August 1914.

49. BOA DH.ŞFR 437/69, 24 August 1914.

50. The story of their mission is told in the memoir of one of the group: Adil Hikmet Bey, *Asya'da Beş Türk*, Yusuf Gedikli, trans. (Istanbul: Ötüken, 1998).

51. Hanioğlu, *Brief History*, 177.

52. Philip Hendrick Stoddard and H. Basri Danışman, eds., *The Turkish Battle at Khaybar* (Istanbul: Arba, 1997), 31.

53. TNA, FO 157/695, 4 September 1915.

54. Hanioğlu, *Brief History*, 180. On the importance of the Canal going far beyond its purely strategic aspects, see Valeska Huber, *Channelling Mobilities: Migration and Globalisation in the Suez Canal Region and Beyond, 1869–1914* (Cambridge: Cambridge University Press, 2013).

55. Hew Strachan, *The First World War, Vol. I: To Arms* (Oxford: Oxford University Press, 2001), 729.
56. Edward C. Woodfin, *Camp and Combat on the Sinai and Palestine Front: The Experience of the British Empire Soldier, 1916–18* (Basingstoke: Palgrave Macmillan, 2012), 14.
57. Woodfin, 14.
58. EK2, Picture 011.
59. Vahdet Keleşyılmaz, *Teşkilâtı Mahsusa'nın Hindistan Misyonu (1914–1918)* (Ankara: Atatürk Araştırma Merkezi, 1999), 26–7.
60. Djemal Pasha, *Memories of a Turkish Statesman*, 142.
61. Interestingly, Eşref retained a letter in Arabic from Prüfer inviting him to have breakfast at the Grand Hotel Victoria in Damascus on 11 November 1914. Whether this transpired and if so what was discussed remains unknown. Stoddard documents V.
62. Scott Anderson, *Lawrence in Arabia: War, Deceit, Imperial Folly and the Making of the Modern Middle East* (New York: Doubleday, 2013), 93–4.
63. EK2, Picture 009.
64. Polat Safi, "The Ottoman Special Organization—*Teşkilat-ı Mahsusa*: A Historical Assessment with Particular Reference to its Operations against British Occupied Egypt (1914–1915)" (unpublished MA dissertation, Bilkent University, Ankara, 2006), 44.
65. BOA DH.ŞFR 47/346, 6 December 1914.
66. Stoddard, 103–4, 50–51; Polat Safi, "Operations against British Occupied Egypt," 52; Yigal Sheffy, *British Military Intelligence in the Palestine Campaign, 1914–1918* (London: Frank Cass, 1998), 43.
67. EK2, Scan 52.
68. Djemal Pasha, *Memories*, 148.
69. Polat Safi, "The Ottoman Special Organization—*Teşkilat-i Mahsusa*: An Inquiry into its Operational and Administrative Characteristics" (unpublished PhD dissertation, Bilkent University, Ankara, 2012), 46.
70. EK2, Scans 54–5.
71. *Arab Bulletin* 17, 187–8.
72. He later published a detailed account of the campaign, in which he doubtless alluded to Eşref without naming him when he refers to "an infamous Macedonian guerrilla commander" in charge of a large force of volunteers marching towards the canal via Nakhl, which was Eşref's route, as we shall see below. Friedrich Freiherr Kress von Kressenstein, *Mit den Türken zum Suezkanal* (Berlin: Vorhut-Verlag Otto Schlegel, 1938), 85.
73. Tilman Lüdke, *Jihad Made in Germany*, 153.
74. Djemal Pasha, *Memories*, 150.
75. Polat Safi, "Operations against British Occupied Egypt," 49–50; Sheffy, 43.
76. Strachan, 738.

77. Şerif Mardin, "The Ottoman Empire," in K. Barkey and M. von Hagen, eds, *After Empire: Multiethnic Societies and Nation-building in the Soviet Union and the Russian, Ottoman and Habsburg Empires* (Boulder, CO: Westview, 1997), 115.

78. Mesut Uyar, "Arab Officers between Nationalism and Loyalty during the First World War," *War in History* 20:4 (2013), 526–44.

79. Djemal Pasha, *Memories*, 153.

80. TNA WO 32/5620, 160. "Notes of an interview with Enver Pasha."

81. Cemal Paşa, *Hatırat* (Istanbul: Arma, 1996), 146–7.

82. EK Resim, 263, EK (Jaffa) to S Askerî (Istanbul), 23 October 1914.

83. EK Resim, 299, EK (Jaffa) to S Askerî (Istanbul), 30 October 1914. "Ebu Feridun" is Arabic for Father of Feridun, accurate as a patronymic but hardly a secure alias.

84. EK Resim, 4, S Askerî (Istanbul) to EK (Aleppo), 4 November 1914.

85. Polat Safi, "Operations against British Occupied Egypt," 48.

86. EK Resim, 3, EK (El Arish) to 8th Army Corps Commander, 19 December 1914.

87. EK2, Scan 431.

88. EK2, Scans 437–41.

89. EK2, Scans 432–3.

90. Djemal Pasha, *Memories*, 151.

91. EK Resim, 140, Haydar to EK, 27 December 1914.

92. EK Resim, 146, Ali Haydar to EK, 25 December 1914.

93. EK2 Scan 386, 15 January 1915. When advancing over the same Sinai ground in the opposite direction later in the war, British forces would remark on the inhospitable terrain. They called in the "rotten wilderness" and cursed the same extremes of heat, thirst, insects, barrenness of terrain, sandstorms, etc. that their enemies had encountered, but adding another—it pushed some of them beyond sanity. Woodfin, 19 ff.

94. EK Resim 146, Ali Haydar to EK, 25 December 1914.

95. EK Resim, 288, EK to Hasan Ali, Salihli, n.d.

96. EK Resim 37, 27 December 1915.

97. Djemal Pasha, *Memories*, 158.

98. Ibid., 157–8.

99. EK Resim, 149.

100. Peter Englund, *The Beauty and the Sorrow: An Intimate History of the First World War*, trans. Peter Graves (London: Profile, 2011), 82.

101. EK Resim, 144.

102. EK2, Scans 56–9.

103. EK2, Scans 59–60.

104. Presumably the St James, a restaurant later frequented by the likes of Churchill, the Agha Khan, and General Montgomery. http://weekly.ahram.org.eg/2003/642/letters.htm, accessed 8 June 2014.

105. Joseph Maiolo and Tony Insall, "Sir Basil Zaharoff and Sir Vincent Caillard as

Instruments of British Policy towards Greece and the Ottoman Empire during the Asquith and Lloyd George Administrations, 1915–8," *International History Review* 34:4 (December 2012), 827.

106. Parliamentary Archives, Lloyd George Papers, LG/F/6/1.
107. Stoddard, 106–7.
108. EK2, Scan 907.
109. EK2, 908.
110. Strachan, 739–42.
111. *The Times*, 13 February 1915, 7.
112. Stoddard, 107; Strachan, 742.
113. Pervin, 13.
114. EK Resim, 38, Captain Adli (Izmir) to EK (El-Arish), 14 March 1915.
115. EK Resim, 39, 27 March 1915, Haci Sami (Deraliye [Istanbul]) to Eşref (Izmir).
116. Hanioğlu, *Brief History*, 181.
117. Mehmet Beşikçi, *Ottoman Mobilization in the First World War: Between Voluntarism and Resistance* (Leiden: Brill, 2012), 114.
118. See, for example, BOA DH.ŞFR 55A/223, Talat to Adana vilayeti, 13 September 1915. On this civil official, see Hilmar Kaiser, "Shukru Bey and the Armenian Deportations in the Fall of 1915," in M. Talha Çiçek, ed., *Syria In World War I* (London: Routledge, 2016). On occasion disambiguation can be quite difficult, a problem created by the lack of surnames or other means of distinguishing between men with the same first name. For example, one document mentions a man named Çerkes Eşref who was sentenced to three and a half years of hard labor in Bitlis for setting fields on fire. He is subsequently pardoned by imperial decree in late October 1914. BOA İ.MMS 190/15 and DH.ŞFR 46/251, 8 November 1914. But by that point, as we shall see, Kuşçubaşı Eşref was clearly in Jaffa sending telegrams to Süleyman Askerî in preparation for the Canal campaign. The arsonist seems to have been another and heretofore unknown "Circassian Eşref," adding another level of obscurity to the subject.
119. Hilmar Kaiser, *The Extermination of Armenians in the Diarbekir Region* (Istanbul: Istanbul Bilgi Unversity Press, 2014), 362.
120. DH.ŞFR 54/32 DH to Diyarbakır vilayeti, 16 June 1915. Kaiser, 362.
121. Kaiser, 363.
122. DH.ŞFR 61/132.
123. DH.ŞFR 54/231, Enver (Harbiye Nezareti) to Urfa mutasarrıflığı, 30 June 1915.
124. Kaiser, 362, note.
125. TNA, WO 157/695, 2, 4 September 1915.
126. TNA, WO 157/695, 1, 4 September 1915.
127. Stoddard, 110.

6. THE GREAT WAR, PART II: BACK TO ARABIA

1. Philip Hendrick Stoddard and H. Basri Danışman, "The Life of Eşref Sencer Kuşçubaşızade," in Eşref Kuşçubası, *The Turkish Battle at Khaybar*, eds. Philip Stoddard and H. Basri Danışman (Istanbul: Arba, 1997), 32.
2. Stoddard, 147.
3. Nicholas Ajay, "Political Intrigue and Suppression in Lebanon during World War I," *IJMES* 5:2 (April 1974), 155–6.
4. Eliezer Tauber, *The Arab Movements in World War I* (London: Frank Cass, 1993), 39–41.
5. BOA HR.SYS 2415/14, 4 November 1915.
6. Stoddard, 147, 222, n 336.
7. Djemal Pasha, *Memories*, 197, 228 ff.; Ajay, 156.
8. BOA DH.ŞFR 508/101, 11 February 1916. The Ottoman governor in Beirut, Cemal Azmi, had been known as the Butcher of Trabzon due to his role in eliminating the Armenian population from that city the previous year, before his transfer to Lebanon.
9. Kayalı, *Arabs and Young Turks*, 193; M Talha Çiçek, *War and State Formation in Syria: Cemal Pasha's Governorate during World War I*, 1914–17 (London: Routledge, 2014), 49–50.
10. BOA DH.ŞFR 61/132, 27 February 1916.
11. BOA DH.ŞFR 521/61, 30 March 1916.
12. Ernst Rodenwaldt, *Ein Tropenarzt erzählt sein Leben* (Stuttgart: Ferdinand Enke Verlag, 1957), 138. I am grateful to Dr Hilmar Kaiser for this reference.
13. Ibid.
14. Establishing the length and dates of the mission is problematic. Düzdağ says that it began in May 1915 and lasted five months: M. Ertuğrul Düzdağ, ed., *Mehmed Âkif Ersoy* (Izmir: Sütün, 2007). Safi, citing Stoddard, states that Eşref stayed in the Sinai until the end of 1915 and then went to Arabia to counter British influence there: Polat Safi, "The Ottoman Special Organization—*Teşkilat-ı Mahsusa*: A Historical Assessment with Particular Reference to its Operations against British Occupied Egypt (1914–1915)" (unpublished MA dissertation, Bilkent University, Ankara, 2006), 76. Stoddard and Danışman say the mission took place in early 1916: Stoddard and Danışman, 32. Pervin indicates that they were gone for four months: Pervin, 18. The battle of Çanakkale was fought between April 1915 and January 1916; perhaps the best that can be said is that the mission began sometime towards the end of 1915 and ended in the spring or early summer of 1916.
15. Cemal Kutay, *Necid Çöllerinde Mehmed Âkif* (Istanbul: Ercan, 1963).
16. Safi, "History in the Trench: The Ottoman Special Organization—Teşkilat-ı Mahsusa Literature," *Middle Eastern Studies* 48:1 (January 2012): 91.
17. Pervin, 16.
18. Kutay, *Necid Çöllerinde*, 156.

19. The exact date of this meeting is unknown but seems to have taken place some-time during the Mali month of Temmuz 1332, i.e. between 14 July and 13 August 1916. EK, *Turkish Battle*, 228–9. The following sections rely on Eşref's account, the one surviving volume of his memoir.

20. Erik Jan Zürcher, *The Unionist Factor: The Role of the Committee of Union and Progress in the Turkish National Movement* (Leiden: Brill, 1984), 51 n.

21. Pervin, 24.

22. As we have seen elsewhere, Mustafa Kemal's pre-Republican contacts often proved uncomfortable to his later role as statesman.

23. Pervin, 26.

24. Zürcher, *The Young Turk Legacy and Nation Building: From the Ottoman Empire to Atatürk's Turkey* (London: I. B. Tauris, 2010), 132.

25. Zürcher, *Unionist Factor*, 51 n.

26. Pervin, 26. Although the connection between the Yakup Cemil affair and Eşref's being sent to Yemen makes sense, the chronological sequence is somewhat prob-lematic. Eşref's account of his voyage holds that he went to Enver in the Mali month of Temmuz, i.e. between 14 July and 13 August 1916. It may be that he remembered the date of the initial meeting with Enver incorrectly, especially as Pervin's account is quite clear on the sequence of events. Yakup Cemil was arrested and executed on 11 September 1916.

27. Ulrike Freitag, "Modern-Day Saudi Arabia During the First World War: Insights into a Contingent Era," in *Fikrun wa Fann*, www.goethe.de/ges/phi/prj/ffs/the/a100/en12235572.htm, accessed 26 July 2014.

28. EK, *Turkish Battle*, 39.

29. EK, *Turkish Battle*, 40.

30. EK, *Turkish Battle*, 41.

31. EK, *Turkish Battle*, 41.

32. *The Arab Bulletin: Bulletin of the Arab Bureau in Cairo, 1916–1919*, vol. I, no. 26, 16 October 1916, 361.

33. Pervin, 27–8.

34. EK, *Turkish Battle*, 44–5.

35. EK, *Turkish Battle*, 46.

36. On Fahri Paşa, see Martin Strohmeier, "Fakhri (Fahrettin) Paşa and the end of Ottoman rule in Medina," *Turkish Historical Review* 4 (2013), 192–223.

37. EK, *Turkish Battle*, 52.

38. EK, *Turkish Battle*, 53.

39. EK, *Turkish Battle*, 56.

40. EK, *Turkish Battle*, 60.

41. BOA DH.ŞFR 574/59, Fahri (Medina) to Interior Ministry, 14 January 1917.

42. EK, *Turkish Battle*, 61.

43. EK, *Turkish Battle*, 63.

44. EK, *Turkish Battle*, 65.

45. A. Guillaume, *The Life of Muhammad: A Translation of [Ibn] Ishaq's Sirat Rasul Allah* (Oxford: Oxford University Press, 1955), 510 ff.

46. EK, *Turkish Battle*, 72.

47. EK, *Turkish Battle*, 75.

48. EK, *Turkish Battle*, 77.

49. EK, *Turkish Battle*, 80.

50. T. E. Lawrence, *Seven Pillars of Wisdom: A Triumph* (New York: Penguin Books, 1962), 159. Lawrence then provides a potted biography of Eşref, getting a few details wrong, before explaining more or less the same story of the battle, the machine gun and how he came to be captured by Abdallah's men.

51. *The Arab Bulletin* 40 (29 January 1917), 41.

52. Polly A. Mohs, *Military Intelligence and the Arab Revolt: The First Modern Intelligence War* (London: Routledge, 2008), 120.

53. EK, *Turkish Battle*, 241.

7. PRISONER OF WAR

1. Alan R. Kramer, "Prisoners in the First World War," in Sibylle Scheipers, ed., *Prisoners in War* (London: Oxford University Press, 2010), 76.

2. TNA FO 383/347; Kent F. Schull, "Interned on the Isle of Man: Ottoman Citizens in British Concentration Camps during World War One," paper presented at the annual meetings of the Middle East Studies Association, Denver, CO, November 2012.

3. EK, *Turkish Battle*, 90.

4. EK, *Turkish Battle*, 98.

5. EK, *Turkish Battle*, 98–9.

6. EK, *Turkish Battle*, 100.

7. EK, *Turkish Battle*, 102–3.

8. Ussama Makdisi, "Ottoman Orientalism," *American Historical Review* 107:3 (2002), 768–96.

9. EK, *Turkish Battle*, 105.

10. EK, *Turkish Battle*, 127–8.

11. EK, *Turkish Battle*, 130–1.

12. EK, *Turkish Battle*, 132–3.

13. EK, *Turkish Battle*, 135.

14. EK, *Turkish Battle*, 156.

15. www.naval-history.net/WW1Battle1502SuezCanal.htm, accessed 4 September 2014.

16. www.naval-history.net/OWShips-WW1–09-HMS_Lama.htm, accessed 4 September 2014. Storrs, T. E. Lawrence and Aziz Ali al-Masri had traveled on the same ship. Michael Asher, *Lawrence: The Uncrowned King of Arabia* (London: Penguin Books, 1999), 168, 172.

17. For an analysis of Eşref's encounter with the British in comparative perspective, see Selim Deringil, "Intellectual encounters with the west: The cases of Turkey and Japan," *New Perspectives on Turkey* 35 (2006), 65–83.
18. EK, *Turkish Battle*, 171–2.
19. EK, *Turkish Battle*, 180–1.
20. EK, *Turkish Battle*, 184.
21. Stephen M. Miller, *Lord Methuen and the British Army: Failure and Redemption in South Africa* (London: Frank Cass, 1999), 249.
22. www.timesofmalta.com/articles/view/20140817/life-features/The-Salter-album-from-World-War-I.532336, accessed 5 September 2014.
23. EK Resim 154.
24. At the same time, the British jailed Maltese nationalists in Egypt, usually at the Sidi Bishr camp near Alexandria.
25. After the war when the British and French occupied Istanbul many more political prisoners, for example the writer and political acitivist Ziya Gökalp, were sent to Malta, often overlapping with those who were captured during the fighting.
26. Eyüp Sabri was a special case because of his role as one of the Freedom Heroes, along with Enver and Niyazi, in the 1908 revolutions. He was seemingly the only Ottoman prisoner on whose behalf Istanbul intervened to try to secure his release, a fact discussed at the level of the wartime British cabinet. IWM, Papers of Lieutenant General Sir Herbert Belfield. Belfield was British Director of Prisoners of War, 1914–20.
27. On the remarkable story of the *Emden* and the frantic British attempts to put a stop to her spree of raiding across South and South East Asia, see Strachan, 466 ff., 479–80.
28. Franz Joseph Prince of Hohenzollern, *Emden: My Experiences in S.M.S. Emden* (London: Herbert Jenkins, 1928), 267.
29. BOA HR.SYS 2204/70. The report is dated 10 January 1918, in other words just shy of nine months after Eşref's arrival. The author claims to have been granted full access to the prisoners, to have been able to interview them individually and to have inspected their quarters. But Hohenzollern says that this man, a local Maltese, was beholden to the British and that his correspondence "left much to be desired." Hohenzollern, *Emden*, 278.
30. Hohenzollern, *Emden*, 273.
31. BOA HR.SYS 2204/70.
32. http://www.timesofmalta.com/articles/view/20140817/life-features/The-Salter-album-from-World-War-I.532336, accessed 5 September 2014.
33. http://www.timesofmalta.com/articles/view/20140817/life-features/The-Salter-album-from-World-War-I.532336, accessed 5 September 2014.
34. Imperial War Musuem Collections (IWM), "Autograph Book by POWs at Malta, First World War, presented to Captain George Henry Salter" (Documents 3004).

35. An example of such a photograph is one Eşref was given, showing a group of thirty-seven Ottoman subjects, mostly wearing the fez, arranged in three rows for a group photo which was presented inside a folding red leather frame. Eşref's caption indicates that they had been taken from the Hijaz and other places, sent to Malta and housed in one of the tent camps. EK2, Scan 12. Others show a musical group composed of German sailors in uniform, a large group of Muslim prisoners posing for a card captioned with Happy Bayram wishes, etc. EK Resim 127.

36. Sources from Eşref's papers that stem from his time on Malta consist of photographs, letters to and from his family, and some typewritten draft sections of his now lost memoir.

37. EK Resim 131.

38. Eşref refers to him as Signore Ditta, the "famous painter." But it is also possible to read his signature as "Litta". http://www.timesofmalta.com/articles/view/20140817/life-features/The-Salter-album-from-World-War-I.532336, accessed 5 September 2014. Whether he painted under a pseudonym or not is unknown. I have been unable to establish his real identity.

39. EK Resim 5–7.

40. EK Resim 19–21.

41. EK, "Malta hatırası"; EK2 Resim 7 ff.

42. EK, "Malta hatırası"; EK2 Resim 11.

43. That these men were on Eşref's "side" is clear from his descriptions: Sarı Mustafa was later a squad or gang captain during the "National Forces" era and Deli Hasan was a naval captain from Baghdad. The source for this case is Eşref's account called "Our Life on Malta" (Malta Hayatımız), which contains reminiscences of several incidents. Although undated, it was probably written much later as he used, somewhat problematically, the Latin script. EK, "Malta Hayatımız," 137–8 (EK2 Resim 210–11).

44. BOA HR.SYS 2210/44. 3 Eylül 1335 (3 September 1919). The incident had reportedly happened a year before that. Why it took so long to reach the Istanbul authorities is unclear.

45. For a photograph of the plaque, see: https://plus.google.com/10037298521 7770342562/about?gl=uk&hl=en&pid=5685567732449581762&oid=109071 717030654322604, accessed 12 September 2014.

46. EK Resim 36; Resim 126; Resim 129.

47. Eşref also complained about Reşid both before and after he was taken prisoner. Eşref says that once he was on Malta, Reşid ran riot, comparing him to a horse that has the bit between its teeth, the same phrase he used when describing Reşid's running amok in Western Thrace a few years before. Eşref particularly resented Reşid's antics and considered him ungrateful because Eşref had provided him with land and included him on the deeds of some of his land at Salihli. TT DSC00311.

48. Pervin, 30.
49. Pervin, 33.
50. EK Resim 33. EK (Malta) to Pervin, 14 March 1918. The problems with the mail continued. In February 1919 Pervin replies to another of Eşref's letters in which he said he had received no letters for three or four months. EK2, Scan 202, Pervin (Salihli) to EK (Malta), 28 February 1919.
51. EK2, Scan 191, Feridun (n.p.) to Eşref (Malta) (n.d.).
52. EK2, Scan 189. Pervin (n.p.) to Eşref (Malta), 2 August 1918.
53. EK2, Scan 185, Pervin (Salihli) to Eşref (Malta), 25 August 1918.
54. Pervin, 36–7.
55. EK2, Scan 182, Pervin (Salihli) to Eşref (Malta), 13 April 1919.
56. Seza Hanım (Salihli) to EK (Malta), 27 April 1919. EK2, Scan 207. Seza Polar (Üçer), daughter of Hacı Nazmi Paşa, was a journalist and educationalist, the principal of the Circassian Model School (Çerkes Nümüne Mektebi) and a founder of the Circassian Women's Benevolent Association (Çerkes Kadınlar Teavün Cemiyeti) which published the journal *Diyane*.
57. Pervin (Beşiktaş) to EK (Malta), 17 August 1919. EK2, Scans 204–5.
58. ATASE İSH 84/67, Bekir Sami (Eşme) to War Ministry, 14 June 1919.
59. Salihli was also suspected as being a place where the records of the CUP were burned during the final year of the war. Erik Zürcher, personal communication.
60. Zürcher, *Unionist Factor*, 86.
61. Ünal, *Kurtuluş Savaşından Çerkeslerin Rolü*, 27.
62. Gingeras, *Sorrowful Shores*, 79.
63. The kidnapping took place in front of a number of prominent Levantines, including members of the Whittall family, and is described in a letter written the following day by the British Vice Consul to Chios who was visiting Izmir at the time. TNA FO 371/4157, W. Lewis Bailey to Granville, 13 February 1919.
64. TT EK to Asaf Tugay, 22 August 1962 (DSC00311); Murat Bardakçı, *İttihadçı'nın Sandığı: İttihad ve Terakki liderlerinin özel arşivlerindeki yayınlanmamış belgeler ile Atatürk ve İnönü dönemlerinde Ermeni gayrimenkulleri konusunda alınmış bazı kararlar* (Istanbul: Türkiye İş Bankası Kültür Yayınları, 2013), 362.
65. TT EK to Asaf Tugay, 22 August 1962 (DSC00311). Another source says that the ransom demanded was 53,000 gold coins: www.levantineheritage.com/guiffray. htm, accessed 15 September 2014.
66. Bardakçı, 362.
67. TT EK to Asaf Tugay, 22 August 1962 (DSC00311).
68. Bardakçı, 365.
69. Alparslan remained on friendly terms with Eşref's family in subsequent years, for example paying holiday (*bayram*) visits to Pervin.
70. TT EK to Asaf Tugay, 22 August 1962 (DSC00312).
71. TNA FO 371/5090, 25. Eşref's name, rendered as "Eshreff Kushjibashi Zadé," was included on a "List of Turks whose surrender it is recommended should be demanded on account of cruelty to native Christians or for other reasons."

8. RETURN, "NATIONAL STRUGGLE," AND EXILE

1. Pervin, 50–2.

2. Erik Jan Zürcher, *Turkey: A Modern History*, 3rd edn (London: I. B. Tauris, 2004), 139; Andrew Mango, *Atatürk* (London: John Murray, 1999), 190. Ottoman apprehension was exacerbated by the fact that the British army continued to advance on Mosul, and its oil fields, after the armistice was signed. The British occupation of Mosul as well as the port of İskenderun encouraged Ottoman officers to make contingency plans to resist the Allies in Anatolia. Mango, *Atatürk*, 191–2.

3. Hasan Kayalı, "The Struggle for Independence," in Reşat Kasaba, ed., *The Cambridge History of Turkey*, vol. 4: *Turkey in the Modern World* (Cambridge: Cambridge University Press, 2008), 113.

4. Interestingly, in an interview conducted with a British military official in Berlin in early January 1920, Enver indicated that he was still in touch with Mustafa Kemal (via a courier that reached Enver when he was in Switzerland on a recent visit); he said that despite their differences, which went back to their days in Libya (Enver felt that Kemal "had worked against him in Tripoli"), the two had "smoothed over" these disagreements and were now willing to work together for the good of their country. Enver said that Mustafa Kemal had told him that he would be willing to serve under Enver even "as a sergeant if necessary," in organizing a treaty with Britain. TNA WO 32/5620, 161.

5. Zürcher, *Turkey: A Modern History*, 145.

6. Erik Jan Zürcher, *The Unionist Factor: The Role of the Committee of Union and Progress in the Turkish National Movement* (Leiden: Brill, 1984), 104–5. During this period the terms given to the various groups are contentious. From the perspective of the Ottoman government, the movement that would eventually come to be referred to as "nationalist" was seen as a rebellion. The "nationalists" called themselves the Kuva-yı Milliye, a term that can be translated as either the Communal, i.e. Muslim Communitarian Forces, or the National Forces, as it embraced a range of Muslim groups, including Turks, Albanians, Circassians, Laz, etc. This movement, in turn, deemed those who deviated from it or abandoned it to be "rebels" as well, a term used by Ankara to define Çerkes Edhem and Eşref when they split away toward the end of 1920.

7. Zürcher, *Unionist Factor*, 86.

8. On the Karakol, see Zürcher, *Unionist Factor*, 80 ff. It is important to note that its crucial and largely successful role in laying the ground for the "national movement" tends to be slighted in Kemalist accounts because it was established at the instigation of Enver and Talat Paşas at a meeting in Enver Paşa's house in Kuruçeşme in October 1918. Mustafa Kemal had also had connections with some of the more shadowy members of Karakol, a fact that naturally is not given prominence in Kemalist accounts. For details, see Zürcher, *Unionist Factor*, 113–14; Ryan Gingeras, *Sorrowful Shores: Violence, Ethnicity, and the End of the Ottoman Empire, 1912–1923* (New York: Oxford University Press, 2009), 70.

9. ATASE ATAZB 27/42–1, 22 January 1920.

10. Yahya Kaptan was a Special Organization member who had engaged in brigand-age in Macedonia and then gravitated toward Yakup Cemil's plot to overthrow the wartime Unionist cabinet. Yakup Cemil was hanged, but Yahya Kaptan was exiled to Iraq. After returning to the Istanbul region, he operated as a gang/guer-rilla leader under the authority of Mustafa Kemal. He was killed in an inter-Nationalist struggle for control of the area around Kocaeli after the Karakol decided he was harming the national cause. He was captured by troops sent to arrest him, and subsequently killed. Mango, *Atatürk*, 266; Gingeras, *Sorrowful Shores*, 181. Mustafa Kemal devoted many pages of his famous "Speech" to Yahya Kaptan.

11. ATASE ATAZB 27/42–2, 23 January 1920.

12. Pervin, 60.

13. Hüsameddin Ertürk and Samih Nafız Tansu, *İki Devrin Perde Arkası* (Istanbul: Ramadan Yasar, 1969), 197; Gingeras, *Sorrowful Shores*, 214, n 120.

14. Zürcher, *Unionist Factor*, 123.

15. Bardakçı, 478.

16. Gingeras, *Sorrowful Shores*, 79–80.

17. Pervin, 61.

18. Pervin, 64.

19. Gingeras, *Sorrowful Shores*, 9. Further complicating the picture were the changes wrought both by the penetration of Western capital and market relations in the late nineteenth and early twentieth centuries and by the spread of the idea of nationalism. Gingeras, *Sorrowful Shores*, 20–21.

20. Gingeras, *Sorrowful Shores*, 25, citing Arsen Avagyan, *Osmanlı İmparatorluğu ve Kemalist Türkiye'nin Devlet-İktidar Sisteminde Çerkesler* (Istanbul: Belge, 2004), 71.

21. Alexandre Toumarkine, "Entre Empire Ottoman et État-Nation Turc: Les Immigrés Musulmans de Caucase et des Balkans du Milieu du XIXe Siècle à Nos Jours" (unpublished PhD thesis, University of Paris IV—Sorbonne, 2000), 544–5.

22. Mustafa Kemal Atatürk, *Nutuk* (Istanbul: Bordo, 2007), 259.

23. Gingeras, *Sorrowful Shores*, 42 ff.

24. Ibid., 65.

25. Gingeras, *Sorrowful Shores*, 52–4.

26. Ibid., 70.

27. Toumarkine, 518–19.

28. Hacîm Muhittin Çarıklı, *Balıkesir ve Alaşehir Kongreleri ve Hacîm Muhittin Çarıklı'nın Kuvâ-yı Milliye Hatıraları (1919–1920)* (Ankara: Ankara Üniversitesi Basımevi, 2014), 108.

29. Toumarkine, 545.

30. ATASE ATAZB 27/42.10, 3 February 1920.

31. ATASE İSH 728/135.

32. ATASE ATAZB 27/42.10, 23 January 1920.
33. BOA DH.EUM.AYŞ 33/76, 2 Mart 1336 [2 Mart 1920].
34. For example, ATASE ATAZB 27/62.3, 23 February 1920.
35. ATASE ATAZB 27/54–1, 27 February 1920. The telegram indicates that it was actually sent from İzmit. Subsequent correspondence, including that of an intermediary, reveals that Eşref did not arrive in Adapazarı until the next day.
36. ATASE ATAZB 27/58–1, 1 March 1920.
37. ATASE ATAZB 27/57–1, 29 February 1920.
38. ATASE ATAZB 27/58–1, 1 March 1920.
39. Sefer Berzeg, *Türkiye Kurtuluş Savaşı'nda Çerkes Göçmenleri, Cilt II* (Istanbul: Nart Yayıncılık, 1990), 47–8. After serving under Ahmed Anzavur and representing Kandıra in the Near Eastern Circassian Association congress of 1921, Maan Şirin was, like Eşref, placed on "The 150" list and settled in Greece after Turkish independence.
40. Gingeras, *Sorrowful Shores*, 62–3.
41. Toumarkine, 543.
42. ATASE ATAZB 27/58–2, n.d., probably 2 March 1920, because Mustafa Kemal responded on 3 March 1920.
43. Stanford J. Shaw, *From Empire to Republic: The Turkish War of National Liberation*, 5 vols. (Ankara: Türk Tarih Kurumu, 2000), Vol. II, 645.
44. ATASE ATAZB 27/58–3.
45. ATASE ATAZB 27/58–3.
46. ATASE ATAZB 27/58–3.
47. ATASE ATAZB 27/58–6, 3 March 1920.
48. ATASE ATAZB 27/58–6, 3 March 1920.
49. ATASE ATAZB 27/58–6a, 3 March 1920.
50. Gingeras, *Sorrowful Shores*, 104; Toumarkine, 544.
51. ATASE ATAZB 23/113.1 and ATAZB 23/113.1a, 5 March 1920, Şevket (Beşiktaş) to Nuh Bey (Ankara?). The last line indicates that this report was to have been brought to the attention of Eşref.
52. ATASE ATAZB 27/62–1, 13 March 1920 (his telegram indicates that this was not the first time he had requested Eşref's presence in Ankara).
53. BOA DH.KMS 53–4/47, İzmit mutasarrıflığı to Interior Ministory, 18 Nisan 1336 (18 April 1920).
54. This claim was made by Hacîm Muhittin Çarıklı, a high-ranking CUP official who became an important Kuva-yı Milliye organizer (although not without his qualms at Mustafa Kemal's assumption of power among the resistance forces). In his memoir he states that he was in the vicinity of Adapazarı and in the possession of two rifles that had been given to him for safe-keeping that were to be passed to Eşref. But, he said, the Circassians of Adapazarı had revolted against him because of his servile origins and in such an atmosphere Hacîm was captured and taken to Adapazarı and insulted on the way. Çarıklı, 110. Such a claim would have been

strongly rejected by Eşref who claimed descent from the twelfth-century Seljuk sultan Sanjar (Sencer). Of course, the two claims are not mutually exclusive. It seems clear that the Circassian nobility of north-west Anatolia did not consider Eşref to be one of their number. The divisions between noble and servile in Circassian society seem especially stark, but are notoriously difficult for outsiders to discern.

55. Toumarkine, 543.
56. Gingeras, *Sorrowful Shores*, 104.
57. TNA FO 371/5167, 106, 17 April 1920.
58. Toumarkine, 544.
59. ATASE ATAZB 23/113.3, 5 March 1920.
60. ATASE ATAZB 27/61.1, 7 March 1920.
61. ATASE İSH 371/66.1, 12 March 1920.
62. ATASE ATAZB 27/64.3, 12 March 1920.
63. ATASE ATAZB 24/89.1, 5/6 March 1920. In the end Mustafa Kemal decided to give the assignment to the commander of the 1st Division and not to Eşref. ATASE ATAZB 24/89.2, 8 March 1920.
64. ATASE ATAZB 27/64.1, 13 March 1920.
65. ATASE ATAZB 27/66.5, 14 March 1920.
66. ATASE ATAZB 27/66.6, 14 March 1920.
67. EK2, Picture 102.
68. Pervin, 72.
69. EK2, Picture 103; Pervin, 72.
70. BOA DH.EUM.AYŞ 40/20, 6 May 1920.
71. Pervin, 75.
72. Pervin, 76. Nemrut Paşa later signed the warrant condemning Mustafa Kemal and his key associates in Anatolia to death in absentia.
73. ATASE ATAZB 11/35–1, 4 April 1920.
74. Mühittin Ünal, *Miralay Bekir Sami Günsav'ın Kurtuluş Savaşı Anıları 2. baskın* (Istanbul: Cem, 2002), 330.
75. ATASE ATAZB 11/35–4, 7–8 April 1920; ATASE İSH 274/18–5, 7–8 April 1920.
76. ATASE ATAZB 11/35–4, 7–8 April 1920.
77. TNA FO 371/5167, 106, 17 April 1920.
78. ATASE ATAZB 11/37.1, 8 April 1920.
79. ATASE ATAZB 11/37–2, 9 April 1920.
80. Günay Çağlar, "XXIV. Tümen Komutanı Yarbay Mahmud Bey Olayı," *Ankara Üniversitesi Türk İnkılap Tarihi Enstitüsü Atatürk Yolu Dergisi* 3:12 (1993), 357–8.
81. ATASE ATAZB 11/35–1, 4 April 1920.
82. EK2 Resim 23. If true, this would mean that Eşref went to Ankara before he headed to Adapazarı, a detail not mentioned elsewhere. That could explain his delay in arriving in the town.

83. Mango, *Atatürk*, 272.
84. TNA FO 371/5090, 6, 20 May 1920.
85. Zürcher, *Unionist Factor*, 122.
86. ATASE İSH 274/18–3, 8 April 1920.
87. Toumarkine, 543.
88. TNA PRO 371/5167, 106, 17 April 1920.
89. ATASE İSH 274/18–2, 10 April 1920.
90. Toumarkine, 527.
91. ATASE 274/18–1, 11 April 1920.
92. ATASE, *Harb Tarihi Vesikaları Dergisi* 10: 35, Vesika 871.
93. EK2, Picture 012. Salihli was then still accessible, as it would not be occupied by the Greek advance until late June 1920.
94. Mango, *Atatürk*, 278.
95. Ünal, *Miralay Bekir Sami*, 366.
96. Nilüfer Hatemi, *Mareşal Fevzi Çakmak ve Günlükleri*, vol. 2 (Istanbul: Yapı Kredi Yayınları, 2002), 700; ATASE İSH 427/228.1, 3 May 1920.
97. ATASE İSH 874/5–2, 3 May 1920; TİTE 927/31/205, 3 May 1920.
98. ATASE, *Türk İstiklal Harbi Batı Cephesi*, vol. 2, section 2 (Ankara: ATASE, 1999), 232. Thanks to Dr Mesut Uyar for kindly providing this reference, among many other helpful points.
99. ATASE İSH 738/25, 2 July 1920.
100. Barış Metin, ed., *Esaretten Zafere: Uşaklı Bir Muharip Gazi Şükrü Nail'in (Soysal) Birinci Dünya Savaşı ve Milli Mücadele Dönemi Hatıraları* (Uşak: Uşak Akademi Kitap Dağıtım Pazarlama Yayınevi, 2012), 304–5. Thanks to Dr Yiğit Akın for kindly providing me with this source.
101. Ibid., 305.
102. Ibid., 308. The next episode mentions another bandit (*efe*) operating in the region who is opposed to the Kuva-yı Milliye and is forced to flee the area and take up with the Greek army.
103. ATASE İSH 970/72; ATASE İSH 970/73.
104. ATASE İSH 970/73.1, 28 June 1920.
105. ATASE İSH 970/72.3, 28 June 1920; ATASE İSH 970/72.4, 28 June 1920.
106. ATASE İSH 970/72.2, 28 June 1920.
107. Hatemi, *Mareşal Fevzi Çakmak ve Günlükleri*, 723.
108. Ibid., 726.
109. Mesut Uyar, "Greco-Turkish War, 1919–1922," in Richard C. Hall, ed., *War in the Balkans: An Encyclopedic History from the Fall of the Ottoman Empire to the Breakup of Yugoslavia* (Santa Barbara, CA: SBC-CLIO, 2014), 119.
110. ATASE İSH 841/54.1, 26 October 1920.
111. Zürcher, *Turkey*, 164.
112. Mango, *Atatürk*, 301.
113. ATASE İSH 865/98.1.

114. ATASE ATAZB 38/16.1.
115. EK2, Picture 116.
116. EK2, Picture 117.
117. Pervin, 79.
118. Pervin, 85–6.

9. AFTERMATH: A LIFE IN FRAGMENTS

1. ATASE İSH 886/143, 2 February 1921, Hurşid (Söke) to Ankara.
2. ATASE İSH 865/98.1, 9 February 1921, Refet (Afyon Karahisar) to Ankara.
3. My thanks to Dr Dimitris Stamatapoulos for his advice on this point.
4. ATASE İSH 1158/101, 22 June 1921.
5. TCA 30.18.1.1/3.29.16. 5 July 1921. Contrary to the information given in Özoğlu, Eşref was not among those arrested and then released. Cf. Hakan Özoğlu, *From Caliphate to Secular State: Power Struggle in the Early Turkish Republic* (Santa Barbara: ABC-Clio/Prager, 2011), 64.
6. Zürcher, *Unionist Factor*, 128.
7. Ibid.
8. Michael Reynolds, *Shattering Empires: The Clash and Collapse of the Ottoman and Russian Empires, 1908–1918* (New York: Cambridge University Press, 2011), 204.
9. Ibid., 129.
10. ATASE İSH 1167/127, 2 September 1921.
11. Zürcher, *Unionist Factor*, 128.
12. ATASE İSH 1167/128, 5 September 1921.
13. Gingeras, *Sorrowful Shores*, 124.
14. Toumarkine, 917; Efe, 183–4.
15. EK, *Turkish Battle*, 185.
16. Türk İnkilâp Tarih Enstitüsü Arşivi (TİTE) 50/29.
17. TİTE 49/90.
18. Gingeras, *Sorrowful Shores*, 138.
19. Sometimes also referred to as the Ottoman Anatolian Revolutionary Committee.
20. Emrah Cilasun, *Bâki İlk Selam—Çerkes Ethem* (Istanbul: Agora, 2009), 235–8.
21. Efe, 219 ff.
22. Efe, 196.
23. Gingeras, *Sorrowful Shores*, 141.
24. Ibid.
25. TİTE 328/3. n.d.
26. Cilasun, 215.
27. Gingeras, *Sorrowful Shores*, 141.
28. BOA HR.İM 81/57, 23 August 1923.
29. Gingeras, *Sorrowful Shores*, 141.
30. TİTE 27/87.1.

31. A brief attempt to enter into the shipping business in the early 1930s seems to have ended in failure. Sedat Bingöl, *150'likler Meselesi: Bir İhanetin Anatomisi* (Istanbul: Bengi, 2010), 174.

32. Ibid.

33. Ibid., 175.

34. EK to Cuyap, n.d.

35. For a discussion of Greek policy toward its Muslim poulation in this period, see Stefanos Katsikas, "Hostage Minority: The Muslims of Greece (1923–1941)," in Benjamin C. Fortna, Stefanos Katsikas, Dimitris Kamouzis, and Paraskevas Konortas, eds., *State-Nationalisms in the Ottoman Empire, Greece and Turkey: Orthodox and Muslims, 1830–1945* (London: Routledge, 2013), 153–75.

36. For this correspondence, undertaken in 1930, see Kutay, *Yazılmamış Tarihimiz-Seçmeleri 1* (Istanbul: Aksoy, 2000), 113 ff.; and Kutay, *Tarih Sohbetleri* (Istanbul: Halk Matbaası, 1966), 163 ff. The men appear to have remained close. Âkif refers to Eşref as "my Eşref, my friend of my two eyes," a term of endearment in Turkish.

37. EK to Cihangiroğlu İbrahim, 15 June 1952 and 21 December 1953. My thanks to Dr İbrahim Şirin for sharing these papers with me.

38. Vahakn Dadrian and Taner Akcam, *Judgment at Istanbul: The Armenian Genocide Trials* (New York: Bergbahn, 2011), 247.

39. Berzeg, *Çerkes—Vubıhlar*, 468.

40. Philip Stoddard, personal communication, 18 November 2010.

BIBLIOGRAPHY

ARCHIVES

Başbakanlık Cumhuriyet Arşivi (BCA)
Başbakanlık Osmanlı Arşivi (BOA)
    Bab–ı Ali Evrak Odası (BEO)
    Dahiliye Nezâreti
    Emniyet-i Umumiye (DH.EUM)
    Emniyet-i Umumiye Asayiş Kalemi (DH.EUM.AYŞ)
    Emniyet-i Umumiye Levazım Kalemi (DH.EUM.LVZ)
    Emniyet-i Umumiye Muhâsebe Kalemi (DH.EUM.MH)
    Kalem-i Mahsus Müdüriyeti (DH.KMS)
    Şifre Kalemi (DH.ŞFR)
    Hariciye Nezâreti
    İstanbul Murahhaslığı (HR.İM)
    Siyasî Kısmı (HR.SYS)
    İradeler
    İrade Askeri (İ.AS)
    İrade Hususi (İ.HUS)
    İrade Dosya Usulü (İ.DUIT)
    Meclis-i Vükela Mazbataları (MV)
    Rumeli Müfettişliği
    Müteferrika Evrakı (TFR.İ.M)

Cihangiroğlu papers

Private papers of Eşref Kuşçubaşı (EK)

Genelkurmay Askerî Tarih ve Stratejik Etüt Arşivi (ATASE)
    Atatürk Arşivi Ziraat Bankasından Gelen Evrak (ATAZB)
    İstiklal Harbi Kataloğu (İSH)

BIBLIOGRAPHY

Imperial War Museum Collections (IWM), London

Middle East Archive, St Antony's College, Oxford
  Deedes Collection (MEC)

The National Archives (TNA), Kew
  Foreign Office (FO)
  War Office (WO)

Parliamentary Archives, Houses of Parliament, London
  Lloyd George Papers (LG)

SOAS Special Collections, SOAS Library, London

Taha Toros papers Şehir Üniversitesi Kütüphanesi, Taha Toros
  Arşivi (TT)

Türk İnkilâp Tarih Ensitüsü Arşivi (TİTE)

NON-ARCHIVAL MATERIALS

Aarbakke, Vemund, "The Muslim Minority of Greek Thrace" (unpublished PhD dissertation, University of Bergen, 2000).
———, "The Independent Republic of Gumuldjina (1913)–What do the sources tell us?" Paper presented at the international conference organized by the Institute of History at the Bulgarian Academy of Sciences, 10–12, November 2013.
———, "The Report of Petâr Chaulev to Prime Minister Vasil Radoslavov about the Situation in Western Thrace in February 1914", *Balkan Studies* 49 (2014), 47–68.
———, "Uneven nation formation and the disruptive effect of the Balkan Wars", in Dimitris Stamatapoulos, ed., *Balkan* Nationalism(s) and Ottoman Empire, vol. 2 (Istanbul: Isis Press: 2015).
———, Georgios Niarchos, and Vassilis Koutsoukos, "The Independent Republic of Gumuldjina (1913)–A New Test for Young Turk Policy Makers", in Dimitris Stamatapoulos, ed., *Balkan Nationalism(s) and Ottoman Empire*, vol. 3 (Istanbul: Isis Press: 2015).
Adil Hikmet Bey, *Asya'da Beş Türk*, Yusuf Gedikli, ed. (Istanbul: Ötuken, 1998).
Ajay, Nicholas, "Political Intrigue and Suppression in Lebanon during World War I", *IJMES* 5:2 (April 1974), 140–60.
Akcam, Taner, *A Shameful Act: The Armenian Genocide and the Question of Turkish Responsibility* (New York: Macmillan, 2006).
Aksakal, Mustafa, *The Ottoman Road to War in 1914: The Ottoman Empire and the First World War* (Cambridge: Cambridge University Press, 2008).
Akyol, Taha, *Rumeli'ye Elveda: 100 Yılında Balkan Bozgunu* (Istanbul: Doğan Kitap, 2013).

BIBLIOGRAPHY

Anderson, Scott, *Lawrence in Arabia:War, Deceit, Imperial Folly and the Making of the Modern Middle East* (New York: Doubleday, 2013).

The Arab Bulletin: Bulletin of the Arab Bureau in Cairo, 1916–1919 (Cairo).

Asher, Michael, *Lawrence: The Uncrowned King of Arabia* (London: Penguin Books, 1999).

ATASE, Askeri Tarih Belgeler Dergisi (Ankara).

———, *Türk İstiklal Harbi Batı Cephesi* (Ankara: ATASE, 1999).

Atatürk, Mustafa Kemal, *Nutuk* (Istanbul: Bordo, 2007).

Bardakçı, Murat, *İttihadçı'nın Sandığı: İttihad ve Terakki liderlerinin özel arşivlerindeki yayınlanmamış belgeler ile Atatürk ve İnönü dönemlerinde Ermeni gayrimenkulleri konusunda alınmış bazı kararlar* (Istanbul: Türkiye İş Bankası Kültür Yayınları, 2013).

Bayar, Celâl, *Ben de Yazdım: Millî Mücadele'ye Gidiş*, 4 vols. (Istanbul: Baha, 1967).

Baykal, Erol, "Istanbul During the Balkan Wars (1912–1913): Cholera, Medicine and the Press", *Turkish Historical Review* 5:2 (2014), 141–64.

Berzeg, Sefer E., *Çerkes–Vubıhlar: Soçi'nin İnsanları (Portreler)* (Ankara: Kuban, 2013).

———, *Türkiye Kurtuluş Savaşı'nda Çerkes Göçmenleri, Cilt II* (Istanbul: Nart Yayıncılık, 1990).

Beşikçi, Mehmet, "Mobilizing Military Labor in the Age of Total War: Ottoman Conscription during the Great War", in Erik-Jan Zürcher, ed., *Fighting for a Living: A Comparative History of Military Labor 1500–2000* (Amsterdam: Amsterdam University Press, 2013), 547–80.

———, *Ottoman Mobilization in the First World War: Between Voluntarism and Resistance* (Leiden: Brill, 2012).

Besleney, Zeynel Abidin, *The Circassian Diaspora in Turkey: A Political History* (London: Routledge, 2014).

Bilmez, Bülent, "A Nationalist Discourse of Heroism and Treason: The Construction of an 'Official' Image of Çerkes Ethem (1886–1948) in Turkish Historiography, and Recent Challenges", in Amy Singer, Christoph K. Neumann, and Selçuk Akşin Somel, eds., *Untold Histories of the Middle East: Recovering Voices from the 19th and 20ᵗʰ Centuries* (London: Routledge, 2011).

Bingöl, Sedat, *150'likler Meselesi: Bir İhanetin Anatomisi* (Istanbul: Bengi, 2010).

Birbudak, Togay Seçkin, "Osmanlı Basınında Mahmud Şevket Paşa Suikastı", *Bilig* 65 (Bahar, 2013).

Bıyıklıoğlu, Tevfik, *Trakya'da Millî Mücadele*, 2 vols. (Ankara: Türk Tarih Kurumu, 1955).

Çağlar, Günay, "XXIV. Tümen Komutanı Yarbay Mahmud Bey Olayı", *Ankara Üniversitesi Türk İnkılap Tarihi Enstitüsü Atatürk Yolu Dergisi* 3:12 (1993), 355–62.

BIBLIOGRAPHY

Çarıklı, Hacîm Muhittin, *Balıkesir ve Alaşehir Kongreleri ve Hacîm Muhittin Çarıklı'nın Kuvâ-yı Milliye Hatıraları (1919–1920)* (Ankara: Ankara Üniversitesi Basımevi, 2014).

Carnegie Endowment for International Peace, *Report of the International Commission to Inquire into the Causes and Conduct of the Balkan Wars* (Washington, DC: Carnegie Endowment for International Peace, 1914).

Cemal Paşa, *Memories of a Turkish Statesman, 1913–1919* (New York: Arno, 1973).

———, *Hatırat* (Istanbul: Arma, 1996).

Çetinsaya, Y Doğan, "Atrocity Propaganda and the Nationalization of the Masses in the Ottoman Empire during the Balkan Wars (1912–13)", *IJMES* 46:4 (2014), 759–78.

Çiçek, M. Talha, *War and State Formation in Syria: Cemal Pasha's Governorate During World War I, 1914–17* (London: Routledge, 2014).

Çiçek, Nazan, "More History Than They Can Consume?" in M. H. Yavuz and I. Blumi, eds., *War and Nationalism: The Balkan Wars, 1912–1913, and Their Sociopolitical Implications* (Salt Lake City: University of Utah Press, 2013), 777–804.

———, "'Talihsiz Çerkesleri İngiliz Peksimeti': İngiliz Arşiv Belgelerinde Büyük Çerkes Göçü (Şubat 1864–Mayıs 1865)", *Ankara Üniversitesi Siyasal Bilimler Fakültesi Dergisi* 64:1 (2009), 57–88.

Cilasun, Emrah, *Bâki İlk Selam–Çerkes Ethem* (Istanbul: Agora, 2009).

Clark, Christopher, *The Sleepwalkers: How Europe Went to War in 1914* (London: Penguin Books, 2013).

Dadrian, Vahakn, "Ottoman Archives and Denial of the Armenian Genocide", in Richard G. Hovannisian, ed., *The Armenian Genocide: History, Politics, Ethics* (New York: Macmillan, 1992).

——— and Taner Akcam, *Judgment at Istanbul: The Armenian Genocide Trials* (New York: Bergbahn, 2011).

Deringil, Selim, "Intellectual encounters with the West: The Cases of Turkey and Japan", *New Perspectives on Turkey* 35 (2006), 65–83.

Düzdağ, M. Ertuğrul, ed., *Mehmed Âkif Ersoy* (Izmir, Sütün, 2007).

Efe, Ahmet, *Efsaneden Gerçeğe Kuşcubaşı Eşref* (Istanbul: Bengi, 2007).

Englund, Peter, *The Beauty and the Sorrow: An Intimate History of the First World War*, trans. Peter Graves (London: Profile, 2011).

Enver Pascha, *Um Tripolis: Feld-Ausgabe* (München: Hugo Bruckmann Verlag, 1918).

Erdem, Nilüfer, "1913 Yılının Temmuz–Ekim Ayları Batı Trakya Türkleri ile ilgili Gelişmelerin Yunan Basınındaki Yansımaları", *History Studies* 6:2 (February 2014), 67–89.

Erickson, Edward J., *Ordered to Die: A History of the Ottoman Army in the First World War* (Westport, CT: Greenwood Press, 2001).

BIBLIOGRAPHY

————, *Defeat in Detail: The Ottoman Army in the Balkans, 1912–1913* (Westport, CT: Praeger, 2003).

————, *Ottomans and Armenians: A Study in Counterinsurgency* (New York: Palgrave Macmillan, 2013).

Erkan, Aydın Osman, *Turn My Head to the Caucasus: The Biography of Osman Ferid Pasha* (Istanbul: Çitlembik, 2009).

Erol, Emre, "Organised Chaos as Diplomatic Ruse and Demographic Weapon: The Expulsion of the Ottoman Greeks (*Rum*) from Foça, 1914", *Tijdschrift voor Sociale en Economische Geschiedenis* 10:4 (2013), 66–96.

————, "Preparing for the First World War: Forced Migration as a Tool of 'Demographic Warfare' in the Pre-War Western Anatolia", paper presented to the international conference "Not All Quiet on the Ottoman Fronts: Neglected Perspectives on a Global War, 1914–1918", Istanbul, April 2014.

Ertürk, Hüsameddin and Samih Nafız Tansu, *İki Devrin Perde Arkası* (Istanbul: Ramadan Yasar, 1969).

Evans-Pritchard, E. E., *The Sanusi of Cyrenaica* (Oxford: Oxford University Press, 1949).

Farge, Arlette, *The Allure of the Archives* (New Haven: Yale University Press, 2013).

Featherstone, Kevin et al., *The Last Ottomans: The Muslim Minority of Greece, 1940–1949* (London: Palgrave Macmillan, 2011).

Fortna, Benjamin C., *Learning to Read in the Late Ottoman Empire and the Early Turkish Republic* (London: Palgrave Macmillan, 2010).

Franz Joseph, Prince of Hohenzollern, *Emden: My Experiences in S.M.S. Emden* (London: Herbert Jenkins, 1928).

Freitag, Ulrike, "Modern-Day Saudi Arabia During the First World War: Insights into a Contingent Era", in *Fikrun wa Fann*, www.goethe.de/ges/phi/prj/ffs/the/a100/en12235572.htm, accessed 26 July 2014.

Gawrych, George, *The Young Atatürk: From Ottoman Soldier to Statesman of Turkey* (London: I. B. Tauris, 2013).

Georgelin, Hervé, *La fin de Smyrne* (Paris: CNRS, 2006).

Gilmour, David, "He Dared the Undarable", *New York Review of Books* LXI: 4 (6–19 March 2014), 22.

Gingeras, Ryan, *Sorrowful Shores: Violence, Ethnicity, and the End of the Ottoman Empire, 1912–1923* (New York: Oxford University Press, 2009).

Ginio, Eyal, "Paving the Way for Ethnic Cleansing: Eastern Thrace during the Balkan Wars (1912–1913) and their Aftermath", in Omer Bartov and Eric D. Weitz, eds., *Shatterzone of Empires: Coexistence and Violence in the German, Hapsburg, Russian and Ottoman Borderlands* (Bloomington: Indiana University Press, 2013), 283–97.

BIBLIOGRAPHY

Giustozzi, Antonio, *The Art of Coercion: The Primitive Accumulation and Management of Coercive Power* (London: Hurst & Co., 2011).

Göçek, Fatma Müge, "What is the Meaning of the 1908 Young Turk Revolution? A Critical Historical Assessment in 2008", *İstanbul Üniversitesi Siyasal Bilgiler Fakültesi Dergisi* 38 (2008), 179–214.

Guillaume, A., *The Life of Muhammad: A Translation of [Ibn] Ishaq's Sirat Rasul Allah* (Oxford: Oxford University Press, 1955).

Gündağ, Nevzat, *1913 Garbî Trakya Hükûmet-i Müstakîlesi* (Ankara: Kültür ve Turizm Bakanlığı, 1987).

Hall, Richard C., *The Balkan Wars, 1912–1913: Prelude to the First World War* (London: Routledge, 2000).

Hanioğlu, M. Şükrü, Kendi Mektuplarında Enver Paşa (Istanbul: Der, 1989).

————, *Preparation for a Revolution: The Young Turks, 1902–1908* (New York: Oxford University Press, 2001).

————, *A Brief History of the Late Ottoman Empire* (Princeton: Princeton University Press, 2008).

————, "The Second Constitutional Period, 1908–1918", in Reşat Kasaba, ed., *The Cambridge History of Turkey*, vol. 4: *Turkey in the Modern World* (Cambridge: Cambridge University Press, 2008), 62–111.

————, *Atatürk: An Intellectual Biography* (Princeton: Princeton University Press, 2011).

Hatemi, Nilüfer, *Mareşal Fevzi Çakmak ve Günlükleri*, 2 vols. (Istanbul: Yapı Kredi Yayınları, 2002).

Huber, Valeska, *Channelling Mobilities: Migration and Globalisation in the Suez Canal Region and Beyond, 1869–1914* (Cambridge: Cambridge University Press, 2013).

Ihrig, Stefan, *Atatürk in the Nazi Imagination* (Cambridge, MA: Belknap Press, 2014).

Kağan, Hakan, *İmparatorluğun Son Akşamı* (Istanbul: Timas, 2008).

Kaiser, Hilmar, *The Extermination of Armenians in the Diarbekir Region* (Istanbul: Istanbul Bilgi Unversity Press, 2014).

Kasaba, Reşat, *A Moveable Empire: Ottoman Nomads, Migrants and Refugees* (Seattle: University of Washington Press, 2009).

Katsikas, Stefanos, "Hostage Minority: The Muslims of Greece (1923–1941)", in Benjamin C. Fortna, Stefanos Katsikas, Dimitris Kamouzis, and Paraskevas Konortas, eds., *State-Nationalisms in the Ottoman Empire, Greece and Turkey: Orthodox and Muslims, 1830–1945* (London: Routledge, 2013), 153–75.

Kayalı, Hasan, *Arabs and Young Turks: Ottomanism, Arabism, and Islamism in the Ottoman Empire, 1908–1918* (Berkeley: University of California Press, 1997).

————, "The Struggle for Independence", in Reşat Kasaba, ed., *The*

BIBLIOGRAPHY

Cambridge History of Turkey, vol. 4: *Turkey in the Modern World* (Cambridge: Cambridge University Press, 2008),112–46.

Keleşyılmaz, Vahdet, *Teşkilâtı Mahsusa'nın Hindistan Misyonu (1914–1918)* (Ankara: Atatürk Araştırma Merkezi, 1999).

Kevorkian, Raymond, *The Armenian Genocide: A Complete History* (London: I. B. Tauris, 2011).

Kramer, Alan R., "Prisoners in the First World War", in Sibylle Scheipers, ed., *Prisoners in War* (London: Oxford University Press, 2010).

Kress von Kressenstein, Friedrich Freiherr, *Mit den Türken zum Suezkanal* (Berlin: Vorhut-Verlag Otto Schlegel, 1938).

Kuşçubası, Eşref, *Kanuna, aklıselime ve hukuk devleti devri iddialarına rağmen devam halindeki bir zülmün acı hikayesi* (Istanbul: Tan, 1953).

———, *The Turkish Battle at Khaybar*, eds. Philip Stoddard and H. Basri Danışman (Istanbul: Arba, 1997).

———, *Hayber'de Türk Cengi* (Istanbul: Arba, 1997).

Kutay, Cemal, *Türkiye İstiklâl ve Hürriyet Mücadeleri Tarihi*, vol. X (Istanbul: Nurgök Tarih Matbaası, 1957).

———, *1913 de Garbî Trakya'da İlk Türk Cumhuriyeti* (Istanbul: Tarih Yayınları, 1962).

———, *Ana-Vatan'da Son Beş Osmanlı Türk'ü* (Istanbul: Bahadır Matbaası, 1962).

———, *Birinci Dünya Harbinde Teşkilat-ı Mahsusa ve Hayber'de Türk Cengi* (Istanbul: Tarih Yayınları, 1962).

———, *Necid Çöllerinde Mehmed Âkif* (Istanbul: Ercan, 1963).

———, *Tarih Sohbetleri* (Istanbul: Halk Matbaası, 1966).

———, *Yazılmamış Tarihimiz–Seçmeleri 1* (Istanbul: Aksoy, 2000).

Lawrence, T. E., *Seven Pillars of Wisdom: A Triumph* (New York: Penguin Books, 1962).

Lüdke, Tilman, *Jihad Made in Germany: Ottoman and German Propaganda and Intelligence Operations in the First World War* (Münster: Lit Verlag, 2005).

Macar, Oya Dağlar, "Epidemic Diseases on the Thracian Front of the Ottoman Empire during the Balkan Wars", in H. Yavuz and I. Blumi, eds., *War and Nationalism: The Balkan Wars, 1912–1913, and their Sociopolitical Implications* (Salt Lake City: Utah University Press, 2013), 272–97.

McCarthy, Justin, *Death and Exile: The Ethnic Cleansing of Ottoman Muslims, 1821–1922* (Princeton, NJ: Darwin Press, 1995).

Mahmut Şevket Paşa, *Sadrazâm ve Harbiye Nazırı Mahmut Şevket Paşa'nın Günlüğü* (Istanbul: Arba, 1988).

Maiolo, Joseph and Tony Insall, "Sir Basil Zaharoff and Sir Vincent Caillard as Instruments of British Policy towards Greece and the Ottoman Empire during the Asquith and Lloyd George Administrations, 1915–8", *International History Review* 34:4 (December 2012), 819–39.

BIBLIOGRAPHY

Makdisi, Ussama, "Ottoman Orientalism", *American Historical Review* 107:3 (2002), 768–96.

Mango, Andrew, *Atatürk* (London: John Murray, 1999).

Mardin, Şerif, *Religion and Social Change in Modern Turkey: The Case of Bediüzzaman Said Nursi* (Albany, NY: State University of New York Press, 1989).

————, "The Ottoman Empire", in K. Barkey and M. von Hagen, eds., *After Empire: Multiethnic Societies and Nation-building in the Soviet Union and the Russian, Ottoman and Habsburg Empires* (Boulder, CO: Westview, 1997).

Metin, Barış, ed., *Esaretten Zafere: Uşaklı Bir Muharip Gazi Şükrü Nail'in (Soysal) Birinci Dünya Savaşı ve Milli Mücadele Dönemi Hatıraları* (Uşak: Uşak Akademi Kitap Dağıtım Pazarlama Yayınevi, 2012).

Miletich, Lyubomir, *Istoriyata na Giumiurdjinskata* avtonomiya (The History of the Giumurdjina Republic) (Sofia, 1914).

————, *Razorenieto na trakiĭskite Bălgari prez 1913 godina* (The Destruction of the Thracian Bulgarians in 1913) (Sofia, 1918).

Miller, Stephen M., *Lord Methuen and the British Army: Failure and Redemption in South Africa* (London: Frank Cass, 1999).

Mohs, Polly A., *Military Intelligence and the Arab Revolt: The First Modern Intelligence War* (London: Routledge, 2008).

Norton-Taylor, Richard, "First world war abridged", *Guardian*, 13 August 2013, 28.

Ortaylı, İlber, *İmparatorluğun En Üzün Yüzyılı* (Istanbul: Timas, 2008).

Özbek, Nadir, "Policing the Countryside: Gendarmes of the Late 19th-Century Ottoman Empire (1876–1908)", *IJMES* 40:1 (2008), 47–67.

Özkan, Behlül, *From the Abode of Islam to the Turkish Vatan: The Making of a National Homeland in Turkey* (New Haven, CT: Yale University Press, 2012).

Özoğlu, Hakan, *From Caliphate to Secular State: Power Struggle in the Early Turkish Republic* (Santa Barbara: ABC-Clio/Prager, 2011).

Philliou, Christine M., *Biography of an Empire: Governing Ottomans in an Age of Revolution* (Berkeley: University of California Press, 2011).

Pope, Nicole and Hugh Pope, *Turkey Unveiled: Atatürk and After* (London: John Murray, 1997).

Presland, John (pseudonym of of Mrs Gladys Skelton), *Deedes Bey: A Study of Sir Wyndham Deedes, 1883–1923* (London: Macmillan, 1942).

Reynolds, Michael, *Shattering Empires: The Clash and Collapse of the Ottoman and Russian Empires, 1908–1918* (New York: Cambridge University Press, 2011).

Rodas, Mihail, *Almanya Türkiye'deki Rumları Nasıl Mahvetti* (Istanbul: Belge Yayınları, 2011).

Rodenwaldt, Ernst, *Ein Tropenarzt erzählt sein Leben* (Stuttgart: Ferdinand Enke Verlag, 1957).

BIBLIOGRAPHY

Safi, Polat, "The Ottoman Special Organization—*Teşkilat-ı Mahsusa*: A Historical Assessment with Particular Reference to its Operations against British Occupied Egypt (1914–1915)" (unpublished MA dissertation, Bilkent University, Ankara, 2006).

————, "The Ottoman Special Organization—*Teşkilat-ı Mahsusa*: An Inquiry into its Operational and Administrative Characteristics" (unpublished PhD dissertation, Bilkent University, Ankara, 2012).

————, "History in the Trench: The Ottoman Special Organization–Teşkilat-ı Mahsusa Literature", *Middle Eastern Studies* 48:1 (2012), 89–106.

Schull, Kent F, "Interned on the Isle of Man: Ottoman Citizens in British Concentration Camps during World War One", paper presented at the annual meetings of the Middle East Studies Association, Denver, CO, November 2012.

Shaw, Stanford J., *From Empire to Republic: The Turkish War of National Liberation*, 5 vols. (Ankara: Türk Tarih Kurumu, 2000).

Sheffy, Yigal, *British Military Intelligence in the Palestine Campaign, 1914–1918* (London: Frank Cass, 1998).

Simon, Rachel, *Libya between Ottomanism and Nationalism: The Ottoman Involvement in Libya During the War with Italy (1911–1919)* (Berlin: Klaus Schwarz Verlag, 1987).

Şimşek, Nurettin, *Teşkilât-ı Mahsusa'nın Reisi Süleyman Askerî Bey: Hayatı, Siyasi ve Askeri Faaliyetleri* (Istanbul: IQ Kültür Sanat Yayıncılık, 2008).

Şirin, İbrahim, "İki Hükümet Bir Teşkilat: Garbî Trakya Hükümet-i Muvakkatesi'nden Cenub-î Garbî Kafkas Hükümeti Muvakkate-î Milliyesi'ne", *History Studies* 6:2 (2014), 125–42.

Slavkov, Iliya and Boryana Dimitrova, *Sachanli—Historical and Ethnographic Study* (Sofia, 1989).

Sohrabi, Nader, "Global Waves, Local Actors: What the Young Turks Knew About Other Revolutions and Why It Mattered", *Comparative Studies in Society and History* 44/1 (2002), 45–79.

————, *Revolution and Constitutionalism in the Ottoman Empire and Iran* (Cambridge: Cambridge University Press, 2011).

Stoddard, Philip Hendrick, "The Ottoman Government and the Arabs, 1911 to 1918: A Preliminary Study of the Teşkilât-ı Mahsusa" (unpublished PhD dissertation, Princeton University, 1963).

————, and H. Basri Danışman, "The Life of Eşref Sencer Kuşçubaşızade", in Eşref Kuşçubası, *The Turkish Battle at Khaybar*, eds. Philip Stoddard and H. Basri Danışman (Istanbul: Arba, 1997).

Stoler, Ann Laura, *Along the Archival Grain: Epistemic Anxieties and Colonial Commonsense* (Princeton: Princeton University Press, 2009).

Strachan, Hew, *The First World War*, vol. I: *To Arms* (Oxford: Oxford University Press, 2001).

BIBLIOGRAPHY

Strohmeier, Martin, "Fakhri (Fahrettin) Paşa and the end of Ottoman rule in Medina", *Turkish Historical Review* 4 (2013), 192–223.

Taçalan, Nurdoğan, *Ege'de Kurtuluş Savaşı Başlarken* (Istanbul: Hur Yayınları, 1981).

Tauber, Eliezer, *The Arab Movements in World War I* (London: Frank Cass, 1993).

Tetik, Ahmet, *Teşkilat-ı Mahsusa (Umûr-u Şarkiye Dairesi) Tarihi Cilt I: 1914–1916* (Istanbul: Turkiye İş Bankası Yayınları, 2014).

Toumarkine, Alexandre, "Entre Empire Ottoman et État-Nation Turc: Les Immigrés Musulmans de Caucase et des Balkans du Milieu du XIXe Siècle à Nos Jours" (unpublished PhD thesis, University of Paris IV–Sorbonne, 2000).

Tuchman, Barbara W., *The Guns of August* (New York: Macmillan, 1962) (repr. Ballantine).

Turfan, M. Naim, *Rise of the Young Turks: Politics, the Military and Ottoman Collapse* (London: I. B. Tauris, 2000).

Turgut, Hulusi, "Nur cemaatinin Türkiye'de 20 bin medresesi var", *Sabah*, 19 January 1997.

Ünal, Muhittin, *Kurtuluş Savaşında Çerkeslerin Rölü* (Ankara: Kafkas Derneği Yayınları, 2000).

———, *Miralay Bekir Sami Günsav'ın Kurtuluş Savaşı Anıları* 2. baskın (Istanbul: Cem, 2002).

Üngör, Uğur Ümit, "'Turkey for the Turks': Demographic Engineering in Eastern Anatolia, 1914–1945", in R. G. Suny, F. M. Göçek, and N. M. Naimark, eds., *A Question of Genocide: Armenians and Turks at the End of the Ottoman Empire* (New York: Oxford University Press, 2011), 287–305.

Uyar, Mesut, "Arab Officers between Nationalism and Loyalty during the First World War", *War in History* 20:4 (2013), 526–44.

———, "Greco-Turkish War, 1919–1922", in Richard C. Hall, ed., *War in the Balkans: An Encyclopedic History from the Fall of the Ottoman Empire to the Breakup of Yugoslavia* (Santa Barbara, CA: SBC-CLIO, 2014), 119–20.

Wasti, Syed Tanvir, "The 1912–13 Balkan Wars and the Siege of Edirne", *Middle Eastern Studies* 40:4 (2004), 59–78.

Woodfin, Edward C., *Camp and Combat on the Sinai and Palestine Front: The Experience of the British Empire Soldier, 1916–18* (Basingstoke: Palgrave Macmillan, 2012).

Yetkin, Sabri, *Ege'de Eşkiyalar* (Istanbul: Tarih Vakfı, 2003).

Yılmazer, Bülent, "Ottoman Aviation, Prelude to Military Use of Aircraft", Appendix A in Edward J. Erickson, *Defeat in Detail: The Ottoman Army in the Balkans, 1912–1913* (Westport, CT: Praeger, 2003).

Zürcher, Erik Jan, *The Unionist Factor: The Role of the Committee of Union and Progress in the Turkish National Movement* (Leiden: Brill, 1984).

———, *Turkey: A Modern History*, 3rd edn (London: I. B. Tauris, 2004).

————, *The Young Turk Legacy and Nation Building: From the Ottoman Empire to Atatürk's Turkey* (London: I. B. Tauris, 2010).

————, "The Balkan Wars and the Refugee Leadership of the Early Turkish Republic", in H. Yavuz and I. Blumi, eds., *War and Nationalism: The Balkan Wars, 1912–1913, and Their Sociopolitical Implications* (Salt Lake City: University of Utah Press, 2013), 665–78.

————, "Macedonians in Anatolia: The Importance of the Macedonian Roots of the Unionists for their Policies in Anatolia after 1914", *Middle Eastern Studies* 50:6 (2014), 960–75.

WEBSITES

www.naval-history.net/WW1Battle1502SuezCanal.htm, accessed 4 September 2014.

www.naval-history.net/OWShips-WW1–09-HMS_Lama.htm, accessed 4 September 2014.

www.levantineheritage.com/guiffray.htm, accessed 15 September 2014.

https://plus.google.com/100372985217770342562/about?gl=uk&hl=en&pid=5685567732449581762&oid=109071717030654322604.

www.timesofmalta.com/articles/view/20140817/life-features/The-Salter-album-from-World-War-I.532336, accessed 5 September 2014.

INDEX

Abadan, Iran, 53
Abbasia, 208
Abd al-Aziz, 186–7
Abd al-Qadir, 69
Abdülaziz I, Ottoman Sultan, 13,
    32
Abdülhamid II, Ottoman Sultan, 2,
    24, 27, 31, 32, 33–4, 36, 43, 44,
    49, 51, 56, 85, 237, 272
Abdülkadir Antepli, 271
Abdülkerim Bey, 161
Abdullah I, King of Jordan, 186,
    195, 198–200
Abdurrahman Bey, 246
Abkhazians, 249
Abu al-Naam, Arabia, 187–8, 195
Abulqadir Gilani, 37
Action Army, 44
Adana, Anatolia, 129, 180
Adapazarı, Anatolia, 233–4,
    236–44, 247–50
Âdil, Hacı 93, 104–5
Adrianople, *see* Edirne
Aegean Sea, 2, 26, 89, 133–4
Afghanistan, Afghans, 60, 88, 123,
    150, 152, 158, 163, 264
Afyon, Anatolia, 40
Afyonlu Ethem Efendi, 180

Agadir crisis (1911), 55, 56
Ahmed, *see* Çerkes Ahmed
Ahmed Ağa, 109
Ahmed Anzavur, 240, 241, 243
Ahmed İzzet Paşa, 88, 95, 123
Ahmed Ratib Paşa, 37
Ahmednagar, India, 213
Ahmet Mücahit, 180
airplanes, 11, 128–31
Akgöl, Eyüb Sabri, 210
Akhisar, Anatolia, 225
Alaşehir, Anatolia, 216, 253
Albania, Albanians, 14, 57, 60, 79,
    83, 233, 237, 238, 240
Aleppo, Syria, 63, 64, 66, 119,
    129, 140, 150, 152, 172, 181–2,
    184
Alexandria, Egypt, 61, 62, 66, 69,
    70, 84, 145, 152, 270
Alexandroupoli, Greece, 94, 111,
    117; *see also* Dedeağaç
Algeria, 53, 60, 62, 70, 72
Ali ibn Husayn, King of Hijaz, 140
Ali Çetinkaya, 59, 60
Ali Paşa, 60, 62, 69
Ali Efendi, 180, 184
Ali Fuad Paşa, 250, 251, 254
Ali Haydar, 157–8

323

INDEX

INDEX

INDEX

Abdullah Mountains, 76–7; returns to Istanbul, 84

1913 deal with Talat for release of colleagues, 48; defense of Istanbul 21, 88–90; battle of Çatalca, 90; captures assassins of Şevket Paşa, 91–2; recapture of Edirne 21, 28, 92–7, 113, 125; campaign for Western Thrace, 101–6, 113; Provisional Government of Western Thrace established, 21, 28, 52, 98, 100, 106–13 declaration of Independent Government of Western Thrace, 21, 28, 52, 98, 100, 113, 125; Bulgaria occupies Western Thrace; returns to Istanbul, 119, 121

1914 marries Pervin, 21, 125–6; assigned to expel non-Muslims from İzmir, 131, 133; outbreak of First World War; mission to Europe, 21, 126–7, 131; given airborne assignment to Egypt, 128–31; expulsion of non-Muslims from İzmir, 132, 135, 217; mission to Arabia, 135–40; Suez Canal campaign begins, 21, 140–57

1915 attacked by British during recon mission, 158; battle for Suez Canal, 162–5; birth of Sencer, 165; raids on French consulates in Beirut and Damascus, 171–3; death of Sencer, 175; Najd mission, 174–6, 270

1916 arrest and execution of Yakup Cemil, 176–7; sets out on Yemen mission, 176–82; meets spy in Damascus,

182–3; enters Hijaz; meets with Fahri Paşa, 183–5; meets with Abd al-Aziz, 186–7

1917 battle with Sharifian force near Khaybar, 190–5, 215; captured by Sharifian force, 21, 195–6; meets Abdullah of Jordan, 197–200; leg wound treated by Shakir of Taif, 200–1; sent to Jeddah; humiliation in Mecca, 202–4; sent to Cairo, 204–8; imprisoned in Malta, 208–15

1918 accused of misappropriating Red Crescent funds, 220–1

1920 returns to Istanbul 22, 228, 229; meets with Karakol organization, 230; joins National Forces; posted to Adapazarı, 233–5; visits Şerife Hanım; Pervin has miscarriage, 235; organizes resistance in Adapazarı, 239–42; Circassian rebellion in Adapazarı, 22, 243–4; marches on Bolu, 244; summoned to Ankara, 242, 245; Maltepe raid, 245; Mahmud Bey appointed to Adapazarı, 247; driven out of Adapazarı, 247–9; summoned to Ankara, 248, 250; declines position in Grand National Assembly, 256–7; captures Göynük, 251; fights Greeks in Uşak, 252–4; accused of harboring opium, 255–6

1921 moves into Greek zone, 257–8, 261

1922 birth of Cuyap, 260, 264; organizes anti-CUP resistance in Thrace, 264; returns to

INDEX

INDEX

INDEX

INDEX

Ömer Fahrettin, 183
Ömer Naci, 62
150ers, The 6, 22, 269–70
opium, 255–6
von Oppenheim, Max, 143
Ortaköy, Anatolia, 252
Ortaköy, Thrace, 101, 104, 112, 121, 176
Osman Ferid Paşa, 24, 32
Ottoman Empire (1299–1923)
  1830 France conquers Algeria, 53
  1853 Crimean war begins, 13, 54
  1856 Treaty of Paris, 54
  1876 Abdülhamid II becomes Sultan 24
  1877 outbreak of Russo-Ottoman War, 56, 99, 237
  1878 Britain conquers Cyprus, 54
  1881 France conquers Tunisia, 54
  1882 Britain conquers Egypt, 54, 146, 209
  1897 Greco-Turkish War, 56
  1903 foundation of Arabian Revolutionary Committee 20, 33
  1908 Young Turk revolution, 2, 17, 20, 42, 49, 55, 59, 70, 88, 95, 100, 128, 237
  1909 anti-Unionist counter-revolution, 29, 44; Law for the Prevention of Brigandage, 40
  1911 outbreak of Italian-Ottoman War, 2, 14, 16, 17, 19, 20–1, 28, 45, 49, 51–71, 175; battle for Derne begins, 71–6, 202
  1912 assault on Benghazi, 77; Treaty of Lausanne, 78; out-

break of Balkan Wars, 2, 10, 16, 17–19, 21, 28, 48, 52, 53, 57, 74, 78, 83
  1913 Raid on the Sublime Porte, 86, 88, 113, 176, 271; fall of Edirne, 85; battle of Çatalca, 90; Treaty of London, 86, 90, 91, 94, 95, 119; assassination of Mahmud Şevket Paşa, 91, 246; recapture of Edirne 21, 28, 92–7, 113, 125; campaign for Western Thrace begins, 101–6, 113; Bucharest Treaty, 112; Provisional Government of Western Thrace established, 21, 28, 52, 98, 100, 106–13; capture of İskece, 108; high command demands fighters accept Bucharest Treaty, 112; declaration of Independent Government of Western Thrace, 21, 28, 52, 98, 100, 113, 125; Treaty of Istanbul, 118–19; Greece cedes Dedeağaç to Western Thrace, 117; Sıçanlı incident, 115–17; Bulgaria occupies Western Thrace, 119
  1914 secret treaty with Bulgaria, 117; secret meetings on non-Muslims in İzmir, 133; outbreak of First World War, 1, 2, 5–6, 8–10, 15, 16, 18, 19, 20–1, 43, 58, 117, 126–8; demonstration flight to Egypt, 128–31; expulsion of non-Muslims from İzmir, 131–5, 217; Five Turks mission leaves for Central Asia, 135–7; alliance with Germany, 137–8; *Goeben* and *Breslau* granted passage through Dardanelles,

336

INDEX

Pozantı, Anatolia, 180, 184
prostitution, 144
Provisional Government of South-Western Caucasia, 270
Provisional Government of Western Thrace, 17, 100, 106–13
Provisional State of Western Thrace, 120
Prüfer, Curt, 143, 147

Qal'at al-Nakhl, Sinai, 145, 151, 152, 155
Qantarah, Sinai, 151, 162
Qur'an, 17, 26, 48, 57, 73, 198, 223

Rabigh, Arabia, 202, 204
Rafa, Sinai, 151
Ragıb Bey, 27–8
Rahmi Bey, 132, 133, 135, 226
Raid on the Sublime Porte (1913), 86, 88, 113, 176, 271
railways, 11, 15, 35, 37, 44, 116, 134, 143, 161, 166–7, 173, 175, 180, 181, 184–7, 196, 242
rape, 101, 103, 104, 116–17
Ras al-Laban, Libya, 78
Rashid dynasty, 140, 169, 174, 175, 186
al-Rashid, Abdülaziz, 37
Rauf Bey, 180
Rauf Orbay, 225, 227, 233, 239, 268
Red Crescent Society, 220–1
Red Sea, 136, 178–9, 183, 201
Refet Bele, 261
Reşat Nuri, 45
Reşid, see Çerkes Reşid
Resne, Macedonia, 67
Resneli Niyazi, 69
Rhodope Mountains, 100

Riyadh, Arabia, 186
Rıfai Sufism, 64
Rıza Bey, 251
Rodenwaldt, Ernst, 173–4
Romania, 88, 166
Rum, 10, 18, 131–5, 237, 238, 255, 267
Rumelia, 38, 42, 83, 152; see also Balkans
Rüşdü Bey, 233, 241
Russian Empire, (1721–1917) 2, 12, 15, 21, 24–5, 29, 30, 49, 54, 56, 85, 99, 111, 114, 123, 138, 144, 162, 166, 167, 198, 203, 237, 240
Russian Revolution (1917), 49, 162
Russo-Circassian War (1830–64) 12
Russo-Ottoman War (1877–8), 56, 99, 237

Sabahattin, Prince, 91
Sabit, 118
Sahur tribe, 37
Said Halim Paşa, 104, 123
Said Nursî, 29–31
al-Said, Nuri, 61, 202
Sakallı Ahmed, 185
Sakallı Emin Efendi, 65, 70
Saladin, Sultan of Egypt and Syria, 131
Salih Hoca Mehmedoğlu, 106
Salih Şerif, 60, 61, 69, 70, 71, 174
Salihli, Anatolia, 11, 15, 43–4, 126, 139, 156, 176–7, 181, 216, 221–6, 231, 246, 250–1, 253, 256, 261–2, 271, 273, 231, 246, 250–1, 253, 256, 261–2, 271, 273
Salloum, Egypt, 70
Salonica, Thrace 30, 42, 53, 85, 132

INDEX